Halal Cryptocurrency Management

Mohd Ma'Sum Billah
Editor

Halal Cryptocurrency Management

Editor
Mohd Ma'Sum Billah
Finance, Insurance, Fintech
and Investment, Islamic Economics
Institute
King Abdul Aziz University
Jeddah, Kingdom of Saudi Arabia

ISBN 978-3-030-10748-2   ISBN 978-3-030-10749-9   (eBook)
https://doi.org/10.1007/978-3-030-10749-9

Library of Congress Control Number: 2019932958

This Palgrave Macmillan imprint is published by the registered company Springer Nature Switzerland AG.
The registered company address is: Gewerbestrasse 11, 6330 Cham, Switzerland

This book is dedicated to the remembrance of my most beloved parents Allamah Mufti Nur Mohammad (r) *and* Ustazah Akhtarun Nisa' (r) *who have nourished me with their love and wisdom. May* Allah (swt) *shower them with His Love and Mercy and grant them* Jannat al-Ferdaus Nuzulah. *I would also dedicate this book to my lovely wife Dr. Khamsiah Nawawi and our heart-touching kids Dr. Ahmad Mu'izz Billah, Ahmad Mu'azz Billah, Ahmad Muniff Billah and Akhtarun Naba' Billah for their continuous support and sacrifices. May all be blessed with* Muwaddau Wa Rahmah, Qurratu A'yun *and* Mardhaati Allah (swt) *in the life and the next.*

This book is also dedicated to the Ummah, *the whole of humanity and creatures.*

Mohd Ma'Sum Billah

FOREWORD

From the early days of bartering, man was looking for a means to easily exchange when selling or buying basic goods such as food, medicine and clothing. The use of precious metals and stones solved such need until the second half of the seventeenth century when banknotes were officially introduced in Sweden by a full backing of the state and gradually spread in other European countries to solve the multiple problems of using gold and silver. The establishment and growth of money exchange service providers and banks later with their networks encouraged saving, investment and money transfers, subsequently enhanced cross-border trade. The issuance of banknotes was always based on gold and silver, and issuers were printing on their issued banknotes their undertaking to exchange the units of their currency with a specific weight of gold to ensure the trustworthiness of their banknotes which must carry the seal of the issuing country's central bank and the signature of its governor. The use of gold and silver complies with Islamic *Shari'ah* jurisprudence, therefore, banknotes, as well, were accepted as they were based on gold and silver and later special drawing rights SDR which is issued by the IMF and recognized by its member countries.

Islamic financial institutions are thriving to establish and promote *Shari'ah* compliant products, and for the last 55 years, the Islamic finance has significantly secured its global platform with utmost success. Today, Islamic financial products are not confined within Muslim countries and Islamic banking institutions, but crossing the border to non-Muslim world and conventional banks. The asset size of Islamic finance hits USD 2.3 trillion while its annual growth rate is about 18% with a significant achievement as compared to what in the conventional counterparts.

Cryptocurrency is a new dimension in the contemporary economic era, which has been rapidly growing with utmost appreciation from different classes of the global market despite numerous shortcomings that are surrounding it. There are number of cryptocurrencies offered in the cyberspace, among them are: Litecoin (LTC), Ethereum (ETH), Zcash (ZEC), Dash (DASH), Ripple (XRP), Monero (XMR), Bitcoin Cash (BCH), NEO (NEO), Cardano (ADA) and EOS (EOS). All those digital currencies offer their coins or tokens in their respective platforms relying on their decentralized policies and strategies.

Although the people across the world and particularly the Muslim communities are expecting a *Shari'ah* alternative cryptocurrency model to meet the demand in the market, it has been observed that, no *Shari'ah* model of cryptocurrency has so far been effectively in use yet. It is worth noted here that, there are numerous players in the cyberspace claimed to have designed *Shari'ah* model of cryptocurrency, perhaps in the conceptual level, but not in reality with effective paradigm yet.

However, in the Gulf region, Saudi Arabia and the UAE have launched, recently, a joint cryptocurrency which will be limited to banks during its first stages. The currency operates on the use of a distributed database between the central banks and the participating banks from both sides, among which several *Shari'ah* compliant banks that have to observe directions set by their *Shari'ah* boards in this respect.

There are writings, comments, views and thoughts on Islamic model of cryptocurrency available particularly in the social media, but comprehensive academic or professional writing is not sufficiently produced yet in meeting the global desire among the academia, industries or policy makers.

Thus, the initiative of Prof. Dr. Mohd Ma'Sum Billah (a renowned Islamic finance scholar) in producing this book *Halal Cryptocurrency Management* is timely to meet the demand of the contemporary world to be benefited with *Halal* Cryptocurrency solution. I found this book, which addresses the subject with comprehensive analysis, intellectual discussion and empirical solution as a pioneer guide and reference for the academia, researchers, professionals, industrialists, entrepreneurs, decision makers, promoters, programmers, students and people in general who are involved or have interest in cryptocurrency, digital currency or *Halal* cryptocurrency.

Further, I urge him to expand on this interesting subject by writing on a practical solution for Halal Cryptocurrency endorsed by the Islamic Development Bank IDB using its nominal Islamic Dinar (ID), which is a recognized, unissued, currency by its 57 country members and can be used as the base for secured new *Shari'ah* compliant cryptocurrency.

Finally, it is to my great honor to write this foreword for this prestigious title. May we all be blessed with true knowledge and its rightful practices.

Kingdom of Saudi Arabia   Saleh A. Alawaji Alghamdi
March 2019   Secretariat of the Council of Ministers
                                          Office of the Advisor

PREFACE

Halal cryptocurrency is a *Shari'ah* compliant digital currency operated within the ambit of *Maqasid al-Shari'ah* (divine objectives) through cryptography based on a blockchain technology (platform). A cryptocurrency business is a peer-to-peer transaction by encryption thus enabling the transaction to be nodded and recorded in the ledger account. Through such action of encryption the user creates own e-wallet for enabling him or her to manage own account in the cyberspace within the ledger. Its blockchain technology, system, model, objectives, operational mechanisms, technicalities, culture and all activities shall be in total compliance with the *Shari'ah* principles (*Halal* standard), which shall regularly be advised by the company's board of advisors, screened through by the company's technical experts prior to the approval by the *Shari'ah* advisory board (SAB) of the company and thereafter shall be operated or executed accordingly.

Cryptocurrency through the blockchain technology is a cyber-space economic revolution in the twenty-first century. Numerous players are in the market globally to offer cryptocurrency platforms, but with many shortcomings like, lack of regulatory supports, poor strategic planning, uncertainty and mostly with no backing asst, but only on virtual assumption. The *Halal* model of cryptocurrency is timely to fill the gap of the ongoing shortcomings in the cryptocurrency market. A *Halal* cryptocurrency model thus shall be backed by valued asset or be an asset-backed platform, operated based on valued assets (coins); transactions are based on *Shari'ah* hybrid instruments of *al-Bai wa al-Shira'* (trading),

xi

al-Wadiyah (deposit), *al-Amanah* (trust), *al-Ijarah* (service charge), *al-Mudharabah* (co-partnership), *al-Wakalah* (agency), *al-Ju'alah* (reward) and *al-Tabarru'at* (donation), concerns about humanitarian well-beings, regulated by the standard *Shari'ah* principles *al-'Aqd* and other related rules, opposes to uncertainty in any component and liberty in enjoying with legitimate (*Halal*) investment return. Thus, the *Halal* cryptocurrency model has the greater opportunity to attract the global cryptocurrency market with sustainable existence in the emergence of blockchain technology.

The prime objective of a *Halal* cryptocurrency model is to create an enterprising and entrepreneuring based community for all across the world through *Halal* cryptocurrency management and participation globally. This may ultimately fight the poverties, jobless, domestic economic crisis and world eco-catastrophe. A *Halal* cryptocurrency management is with universal character welcoming, encouraging and benefiting to all mankind regardless of one's religion, race, status, gender, color or even nationality. A *Halal* cryptocurrency operation does not concern only money making, but part of its income in each transaction shall mandatorily be deducted as *Tabarru'at* (donation) for the humanitarian causes based on the holistic principles of solidarity. Furthermore, all gross income in every transaction, account, management, activities, income and services of a *Halal* cryptocurrency management shall be subjected to 2.5% compulsory deduction as *Zakat* (alms).

This title *Halal Cryptocurrency Management* is timely as among the pioneers of the subject in the contemporary economic era with a comprehensive solution to core components of cryptocurrency within *Maqasid al-Shari'ah*. The book, however, is divided by specialized sub-areas of cryptocurrency in to six parts with nineteen chapters besides an introduction.

Part I provides an overview of *Halal* cryptocurrency management, which consists of four chapters addressing different issues. Chapter 1 contributes a Halal alternative model of cryptocurrency with its different aspects as a corporate understanding. Chapter 2 provides a SWOT analysis of both conventional and *Halal* model of cryptocurrency with a possible comparative treatment. Chapter 3 focuses on innovative culture of *Halal* cryptocurrency management, which may be essential to attract the market with dynamism and sustainable existence. Chapter 4 analyzes on the *Halal* cryptocurrency paradigm and its impact toward the global financial stability.

Part II focuses on technicalities and blockchain technology that a *Halal* cryptocurrency management is based, which consists of three chapters contributing different components of the theme. Chapter 5 analyzes the blockchain technology and its mechanisms on how it facilitates a *Halal* cryptocurrency management. Chapter 6 presents a paradigm of blockchain technology and its *Shari'ah* compliant structure. Chapter 7 goes on analyzing the cryptocurrency along with its characterization and reality concern.

Part III contributes on regulatory frameworks facilitate a *Halal* cryptocurrency management. The part consists of six chapters, which focus on different core issues of the subject. Chapter 8 analyzes the cryptocurrency paradigm within *Maqasid al-Shari'ah*. Chapter 9 provides a comprehensive analysis of various *Fatwa* (juristic opinion) on bitcoin. Chapter 10 discovers the *Shari'ah* code that may facilitate cryptocurrency management. Chapter 11 discusses on the *Shari'ah* regulatory standard governing cryptocurrency management. Chapter 12 analyzes on the existing regulatory frameworks facilitate cryptocurrency management in different jurisdictions of the world. The chapter also provides a *Shari'ah* alternative regulatory standard, which may facilitate *Halal* cryptocurrency operation within the *Maqasid al-Shari'ah*. Chapter 13 contributes a regulatory and *Shari'ah* frameworks governing cryptocurrency with a comparative treatment.

Part IV focuses on empiricality of *Halal* cryptocurrency management. The part consists of two chapters with different issues within the core subject. Chapter 14 provides a fundamental discovery of various stages and components of the establishment and operational mechanisms of a *Halal* cryptocurrency management. Chapter 15 contributes with a case analysis of bitcoin and its *Halal* alternative dimension.

Part V analyzes on the social financing mechanisms through *Halal* cryptocurrency management. The part consists of three chapters contributing different components of the theme. Chapter 16 discusses on the paradigm of Islamic social financing through cryptocurrency platform. Chapter 17 contributes on how *Zakat* standard frameworks in *Halal* cryptocurrency business can be. Chapter 18 provides a *Waqf* led *Halal* cryptocurrency model with possible structure.

Part VI focuses on risk management in *Halal* cryptocurrency platform. The part consists of two chapters. Chapter 19 analyzes on the *Shari'ah* model of risk management with divine justifications facilitate the practical reality. Chapter 20 discovers various potential risk factors in cryptocurrency management and two *takaful* schemes as a solution to cryptocurrency risks.

It is submitted that, most of the chapters are contributed by learned academia, industrialists, researchers and experts in the field of Islamic finance from different parts of the world, I truly appreciate their kind contributions and greater supports in completing the title with successful results.

Lastly, it is admitted that, the idea of cryptocurrency or its *Halal* alternative is in its infancy stage with no reliable research works or empirical solution yet that can be used as a reference for continuing academic or industrial research, except some thoughts available in the social media. Thus, this title *Halal Cryptocurrency Management* is among the pioneers of the subject with possible academic, empirical and hypothetical solutions, which may be a guide academia, researchers, practitioners, decision makers, programmers, professionals, promoters and students for their future research and development of the model of *Halal* cryptocurrency. It is not impossible for the book contains any shortcoming. We are thus grateful to all readers should any shortcoming be notified to us for further improvement.

Jeddah, Kingdom of Saudi Arabia   Mohd Ma'Sum Billah, Ph.D.

ACKNOWLEDGEMENTS

There is no strength and power except in *Allah (swt)*, To Him comes the praise, the Savant, the Wise, the Omniscient, the most beautiful names belong to Him. May the blessing of Allah (swt) and peace be upon *Muhammad (saw)* and all the Prophets *(aws)* from the first to the last.

First of all, I would humbly like to acknowledge King Abdulaziz University, Kingdom of Saudi Arabia, and its prestigious wing Islamic Economics Institute for supporting us with every facility in research, academic, human capital and professional development activities out-reaching the global *Ummah*. It is also a great honor for me to humbly acknowledge His Excellency Professor Dr. Abdulrahman Obaid AI-Youbi, the President of King Abdulaziz University, Professor Dr. Yousef Abdul Aziz Al Turki, the Vice President of King Abdulaziz University, and Dr. Abdullah Qurban Turkistani, the Dean of the Islamic Economics Institute (IEI), King Abdulaziz University (KAU),

Dr. Mohammad A. Naseef (Vice Dean, IEI-KAU), Dr. Marwan G. A. Andejani (Vice Dean, IEI-KAU), Dr. Hasan Mohammad Makhethi (Vice Dean, IEI-KAU), Dr. Maha Alandejani (Vice Dean, IEI-KAU), Dr. Faisal Mahmoud Atbani (Head, Department of Insurance, IEI-KAU), Dr. Adnan M. A. Al-Khiary (Head, Department of Finance, IEI-KAU) and Dr. Albara Abdullah Abulaban (Head, Department of Economics), for their continuous generous support and encouragement toward excellent academic contributions, specialized advance scientific research activities and dynamic professional development. Humble acknowledgment is also extended to my respected fellow colleagues from the IEI, King Abdulaziz University, including Dr. Ibrahim M. S. Abolola, Dr. Omar Hafiz, Prof. Dr. Abdulrahim Al-Saati, Sheikh Dr. Ali Ahmed Al-Nadwi, Prof. Dr. Abdul Azim Islahi, Dr. Ahmed Mahdi Belouafi, Dr. Fadul AbdulKarim Al-Bashir, Dr. Abdul Razzaq Belabes, Dr. Hichem Salem Hamza and my talented colleague Mr. Mohammed Alabdulraheem, Lecturer (Islamic banking and finance), IEI-KAU. Further acknowledgment is extended to other universities, industries and professional firms including my research assistant Hafiz Akram bin Mohd Ghani whose direct and indirect support with knowledge, experiences and resources are full-heartedly recorded.

Mohd Ma'Sum Billah

CONTENTS

NOTES ON CONTRIBUTORS

Faraz Adam, M.A. is a Shari'ah Scholar and Director of Amanah Finance Consultancy from where he actively advises several global organizations in Islamic finance, banking, zakat management and other sectors. He has studied Shari'ah with scholars for almost a decade and completed a Master's degree in Islamic finance and banking in the UK. He has further attained a number of industry qualifications. Faraz has authored many research papers on cryptocurrencies and blockchain from a Shari'ah compliance perspective and advises a number of crypto-asset management and crypto-exchange platforms. Faraz is passionate about establishing an economy which upholds justice, equity and growth for all members of society.

Salami Saheed Adekunle, M.Sc. is presently pursuing a Ph.D. in Islamic Finance at INCEIF, Malaysia. He holds both professional and academic Master's degrees (MIFP and M.Sc.) in Islamic Finance at INCEIF. He has presented papers in many conferences on Islamic finance both in Nigeria and internationally. He has worked as research assistant on various Islamic finance issues with many professors and organizations including International Shari'ah Research Academy for Islamic Finance (ISRA). He also has long experience in translations of Arabic into English. He holds few undergraduate degrees from including B.A. in Shari'ah from King Faisal University, Chad. His current research areas of interest are in virtual currencies/Bitcoin, blockchain, Maqasid al-Shari'ah, Islamic microfinance and impact assessment of Islamic social finance such as waqf and zakat.

Nafis Alam, Ph.D. is an Associate Professor of finance. His expertise is centered on banking regulation, financial stability and corporate finance. His scholarly articles have been published in leading journals including *The World Economy, Emerging Markets Review, Pacific Basin Finance Journal, Journal of Asset Management, Journal of Banking Regulation, Review of Islamic Economics* and *Journal of Financial Services Marketing*, among others. He has co-authored five books in Islamic finance—among them is *Encyclopedia of Islamic Finance* which is the first of its kind and has sold over 1000 copies worldwide. As a frequent traveler, he has given lectures on finance and Islamic finance across the world, including Harvard Islamic Finance Forum at Harvard Law School; a Gulf Research Meeting at Cambridge University, UK; Durham University Summer School; Seoul International Finance Conference (SIFIC); World Islamic Economic Forum (WIFE); and OIC Asia Trade and Economic Forum. Alam has served as a visiting associate professor at various universities in the UK and Indonesia. He was featured as a Professor of the Month by Financial Times (FT) in 2014 and received an award for Upcoming Personality in Islamic Finance in 2016 presented by GIFA and hosted by the Indonesian government.

Mohammed Fawzi Aminu Amadu, M.B.A. is a Management Consultant and Social Commentator with 18 years of experience. His consultancy covers work with Government of Ghana, Private Corporations—both local and international, as well as local NGOs. Currently, he is Director of Business Development for GM Ambassadors—a management consulting firm. Amadu is also a Director with Africa Islamic Economic Foundation, an international NGO. Through his office at the Africa Islamic Economic Foundation, he currently is working with the Government of Ghana (through the Ministry of Foreign Affairs and the Bank of Ghana) to develop an enabling environment for the adoption of Islamic finance. His consultancy has covered a wide range of fields including information technology issues, education, commodity trading, real estate development, finance—especially with regard to Islamic finance, agriculture as well as transport and logistics.

Mohamed Cherif El Amri, Ph.D. is working as an Assistant Professor at the Faculty of Business and Management Sciences Specialized Islamic Economics and Finance, at Sabahattin Zaim University. He completed his Bachelor's degree in Islamic Studies from Ibn Tofail University in Morocco. He had his Master's in Islamic Jurisprudence and its principles, while his Ph.D. in Islamic Banking and Finance from International

Islamic University Malaysia. He worked as an intern at several Islamic Financial Institutions, such as the Islamic Capital Market Business Group, Securities Commission, Kuala Lumpur Malaysia and Maybank Islamic. He worked as a Researcher at the Institute of Islamic Banking and Finance, Malaysia. He was an Associated Consultant at Amanie Advisors, Kuala Lumpur, Malaysia. He is a member of the Scientific Committee of the *International Review of Entrepreneurial Finance Journal* and *Journal of Islamic Economics and Finance*. He has multiple research publications and presentations in the field of Islamic finance and economics.

Houssem eddine Bedoui, Ph.D. is a Global lead Islamic finance expert at the Islamic Development Bank (IDB). As part of his work at the Islamic Development Bank, he actively contributes to the structuring, launch, and implementation of innovative products and processes for the market. Besides, Bedoui is ATD certified trainer (MTP: Master Trainer Program). He has several entrepreneurial experiences putting Islamic finance principles and products into practice. Prior to his job at the IsDB, he was a consultant in Europe in management advisory and ethical/sustainable finance and worked with many think tanks to develop Islamic finance in France. He has a Master's from Telecom SudParis Engineering School (INT), France; an M.B.A. from IE Business School (Spain); a Ph.D. from ENS (École Normale Supérieure, France); he is also an Alumni from Harvard Kennedy School (CID, Center for International Development). Bedoui is the co-editor of *IRTI's French* journal. His research interests comprise Islamic capital markets, fintech, social entrepreneurship and finance, competitiveness and Islamic banking; he has published in several academic journals and presented his research works at various international conferences.

Irfan Syauqi Beik, Ph.D. is an Associate Professor at the Department of Islamic Economics, Bogor Agricultural University (IPB), Indonesia, and holds the position of the Director of the Centre of Islamic Business and Economic Studies (CIBEST) at IPB. Beside as an academician, Irfan has been appointed as the Director of the Centre of Strategic Studies at the National *Zakat* Board of the Republic of Indonesia (BAZNAS) since August 2016. He is also a member of the National Shari'ah Board of the Indonesian Council of Ulama (DSN-MUI) and the Deputy Chairman of the Indonesian Association of Islamic Economist (IAEI). Irfan is member of Shari'ah supervisory council in several Islamic financial institutions. In addition, Irfan has published books and scientific articles at both national and international journals and has contributed regularly in various national newspapers in Indonesia.

Mohd Ma'Sum Billah, Ph.D. is a Professor of finance, insurance, fintech and investment, Islamic Economics Institute, King Abdul Aziz University, Kingdom of Saudi Arabia. Billah had been serving and contributing both academic and corporate industries for more than 20 years with management, teaching, research, solution proving and sharing of strategic and technical thoughts toward the advancement of Islamic finance and insurance (*Takaful*) besides *Halal* standard. Billah has published 31 books and chapters in books besides more than 200 articles in journals and social media. He had been presenting in more than 300 conferences, seminars, executive workshops and industrial trainings in different parts of the world. In addition, he had also been affiliated with corporate, academic and financial industries besides NGOs in his capacity as a member in boards, advisor, strategic decision maker, transformer and reformer with strategic solutions. Among the areas of his interest and contributions are: Islamic finance, insurance (*Takaful*), fintech, investment, capital market (*Sukuk*), social finance, petroleum trade and finance, models and standards.

Ahmet Suayb Gundogdu, Ph.D. is an accomplished and internationally experienced seeker of knowledge with a first-class academic grounding in international trade, finance and economics. Currently working for the Islamic Development Bank Group, he holds a B.A. in International Trade from Bogazici University and an M.A. in International Development from the International University of Japan. He was pursuing his Ph.D. in Economics at Virginia Tech, USA, before joining to IDB Group and completed his Ph.D. in Islamic Finance at Durham University, UK. Gundogdu has held several positions within IDB Group; he served as a Senior Program Manager and Country Representative at Islamic Solidarity Fund for Development and managed a portfolio of about $1 billion at the International Islamic Trade Finance Corporation. Presently, he is Senior Technical Specialist of Chief Economist & Director General of Global Practices at Islamic Development Bank and Associate Professor of Finance at Istanbul Zaim University.

Farrukh Habib, Ph.D. is a Shari'ah (Islamic jurisprudence) and Islamic finance expert. He is Researcher at International Shari'ah Research Academy for Islamic Finance (ISRA); Shari'ah Advisory Board Member of Salihin Shari'ah Advisory Sdn Bhd; Co-editor of *ISRA International Journal of Islamic Finance* (IIJIF); and Reviewer of various well-reputed academic journals. He has been involved in numerous researches, corporate trainings, workshops and consultation work on Islamic finance. He has been a prolific contributor in numerous academic journals, reports, research papers and business magazines, and presented in several international conferences and seminars. He has also been invited to many Islamic finance events as a guest speaker. His current interests are capital markets, sukuk, fintech, blockchain, virtual currencies/Bitcoin, crowdfunding, ethical and social finance. He holds a Ph.D. degree in Islamic Finance from INCEIF, Kuala Lumpur. He acquired a Master's degree (M.Sc.) in banking and finance from Queen Mary, University of London, UK. Prior to that, he obtained Master's and Bachelor's degrees from University of Karachi, both in economics. He also received traditional Islamic (Shari'ah) knowledge through an extensive eight years' course in Jamia Uloom-E-Islamia, Karachi, acquiring Bachelor's and Master's degrees in Islamic studies.

Asma Hakimah Ab Halim, Ph.D. is a Senior Lecturer at the Faculty of Law, the National University of Malaysia. She holds L.L.B. Hons and L.L.B. (Shari'ah) (UIAM), L.L.M. (UKM) and Ph.D. in Law (University of Glasgow Caledonian). Her research interest is Islamic capital market regulation.

Rusni Hassan, Ph.D. is a Professor at the IIUM Institute of Islamic Banking and Finance, IIUM. She graduated with L.L.B. (Hons), L.L.B. (Shari'ah) (First Class), Master of Comparative Laws (MCL) and Ph.D. in Law. She is actively involved in various Islamic Financial Institutions as the Shari'ah Committee locally and internationally. She has spoken extensively in conferences, workshops and trainings on various Islamic finance issues. She has published books on Islamic Banking and Takaful, Islamic Banking under Malaysian Law, Islamic Banking Cases and Commentaries, Corporate Governance of Islamic Financial Institutions and Remedies for Default in Islamic Banking. She has more than 100 articles in local and international journals. She received a few awards for her contribution in Islamic finance such as Top 10 Women in Islamic Finance (2013); Most Talented Women Professional in Islamic Banking (2014); Women of Distinction in Islamic Finance and Law (2016); Distinguished Woman in Management (2017); 100 Influential Women in Islamic Finance (2017); and recently as The Top 50 Most Influential Women in Islamic Finance (2018).

Hylmun Izhar, Ph.D. is currently affiliated with the Islamic Research and Training Institute (IRTI), Islamic Development Bank (IsDB) as Senior Economist. His publications range from international refereed journals, book chapters, policy-oriented papers and reports, book reviews and articles in academic and professional magazines. Prior to joining IsDB, he was a Lecturer at the Markfield Institute of Higher Education (MIHE), Leicester, UK, following a research fellowship at the Oxford Centre for Islamic Studies (OXCIS), Oxford, UK. He has been honored with the prestigious award of 'Upcoming Personality in Global Islamic Finance (Academic)' during the annual Global Islamic Finance Awards (GIFA), 2017. He provides his expertise to a range of policymakers, multilateral organizations and institutional clients worldwide in different issues of Islamic finance. He is the co-author of *I for Impact: Blending Islamic Finance and Impact Investing for the Global Goals* (by UNDP and IDB Group), *Global Report on Islamic Finance: A Catalyst for Shared Prosperity* (by the World Bank and IDB Group) and textbook on *Islamic Capital Markets: Principles and Practices* published by ISRA and Securities Commission Malaysia. His latest book on *Critical Issues in Islamic Economics and Finance Development* is published by Palgrave Macmillan. He currently represents IDB Group at the IFSB Working Group on the Revised Standard on Disclosures to Promote Transparency and Market Discipline for Institutions Offering Islamic Financial Services. Izhar earned his Ph.D. in Islamic Finance at Durham University during which he was honored Distinguished Doctoral Fellowship by Graduate School, Durham University, UK.

Shajahan K. Kakkattil, M.C.A. is presently heading Cyber Security, IT Quality at Dubai Chamber of Commerce & Industry, with lead role in defining and executing technology strategy and governance. He has decades of active involvement in driving technology innovations and early adoptions for various organization and industries, including Indian Navy, Microsoft & Dubai Government. He is pioneer in setting result-oriented organization strategies with innovative technologies and executing challenging portfolios and expert in .com, e-commerce, smart systems to blockchain—from strategy to coding with hacker-level insights.

Aminurasyed Mahpop, L.L.M. is a Senior Lecturer at the Faculty of Law, the National University of Malaysia. He holds L.L.B. Hons (UKM), L.L.M. (Malaya) and Master's in Islamic Economics (UKM). Before joining the university, he was a practicing lawyer for almost 14 years, and during his practice, he served as a member of Islamic finance committee of Malaysian Bar Council. His research interest is Islamic banking regulation.

Mustafa Omar Mohammed, Ph.D. is presently the Head and an Associate Professor at the Department of Economics, International Islamic University Malaysia [IIUM], where he has been teaching for more than 15 years now. He has published more than 50 refereed journal articles and presented more than 70 papers, mostly at international conferences. He is actively involved in funded and commissioned research projects. His present research areas of interest are in *waqf*, *zakat*, Islamic microfinance and *Maqasid al-Shari'ah*. He has supervised more than 45 dissertations at Ph.D. and Master Levels. He is also a journal editorial member and reviewer panel to 11 academic entities. He has received several quality awards for teaching and research. He was part of a committee responsible for setting up the Institute of Islamic Banking and Finance and recently, the Department of Islamic Finance at IIUM. He also has long experience in translations, Arabic and English. He undertook projects for several organizations, including MIFC, IBFIM, AIBIM, IFSB—affiliates of the Central Bank of Malaysia. He offers consultancy and has conducted several trainings on Islamic economics, banking and finance in several countries including Kazakhstan, Singapore, Sri Lanka, Bangladesh, Philippines, Indonesia, South Africa and Uganda. Dr. Mustafa holds a Bachelor's and Master's degrees in Economics from IIUM and Ph.D. in Finance from Universiti Sains Malaysia.

Aishath Muneeza, Ph.D. is an Associate Professor at INCEIF. She is the first female Deputy Minister of Ministry of Islamic Affairs and is the Deputy Minister of Ministry of Finance & Treasury of Republic of Maldives. She is also the chairwoman of Maldives Center for Islamic Finance. She is considered as the founder of Islamic finance in Maldives. Her contribution to Islamic finance includes structuring of the corporate sukuks and sovereign private sukuk of the country including the Islamic treasury instruments. She also drafted the Islamic Capital Market framework of the country and is the only registered Shari'ah adviser for Islamic capital market in the country since 2013. She played a key role in setting up of the Tabung Haji of Maldives, Maldives Hajj Corporation, and was the first chairperson of it. She sits in various *Shari'ah* advisory bodies nationally and internationally and is chairman for many of these *Shari'ah* advisory bodies including the apex Shari'ah Advisory Council for capital market in Maldives. She has assisted more than eleven institutions to offer Islamic financial products/services. She won various national and international awards for her contribution made toward the development of Islamic finance industry. She is also a role model and a mentor for females who aspire to build their careers in Islamic finance industry and is the Vice President of Women on Boards, an NGO advocating women representation on boards of companies. She is an invited speaker in Islamic finance conferences and events held in different parts of the world. She was listed in 2017 as number seven among the 50 Influential Women in Business and Finance by ISFIRE which is an official publication of Islamic Bankers Association based in London and she is among the most influential 500 in Islamic Economy. She is a member of the Association of Shari'ah Advisors in Islamic Finance Malaysia (ASAS), Malaysia. She holds a doctorate in law from International Islamic University of Malaysia.

Zakariya Mustapha, L.L.M. practices law in Nigeria where he is an advocate and solicitor of Nigeria's Supreme Court since 2008. In 2010, he joined Faculty of Law Bayero University, Kano, Nigeria, as a lecturer where he taught conventional and Islamic banking and finance law, alongside other Islamic law courses until 2017. He specializes in legal and *Shari'ah* issues in Islamic banking and finance and offers legal and Islamic financial advisory services about legal framework, dispute resolution and Shari'ah compliant product development in Islamic banking and finance. He has published numerous articles, and he has presented research papers in national and international conferences. He holds a L.L.B., L.L.M., B.L., with membership of Nigerian Bar Association and Nigerian Institute of Management (Chartered). He is currently pursuing his Ph.D. in Islamic Finance Law at Faculty of Law University of Malaya, Kuala Lumpur.

Rizal Mohd Nor, Ph.D. is an Assistant Professor at the Department of Computer Science, KICT, IIUM. He holds Ph.D. in Computer Science and M.Sc. (Kent State University), M.B.A. (IIUM) and a double degree in B.Sc. Computer Engineering and Electrical Engineering (Johns Hopkins University). His research is in fintech and blockchain in areas such as self-stabilizing algorithms in blockchain consensus, blockchain applications in IoT, blockchain applications in Islamic finance, blockchain applications in edutech, Internet of thing (IoT), cryptocurrencies and machine learning for financial robo-advisors. He has published several journals in blockchain, IoT and fintech which have received international awards and research grants both local and international. Professionally, he has served as a consultant for several fintech and blockchain companies in Malaysia in their fintech, blockchain, IoT and AI initiatives. He currently owns a patent filed in 2018 relating to blockchain technology. He is a frequent speaker in local and international conferences and a trainer for several agencies.

Nadiyah Syahira Nordin, M.Sc. holds her M.Sc. in finance from the Institute of Islamic Banking and Finance (IIiBF), International Islamic University Malaysia (IIUM). She also holds a Bachelor's Degree in Shari'ah (Islamic Banking and Economics) from Yarmouk University, Irbid, Jordan. She is a recipient of Shari'ah Scholarship Award from International Shari'ah Research Academy in Islamic Finance (ISRA) in 2015. Prior to joining the Islamic finance industry, she indulged in research relating to cryptocurrency from Shari'ah perspective. Her core research interest is in the area of policy making and innovation in Islamic finance, which encompasses fintech, blockchain and cryptocurrency.

Mohammad Soleh Nurzaman, Ph.D. is a Lecturer at the Department of Islamic Economics, Faculty of Economics and Business, University of Indonesia. He is also working as a Deputy Director for the Center of Strategic Studies, National Board of *Zakat*, the Republic of Indonesia. He holds degrees from University of Indonesia (B.Sc. Economics), Australian National University (Master of International and Development Economics) and International Islamic University Malaysia (Ph.D. Islamic Economics). His research interests are in the areas of Islamic economics and finance, Islamic social finance and development economics. Out of academic and research activities, he worked as a consultant in the area of Islamic economics and finance for some regulatory institutions in Indonesia such as Ministry of Finance, House of Representative of Republic of Indonesia, Coordinating Ministry for Economic Affairs and for some international institutions such as United Nation Development Program and Asian Development Bank.

Priyesta Rizkiningsih, M.Sc. is a Senior Researcher in Center of Strategic Studies, the National Board of *Zakat*, the Republic of Indonesia (Puskas BAZNAS). Previously, she worked as a research assistant at the Central Bank of Indonesia. She earned her Master's degree in Islamic Finance and Management from Durham University, UK, with a full scholarship from Indonesia Endowment Fund for Education. Her research interests are Islamic social finance as well as governance and social reporting. She can be contacted at priyesta.rizkiningsih@puskasba-znas.com.

Aroua Robbana, M.Sc. is a holder of M.Sc. in Islamic finance from the International Centre for Education in Islamic Finance (INCEIF). Currently, she is pursuing her Ph.D. at the International Islamic University Malaysia (IIUM). Her research interests comprise Islamic finance, Islamic economics, *zakat* and fintech.

Aisha Putrina Sari, M.A. is a Senior Researcher in Center of Strategic Studies, the National Board of Zakat, the Republic of Indonesia (Puskas BAZNAS). She graduated from Tazkia University College of Islamic Economics (Bachelor's degree) and University of Indonesia (Master's degree). Her research interests are Islamic social finance, Islamic endowment and Shari'ah banking.

Muhammad Hasbi Zaenal, Ph.D. is a Deputy Director in Center of Strategic Studies, the National Board of Zakat, the Republic of Indonesia (Puskas BAZNAS), and Research Fellow in Islamic Economic Studies and Thoughts Centre (IESTC). He graduated from Al-Azhar University (Bachelor's degree) and Universiti Kebangsaan Malaysia (Master and Ph.D.). His previous experiences include as Researcher at Research Center for Islamic Economics and Finance, School of Economics, Universiti Kebangsaan Malaysia, from 2011 to 2014, and Research Assistant at Islamic Research and Training Institute, Islamic Development Bank from, 2013 to 2017.

Abdolhossein (Pejman) Zameni, Ph.D. is a Lecturer of Finance. He obtained a B.Sc. in Industrial Engineering at Mazandaran University of Science and Technology in Iran. In 2006, in order to pursue his education in an international environment, he moved to Malaysia and obtained his M.B.A. in Finance at Multimedia University. In 2014, he was awarded a Ph.D. in Finance by the National University of Malaysia (UKM). He has experience in the delivery of educational programs at undergraduate levels, as well as business experience within the fields of finance, accounting and industry.

Muhamed Zulkhibri, Ph.D. is a Senior Economist at the Islamic Research and Training Institute (IRTI) and earlier he worked in the Economic

Research and Policy Department, Islamic Development Bank, Saudi Arabia. Prior to joining the IRTI-IsDB, he worked at the Central Bank of Malaysia in various capacities and also attached to policy research institutions as a research fellow. He involved in many task forces, training and research, spoke at various conferences/workshops and provided advisory/consulting services to various organizations worldwide. Previously, he lectured at the University Putra Malaysia, Malaysia, and University of Nottingham, UK. He published extensively in various publications in leading academic journals, industry reports, edited books, etc. His most recent books include *Macro prudential Regulation and Policy for Islamic Financial Industry* (Springer, 2016) and *Financial Inclusion and Poverty Alleviation: Perspectives from Islamic Institutions and Instruments* (Palgrave, 2017). His current research focuses on monetary economics, macroeconomics, Islamic economics and finance. He is the co-editor of the *Islamic Economic Studies* journal. He received his Ph.D. in Economics from the University of Nottingham, UK.

About the Author/Editor

Mohd Ma'Sum Billah, D.B.A., Ph.D., M.C.L., M.M.B., L.L.B. (hons) Professor of finance, insurance, fintech and investment, Islamic Economics Institute, King Abdul Aziz University, Kingdom of Saudi Arabia. Billah had been serving and contributing both academic and corporate industries for more than 20 years with management, teaching, research, solution proving and sharing of strategic and technical thoughts toward the advancement of Islamic finance and insurance (*Takaful*) besides *Halal* standard. Billah has published 32 books and chapters in books besides more than 200 articles in journals and social media. He had been presenting in more than 300 conferences, seminars, executive workshops and industrial trainings in different parts of the world. In addition, he had also been affiliated with corporate, academic and financial industries including central banks, international corporate organizations, governments and NGOs in his capacity as a member in boards, advisor, strategic decision maker, transformer and reformer with strategic solution provider. Among the areas of his interest and contributions are: Islamic finance, insurance (*Takaful*), crowdfunding, investment, capital market (*Sukuk*), social finance, petroleum finance, trade, fintech and cryptocurrency models and standards.

LIST OF FIGURES

LIST OF TABLES

INTRODUCTION

Cryptocurrency generally means a virtual, digital or cyber complimentary money with intrinsic commercial value, which takes the form of tokens or coins. Some cryptocurrencies have ventured into the physical world with debit or credit cards or other instruments, the large majority remains entirely intangible or virtual existence in the cyberspace. The term 'crypto' in cryptocurrencies refers to sophisticated cryptography, which allows for a particular e-coin or e-token to be generated, stored and transacted anonymously typically, securely and smartly by digital encryption. The essence of 'crypto' feature of these digital currencies is, a common undertaking to decentralization; all cryptocurrencies are typically designed and developed as a specific hash code by teams who build in mechanisms for issuance through a process called 'mining' in most cases and other virtual devices. In the contemporary practices, cryptocurrencies are commonly designed to be free from government manipulation, control and influence, despite they (cryptocurrencies) have grown rapidly with global market appreciation. Cryptocurrencies, which modeled after bitcoin, are collectively known as altcoins and have tried to appear in the cyber market as hybrid versions of bitcoin. Some of those digital currencies are easier to be managed than a bitcoin with complexity. Today, there are more than 1600 cryptocurrencies exist, which are offered in the cyberspace through blockchain technology, and many of those tokens or coins are popular in their micro-capacities or attributes among the virtual communities of investors and traders in the cyberspace.[1]

A *Halal* alternative cryptocurrency is a *Shari'ah* compliant digital currency activated by the application of cryptography through a blockchain technology within the ambit of *Maqasid al-Shari'ah* (divine objectives). The fundamental dichotomy between the conventional practices and the Halal alternative model is the core objectives and the mechanisms adapted. In a *Halal* cryptocurrency, its blockchain system, technology, model, objective, operational mechanisms, technicalities, culture, functions and all activities shall be in total compliance with the *Shari'ah* principles (*Halal* standard), which shall regularly be advised by the board of advisors, screened through and duly approved by the *Shari'ah* advisory board (SAB) of the company before any implementation takes place.

The cryptocurrency through the blockchain technology is a cyberspace economic revolution in the twenty-first century. Numerous players are in the market globally to offer different categories cryptocurrencies, but with many shortcomings like, lack of regulatory supports, poor strategic planning, uncertainty and mostly with no backing asset, but on virtual assumption. Whereas a *Halal* model of cryptocurrency is a *Shari'ah* compliant cryptocurrency model is a timely to fill the gap of the ongoing shortcomings in the cryptocurrency market. A *Halal* Cryptocurrency model is thus backed by valued asset and operated based on valued assets (coins or tokens); transactions are based on *Shari'ah* instruments like, *al-Bay wa al-Shira'* (trading), *al-Musharakah* (partnership), *al-Mudharabah* (co-partnership), *al-Wakalah* (agency), *al-Ujrah* (service charge), *al-Ju'alah* (reward), *al-Wadiyah* (deposit), *al-Amanah* (trust), *al-Tabarru'at* (charity) and *Zakat* (alms), concerns about humanitarian well-beings regulated by the standard *Shari'ah* principles, opposes to uncertainty (*Garar*) in any component and liberty in enjoying with legitimate (*Halal*) investment return. Thus, the *Halal* cryptocurrency model has the greater opportunity to attract the global cryptocurrency market with sustainable existence in the emergence of blockchain technology.

The prime objective of a *Halal* cryptocurrency model is to create an enterprising and entrepreneuring based community across the world through *halal* cryptocurrency management and participation therein

---

[1]https://www.investopedia.com/tech/most-important-cryptocurrencies-other-than-bitcoin.

globally. This may ultimately fight the poverties, jobless, domestic economic crisis and world eco-catastrophe. *Halal* cryptocurrency management is with universal character welcoming, encouraging and benefiting all mankind regardless of one's religion, race, status, gender, color or even nationality. Its operation does not concern only money making, but part of its income with 2.5% in each transaction shall be deducted for the humanitarian or charitable causes based on the holistic principles of *Zakat*. Additionally, it is also recommended that all gross income in every transaction, account, management, activities, income and services shall be subjected to a reasonable deduction as *al-Tabarru'at* (charity) for the noble causes of charity and solidarity.

The basic features of *Halal* cryptocurrency model is that it shall be operated based on the *Halal* standard (compliant with the *Shari'ah* principles) closely supervised and duly screened through by a qualified *Shari'ah* advisory board, advised by a team of scholars as a board of advisors. The management of *Halal* cryptocurrency operation shall strictly be obliged to abide by the standard *Shari'ah* guidelines and ethical standard in its all activities, policies and functions within the rules of *Maqasid al-Shari'ah* (divine objectives). All investors (coin or token holders) shall be protected by transparence transactions and are formalized based on the *Shari'ah* justified doctrines and mechanisms.

A *Halal* cryptocurrency model shall be based on the following dimensions and philosophy: The model shall be operated based on the principles of *Shari'ah* (*Halal* standard). The total operation of the model shall be facilitated by a *Shari'ah* compliant hybrid structure. It evolves as both an asset-backed and also an asset-based operation within the *Shari'ah* frameworks. The company shall be backed by a valued asset equivalent to the value of the initial coin offering (ICO) at least, while its products and services (business operations) are based on asset (valued coins/tokens). The total operation shall be facilitated by *Shari'ah* justified instruments and divine principles like, *al-Mudarabah* (co-partnership), *al-Musharakah* (partnership or joint-venture), *al-Wakalah* (agency with commission), *al-Wadiyah* (deposit), *al-Ju'alah* (reward or service charge), *al-Amanah* (trust), *al-Ujarah* (service charge), *al-Tabarru'at* (donation) and *al-Zakat* (alms or compulsory tax). The structure of a *Halal* model is that it is a *Shari'ah* compliant hybrid platform of cryptocurrency backed by valued asset.

The operation of a *Halal* cryptocurrency model is facilitated and dully operated mainly based on the *Shari'ah* principles with the concept of 'issuer coin or token' or of an 'exchange platform.' An operation based on 'Issuer Coin or Token' shall primarily be executed by trading platform, a decentralized direct (one-to-one) buying and selling (*Bai' wa al-Shira'*) mechanisms. However, it may exceptionally be operated through exchange platform based on a *Shari'ah* hybrid mechanism, facilitated by the doctrines of *al-Shuftaza* (exchange), *al-Hewalah* (transfer), *al-Kafalah* (custodianship), *al-Amanah* (trust), *al-Wakalah* (agency by commission), *al-Ju'alah* (reward for services) and *al-Ujrah* (service charge) within the *Shari'ah* frameworks.

This book, however, contributes a series of specialized chapters addressing various core components of *Halal* model of cryptocurrency by intellectual and industrial analyzes with academic and empirical treatments besides possible recommendations.

PART I

An Overview of Halal Cryptocurrency Management

CHAPTER 1

Cryptocurrency? Its Halal Alternative Model

Mohd Ma'Sum Billah

BACKGROUND

The central idea of Bitcoin was first initiated by Satoshi Nakamoto in 2007 by using SHA-256 cryptocurrency hash function as its proof of work scheme through the blockchain technology. Nakamoto was born on April 5, 1975 and has claimed to be a man of Japan origin living in the USA and Europe. He has mostly focused on a number of cryptocurrencies and computer science. In August 2008 by Bitcoin.org, domain registration took place. In October 2008, the Bitcoin whitepaper was introduced. The first trial of Bitcoin was recorded on January 3, 2009 through a code: XBT. Bitcoin is known as decentralized digital currency by peer-to-peer network. IOTA was the first cryptocurrency introduced not through blockchain technology, but by using the tangle. In the process of all categories of digital currencies, which where aimed at resolving the double expanding problem.

Among the top cryptocurrencies are: Bitcoin, Litecoin (LTC), Ethereum (ETH), Zcash (ZEC), Dash, Riplle (XRP) and Monero (XMR). The testing period of the Bitcoin, however, continued till 2010. The preparation for the execution continued till 2013 when the first real operation of Bitcoin took place. As of May 24, 2017, Nakamoto is

M. M. Billah (✉)
Finance, Insurance, Fintech and Investment, Islamic Economics Institute,
King Abdul Aziz University, Jeddah, Kingdom of Saudi Arabia
URL: http://www.drmasumbillah.blogspot.com

© The Author(s) 2019
M. M. Billah (ed.), *Halal Cryptocurrency Management*,
https://doi.org/10.1007/978-3-030-10749-9_1

3

believed to own up to roughly one million Bitcoin with a value estimated at approximately USD 7 billion as of November 2017. On December 31, 2017, Bitcoin's value reaches USD 15,939.1348 and thus makes Bitcoin among the fastest growing financial engineering with 151.082% p.a. Current price of Bitcoin is tremendously decreased to USD 9532.18 as at May 6, 2018. It is further recorded that the initial token price of Bitcoin was USD 0.007, but the value increased to USD 10.85 within a year. Bitcoin began a roaring price 1 BTC = USD 770, but as at December 31, 2017, the price hit with 1 BTC = USD 15,939.1348. Through such growing track record, the Bitcoin is capturing the market on its own magnetic power without being controlled by any sovereign or specific regulatory standard. However, the issuer or the originator or the receiver positions as a virtual sovereign with vague identity. As a result, it has been observed that the users or expenders or investors participate in Bitcoin with no illegal or ethical protection.

Cryptocurrency Technology

In recent history, the cryptocurrency has been developed through a blockchain technology using the SHA256, a cryptographic hash function as is proof of work scheme. It is decentralized digital currency by peer-to-peer network, but IOTA was among the first cryptocurrencies not based on blockchain technology, but using tangle instead. Cryptocurrency through the blockchain technology is a virtual shared public leisure on which Internet network is based. All encrypted confirmed transactions are nodded and recorded in the blockchain as a proof of transactions. Each transaction is a chain and connected to each other thus enables a cryptocurrency digital wallet in calculating one's spendable balance, and new transactions can be verified to be expanding cryptocurrency that is actually owned by the spender or user.

Market Scenario

A cryptocurrency is costless, fastest and easiest digital currency business, creating an opportunity for all across the world into this economic environment. The cryptocurrency moves with its promising potential to encourage all levels of mankind to participate in the digital marketplace to maximize one's enterprising and entrepreneurial opportunities without unnecessary obstacles. Cryptocurrency may be a solution in the contemporary economic reality as an alternative currency to attribute a dual currency system in any jurisdiction in easying the day today commercial dealings. Despite the existence of the cryptocurrency with numerous comfortnesses, it encounters risks if one does not comply with the standard regulatory frameworks and also the ethical standard. It is submitted that the cryptocurrency can only be successful should one is governed by the acceptable regulatory standard.

In the contemporary global cyberspace, there are numerous cryptocurrencies offered through blockchain technology, most of which are moving ahead with significant results, particularly with commercial gain. Among those cryptocurrencies, the most popular are 10, namely[1] Bitcoin Cash (BCH), NEO (NEO), Monero (XMR), Dash (DASH), EOS (EOS), Ethereum (ETH), Cardano (ADA), Zcash (ZEC), Litecoin (LTC) and Ripple (XRP).

Confusion-Position-Reasons

There are numerous confusions arising out in cryptocurrency as to whether it is a currency or commodity or product? Is it a transaction with privity or with uncertainty? Does it survive on its sovereignty or on own existence? Is the receiver registered or based on virtual existence? Is the receiver known or vague behind the curtain? Is the transaction formalized by encryption or digit? Does it concern about the risk plan or moves on with no risk concern? Does the source of income in cryptocurrency is known or uncertain? Does cryptocurrency comply the standard or regulatory policies?

To response to those queries with appropriate solutions are: A cryptocurrency is recommended to be treated as a commodity, because of the nature of the transaction by buying and selling in the open digital market. In a cryptocurrency platform, the receiver shall be registered and known so to establish a privity between the user and the receiver. A cryptocurrency is recommended to be with coin or token-based offering through initial coin offering (ICO), but not through exchange platform, because it may encourage money laundering activities. Encryption may not be sufficient to protect the users in a cryptocurrency; thus, additionally a biometric process shall also be required to create a better authentication and security for the user. A cryptocurrency transaction

---

[1] https://www.investopedia.com/tech/most-important-cryptocurrencies-other-than-bitcoin/.

shall also be protected through a appropriate risk plan. It is essentially recommended that establishment, system, management, operation and all activities shall be governed by standard regulatory frameworks, policies and guidelines so to ensure a sustainable existence of cryptocurrency benefitting all within the legitimate frameworks.

REFORM STRATEGY

It has been observed in recent years that the cryptocurrency has been growing rapidly with mixed appreciation from different parts of the world. Even though it gains a significant market across the globe, yet it evolves around with numerous shortcomings that is a long-term threat to the growth of cryptocurrency. Therefore, it is timely and strongly recommended that the cryptocurrency model shall be reformed so to make it a globally acceptable alternative or complimentary currency or a digital monetary commodity. Hence, a reform strategy of cryptocurrency may be as follows:

Cryptocurrency shall be standardized with acceptable regulatory frameworks, policies and guidelines. Encryption shall further be strengthened by biometric signature of the user as an additional requirement. Ethical standard shall also be developed to regulate all levels of participants in the cryptocurrency platform, so to avoid any form of malpractices in the system and the market as well. There shall be central depository or sovereignty both at the international level and also in the local jurisdiction by respective central banks. A cryptocurrency shall be limited to the coin or token offering through ICO, but shall be opened to any of its activities through exchange platform, so to avoid possibilities of malpractices or money laundering by cryptocurrency. The payment system shall be reformed with guided digital payment method, such as electronic transfer which can also be activated through mobile to mobile and shall be formalized through a digital code by encrypted signature enabling the user to apply for any form of transaction within the creditability. A cryptocurrency space is a borderless platform thus its entity and operation are recommended to be based on offshore without being hindered by any local jurisdiction. Cryptocurrency operation shall be bound by a standard policy to segregate part of its income for the humanitarian or charitable causes, which can be through the compulsory *Zakat* (alms) provision and also *Tabbarru'at* (charitable) provision. All activities in cryptocurrency may also be exposed to risk due to technical failure, hackings, unforeseeable catastrophe and malpractices. Such unpredicted risks may be threat to the whole blockchain technology and cryptocurrency system besides discouraging the market and its participants. Therefore, it is strongly recommended that a standard risk plan shall be established for each cryptocurrency management.

HALAL ALTERNATIVE CRYPTOCURRENCY

Despite a rapid growth of cryptocurrency in the contemporary socioeconomic environment, there is not much solution yet for a *halal* alternative of cryptocurrency though there are some players trying to introduce *Shari'ah* model of cryptocurrency, but not successful yet. It is perhaps because of a *halal* alternative cannot simply be confirmed by mere changes of terminology without fulfilling the requirements for an effective *Shari'ah* model. A *halal* alternative model of cryptocurrency shall therefore be in conformity with the followings.

A *halal* model of cryptocurrency shall ensure its objectives compliant with the spirit of *al-Maqasid al-Shari'ah* (divine objectives). If the objective of the platform maintain in the paper by complying the *Shari'ah* principles, but in reality otherwise, may make the whole system non-compliant to the *Maqasid al-Shari'ah*. Therefore, to be a *halal* model, one shall be with *Shari'ah* spirit both in paper and in reality. A *halal* cryptocurrency model shall be governed and guided by the standard *Shari'ah* justified guidelines, policies and systems. It must be closely supervised by qualified *Shari'ah* board, all activities of it shall be screened through by a *Shari'ah* audit to ensure all activities and functions are compliant to the *Shari'ah* principles. While an advisory body shall contribute closely in advising the management and their activities in line with the *Shari'ah* principles and the divine ethical standard.

The blockchain technology along with its ledger and other technological components shall be screened through to ensure one is compliant to the divine spirit of *Shari'ah*. The operation shall be centralized by sovereignty. In Islamic business activities, the true sovereignty is with almighty *Allah (swt)*, but in practical, reality of cryptocurrency there should be a central depository with international regulatory control, government control at locality through the central bank and offshore regulatory control shall be maintained at the offshore level, which all shall be within a *Shari'ah* justified code or standard. Even though the operation of a *halal* cryptocurrency model takes place in the cyberspace with borderless activities, but to avoid unpredicted risk and malpractices, the operator shall be registered and duly incorporated as a company in any legal jurisdiction. Through such incorporation, the receiver is identified and privity is maintained between the receiver and users with a transparence culture.

There is confusion on whether the cryptocurrency (coin or token) shall be treated as currency or product or commodity. It is recommended that the cryptocurrency may be treated as a complimentary currency to be used as a medium of exchange of value. It may also be treated as a commodity or product, because one has the intrinsic virtual value. Thus, the *halal* alternative cryptocurrency may be used as a complimentary currency or a commodity or product so long one is compliant with *Shari'ah* principles. In any commercial activity under *Shari'ah* principles, shall be free from the element of uncertainty (*Garar*) thus, in *halal* cryptocurrency model the receiver, user, technology and activities shall be transparence and be free from uncertainty (*Garar*). In *halal* model of cryptocurrency, its total activities and transactions shall be facilitated by *Shari'ah* instruments and doctrines. For example, the investment by the users is based on principles of *al-Mudharabah* (co-partnership) or *al-Musharakah* (partnership) where the user receives return as income sharing with the receiver or other users through trading activities. The receiver receives the service charge based on the principles of *al-Jualah* (reward) or *al-Wakalah* (agency) or *al-Ujrah* (charge). Meanwhile, the transaction takes place in the blockchain platform is based on the principles of *al-Bay wa al-Shira* (buying and selling). The halal model of cryptocurrency shall be subjected to pay compulsory taxes with *Zakat* (alms). Besides, a voluntary segregation over the income shall be provisioned for humanitarian causes based on the principles of *al-Tabarruat* (charity).

In a *halal* model of cryptocurrency, a transaction by an encryption is not sufficient to protect the user from any unpredicted risk might be due to technical failure by hacks and or other catastrophes. Thus, additionally it is recommended to require a digital signature by biometric of the user simultaneously with the action of encryption in all levels of transaction. This may be a better authentic as to nodding and recording. In a *halal* cryptocurrency management, the divine ethical standard shall strictly be observed. No dishonesty, fraud, misrepresentation, deceiving, falsehood and other form of malpractices are intolerable, because of those moral hazards may defeat the purpose of *al-Maqasid al-Shari'ah*. In a *halal* cryptocurrency management, multi-currency basket model may also be allowed to make comfort among the users in the global cyber platform.

The establishment, operation and management of a *halal* cryptocurrency model are more recommended to be based on offshore, so that the total activities shall be bound by the offshore regulations without being interrupted by the local authorities, provided that all regulatory frameworks, policies and activities are within the *Shari'ah* justified standard. It shall also be worth noted that either receiver or user or technical supporter or anyone in the system shall in no situation be allowed to gain unlawfully at the expense of others, because there is no room for anyone gaining at the expense of others in the Islamic commercial activities. A *halal* cryptocurrency management is not free from risk be one due to technical failure, technology disaster by hacks, receiver bankruptcy or fraud activities. In those unforeseeable circumstances, the risk shall be minimized by a *Shari'ah* justified *takaful* (insurance) scheme aiming at protecting both the user and also the receiver against unpredicted catastrophe.

DICHOTOMY

Even though the cryptocurrency management in the conventional practices in recent days receives greater popularity and appreciation globally, the model is yet surrounded by numerous shortcomings and criticisms from different levels. A *halal* model of cryptocurrency on the other hand, despite being a new dimension, but one ought to be designed carefully by complying with the *Shari'ah* ethical and commercial principles. However, a dichotomy analysis is provided here to show how conventional cryptocurrency is different from the one designed under the *Shari'ah* normative principles (Table 1.1).

CONCLUSION

Cryptocurrency is a new chapter in the contemporary economic environment with rapid growth and greater appreciation across the world. Despite its greater popularity with perhaps emotional action and less rational way forward, it is somehow a risk yet due to availability of lack of regulatory standard, poor risk plan, unstable system, less concern on rights and obligations and minimum care as to moral responsibility. For a sustainable existence, the model shall be compliant to standard legal requirement, ethical principles, acceptable operational mechanisms and risk plan. A *halal* alternative cryptocurrency model on the other hand

Table 1.1 Conventional cryptocurrency and halal cryptocurrency

Issues	Conventional cryptocurrency	Halal cryptocurrency
Law and policies	In conventional cryptocurrency practices, the regulatory frameworks as to law, policy and orders are not quite concerned over the competitive commercial gain	The regulatory concern with Shari'ah standard in *halal* cryptocurrency model shall be among the prime requirements, so to make sure every activity are within the spirit of *al-Maqasid al-Shari'ah*
System	In the cryptocurrency practices, the blockchain technology and the total system are decentralized with private control by the receiver	The system of blockchain technology shall be controlled by systematic body for the common benefit with no personal agenda and be screened through by the *Shari'ah* board
Receiver	The receiver's identity is not necessarily to be registered in any onshore or offshore jurisdiction, but a cyber-registered entity is the common basis. In this culture, the receiver's identity remains unknown and uncertain, which may create a fundamental risk against the user	The receiver is required to be a registered entity either in onshore or offshore. In such requirement the receiver's identity shall be known and be free from uncertainty (*Garar*). This may create a confidence among the users in being protected from any fraud
Sovereignty	There is no sovereignty in cryptocurrency management as to be controlled by any central bank or central depository in the international jurisdiction. Its sovereignty is realized only by a private control of the receiver with no legal recognition	The actual sovereignty is with almighty *Allah (swt)* by complying with the regulatory and ethical principles of the *Qur'an* and the *Sunnah*. In addition, the central bank of the local jurisdiction and also the international central depository shall be recognized as the sovereignty in the practical reality, so to avoid any malpractices within the activities
Privity	The privity in cryptocurrency management between the user and the receiver seems quite remote by no visual legal contractual relation. This may result in avoidance of one's responsibility and accountability	The privity with contractual relationship between the user and receiver shall be maintained and known through cyberspace visual contractual relation, so that the accountability and responsibility of the parties are recorded
Control	Conventional cryptocurrency is controlled by private initiative of blockchain technology	A *halal* cryptocurrency management is controlled by divine principles within *al-Maqasid al-Shari'ah*, law and sovereignty

(continued)

Table 1.1   (continued)

Issues	Conventional cryptocurrency	Halal cryptocurrency
Growth	The growth of cryptocurrency practices is quite emotional without bothering to much of legal or ethical concern	The growth culture shall be rational with sustainability by complying with the *Shari'ah* concern and legal sensitivity
Subject matter	The subject matter is a digital coin or token and be treated as digital currency which can be convertible in any exchange platform	It may be treated as an alternative digital currency or digital commodity or digital product, because a digital coin or token carries digital value, which can also be defined as intrinsic value
Operational mechanisms	The operation takes place based on any self-designed mechanisms with no concern of standard regulatory frameworks yet. It is by a "coin or token" offering, traded in the trading platform through a blockchain technology. It is also practiced based on an exchange platform as "cryptocurrency exchange", but no standard guidelines yet in supporting such mechanisms	The operation of a *Halal* cryptocurrency model is facilitated and dully operated mainly based on the *Shari'ah* principles with the concept of "issuer coin or token" or of an "exchange platform" through a *Shari'ah* screened block-chain technology An operation based on "Issuer Coin or Token" shall primarily be executed by trading platform, a decentralized direct (one-to-one) buying and selling (*Bai' wa al-Shira'*) mechanisms However, It may exceptionally be operated through exchange platform based on a *Shari'ah* hybrid mechanism, facilitated by the doctrines of *al-Shuftaza* (exchange), *al-Hewalah* (transfer), *al-Kafalah* (custodianship), *al-Amanah* (trust), *al-Wakalah* (agency by commission), *al-Ju'alah* (reward for services) and *al-Ujrah* (service charge) within the *Shari'ah* frameworks
Income	The sources of income in the conventional cryptocurrency management are unknown	In *halal* cryptocurrency management, the sources are known to both receivers and users through legitimate trading
Tax	There is nether concern of tax over the income in the conventional cryptocurrency management nor there is any tax plan or policy	In Islamic cryptocurrency management, it is mandatory to establish a *Zakat* provision over any income, if the income is Zakatable. In addition, the tax also be payable as per the statutory requirement

(continued)

Table 1.1   (continued)

Issues	Conventional cryptocurrency	Halal cryptocurrency
Risk	There is no risk plan in conventional cryptocurrency management yet, to protect either the user or the receiver against any unpredicted catastrophe	The risk plan is required in *halal* cryptocurrency management to protect receiver, user and the system against unpredicted risk; thus, a *takaful* scheme is strongly recommended to be established in managing unpredicted risk against *halal* cryptocurrency management
Formality	In the conventional cryptocurrency management, the transaction is confirmed by the encryption only so to nod and record the transaction. By encryption with digit alone may not be an enough protection for the user if incase the digit is known to someone else or being hacked	For the *halal* cryptocurrency management, to protect the user in a better way, it is recommended that there shall be two requirements for the formalization of a transaction and that is encryption by digit and simultaneously by biometric of the user, so to nod and record the transaction with legal status
Backing asset	A cryptocurrency if so operated without being backed by any valued asset (at least equivalent to the total ICO value) may lead to high risk for the investors with any unforeseeable catastrophe. In the current practices of cryptocurrency, there is no such requirement of backing asset to back the total operation	In the *halal* cryptocurrency management, a valued backing asset with legitimate proof of product or proof of asset or proof of property or proof of commodity (POP) with at least an equivalent value of the ICO, to back the total operation. The objective of this requirement is among others to create a legitimate confidence in the market and among the market participants
Instrument	There is no specific instrument used in the cryptocurrency management except buying and selling with unauthorized traditional mechanism	There are numerous *Shari'ah* justified instruments recommended to facilitate a *halal* cryptocurrency management. Among them are: *al-Mudharabah*, *al-Wakalah*, *al-Jualah*, *al-Bai' wa al-Shira'* and *al-Tabarruat*
Moral hazard	There is no specific regulation or standard policy to regulate moral hazards or malpractices. Thus, it is left as an option to the personal responsibility	It is among the primary requirements of a *halal* cryptocurrency management to strictly concern and observe ethical compliance within the *Maqasid al-Shari'ah* in all levels of personality, decision making and execution

(continued)

Table 1.1 (continued)

Issues	Conventional cryptocurrency	Halal cryptocurrency
Objective	The prime objective in cryptocurrency management is to make money and maximize self-opportunities	The objective shall be within the holistic spirit of *Shari'ah*. Commercial gain within the legitimate frameworks is one of the objectives while the other is to create an entrepreneurship opportunities for all by complying with the *halal* standard. It also aims at caring for humanitarian causes through the doctrine of *al-Tabarruat*
Humanitarian concern	There is no humanitarian concern in conventional cryptocurrency management as a requirement	In *Halal* cryptocurrency management, humanitarian concern is among the objectives in helping others out of the income
Nature	It offers coins or tokens, which can be traded in the cyber platform or be in the exchange platform	It has some similarities with conventional practices to offer through coin or token and be traded in digital platform. The coin can be converted in the exchange platform, but is not encouraged, so to avoid any illegal money laundering. The digital coin can be used as an alternative or complimentary currency in buying commodities or paying dues without having opportunity to treat the coin as a real currency to be exchanged in the foreign exchange platform, so to avoid the possibility of money laundering in the cyberspace
ICO	It offers with initial coin offering (ICO) with a value determined by the receiver on its own discretion	It can be offered either with initial coin offering (ICO) or initial token offering (ITO) or initial product offering (IPO) or initial commodity offering (ICO) with a justifiable value affordable to all levels of mankind, so to maximize an opportunity of entrepreneurship in the cyberspace for all
Currency	It is a coin or token, which is treated as a non-intrinsic currency	Even though it is a coin or token used in the digital platform may also be recommended to be treated as an alternative currency for trading or payment of dues

is conceptually vibrate the global environment though not in effective operation yet. It is in no excuse as to *Shari'ah* compliance, legal requirements, divine code of ethics, standard system, operational mechanisms and activities within the divine objectives. In the *halal* model, mere commercial gain shall not be a prime objective over the socioeconomic and humanitarian concern within the *al-Maqasid al-Shari'ah*.

CHAPTER 2

SWOT Analysis
of Halal Cryptocurrency Structure

Mohd Ma'Sum Billah

SWOT Analysis on Cryptocurrency: An Overview

A SWOT analysis on cryptocurrency in the contemporary era reveals a META view that, a cryptocurrency is strengthened by its unique characters as it is costless and easiest as to its procedural requirements, common opportunities for all, safe and secured way of buying and selling through block-chain platform, not banking obstacles, friendly with sustainability and borderless operation with minimum threat. It creates huge opportunities for all levels of mankind with no restriction as to one's age, status, religion, color, gender or even nationality, to maximize the opportunity of enterprising and entrepreneurship through cryptocurrency. Such potential in cryptocurrency may contribute to rebuilding the global economic atmosphere.

Among the weaknesses in cryptocurrency are, it evolves around the element of uncertainty, less focus on regulatory requirement, zero risk plan, no financial sovereignty, no systematic management, emotional market competition, no humanitarian concern, poor realization of privity

M. M. Billah (✉)
Finance, Insurance, Fintech and Investment, Islamic Economics Institute,
King Abdul Aziz University, Jeddah, Kingdom of Saudi Arabia
URL: http://www.drmasumbillah.blogspot.com

© The Author(s) 2019
M. M. Billah (ed.), *Halal Cryptocurrency Management*,
https://doi.org/10.1007/978-3-030-10749-9_2

15

and less concern on accountability. This all weaknesses, if so allowed to be continued, the cryptocurrency movement may seriously be hindered till those shortcomings are not seriously attended with appropriate improvement.

Among the opportunities in cryptocurrency are, it is profitability with minimum efforts and less cost, unrestricted commercial gain to build up one's economic strength through enterprising and entrepreneurship, borderless participation, common economic eradication, world peace with economic stability for all and to create a matured economic nation.

Among the challenges in cryptocurrency are, it is a threat to the existing banking system, the federal reserve and international banking system are exposed to threat, challenges to the standard laws and orders, undermining the public revenue, no legal protections to entrepreneurs, the market participants encounter uncertainty, no sovereignty, but on individual initiative monetary movement. Opening the door for the money laundering through the exchange platforms, system hazardous by hacks, moral hazardous by non-compliance to the laws and orders and emotional competitions with not much of ethical concern. It is thus concluded here that, despite the rapid growth of the cryptocurrency movement it encounters numerous weaknesses and threats. It is utmost essential to identify all those negative components and find the ways of standardization, so to maximize the opportunities in cryptocurrency with sustainable existence.

Scrutinizing Over SWOT Analysis

A further investigation over the ongoing cryptocurrency management and its structure by comparing with the *halal* alternative model as follows.

Technology

The block-chain technology is the standard digital platform to operate cryptocurrency management. The block-chain platform for the conventional cryptocurrency management is not regulated by standard laws and policies, but an individual initiative in the cyberspace with no concern in complying to any standard law or policies. Each component of the block-chain platform is functioned at the choice of the receiver or technology provider. A *Halal* alternative on the other hand, even though operates its model on the block-chain platform, but every component of the technology, its functions and activities shall be inconformity with the divine spirit of *Shari'ah*. Such *Shari'ah* compliance shall be confirmed by the *Shari'ah* advisory board, which shall be established by the operator as a prerequisite.

Establishment

Currently, most of the cryptocurrencies operators are based on the cyberspace domain registration without being properly formalized at any jurisdiction. Such practices may lead to a high risk by letting the receiver uncertain and unknown to the users. This may also give a chance for the receiver to escape free from any liability while victimizing the users with no legal rights. In *Halal* cryptocurrency management, it is prerequisite that the operation shall be registered as a company and duly incorporated in any jurisdiction either in the offshore or onshore. The company's identity accounts with the banks and activities shall be known to users without being vague. A registered company may also contribute to help both the users and the receiver in the cryptocurrency management free from malpractices by unlawful gain at the expense of others.

Law and Policies

The conventional cryptocurrency management does not really concern in complying any law or standard policy in its establishment, functions and operations. Rather one relies on individual preferred policies, standard and culture in the total establishment, operations and activities of cryptocurrency. This may lead to a threat to the standard laws, policies and orders and thus may eventually be weakening the global financial system. In the *halal* alternative cryptocurrency model, each and every component of one's establishment, operations and management shall be in conformity with the *Shari'ah* principles, ethical standard and the laws and policies of the local jurisdiction besides the cyberspace regulation. A *halal* alternative model, therefore, is required to establish standard policies and guidelines as prerequisite.

Sovereignty

In the current practices of cryptocurrencies, there is no provision of sovereignty in centralizing one's activities. Financial activities with no sovereignty may lead to a huge catastrophe with malpractices and opening the door for gaining unlawfully at the expense of others. In a *halal* alternative cryptocurrency, on the other hand, the sovereignty shall first be with almighty *Allah (swt)* and thus every activity of it shall be in conformity with the rules of *Maqasid al-Shari'ah*. Secondly, a qualified advisory board shall be established to ensure all activities of the operation are compliant to *Shari'ah* principles. Hence, the *Shari'ah* advisory board shall function as an internal sovereignty. Thirdly, all activities shall be regulated and controlled by the central bank of local jurisdiction within the principles of *Shari'ah* compliance. Fourthly, the total operation shall generally comply with the international monetary authority and principles.

Regulatory Authorities

In the current practices of cryptocurrency, there is no specific regulatory authority, regulating the activities of cryptocurrency. This may be a danger to the whole economic system generally and particularly a threat to the sustainable growth of cryptocurrency. In a *Halal* cryptocurrency management, even though there is no specific law enacted yet, the establishment, system, technology, operation and all activities are subject to the total compliance of the *Shari'ah* principles. Such conformity shall be ensured by the *Shari'ah* advisory body, *Shari'ah* compliance policies and guidelines, management responsibilities and corporate governance by complying with the divine ethical principles.

Backing Asset

In the contemporary cryptocurrency practices, one does neither hold any backing asset to back the total operation nor does it require any backing asset. A financial operation without a backing asset may lead to numerous catastrophes and may eventually weaken the total financial system. In a *Halal* cryptocurrency management, it shall be prerequisite to hold a valued asset as backing asset for the total operation. The backing asset shall have an estimated value more than the initial coin offering (ICO). Such backing asset shall back the whole operation to create a confidence in the market among the investors and also to act as a safeguard for the operation if incase of any catastrophe undesirably be faced.

Authenticity of Transaction

In current practices of cryptocurrency, the transaction is confirmed by the encryption of the users. Mere digital encryption with digit may alone not be sufficient to protect the user from any digital catastrophe like hacks, system crash or natural disaster. In a *halal* cryptocurrency management, it is suggested that the transaction activated by encryption shall additionally be signed by digital biometric, so that it may provide a better protection for the users against any form of catastrophe. Therefore, it is recommended that each transaction shall be confirmed with nodding and recording by encryption with digit and also signature by biometric of the users.

Ethical Concern

In the contemporary practices cryptocurrency, the ethical concern is not a primary one, but dominated by the commercial gain. Everyone is concerned how to make money in no matter whether one is concerned with the ethical principles or otherwise. Less concern on ethical principles in any commercial or financial activities may be a threat to the sustainable growth and existence of the system and thus may compel the world of economy to pay unforeseeable damages. In *Halal* cryptocurrency management, it is a prerequisite to care and concern about the divine ethical principles in one's all activities of the operation within the *Maqasid al-Shari'ah*. So that no malpractices, unlawful gain, greediness, unjust enrichment and fraud may not have any place in the *Halal* cryptocurrency management.

Risk Plan

There is no risk plan in the contemporary cryptocurrency management against any unpredicted risk, be one against the system, operation, users or even receivers. In the cryptocurrency management, their numerous risks are awaiting namely system collapse by crash or hacks, natural disasters, deceive or malpractices by the receiver or unethical activities adopted in the trading among the users. All those are among the risks, but no protection plan as yet. In *Halal* cryptocurrency management, risk plan is one of the prime concern to protect both the user and the receiver against unpredicted catastrophe be one either by system crash, hacks, unethical actions or natural disaster. In all circumstances, it is recommended that, there may be two categories of risks plan designed namely; user's Takaful plan and receiver *takaful* plan. Both categories of plans will be discussing in detail under the Chapter 20 of this book.

Tax Provision

There is no tax provision over the income of the contemporary crypto-currency management neither by law nor by internal policies. Any financial or commercial activities if so ignores the tax provision, might be a threat to the public policy. In a *Halal* cryptocurrency, on the other hand, 2.5% *Zakat* is required to be paid over the net income should the *Zakat* requirement is fulfilled besides a percentage of tax over one's net income required by the applicable laws of the jurisdiction concerned. It is clarified that *Zakat* can be adjusted with the income tax subject to the applicable laws.

Humanitarian Concern

In the conventional cryptocurrency management, there is neither provision nor a concern generally to care about humanitarian issues out of its income. In any economic or financial operation, it is a common culture to care about the humanitarian issues out of one's income. Failure to humanitarian concern, the economic justice with fair distribution by caring about others may be defeated. In *Halal* cryptocurrency management, it is strongly recommended that part of the income shall be segregated on the basis of the principles of *al-Tabaruat* (charity) for the humanitarian care. It is to ensure that, through a humanitarian provision, the economic justice is upheld.

Market Niche

It is undoubtedly agreed that the cryptocurrency captures a promising global market as one of the fastest growing digital economic components or fin-tech through the block-chain technology. Because, it is one of the easiest, fastest and comfort financial mechanisms benefiting all with universal character. Its foreseeable future is great. But, the true result with sustainable existence is still under threat due to weaknesses in the regulatory frameworks, less concern on risk management, standardizing the system and ethical compliance. To achieve the goal of a niche market, all aspects of weaknesses shall be ratified by upgrading the total system and activities by complying the standard laws and policies. A *Halal* cryptocurrency management thus shall in no situation be allowed to be operated without complying the true principles of *Maqasid al-Shari'ah* and that may confirm a true achievement of global market niche with utmost appreciation.

Common Entrepreneurship

A cryptocurrency platform under both the conventional and the *Halal* model is a common digital entrepreneurship platform for all with utmost comfort level to establish one as an entrepreneur and gain lawfully. Thus, a cryptocurrency platform may contribute to the development of micro-entrepreneurship opportunities for all mankind with no tension of unnecessary cost, but with less effort, with no time waste and not much of formalities ought to be experienced through. To conclude here, a cryptocurrency platform is a common digital entrepreneurship platform.

Enterprising

There are huge number of population in the world with no proper sources of income due to retrenchment, jobless, poverty, students, housewife, poor income and other factors. The cryptocurrency platform in the contemporary socioeconomic environment is timely to create an easy opportunity for all those of less fortunate ones to be enterprising and entrepreneuring by making one self-reliant. This may eventually contribute to the poverty eradication, creating an enterprising and an entrepreneurship-based community, so to create a true world peace with a reasonable and sustainable eco-victory.

Compliment to Eco-Strength

A cryptocurrency platform of both the conventional and the *Halal* model are compliment to the economic growth and its global sustainable strength. All levels of mankind with no restriction have the common opportunity to participate in the cryptocurrency platform and maximize one's economic goal within the legitimate frameworks.

Thus, the common participation in the cryptocurrency platform may be a significant contribution and compliment to the economic strength of the world community.

Economic Opportunity for All

The contemporary banking and financial system or corporate activities do not create an opportunity for all mankind due to limitation by policies and cultures. Therefore, in the ongoing commercial system and activities, which fail to create an economic well-being for all mankind with universal value. The cryptocurrency platform, on the other hand, is costless with minimum formalities, less effort, less obstacles and less restriction creates a global opportunity for all mankind regardless of one's status, religion, age or nationality, but with universal value to maximize one's source of legitimate income.

Economic Sustainability

The cryptocurrency platform wakes up all level of mankind be one entrepreneur, employee, jobless, less fortunate or even disable ones to be motivated, skilled, smarter, responsible, laborious and participant in the commercial activities through the cryptocurrency platform to make one enterprising and entrepreneur in view of gaining legitimate income with less cost and less effort, but through a smart management. Thus, eventually, it may contribute to building up a community with sustainable economic existence and be a self-reliant thus may contribute to an economic sustainability.

CONCLUSION

It is submitted that despite the cryptocurrency platform is promising component in the contemporary economic chapter to create an opportunity for all with universal character to maximize one's source of income and gain legitimately with less effort and less cost. But, existing model and activities are haunted with numerous weaknesses and threats. The true achievement can only be realized if the above SWOT analysis results are closely observed with careful improvement of the total system and activities and, for the *Halal* model, which shall observe within the *Maqasid al-Shari'ah*.

CHAPTER 3

Innovative Action of Halal Cryptocurrency Management

Mohd Ma'Sum Billah

INTRODUCTION

The success of any corporate industry including financial institutions depends on mainly innovation in reality. The innovation shall be maintained through in policies, culture, corporate management, operation and management, products and services. Cryptocurrency management is no exception, which requires to be maintained with innovative character in technology, system, policies and guidelines, products and services, management and operation towards its sustainable existence. In *Halal* cryptocurrency management, it is among the prime concerns to upheld innovative characters and cultures within *Maqasid al-Shari'ah*.

The innovation shall be in the establishment of the entity with strategic mission and vision. Policies, guidelines and regulatory compliance are to ensure an effective and legitimate operation and offerings. The blockchain technology and the model structure in creating a digital platform shall be with careful concern so that technical failure do not easily come in as an obstacle. The system, management and operational mechanisms

M. M. Billah (✉)
Finance, Insurance, Fintech and Investment, Islamic Economics Institute, King Abdul Aziz University, Jeddah, Kingdom of Saudi Arabia
URL: http://www.drmasumbillah.blogspot.com

© The Author(s) 2019
M. M. Billah (ed.), *Halal Cryptocurrency Management*,
https://doi.org/10.1007/978-3-030-10749-9_3

23

shall be a friendly one, but sustainable character, thus may create an utmost confidence among the users in the cryptocurrency platform. It is also important for the users to be motivated and trained with at least a basic knowledge on technical know-how, so that the users may function their activities in the platform with less risk. This may eventually strengthen the industrial growth. The pricing of the coin or token and its quantity in the initial coin offering (ICO) are also among the innovative concerns with possible lowest price and minimum quantity so that everyone can afford to participate in the platform. The confirmation of the transaction by the user through encryption alone may not be sufficient to protect the users from any digital catastrophe. Thus, in addition to encryption, a biometric signature is recommended to record and node the transaction. For a sustainable growth of the industry and creating confidence among the users and the receivers in the cryptocurrency platform, the risk plan is also an innovative strategy against any unpredicted catastrophe, be one is by capital risk, management risk, technology failure or malpractices.

Innovative Cryptocurrency Within *Maqasid al-Shari'ah*

As has been highlighted earlier that, the cryptocurrency movement in today's economy is moving faster perhaps emotionally by applying less rational principles. It is thus, with utmost concern to recommend that, a *Halal* cryptocurrency management shall ensure an innovation in its every component within the *Maqasid al-Shari'ah*, so this may lead the platform with sustainable growth and success in appreciating among the global market. Followings are among the innovative concerns of the *Halal* cryptocurrency platform.

Corporate Innovation

A *halal* cryptocurrency management shall establish its result oriented objectives within *Maqasid al-Shari'ah*. The establishment of the company, website and other digital networks are recommended to be based on an offshore jurisdiction. Because, a cryptocurrency management is a digital-based borderless operation outreaches the globe. Thus, it is not wise or rational to be subject to any local law or policy, but an offshore law with global impact. The location of the registration of the company shall be carefully identified by looking at the comfort of operation within the legitimate frameworks. The corporate communication shall be friendly and accessible with no network disruption so that the trading activities in the platform run smoothly.

Regulatory Innovation

The world witnesses that there is no any established regulatory frameworks, policies or guidelines available yet in regulating the cryptocurrency management. It is a high risk in any commercial or financial environment if one is moving forward with activities, but no regulatory backup and the cryptocurrency is no exception. For *Halal* cryptocurrency management, it is among the prime concerns to ensure its establishment, system, technology, management, operation and activities of the platform are accurately compliant to the applicable laws, policies, guidelines and standard justified by the *Shari'ah* principles and divine code of ethics within the *Maqasid al-Shari'ah*. Failure to comply the standard regulatory frameworks, a *Halal* cryptocurrency management may not be recognized as a legitimate platform within the ambit of the *Shari'ah*.

Innovative Technology

Cryptocurrency is developed and operated based on cryptography supported by a digital platform called block-chain technology. The block-chain technology is required to be tested in ensuring that none of its components is threatened to be hacked or failure by technical error. To provide a reliable service through a block-chain technology for the cryptocurrency management, the technology, system and the mechanisms shall be tested prior to launching the ICO and continue with review on regular routine so that no default can hinder the operation. Thus, ensuring a reliable technology is an innovative step in cryptocurrency management for a sustainable growth by creating confidence in the market.

Innovative System

Despite the rapid growth of the technology and its digital operation be one is commercial or otherwise with no exception to cryptocurrency, there are numerous failures in the system due to careless designation, poor devices, unskilled operation and less appropriateness. As a result, the system is under threat. For a sustainable growth of cryptocurrency management, the system shall be efficiently managed by ensuring that the designation and application are tested and reviewed, managed by skilled professionals and to be updated in line with the global growth, is an innovative system. For a true success of a *Halal* cryptocurrency management, an innovative system is among the prerequisite.

Human Resource Innovation

Human resource is among the prime factors in any corporate and non-corporate industries. Skilled professionals, efficient, committed and honest human resources are the goodwill of the industry. Failure to select right human resources may result in numerous disasters in the industry leading to its future. For a successful cryptocurrency management, it is an undeniable fact that the total human resources including the decision-makers, management, system operator, marketing arm and other facilitators shall be with appropriate skills, professional personality, smart management skill, talented programmers, honest and committed ones so that the industry moves forward with its true success.

Innovative Corporate Governance

A good corporate governance of any industry leads to a dynamic success of the industry in general. Teamwork with utmost commitment, smartness with sincerity and prioritizing the corporate interest over personal benefit are among the core characteristics of dynamic corporate governance. A true corporate governance culture shall be reviewed, upgraded, enriched with new dimension and ranked with appropriateness on a regular routine, is a corporate governance innovation. Unprofessional competition, jealousy, selfishness, deceiving, and dishonesty among the employees or the employer and the employees, maybe a danger to a corporate future. Thus, an innovative corporate governance is among the prime concerns in a cryptocurrency for its growth and success with market confidence.

Innovative Planning and Strategy

The idea of cryptocurrency is developed through smart digital knowledge by intellectual power. It does not involve much of paperwork by traditional style. It is thus a cyber-invention in this modern socio-economic culture. A successful journey of cryptocurrency depends on innovative planning and smart strategies. A *Halal* cryptocurrency model shall be designed, structured and executed through innovation and strategies within the *Maqasid al-Shari'ah*. The planning and strategies shall not primarily aim at a commercial gain, but to create an opportunity of enterprising and entrepreneurship for all towards a common economic wellbeing by mutual cooperation within the legitimate frameworks. Therefore, the planning and the strategies in a *Halal* cryptocurrency management shall aim a holistic approach with care and concern, but not gaining at the expense of others and that is, an innovative action plan.

Innovative Decision-Making

In the commercial or financial industries, the decision made mostly for the interest of own industry as a primary concern whilst the consumers' benefits are secondary one. Such culture develops corruption, nepotism, selfishness and unfair gain, which eventually become a threat to the industry in general as to its original objective. For a true success in any industry, the decision shall be based on rational principles to protect both the industry and the consumers as well with a just treatment. In cryptocurrency management today, it has been observed that the most of the operators offered their products and services through blockchain technology aiming at their own interest as a primary concern while the users' interest is treated as a secondary. It is due to poor regulatory frameworks, self-created policies and guidelines, no risk plan, no humanitarian concern, no standard ethical principles and no sovereign concern, which may result an uncertainty for the users protection.

Therefore, in an acceptable cryptocurrency management, the decision-making in all levels shall be innovative and compliant to the standard laws and policies. A *Halal* cryptocurrency management likewise, shall ensure its legitimate operation through all levels of its decision making, are compliant to or in harmony with the *Shari'ah* principles thus, in a *Halal* cryptocurrency management, the total operational mechanisms, policies and guidelines shall closely be screened through by a qualified *Shari'ah* board in ensuring that all activities are within the *Maqasid al-Shari'ah*. The decision-making by the board, *Shari'ah* board and the management shall time to time be reviewed with innovative culture within the *Maqasid al-Shari'ah*.

Innovative Management

The management and operation in cryptocurrency management shall be smart, intelligence, wise and dynamic so that the company's future is flourished and that eventually brings dynamic results both for the industry and the users as well. The management's honesty with fair treatment to all users is an innovative culture to attract the market with sustainability. The management or operation team shall maintain a good manual, policies and guidelines for the decision making, planning and strategies, operation and interaction in all levels of its activities. The management shall review its policies, methods and cultures to suit the market niche. A *Halal* cryptocurrency management is no exception, but shall maintain an innovative culture in its management and operation within the *Maqasid al-Shari'ah*.

Cultural Innovation

It is among the prime concerns for any corporate industry to maintain a cultural innovation, so to cope with a competitive market. Many industries collapsed in the history are mainly just because of, failure to maintain an acceptable innovative culture within the industry. Even though the cryptocurrency is in its infancy stage, initiated in the twenty-first century with a bit of emotional movement with no concern much of innovative culture. Such ignorance to innovative culture may hinder the dynamic growth of the industry eventually. For a *Halal* cryptocurrency management, it is strongly recommended that, in any level of its operation, no emotionalism shall influence, but rational principles and cultures shall be adapted and duly appreciated. It is thus concluded that, in a *Halal* cryptocurrency management, all stages of its corporate culture either individual or group, shall be innovative ones by complying the holistic principles of *Shari'ah* within *Maqasid al-Shari'ah*.

Asset-Back Operation by Backing Asset

A commodity or currency transaction shall be backed by valuable asset except in debt trading. In current practices of cryptocurrency management, the total operation is seemed to be not backed by any valuable asset, but on virtual imagination only. Some operators use asset-back operation, but only in paper while some are operating on asset base by imagining the coins are asset. If the operation is without any backing asset may be a high risk with uncertainty for both the receiver and the users. For a *Halal* cryptocurrency management, to avoid uncertainty (*Garar*) and unforeseeable catastrophe, asset-back operation shall be a prerequisite. The asset shall be physically valued one, not by virtual imagination. The backing asset with its proof of product (POP) shall maintain a certified value not less than the total value of the ICO. The valued asset may be any form of asset, product, intellectual property, knowledge-based asset, IT, software, system, project, program and or others, so long one carries the certified commercial value. If in case, the cryptocurrency system collapses, the users maybe protected by the underlying backing asset. Furthermore, the backing asset shall be valuable commercially within the *Shari'ah* definition and shall maintain a certified POP.

Product Innovation (Coin or Token)

In the cryptocurrency practices today, the roaring price of some offered coin through ICO is, unreasonably expensive that, does not encourage the participants to participate with common affordability. For a sustainable growth of cryptocurrency management, the value of the coin in the ICO shall be as low as possible affordable to everyone and that is product innovation in the cryptocurrency management. In a *Halal* cryptocurrency management its recommended that the coin in the ICO shall be priced as low as USD1.00 so to make it affordable for everyone in benefiting from a *Halal* cryptocurrency management. In a *Halal* cryptocurrency management furthermore, the product shall be on coin or token-based trading through block-chain platform, but may not be recommended on exchange platform unless an exchange platform is strictly guided and controlled by a standard regulatory frameworks. Because, trading activities through an exchange platform may lead to money laundering or other form of unethical digital activities.

Innovative ICO

In a *Halal* cryptocurrency management, the ICO shall be well planned with an affordable price through reliable system and on convenient platform. Prior to the ICO, the public awareness through summit or media shall be made so that everyone in the market is aware about the forthcoming ICO. An ICO can be made available in multiple phases depending on the market niche, jurisdiction and creating common opportunity for all. In the process of ICO, monopolism, malpractices, nepotism and dishonesty are among those unethical cultures, which shall be avoided to ensure an innovative ICO.

Innovative Summit

For a cryptocurrency management, it is prerequisite to hold a physical summit or operational briefing in several jurisdictions to ensure that the ICO is outreached in all levels of the market. Alternatively, a media summit can be organized to achieve the purpose. A media summit may comprise of both printing and digital media group to be invited in a briefing to be called media summit. The media group is expected to carry the offer ICO brief and publish widely prior to the launching of the ICO so that the information outreaches the world at large. The media summit is recommended to be held at least a week before the ICO takes place. Because, the soft information through the media summit may help the participants to be aware about the upcoming ICO, and thus, enables the market to participate in the platform with wise decision. For a *Halal* cryptocurrency management, it is recommended that a media summit in different jurisdictions with simultaneous effect shall be organized at least a week before the ICO takes place so that the market may have a chance to make a good decision in participating in the *Halal* cryptocurrency platform and benefit rationally.

Smart Marketing

Cryptocurrency is a new arriving financial platform, which is promoted smartly without following the traditional method. Its marketing strategy is basically confined within the cyberspace through technological tools and that is social media and electronic communications. It is prerequisite for a cryptocurrency to be introduced to public at large by crypto summit with a traditional physical crowd before launching the ICO. Such a traditional summit may not be effective with significant results thus, a smart summit through media flash and cyber communications is recommended. For a smart marketing strategy in a *Halal* cryptocurrency management, it is recommended that a public awareness shall be made through organizing a media summit highlighting the model structure, objectives, methodologies, prospects of ICO and the future protection of the investors along with beneficial results prior to the launching of the ICO. This smart strategy may contribute to a large marketing opportunity with global awareness in a short period of time with less cost and efforts while the result is significant.

Innovative Trading Platform

A traditional trading platform requires numerous procedures and formalities besides costs, efforts and timing. In a cryptocurrency management where the coins or the tokens are traded in the cyberspace trading or exchange platforms through a standard system in the block-chain technology based on respective digital wallet. In a *Halal* cryptocurrency management, the trading platform shall be innovative within the spirit of the *Maqasid al-Shari'ah*. The traders shall not aim at gaining at the expense of others to be called an unethical gain, but the trading environment shall be enshrined by the spirit of mutual cooperation and brotherhood within the *Halal* frameworks. The spirit of capitalism or causing the market crash by maximizing self-opportunity does not in fact have room in the *Shari'ah* teachings. In other word, a trading platform in a *Halal* cryptocurrency management shall be innovated by smartness, honesty and care about others with concern within the ambit of *Maqasid al-Shari'ah*.

Dynamic Risk Management

A cryptocurrency management in fact exposes to numerous risks, be one in the cyberspace or otherwise. A risk in cryptocurrency management may be anticipated due to system crash, hacking, failure to compliance, market crash, war risk, natural disasters, malpractices and or others. In the contemporary practices of cryptocurrency, there is neither any risk plan by the receiver or the users or a regulatory requirement exist yet. In the absence of an appropriate risk plan in the cryptocurrency management, the total system may be exposed to undesirable threat. In a *Halal* cryptocurrency management, it is thus recommended that the risk plan shall be a prerequisite for the operation and that is, based on the principles of *Takaful*. Two schemes of *Takaful* for cryptocurrency management may be recommended namely;

1. *Cryptocurrency User Takaful Scheme.*
2. *Cryptocurrency Receiver Takaful Scheme.*

The user Takaful scheme shall protect the user against unpredicted catastrophe might because by unlawful hackings, capital loss, system crash and disasters by fraudulent. In all those unpredicted catastrophes, the users may be protected by a defined cryptocurrency user Takaful scheme. The receiver Takaful scheme moreover, shall be protected against any unforeseeable risk due to technological failure, regulatory sanction, system hacks, war risk, insolvency, natural disaster and others. The receiver in those unexpected circumstances may be protected by a defined receiver Takaful scheme.

Humanitarian Concern

In any commercial or financial venture or activity, the humanitarian concern out of one's legitimate income is traditionally ruled out as a cooperate customary culture. In the contemporary cryptocurrency management, there is no any written humanitarian concern over the income guided by the standard policy or regulatory requirement yet. In a *Halal* cryptocurrency management, the humanitarian concern over the legitimate income shall be among the prerequisites, which shall be ruled out by a standard policy. The provision of 2.5% *Zakat* over the income is mandatory as the *Shari'ah* requirement. In addition, a provision shall be established in segregating a percentage of the income as *al-Tabarruat* (charity) for the humanitarian causes. So that the poor, destitute, disabled, helpless, jobless and other categories of unfortunate people in any society are cared or any humanitarian sectors, be one health care, education, shelter, food, public welfare and or others may have the right to be benefitted out of the income of a *Halal* cryptocurrency business.

CONCLUSION

It is indeed submitted that a cryptocurrency management either in the conventional economy or the *Shari'ah* model shall be integrated with an acceptable innovative culture for one's sustainable existence with true goals. The recognition, appreciation and success of a *Halal* cryptocurrency management shall ensure its innovative culture as to system, activities, effectiveness and operation with dynamic corporate governance and divine culture within the *Maqasid al-Shari'ah* are among the prerequisites. Failure to observe the innovative culture, the system may expose to weakening the future growth of the total system.

CHAPTER 4

Halal Cryptocurrency and Financial Stability

Muhamed Zulkhibri

INTRODUCTION

The development of electronic means of payment has shown a new perspective: it is now possible to think about financial processes without the need for a traditional, trusted intermediary, e.g. a bank or an online payment service. As part of the new technology, there is an emergence of privately developed digital currencies so-called a cryptocurrency[1] using new decentralized technologies. Fundamental to these cryptocurrencies is the establishment of a new asset, the unit of the cryptocurrencies, i.e. a Bitcoin and a new record-keeping and transfer mechanism that enables users to store and trade those units, i.e. a blockchain, often without reliance on traditional financial institutions. Several thousand cryptocurrencies have joined the ecosphere around Bitcoin. Although Bitcoin was the first cryptocurrency and the most popular cryptocurrency, it is not the only cryptocurrency using blockchain technology. There are many

[1]The terms cryptocurrencies, virtual currencies and digital currencies are often used interchangeable, but they are different. However, in this chapter, we use these terms interchangeably.

M. Zulkhibri (✉)
Islamic Research and Training Institute (IRTI), Islamic Development Bank, Jeddah, Saudi Arabia

M. M. Billah (ed.), *Halal Cryptocurrency Management*,
https://doi.org/10.1007/978-3-030-10749-9_4

35

Table 4.1   Top 10 cryptocurrencies

Rank	Name	Market cap. (in billion)	Price	Circulating supply
1	Bitcoin	$125.3	$7393.22	$16,956,962
2	Ethereum	$40.1	$407.32	$98,605,116
3	Ripple	$21.1	$0.54	$39,094,520,623
4	Bitcoin cash	$11.8	$695.07	$17,054,350
5	Litecoin	$7.2	$130.15	$55,928,269
6	EOS	$4.6	$6.01	$770,312,732
7	Cardano	$4.5	$0.17	$25,927,070,538
8	Stellar	$4.2	$0.23	$18,550,910,262
9	NEO	$3.3	$51.78	$65,000,000
10	IOTA	$2.9	$1.07	$2,779,530,283

Note Data as of April 2018
Source CoinMarketCap (2018)

alternative cryptocurrencies, commonly known as altcoins. While some altcoins have fundamental technological innovations, many are merely copies of Bitcoin or other projects. As of 4 April 2018, there were 1600 cryptocurrencies with US$278 billion market capitalization.[2] Table 4.1 shows the top 10 cryptocurrencies based on the market capitalization.

To give a clear definition of what constitutes a cryptocurrency is difficult. A possible definition is given by Baur et al. (2015) identifies four key features of a cryptocurrency: (i) absence of external regulatory barriers; (ii) establishment of peer-to-peer functions; (iii) usage of public Internet infrastructures; and (iv) implementation of private-public-key cryptography for secure transactions. On the other hand, the technical definition of cryptocurrency is a computer readable program protocol built around a single (or a set of specific) cryptographic function(s).[3] Cryptocurrency issues electronic tokens denominated in their own unit of account according to the rules set out in the protocol. While tokens are intrinsically worthless, it intended to represent values within a specific community. Cryptocurrencies are issued as electronic economic instruments with monetary features enabling users to transfer these tokens fast and secure.

---

[2] Listed on coinmarketcap.com.

[3] According to Dwyer (2015), Bitcoin and similar digital currencies are called cryptocurrencies by some because the underlying algorithms and security are intimately related to digital cryptographic algorithms.

There is no empirical evidence on the economic impacts of cryptocurrency and there is scarcely any academic research on the financial stability issues related to cryptocurrency. While these cryptocurrencies may not pose major concerns at their current levels of use, more serious financial stability issues may result if they achieve wide-scale usage. Risk management can act as a mitigant, if the central asset in a payment system cannot be predictably redeemed for the paper currency, which in turn can have spillovers effects to other areas of the financial system. Therefore, this chapter examines the nature of *halal* cryptocurrency and the impact on financial stability. The chapter also helps to understand the fundamental economic-*Shari'ah* trade-offs and address relevant policy issues. This chapter is set out as follows: Section "What Is Digital-Cryptocurrency?" provides a brief review of cryptocurrency developments. Section "Role of Regulation and Financial Stability" provides the relationship between cryptocurrency and financial stability. Section "Cryptocurrencies and *Shari'ah*" outlines the *Shari'ah* aspects of cryptocurrencies and Section "Conclusion" provides the conclusion.

WHAT IS DIGITAL-CRYPTOCURRENCY?

Since the introduction of Bitcoin by Nakamoto (2008), the number of cryptocurrencies available has largely increased. The development of cryptocurrencies might be related to the price development of Bitcoin in recent years. The study of Kristoufek (2013) suggests that there is a relationship between the price and the interest into a cryptocurrency, thereby generating both positive and negative feedback effects. The interest generated by the price dynamics of Bitcoin might not only be limited to Bitcoin, but it might also transfer to the whole cryptocurrency ecosphere. Hence, this would lead to the conclusion that higher prices and media attention on Bitcoin should also lead to higher numbers of newly created cryptocurrencies. Moreover, real-world developments like the legalisation of Bitcoin in Japan and the formation of the Bitcoin derivatives might have lowered the hurdle to invest into cryptocurrencies (Sapuric et al. 2017). Moreover, founding a cryptocurrency does not necessarily require being a tech expert. There have been online tools around which adapt the code to the creator's preferences. Copying the source code of an existing project is simple and naming the new cryptocurrency can then result in the creation of a new one.

Table 4.2   Type of currencies

	Public-state currency	*Non-state currency*
Fiat currency	US$, GBP, EUR, etc.	• Ithaca hours (type of labour voucher) • Time dollars
Asset-backed currency	Currency US$ currency (1863–1933)	• Liberty dollar (1998–2009) • Digital currency

As defined by the school of monetary economics, money or currency must meet three criteria: (i) a store of value, (ii) a medium of exchange, and (iii) a unit of account. Currencies can be classified according to the nature of the issuing entity and to the underlying backing of the currency value. The current global monetary system is called a *fiat system* in which money is a storage medium for purchasing power. This approach differs from whose value is underpinned by some physical good such as gold or silver which is called commodity money. Moreover, over the last decades, currency system has in most cases been a centralized system, mostly state issued even though electronic payments got more important in recent years (Bagnall et al. 2016). Table 4.2 shows that currencies may be either public/state or non-state and either fiat or asset-backed:

- Public currencies, known as tax-driven money, are issued by central authorities in monopoly and recognized as the unique valid means of payment.
- Non-state currencies are issued by a private centralized or decentralized community-based organization. They are not backed by any government, central bank or sovereign note.
- Fiat currency is intrinsically valueless money. It derives its value from government regulation or law and backed by the government that issued it.
- Asset-backed currencies are currencies whose value is based on a good, often a precious metal such as gold or silver.[4]

---

[4]Similar to commodity currencies, which are made of the commodity, i.e. a gold coin is made of gold.

Digital currencies are money expressed as a string of bits sent as a message in a network that verifies the authenticity of the message via different mechanisms, such as proof-of-work (PoW) or proof-of-stake (PoS) that we briefly explain here below. Most digital currencies exhibit a publicly visible distributed ledger which is shared across a computing network. What distinguishes each digital currency is the process by which its users agree on changes to its ledger (in other words, which transactions to accept as valid) and the mechanism according to which the validation process is rewarded from payment obligations. Historically, most of the countries have forbidden or restricted payments made by other means than by legal tender which is recognized within their jurisdiction. Nakamoto's (2008) design of Bitcoin, as a "peer to peer electronic cash system", that would allow online payments to be sent directly from one party to another without going through a financial institution.

ROLE OF REGULATION AND FINANCIAL STABILITY

The reactions from regulatory authorities to cryptocurrencies vary, partly depending on the part of the world these originate from and on the type of authority. Responses range from warnings about risks, statements and clarifications on the legal status, licensing and supervision of cryptocurrencies related activities or the banning of those. More recently some countries have adopted a hostile attitude towards the propagation and adoption of Bitcoin specifically and cryptocurrencies in general, especially to contain money laundering activities and combat the lack of banking supervision. Table 4.3 provides some countries have become global advocates, while others have actively banned cryptocurrencies completely. In April 2017, Japan passed a law recognizing Bitcoin as legal tender, whereas Bangladesh passed a law in 2014 stating that anybody caught using the virtual currency could be jailed for up to 12 years under the country's strict anti-money-laundering laws. The decentralized and anonymous nature of cryptocurrencies means that it is difficult to protect the public against potentially exploitive behaviour via traditional consumer protection mechanisms. It is unlikely that anyone jurisdiction or central party (e.g. a central bank) will have the ability to impose comprehensive regulation. Rather, the central party is replaced by a framework of internal protocols that govern the operation of the system and allow the verification of transactions to be performed by the system participants themselves. In contrast to fiat currency, a cryptocurrency does not represent a liability on anyone.

Table 4.3   Approach towards crypto-regulations

Countries	Regulatory attitudes
Canada	In November 2013, the Canada Revenue Agency declared that Bitcoin payments should be treated as barter transactions. The Canadian federal government also announced its intention to regulate Bitcoin through its anti-money-laundering and counterterrorist financing legislation
Mexico	The Mexican government has not banned the use of alternative digital currencies outright, but instead is in talks with government regulators to try and introduce their own form of Bitcoin and their own block-chain specific to Mexico
Colombia	It has decreed that cryptocurrency is not illegal, but at the same time, it won't be getting legal recognition anytime soon
Bolivia	The Bolivian government has banned the use of Bitcoin in the belief that it will allow tax evasion and monetary instability
Belgium	It has refused to issue any stance regarding Bitcoin and along with a whole host of other countries is waiting for European-wide guidance. They have issued a public warning no government oversight
Poland	The Polish government has officially recognized the trading and mining of virtual currencies as an "official activity" but has said that regulation should come from the EU
Russia	The Russian Deputy Finance Minister has stated that regulators will be looking to recognize Bitcoin and other cryptocurrencies legally
Ukraine	Despite vague government regulation and political uncertainty in some areas, a major bank announced the ability to purchase Bitcoins in any of its nationwide ATM terminals
India	While Bitcoin is already widely used, there is still "no clear law stating whether Bitcoin and other cryptocurrencies are legal in India"
China	Chinese authorities have banned token sales and local exchanges are closing down
Malaysia	Bitcoin is not recognized as legal tender and Bank Negara Malaysia does not regulate the operations of Bitcoin
Australia	Removing Bitcoins from double taxation policies, the government also legalized Bitcoin and said it can be used just like money
New Zealand	The Reserve Bank regards cryptocurrencies as a "vulnerability" and considers cryptocurrency as a payment system rather than a currency
Japan	Japan eliminated the consumption tax on Bitcoin trading on April 2017, when it officially declared Bitcoin as legal tender. Japan also eliminated the possibility of double taxation on trading of Bitcoins
Iceland	The government worried about capital flight, has banned Bitcoin
United States	The USA has no coherent direction on its cryptocurrency regulation other than that there will be some soon. The Securities and Exchange Commission (SEC) has warned investors of cryptocurrency investing risks, halted several ICOs and hinted at the need for greater cryptocurrency regulation

(continued)

Table 4.3 (continued)

Countries	Regulatory attitudes
Singapore	The government has been relatively lax compared to many of its Asian counterparts on cryptocurrency regulation. The Monetary Authority of Singapore (MAS), like many financial regulators, warned of risks of speculating in the cryptocurrency markets
South Korea	Despite having a significant cryptocurrency presence in the past, Korean authorities began enforcing a rule disallowing anonymous accounts from trading cryptocurrencies
European Union	The European Union had made plans aimed at ending anonymity for cryptocurrency traders, citing anti-money laundering and tax evasion crackdowns. The EU plan would require cryptocurrency platforms to conduct proper due diligence on customers and report any suspicious transactions

Source Various regulatory authorities, author's own compilation

The status of not being a legal tender has some practical real-life consequences. For example, users cannot compel merchants or vendors to accept their coins. The no-legal-tender status is also associated with the absence of a public governing authority in charge of establishing and governing the rules for the use of a cryptocurrency. Cryptocurrencies have made it all but impossible to distinguish between state and private-sector criminality. Hence, this authority should in principle: (1) be responsible for the overall functioning of the cryptocurrency infrastructure as a payment system; (2) be accountable for maintaining the integrity of the central transaction ledgers, the protocols, and any other core functional component of digital currency schemes; (3) be responsible for ensuring that all the actors involved comply with the scheme's rules and that the scheme complies with oversight standards; (4) provide exchange rate stability among cryptocurrencies and between cryptocurrencies and fiat currencies; and (5) eventually act as redeemer of last resort.

Since cryptocurrencies are not issued by public authorities, there is no reason for governments to assign legal tender status to cryptocurrencies that are beyond their control or to establish a central authority that enforces exchange rate stability and acts as redeemer of last resort. Unless a currency has been authenticated by a government, it is unlikely to be fully trusted. Technically, these functions could indeed be directly embedded into the protocol of cryptocurrencies by implementing the rules that governs the money supply and transaction mechanisms at the source code level. Already in place are experimental ledgers that come with a built-in Turing-complete programming language, which can be used to implement any monetary constraint or payment system feature. Cryptocurrencies are not media of payment allowed by law or recognized by any legal system as valid for meeting financial obligations. The following features that are peculiar to any legal tender are not met by cryptocurrencies: (1) mandatory acceptance, where the creditor of a payment obligation can in no way refuse the currency except if the parties have agreed on alternative means of payment; (2) acceptance at full face value, meaning the monetary value is simply equal to the indicated amount; and (3) the currency has the power to release debtors.

The recent development of cryptocurrencies and the novelty of their design mean that they may not be specifically regulated and do not fit easily into existing regulatory definitions and structures. Indeed, the borderless online nature of cryptocurrencies, and the absence of an identifiable "issuer" of the instrument, pose particular challenges to attempts at regulation that a national authority might make (although other identifiable third-party providers might be more easily regulated). These types of system have also raised important concerns by law enforcement authorities about the use of these systems for illegal activity, as well as compliance with AML/CFT obligations that apply to traditional payment methods and intermediation. Regulation naturally imposes costs on payment system providers and intermediaries; digital currency providers may benefit from not being subject to these costs. Regulatory costs may arise in particular from obligations placed upon the issuer of a payment or financial instrument; several countries have begun to adjust existing regulations or pass new regulations to address concerns of law enforcement and other authorities.

Many digital currency schemes with the underlying distributed ledger technology could have a much broader impact on financial stability. The use of distributed ledgers may induce changes in trading, clearing and settlement as they could foster disintermediation of traditional service providers in various markets and infrastructures. Widely used cryptocurrencies may challenge the intermediation role of banks in the financial system. In addition, a widespread substitution of banknotes with cryptocurrencies could lead to a decline in central bank non-interest paying liabilities. The result could be a reduction in central bank earnings that constitute central bank seigniorage revenue. If the adoption and use of

cryptocurrencies were to increase significantly, the demand for existing monetary aggregates and the conduct of monetary policy could be
affected similar to the potential impact of e-money. The effect of cryptocurrencies on the implementation of monetary policy will depend on
the change in demand for bank reserves and the degree of economic and
financial interconnection between the users of sovereign currency and
the users of the digital currency. If the substitution is large and the interconnection is weak, then monetary policy may lose efficacy.

CRYPTOCURRENCIES AND *SHARI'AH*

Generally, *Shari'ah* scholars allow anything used by people as money: (i)
gold, silver, wheat, barley, salt, dates etc.; (ii) paper currencies and coins;
and (iii) electronic money and cryptocurrencies. However, once used
as money, rules of *Sarf*[5] and *riba* would apply. Most *Shari'ah* scholars
unanimously agree upon the factor that currency or money is a medium
of exchange. This is because money has been used over time to trade
commodities and services. Currency, having no intrinsic utility, is that
specified nature of currency, which makes it different from consumption
and production goods. According to Islamic jurisprudence, one cannot
treat currency as goods, also this is a reason why one cannot give it on
lease, unlike goods, which can be given on lease and have rent charge
on them. This concept within Islam about currency or money being a
medium of exchange is different from the concept of goods and this has
been accepted by many economists as well.

The creation of *dirhams* (coin made of silver) and *dinars* (coins
made of gold),[6] fit the reality of time that the entire economic transaction was based on these two kinds of currencies. Prior to this period,
there are nothing except stones with no benefits. However, people

---

[5] *Bay al-Sarf* is a contract of exchange of money for money. The rules of *bay al-Sarf*
derive largely from the well-known Hadith: "Gold is to be paid for by gold, silver by silver,
wheat by wheat, barley by barley, dates by dates, and salt by salt - like for like, equal for
equal, payment being made on the spot. If the species differ, sell as you wish provided that
payment is made on the spot" (Hadith Muslim).

[6] At the time of the Prophet, Muslims used raw metal or Byzantine coins as money.
Three sorts of metal were used for economic transactions: gold (*Dinar*), silver (*Dirham*)
and copper (*fals*, pl.: *fulus*).

need them to exchange for different things food, clothing and other goods (Al-Ghazali 1993). Imam al-Ghazali presented the view that money is not wanted for its own sake. His view has been supported by many *Shari'ah* scholars such as Ibn Taymiyyah, who states that money is not something which is wanted for itself, but it is rather a medium of exchange (Taymiyyah, 1961–1963). Moreover, Crowther (1941) defines similar principle by Al-Ghazali that "the essential characteristics of money, which sets it apart from all other substances, is that it is not desired for itself. It is in the fullest sense, a medium or means, or mechanism of exchange".

The question then becoming much more relevant that Al-Ghazali's emphasizes on the trading of these commodity currencies as: "one who opens the business of purchase and sale of gold and silver in order to earn profit or to take interest will be working against the plan and object of Allah and therefore commit sin. He is ungrateful to the gift of god as these coins are created for other purposes and are not needed for themselves. When someone is trading in dirhams and dinars themselves, he is making them as his goal, which is contrary to their objectives. Money is not created to earn money, and doing so is transgression..... The two kinds of money are means to acquire other things; they are not meant for themselves" (Al-Ghazali 1993). The dilemma of the question doesn't end here, because one of the famous types of sale contracts, which is known as *Ba'i al-Sarf* is wholly based on the trade and exchange of these metals.

Al-Ghazali (1993) deliberates on this specific issue that: "If it is asked why one of the two kinds of money is permitted to be exchanged for the other and why exchanging dirham is permitted with the same amount of it? Then, you should know that the two kinds of money are different from each other in being means of obtaining something else. Sometimes, one of them is more useful in being because it is in larger quantity, like dirham, which is disbursed on different needs in smaller units. If this exchange is forbidden, then their special purpose, i.e. their use as means of getting other things is destroyed" (Al-Ghazali 1993). In the light of these opinions, currency is a medium of exchange and not a type of goods. Therefore, it clear that Islam prohibits treating currency as goods, but allows exchanges under certain conditions. This very nature of currency has also been accepted by many other economists around the world.

Types of Currency in Islam

There are two types of money or currency according to Islamic jurisprudence:

1. *Al-Thaman-ul-Khilqi'* or *Al-Nuqood-ul-Khilqiyyah*: it is a type of currency which is created to work in a form of currency or price or medium of exchange in contracts and trades for us buy commodities and services by using it as a medium of exchange. It is "Natural Money" or "Intrinsic Money" and "Created Currency". As their value of being a currency or a power of being a medium of exchange is not based on tradition, custom or common agreement. Islam does not recognize anything as a natural or intrinsic currency except for gold and silver.[7]
2. *Al-Thaman-ul-Istilahi* or *Al-Nuqood-ul-Istilahiyya*: it is a type of currency where its currency value is established through a common agreement, custom or tradition. It is "Artificial Currency" or "Token Money" as its validity as currency is not constant, because this quality of being currency can be removed any time by the government. Many Islamic scholars used to present *"Fulus"* (Pices/Coins) as an example for artificial currency. In our modern era, one can present the paper currency as the best example of *"Al-Thaman-ul-Istilahi"*. These both types of currencies have their own rulings and injunctions which have been substantiated by *Shari'ah* (Table 4.4).

Islamic Views on Cryptocurrency

Imam Malik defines money as "any merchandise commonly accepted as a medium of exchange" means that people are free to choose their medium of exchange. In the debate on *Fulus* and different opinions of religious scholars were mainly in the time where gold and silver were being used as medium of exchange and standard for payment.

---

[7] Islamic Fiqh Academy in its 5th session held in the city of Makkah Al-Mukarramah issued a ruling on paper money have decided that the paper currency is a stand-alone currency, which takes all the laws of gold and silver. That includes the legal prohibition of the *riba al-fadl* and *riba al-nasiah*, the compulsory zakat and other laws. This is based on qiyas (analogy) of the existing currency against gold and silver. Paper money has replaced gold and silver and serves as a store of value and a medium of exchange in the market. The rules of *riba*, *zakat*, and *sarf* (currency exchange) apply to it equally.

Table 4.4   *Shari'ah* opinion on paper currency

Opinion 1	Opinion 2	Opinion 3
Characteristics		
• Paper currency can be viewed as a bond (certificate of debt) on the deposit of gold or silver • The issuer is obliged to pay to the holder (promise of payment of debt) • There is no gold or silver behind these papers, this written promise on the face of currency notes is totally meaningless	• Artificial currency (*Al-Nuqood-ul-Istilahiyya*) • Currency value establishes through common agreement or custom is commonly agreed upon currency like *Fulus*	• Paper money became well-accepted as currency • Gold and silver lost their existence as currency
Jurist opinions		
• Money cannot be exchanged for money because that would be *dayn bi-ldayn*, which is forbidden due to the immanent *riba* • It cannot be capital currency, i.e. real capital • Exchange is impossible—money cannot be exchanged for money • It is not being able to purchase gold or silver through notes	• It is allowed to exchange *Fulus* in non-equal amount in Shafi school • It is allowed if they are specified in • Hanbali school • It will for *riba* in the economies	• Rulings of *riba* are applicable • Necessary to fulfil the requirements of *Sarf* sale in currency exchange • Using as the capital amount in *Salam* transaction is permissible

Gold and silver at that time were the frequently used currency in general and big transactions, while *Fulus* were meant for the small transactions only. After this stage, currency has seen a notable revolution and vicissitude which consists metallic money system, gold specie standard, gold bullion standard and the era of fiduciary money and gold exchange standard. However, today we are unable to find currency which made of gold or silver, they have lost their existence as currency, because paper currency having no gold or silver behind it, replaced them long ago. In the case of Bitcoin and other cryptocurrencies, some scholars have issued a *fatwa* comparing investing in cryptocurrency

Table 4.5   Comparison between fiat currency and digital-cryptocurrency

	Fiat/ paper currency	*Digital-cryptocurrency (not assets-backed)*	*Digital-cryptocurrency (assets-backed)*
Maysir	Medium	High	Low
Gharar	Medium	Low	Low
Maqasid al-*Shari'ah*	No	No	Yes

Source Meera (2018)

to gambling that is forbidden in Islam.[8] The evolution of Bitcoin and other cryptocurrencies along with the adoption of technological advancement has led many Islamic scholars towards the new research and adoption of different opinions to decide the *Shari'ah* status of currency including digital-cryptocurrency (see Table 4.5).

CONCLUSION

The future path of the money supply of cryptocurrency is pre-determined and finite by design. By contrast, traditional currencies are backed by a central bank and money supply can change to counteract inflationary and deflationary pressures on prices. This is because the primary role of central banks is to manage inflation through monetary tools. Central banks favour low but positive inflation for a reason—wages are considered 'sticky' meaning that it is highly unlikely that firms have the ability to cut their employee's wages. With low, positive inflation, this has the same effect as lowering wages if the pace of a worker's wage rises slower than inflation. In an economy with fixed money supply, as is the case in the cryptocurrency system, this may harm the macroeconomy by contributing to deflation of prices of goods and services.[9]

With a finite money supply, effectively consumers will be able to purchase more goods and services with the same amount of digital currency, inherently lowering the price of goods and services. In addition, workers

[8]For example, Diyanet, the Turkish religious authority; Shawki Allam, Grand Mufti of Egypt; Sheikh Assim al Hakeem, a Saudi scholar; Dr. Daud Bakar, Malaysia scholar in Islamic banking; Sheikh Dr. Haitham al-Haddad, UK-based Islamic scholar.

[9]Once money supply reaches its maximum potential then prices will naturally begin to fall.

with "sticky wages" (most employees) become increasingly costly and as this momentum continues, unemployment may rise. For cryptocurrency to retain long-term value, there must be trust in the system as well as widespread adoption. There are significant barriers to any cryptocurrency becoming the dominant form of money in an economy. Unless traditional currencies suffered from a total collapse in confidence, there is little incentive for the prices of goods and services to move away from traditional currencies. Currently, cryptocurrencies do not play a substantial role as money in society, but the status of cryptocurrencies as money has the potential to develop over time.

Although cryptocurrencies such as Bitcoin do not currently pose a material risk to global monetary stability, central banks can be expected to continue to monitor cryptocurrencies and assess any future risks they may cause to the economic environment. Incidents of digital wallets being hacked can clearly affect confidence in a relatively new currency system and can ultimately lead to a decline in usage. As technologies are developed and refined, old issues are resolved, and new issues arise. Other countries may have different environments and experiences. Therefore, research into digital currency issues, including highly liquid and secure limited-purpose digital currencies for use as a settlement asset for wholesale payment systems, should continue.

References

Al-Ghazali. (1993). *Imam Ghazali's Ihya Ulum-Ud-Din: The Revival of Religious Learnings*. Translated by Fazl-ul-Karim. Karachi: Darul-Ishaat.

Bagnall, J., Bounie, D., Kosse, A., Huynh, K.P., Schmidt, T., Schuh, S., & Stix, H. (2016). Consumer Cash Usage and Management: A Cross-Country Comparison with Diary Survey Data. *International Journal of Central Banking*, 12(4), 1–61.

Baur, A.W., Buhler, J., Bick, M., & Bonorden, C.S. (2015). Cryptocurrencies as a Disruption? Empirical Findings on User Adoption and Future Potential of Bitcoin and Co. In Janssen, M., Mantymaki, M., Hidders, J., Klievink, B., Lamersdorf, W., van Loenen, B., & Zuiderwijk, A. (Eds.), *Open and Big Data Management and Innovation*, 63–80. Cham: Springer International Publishing.

CoinMarketCap. (2018). Top Cryptocurrencies by Market Capitalization. Retrieved April 4, 2018, from https://coinmarketcap.com/6.

Crowther, G. (1941). *An Outline of Money*. London: Thomas Nelson and Sons Limited.

Dwyer, P.G. (2015). The Economics of Bitcoin and Similar Private Digital Currencies. *Journal of Financial Stability*, 17, 81–91.

Kristoufek, L. (2013). Bitcoin Meets Google Trends and Wikipedia: Quantifying the Relationship Between Phenomena of Internet Era. *Scientific Reports*, 3(3415), 1–7.

Meera, A.K.M. (2018). *Cryptocurrency from Islamic Perspectives: The Case of Bitcoin*. Unpublished.

Nakamoto, S. (2008). *Bitcoin: A Peer-to-Peer Electronic Cash System*. http://www.bitcoin.org.

Sapuric, S., Kokkinaki, A., & Georgiou, I. (2017). In Which Distributed Ledger Do We Trust? A Comparative Analysis of Cryptocurrencies. *MCIS 2017 Proceedings*, 21.

PART II

Technicalities of Halal Cryptocurrency Management

CHAPTER 5

Blockchain Technology in Managing Halal Cryptocurrency

Shajahan K. Kakkattil

INTRODUCTION

Status of global wealth management is not based on halal principles, and the halal institutions including Islamic banking industry are trying hard to find its space. Although Islamic banking is well known to the financial world, the halal principles are not that very much applied at its roots but only on periphery even by these Islamic institutions. Islamic wealth management is intruding to find its space in the direction of less halal to more halal, taking a continual step accelerated by halal demand, survival requirements and importantly opportunities that come across. The opportunity for Islamic banking to make a giant leap toward the root of financial and banking industry at our time is presumably blockchain. The blockchain has been visualized as the revolutionary technology for many aspects of human life and interactions. Finding opportunities for blockchain to improve Islamic banking and other halal activities is way more than a technology adoption due to the fact that the blockchain is deep rooted on truthfulness and transparency—the same founding elements of

S. K. Kakkattil (✉)
Dubai, United Arab Emirates

© The Author(s) 2019
M. M. Billah (ed.), *Halal Cryptocurrency Management*,
https://doi.org/10.1007/978-3-030-10749-9_5

53

Islamic banking stemmed from Islamic principles. This chapter explores concepts, methods and options on how the blockchain can be used to initiate and manage halal cryptocurrency.

BLOCKCHAIN: ITS AUTHENTICATION

The truthful nature of blockchain is an important factor that needs to be dissected further in the discussion of halal cryptocurrency. Blockchain can be viewed as a record that is truthfully recorded which can't be altered. The data recorded in blockchain, by itself, testify its truthful existence and preserved forever, without needing to have a further witness to testify its correct recording. This has a striking similarity to the "record of actions" given at the day of judgment as per Islamic teachings. The angels record every action truthfully and the same is evidenced at the day of judgment. Until few decades ago, it was hard to visualize the size of this book; it would be gigantic and hard to comprehend as every nitty-gritty of men's action is supposed to get written in finer details. However, with the advent of digital storage, the size of this book or the way of presentation as an iPad like "tab" is easy to comprehend. In this way of recording, now we could further visualize as a blockchain too.

HASHED PAST

The core of blockchain is a method of encapsulating the past records as a hash and then linking the blocks with specific keys introduced by proof-of-work (or proof-of-"X" in general). The process is recursively used to build and link further blocks to the chain. "Hash" is a digital digest or a miniature but a unique representation of a large chunk of data. The blockchain records the current events in a block along with the hash of past records. This "Hashed Past" helps to preserve the ancestry of the records, tracing back to its root or starting block itself—known as the genesis block.

NATURAL LINEAGE AND DNA EFFECT

Each and every block in the blockchain keeps lineage or its inheritance, much the same way the DNA keeps ancestral trace. Proper analysis of DNA of a living being can help to trace its lineage and ancestral origin right to the first parent(s) and can truthfully verify the ancestry. The hashed past in the blockchain's block provides a similar way of tracing and linking. It is not a mere linked-list; instead, it is a data structure that is much more superior and adapting to the laws of nature. In short, the blockchain is a truthful information recording methodology adapted from the nature; obeying the laws of nature and intern the laws of God is a perfect fit for an autonomous truthful world in general and for halal currency management in specific.

Is QUR'AN BLOCKCHAINED?

It is not required to prove that blockchain is Islamic and referenced in Holy Scriptures to ensure its usage in halal management. However, it is important not to be negligent about the facts that are getting revealed as the generations make continual advancements which support the existence and claims of Holy Scriptures or the theories related to God. The events of *Isra' - Wal-Mi'araj*, the travel of prophet to Palestine and the ascend to heaven, were difficult to understand those days, but the logical thinkers are now able to imagine such a fast transportation. Indeed, the existence of heaven and of God itself is still debatable in such circles; the possibility of a to-and-fro trip between holy lands Mecca and Palestine in a single night is out of question.

Does the blockchain take anything out of question further?

The Quran itself claims that it is a book that was preserved forever and can't be changed. This looks pretty much similar to the claim of blockchain. If this claim—the immutability—doesn't stand for blockchain, then blockchain is not a "blockchain"; instead, it is nothing but a record of information or a database. So the Quran is just a book, like any other book; it can be superior only if the immutability stands. The discussion so far about the immutability of Quran is that it is protected by God. The Quran itself claims that the god will take its guardianship (*Quran* 15:9).

But how?

Based on human logic and the understanding so far, there are many ways narrated such as people by heart Quran for generations, and thus, it is preserved even if someone destroys, corrupts or damages the existing all copies of Quran. This kind of protection by backup or the general ways in which data are protected by continuity plans including disaster recovery is applied in general computing as well as in blockchain-based systems, by means of multisite or peer-to-peer replication.

But the immutability of blockchain is more than this. The way of recording itself lays the foundation of immutability. Once the data are written, the data itself provide the attributes of its correct recording and the elements of its verification, and any element of change is immediately detectable; therefore, alterations are impossible. The hashes and the nonce value mined and inserted in the block linking headers preserve the immutability for blockchain.

Based on this, we are at a juncture of human knowledge expansion to provide another dimension to the un-answered myth of special words and phrases inserted in Quran. That is, the special words and phrases ("Alif -Laam-Meem," "YaSee…n," etc.) found at multiple places at the beginning of different chapters of the Holy Book, much the same way the hashes and nonce inserted at block headers of blockchain. The blockchain nonce and hashes don't carry any natural language meaning and have no reference to any dictionary; the Quranic "hashes and nonce" also don't represent any natural language meanings. Instead, it is been explained by some scholars as the signature of God embedded in Holy Scriptures. Indeed, the hashes and nonce of blockchain have been viewed as the digital signatures of the blocks!

In essence, it is much more meaningful to see that the protection of the Holy Book is derived from its immutability. Any change in letters will corrupt its harmony and will flag the error by itself, much the same way the blockchain keeps its records integrity. Now, what are the algorithms that fit for the Quranic hashes and its blocks (verses or chapters) linkage? This needs a bit of reverse engineering and is definitely going to be harder. This is not an escapism for this hypothesis. Think how hard (if not impossible) it is to find the blockchain hashing and nonce mining algorithm, by just doing reverse engineering based on analyzing the blockchain records. Attempting to find the Quranic immutability will be a much greater effort, but I do feel confident that it is a matter of time that may scale just before the end of world at the maximum or any time sooner.

The confidence is that the human generations to come would witness the finding of proper hashing and nonce mining algorithm (for Quran) that would confirm its correctness, immutability and completeness. The completeness is an additional attribute more than the present-day blockchain, which is a continuously growing record of information blocks.

In the context of Quran, nothing further can be added to it and the algorithm would surprisingly reveal this truth which will be a touchstone for both "the algorithm" and the Holy Book.

The *Qur'an* itself provides a bit of more information or guidance that would lead to the finding of this Linguistic Harmony Algorithm (LHA).

- The language—Arabic—The language of Quran is Arabic, so the reverse engineering efforts would focus based on this language
- The number 19 or similar connectives (The verse "Over it is 19" referenced in *Quran* 74:30)
- The immutability of *Quran* (15:9, 10:64, 6:34, 18:27, 6:115)
- The completeness of *Quran* (6:114, 6:115).

Again, is this important to prove a Quranic linkage of blockchain data structure to use it for halal cryptocurrency management? Not really. But if there is a link, should that be avoided? Not at all. Well it is important for the intrinsic value debate.

The Intrinsic Value Debate

The intrinsic value of gold is a hypothesis in general, but is reliable one as it is been proven by generations. The value of gold is predicatively sustaining for generations to come, as this value is referenced in Holy Quran too. The reliance of Quran on gold as a valuable asset is an important dimension in accepting the gold-backed currencies. In this case, the gold has a value because:

(a) We assume value to it
(b) It is proven by generations
(c) It has value based on Demand and Supply
(d) It is referenced in Holy Book.

The above attributes a, b and c all fit for cryptocurrency. The point d fits as one of the immutability dimensions of Quran (hypothetically) based on a "Linguistic Harmony Algorithm" (LHA) which is blockchain like! Therefore, blockchain-based cryptocurrencies have value by itself, even if it is not supported by gold or any other asset. The intrinsic value of cryptocurrency is nothing but its strength or power of blockchain. There are differently valued blockchain cryptocurrencies, based on its implementation—this is very natural too, much the same way how gold and silver differentiate and valued.

THE MISSING LINK OF ISLAMIC BANKING

The present-day Islamic banking is a branch on the conventional financial and banking system. The pure Islamic banking system calls the less pure ones as Islamic banking "windows." But these "pure" ones are not that very pure as all of them are based on the currency and asset system already established by the conventional banking system, which is not stemmed on the Islamic principles.

It is interesting to note that there were no "high intensity discussions" about halal fiat currency in Islamic banking schools of thought. But when it comes to cryptocurrency, the halal cryptocurrency seems to be a de facto and a must wanted. It implies that Islamic banking accepts the fiat currencies as halal by default, just because it is already established (?). The way of production of fiat currencies and whether it is backed by precious assets doesn't seem to be a matter of importance. At present, many countries' currencies (including US Dollar) are not backed by gold on which Islamic banking operates on. This looks like a double standard as it is very demanding to have halal cryptocurrency but not the halal fiat currency—at least not demanding with the same intensity.

Demand for halal cryptocurrency also implies in a way that "Crypto Currency by itself is not halal and there is something more to be done to make it halal."

This lack of "halal" is due to the lack of intrinsic value primarily. As discussed in the previous sections, the power of blockchain itself, however, has a greater intrinsic value. This is no more a theory as it is evident from the establishment of bitcoin cryptocurrency. The valuation of bitcoin merely based on blockchain's strength or power is a solid proof of its intrinsic value. How much value does this possess have is the only question and the higher volatility does only mean that the market is not yet matured enough to self-evaluate and correct the bitcoin pricing. Obviously, there is a speculation layer that adds more value at the peripheral, but at the core only intrinsic value is left which is directly proportional to the value of blockchain technology. The cryptocurrency market growth is exponential and is getting matured far superior than the conventional assets and currencies. Note that we are comparing cryptocurrency toddler with century's old gold mammoth and fiat currency monsters!

The intrinsic value of cryptocurrency is far superior that it gives courage to initiate discussions of making a halal currency from scratch following the success of bitcoin and other cryptocurrencies based on "transparent truth" which is clearly visible in making, storing, distributing, exchanging and utilizing the cryptocurrency. The gold pegging is not at all a necessity to make cryptocurrency halal—instead, the underlying blockchain value itself would suffice. Some may think that backing with gold would increase the worthiness of cryptocurrency, but it will actually diminish the value of the cryptocurrency to the value of gold. What if the bitcoin was pegged with 1gm of gold at its genesis block? It would have been of great value at that time, because at genesis block time no one was considering any value to it. Since the bitcoin was not pegged with gold, it now possesses more value; 12.5 bitcoins minted at present possess a lot more value than 12.5 gram of gold. Does this mean that bitcoin blockchain has more intrinsic value or not?

Well, I don't want to make a wrong assertion about the intrinsic value V/s speculated value or current market value. Bitcoin's current market price is not its intrinsic value either. Much the same way the gold's market price is not its intrinsic value! Then how much is the intrinsic value of gold? This is a chicken and egg scenario indeed, and finding answer to this (or not finding) will lead to accepting cryptocurrency as equivalent to gold and intern, halal. Cryptocurrency holds the attributes of both gold and fiat currency, but it is more inclined to gold.

Gold and bitcoin (cryptocurrency in general) are similar in following ways:

- *Universally identifiable and acceptable*

Ability to verify gold or its purity is enough to get it accepted, the same is valid for bitcoin too. You don't need to provide any proof of identity of yours to get both of them acceptable anywhere in the world. Well, the bitcoin might not be acceptable in most countries, but to understand this you have to step back to those ancient days when the gold was "invented" and started to gain attention of the people. It is reasonable to assume that gold had underwent for an acceptance lifecycle and was not valuable, legal and acceptable from the day one. About the legality, maybe the legal system itself was started after the invention of gold.

- *Not linked to any government or authority*

Doesn't require much explanation here. Both could mine anywhere in the world. Bitcoin had been an initiative of some government as per many stories behind bitcoin establishment, but now it is pretty much out of anyone's control even from Satoshi Nakamoto.

- *Hard to produce*

Gold is hard to mint and is scarce. Same is the story of bitcoin. The mining difficulty of bitcoin is purposefully made it complicated, hard and time-consuming. The scarcity is set by the known finite availability. Indeed, the transaction confirmation (block chaining) time of bitcoin is higher than electronic transaction system and other cryptocurrencies. Gold is hard to transact than currency, and similarly, bitcoin too is hard to transact in comparison with other currencies in terms of transaction commit time. This is the strength of the bitcoin as it puts extra crypto mechanisms to ensure its purity. Some alt coins improve the speed of this production time but they are getting a lesser valuation than bitcoin.

Other cryptocurrencies take the seat of silver when bitcoin takes the position of gold.

Islamic banking lacks a halal production of currency and left with the choice of relaying on already established currency system. However, blockchain is opening whole lot of possibilities to fill this gap to revolutionize intrinsic value concepts and currency minting.

HALAL MINTING

To start the ideal Islamic banking world from scratch, the halal cryptocurrency too needs to be minted or produced. Presently, the asset reserve or the bond issuance mechanism to produce fiat currencies is no more than a drama or complicated theories behind the jurisdiction of every countries which never come to a public or transparent scrutiny.

We could think of following ways or options to produce halal cryptocurrency based on blockchain.

Option 1—Bitcoin-Like Plain and Simple Cryptocurrency

Simplest of all, start new altcoin or crypto network on a fresh new blockchain, with an ecosystem of miners and full nodes. Following the arguments discussed so far, the intrinsic value is nothing but the power or strength of the blockchain immutability. The rules of currencies to mint per block, the total distribution of currencies, methods to control inflation such as the chain halving or limited distribution, etc., to be set with consensus. Getting such consensus would be a challenge that is what bitcoin ideally breaks with a silent introduction of logically well-placed rule set. Logical stability and dependability of the rule set of the new cryptocurrency are important to withstand the consensus debates. But predominantly it should solve the scalability issues of bitcoin for security, transaction volume and speed to cover an infinite future of technological advancements including quantum computing. But more importantly, other elements based on halal principles need to be set as well. Instead of amending traditional banking concepts, a whole new world of freedom of choice is available to introduce halal rules set at the core. This "opportunity to introduce halal rule set" would be the single important argument to explore this option—otherwise bitcoin itself is there to solve this issue.

There is nothing new in this option than producing a new cryptocurrency to solve issues of current cryptocurrencies and improvising halal aspects by having jurisdiction and authority elements—but without having another asset backing. Challenges definitely will be the consensus across the world; therefore, it would remain in theory and would fight similar survival track other cryptocurrencies are already facing and more consensus debates from halal strategists.

Option 2—Gold/Precious Asset Backed

For those who still need the gold backing to double ensure the "Halalness', this "seems to be" the reasonable best option. This is similar to normal gold-backed currency minting. The central bank takes the gold reserve and mints the cryptocurrency proportional to the value of possessed gold. Each gold bar has to be uniquely identified and linked to the crypto header of the matching currency to ensure a truthful "one to one" minting. The critical questions raised here are, who will be the central bank and how trustworthy they would be to produce equivalent cryptocurrency to be verified in an automated digital world. The central bank can be the already established central banks but the latter part of the question remains unclear. Tokenized assets are not new even in the cryptocurrency world, and government-controlled ones such as "Petro" from Venezuela are already made its debut. This proves that countries could put any mechanism to start its own cryptocurrency but it will remain as a traditional currency mechanism

Option 3—Currency Backed (Currency Crypto)

This would be a migration plan for all currencies across the globe to crypto world with a technology update. Instead of gold, the central banks take back the currency in circulation and reissue an equivalent cryptocurrency, tracing the identity or the serial number of the currency. The currency which is taken back by the central bank freezes forever and never put into circulation. The value of the cryptocurrency recursively refers back to its fiat counterpart and intern to its intrinsic value. This is not the issuance of debit card against your deposit in the conventional bank; instead, an altcoin backed by the fiat currency is generated and its distribution is proportional only to the wealth which is already in circulation in the world. Do not confuse also with current crypto exchange centers which take hot cash and give you the cryptocurrency of your choice.

The new term "Currency Crypto" seems appropriate for this new fiat currency-backed cryptocurrency. Central banks across the world could do this, and indeed, they could accept any countries currency for that matter much the same way they handle the forex reserve. In a broader sense, currency exchange houses could do this currency to crypto conversions too. The exchange houses provide the Currency Crypto in their possession, and upon submitting back to their remittent bank, they get back equivalent crypto in the possession of the bank and ultimately it reaches the central bank and central bank produces new cryptocurrency by freezing the fiat currency and minting new Currency Crypto. This would be halal too, based on tradition intrinsic value concept.

Option 4—Bitcoin-Backed Cryptocurrency

Bitcoin is already established and can be considered as digital-gold and have intrinsic value much similar to gold as discussed so far. The central banks across the world should mint their own cryptocurrency based on "one to one mapping" of bitcoins they acquire. The bitcoin is considered as the gold asset in reserve which never put it back to normal circulation and treats the same way how the gold reserve is treated in traditional fiat currency lifecycle—but with one difference; all these activities are transparent as it is on the blockchain for public to verify. The central banks then issue their cryptocurrency referencing the bitcoins blockchain address. There should be crypto security mechanisms to lock this bitcoin address similar to lightning transactions or "multisig" addresses.[1]

All further transactions of the currency will be by the newly issued cryptocurrency and the bitcoin blockchain will never be a transaction bottleneck. Obviously, the blockchain of the new cryptocurrency should be optimized to address all technology sufferings of bitcoin network. This is much of a cryptocurrency-backed cryptocurrency. Since the bitcoin is powerful enough to disrupt and initiate such a huge market, there are no other cryptocurrencies precious than bitcoin to consider as a backup asset. Bitcoin's logics of minting currencies, distribution and all other related rules are established and accepted. We could see a lot of similarities for both gold and bitcoin as discussed in previous sections. Both are available globally and are held by individuals as well as governments and banks. (Well it is no more secret that governments start to reserve bitcoin as forex reserve.) Which option best suited for halal central bank is discussed further in the next section.

ISLAMIC CENTRAL BANK

It is hard to take out regulatory frameworks and institutional dependency of human beings, much the same way we depend on our family and other relations. Authority and control are appropriate to the level it is required as we analyze any aspects of human interaction and social life. For halal currency discussion, government approval or authorities control is the second mandate after the intrinsic value. Giving the government and central banks an appropriate role in the cryptocurrency world is therefore appropriate. However, it should not kill the tempo set by the blockchain toward an autonomous world. There should be balance between both the worlds to sustain. The above options section "Halal Minting" are meant to bridge this gap right from the currency minting. Which option (of minting the cryptocurrency) to choose is based on the practicality or the scope and breadth of halal banking implementation.

---

[1] The discussion of "bitcoin reserve locking" is outside the scope of this book.

Option 1—New Crypto

This option of creating a new crypto currency from scratch gives complete freedom of implementation, but hard to raise intrinsic value and difficult to win intrinsic value debates. A group of people have to come forward to initially do a crash land implementation of this the same way how the bitcoin introduced. Based on its promises and power of blockchain, the rest of the world will be attracted and insisted to accept this option. This option makes sense only if an implementation of pure halal banking is only possible without winning the approval of established halal banking market.

Option 2 and 3—Gold- and Currency-Backed Crypto

This cannot be introduced by a group of people, like Option 1; instead, the current world dynamics should work to agree upon initiating such efforts. There can be an Islamic central bank window could be started by each central banks, but that would remain as a dream unless the halal rule set embedded on the blockchain is powerful enough to kill the interest-based current financial system similar to the bitcoin rule set of reward-based currency minting and transaction fee allocation crushed the centuries-old currency concepts. However, currency-backed cryptocurrency has immediate benefits to avail in the current banking industry and is a quick shortcut for all countries to shift to cryptocurrency without losing their control. Importantly, the traceability and KYC of the funds are maintained. Pulling the currency from market and reissuing other token are doable as India did its demonetization that rattled the country.

Option 4—Bitcoin-Backed Crypto

Among all the options discussed, this one looks practically possible with or without the consent and support of the established markets. If the established financial institutions support this, it is well and good. Otherwise, someone could introduce this to the market and the worthiness is guaranteed since it is pegged to the bitcoin.

The promise in all these options is that, the underlying blockchain will have extra functionality (the rule set) to automate more valuable halal banking concepts. The halal banking already shifted from banking windows to core banking and this will further move the halal banking from the core banking to central banks level. Currency-backed or the bitcoin-backed cryptocurrencies are meant to bridge this gap, but at the same time to preserve all benefits of cryptocurrencies. It is important to identify that these discussions are not meant to simply digitize the monetary system of countries, which is pretty well done by online banking systems, credit/debit cards and numerous other tokens.

BLOCKCHAINED ISLAMIC BANKS

Following central banks, the banking institutions need also to do a shift to fully autonomous blockchained system. If it is autonomous, why the need to have a banking institution in the middle? These banking institutions are required to trace the identity of the customers or the actors on the halal banking blockchain—mainly the account holders. Identifying the customers is required at this stage through banking institutions as the true identity of the customer should be kept cryptically hidden on the blockchain, but at the same time the customer must be reachable physically to ensure true identity. There can be better mechanisms for this identity verification including the biometrics of the wallet holder on the chain, as well as government institutions, but to preserve a banking institution is important at this stage as there are other ongoing banking activities to be done by this institution, including a coordinated effort to improve the halal blockchain which cannot be left with anonymous enthusiasts or amateurs.

The point is it is better to utilize an already well-established institutional system for the development of autonomous halal banking and get it dismantled as and when the autonomous system gets matured. However, there is no planned effort required to dismantle these institutions; instead, once the powerful blockchain-based autonomous system gets traction, it will be get rejected by itself. And that would lead to a world of autonomous virtual bank, a true natural extension of the banking system which is self-sufficient to function—fully automated truthfully. But more than the identity assurance, there are a lot of other interim activities for the halal banks to fulfill. Mainly, a coordinated effort to kill interest-based system by winning the financial and business battle using its blockchain scripted rules and smart contracts.

When the central bank blockchain concentrates on the transparent and truthful minting and distribution of cryptocurrency, the halal banks should revolutionize all aspects of halal financial dealings and transactions utilizing the blockchain rules set. There are many aspects of banking activity be placed under the blockchain-based management system such as loans, fund settlements, investments and related profit loss sharing. However, following sections discuss examples of important attributes that should be part of a blockchain-based halal banking.

CRYPTO SCRIPT FOR ZAKAT

The bitcoin blockchain shows a great model of reward mechanism using transaction fee. Following this model, one of the reward mechanisms of halal banking should be for zakat management based on the transaction or the wealth kept in crypto account. For instance, a 2.5% amount of zakat can be charged on qualified transactions upon transaction time itself; or can be charged by a smart contract upon reaching the threshold to pay zakath (i.e. Nisab). Not only the collection, the distribution of zakat should also be moved to the eligible receivers autonomously and this mechanism should be inherent to the blockchain's core code. It is important to note that there are no disputes over bitcoin fee collection or distribution as it is truthfully executed as scripted. Therefore, the halal blockchain should also be capable enough to script zakat management logic to the core of the halal banking blockchain. Identifying the account types and transaction type qualified for zakat may involve a "zakat worker" at some points, and the halal bank or the miner would serve this purpose and an incentive need to be scripted for such worker—as this is one of the zakat beneficiaries as specified in the Holy Book. Yes, the incentives for block chaining the zakat transaction should be paid from the zakat amount itself and can be programmed as a variant of transaction fee.

This would indeed lead to kill the interest-based economy by truthfully moving the wealth from rich to the poor—autonomously, truthfully, completely and instantaneously through a publicly verifiable transparent blockchain which is part of the global currency management system. Well, it is important to have this inbuilt to the currency systems itself, should not be an off-chain smart contract extension. The concept of zakat as the foundation of the economy for a well-cherished world is no more a theory and that is the opportunity for the halal banking to establish by realizing the halal cryptocurrency. If this important element of zakat is not there, then there is nothing called halal cryptocurrency—as all cryptocurrencies backed with crypto logic are otherwise halal. The distinction clearly is embarrassing the zakat-based economy to fight out interest-based economy, and the powerful weapon naturally is the blockchain-based cryptocurrency embedded with zakat transaction logic in a clever way.

Smart Inheritance

Islamic law has a supreme pre-scripted inheritance law which is fully compliant for blockchain automation. This should be taken care by an institution and the halal bank's blockchained cryptocurrency should take care this too. Upon triggering the start of the inheritance event (the death of the account holder), all related settlement events should trigger which is pre-scripted on the smart contract based on Shari'ah laws. All the eligible dependents account to get affected based on the Shari'ah principles autonomously and the inheritance chain could get extended to any length and breadth. The halal bank's role of identifying the physical person and its relationship is far more important. This also underscores the need for an institutions engagement than having fully anonymous cryptocurrency dealings.

Conclusion

Blockchain has a greater space in halal wealth management as truthfulness, transparency and preset rule-based execution are common to both. Cryptocurrencies give a space for halal wealth management to reestablish it from scratch, instead of depending on the impure interest-based economy. Instead of doing step-by-step corrective measures and survival tactics in the present-day financial space, the Islamic banking now can build its foundation purely utilizing blockchain and cryptocurrencies by accepting the intrinsic value of cryptocurrencies based on the same principles it applies to gold and precious assets. Using blockchain technology, modern-day Islamic banking is powerful enough to mint its halal currency and take the world by storm by programming halal functions to provide a smart and competitive alternative to the interest-based economy.

CHAPTER 6

Blockchain and Its Shariah Compliant Structure

Aishath Muneeza and Zakariya Mustapha

INTRODUCTION

Islamic finance has gained momentum in the world today. Irrespective of faith conviction, it has been accepted as a mode of financing in the world. The development of Islamic finance was gradual in the past. At the initial stage of its development, Islamic finance was concerned more with Shariah compliance of transactions and contracts used in it. Subsequently, focus was realigned on Shariah harmonisation with respect to juristic views and Shariah governance. Islamic finance encompasses some fundamental religious prohibitions and the promotion of certain virtues enshrined in Islam, to be observed in all ramifications of business dealings, including services provision. Therefore, Islamic finance works in line with Islamic religious principles such as a ban on usury or interest, gambling, uncertainty and outright speculations. This is coupled with upholding Islamic principles on prime virtues in human dealings that seek to promote societal justice, including avoidance and shunning of

A. Muneeza (✉)
INCEIF, Kuala Lumpur, Malaysia
e-mail: muneeza@inceif.org

Z. Mustapha
University of Malaya, Kuala Lumpur, Malaysia

© The Author(s) 2019
M. M. Billah (ed.), *Halal Cryptocurrency Management*,
https://doi.org/10.1007/978-3-030-10749-9_6

dishonesty, exploitation and unjust enrichment. At the same time, these virtues must be pursued on their own as objective of any business dealing. So, regardless of medium and channel of the dealings and providing services and pursuing these virtues, one must guard against indulging in those prohibitions. Accordingly, innovations such as in fintech and the ones based on blockchain are required to conform to these principles in order to be Shariah compliant and be used for purposes sanctioned by the Shariah including Islamic finance.

Today, there are more concern about financial technology (fintech) and information technology (IT) governance of Islamic finance industry. As we are now passing through the era of technology globally, everything, including Islamic finance industry, needs to be fused with the modern technological progress. Accordingly, the buzz phrase used in the Islamic finance industry today is fusing it with blockchain technology, an innovation that has the potential to revolutionise the modus operandi of all human transactions, financial and otherwise. It is worth any innovation that would potentially promote or uphold Islamic virtues in business dealings to be examined before allowing its usage for the lawful pursuit of sustenance or elimination of risks and detriments thereof. This is because it is crucial to maintain the right Shariah image for Islamic finance so that incorporating such innovation, idea or solution would not mar it. Currently, Islamic finance is recording successes in many countries but globally accounts for a negligible percentage of trade financing largely due to non-compliant structures which stifle Islamic finance investment goal. It is therefore desirable and timely to assimilate the demand of Muslim investors for Shariah compliant investment structures so that fintech firms would incorporate Islamic finance to tap the technology-driven global trade financing and financial markets. The blockchain technology is one such idea as well as reality on a global level that might be turned to for such opportunities as well as peculiar challenges to businesses and governments. Acceptance of such an innovative idea or solution into the Islamic finance industry is fast becoming widespread locally and globally. However, it requires a decisive push from national governments and regulators, coupled with international cooperation, as necessary enablers of greater significance in this regard. This is to ensure building stronger and responsible end-to-end Shariah compliance that drives greater stability and higher growth for the industry.

As such, this chapter intends to look at the potential role blockchain technology can play in Islamic finance with view to unravel the technology's features and align same with the underlying principles of Islamic finance. The working of blockchain technology in the realm of finance would be examined using doctrinal methodology. So, documented information on the blockchain technology and fintech generally would be sourced from both print and electronic medium as data for the study. This data would be analysed in relation to the applicability of the technology particularly to Islamic financing. This is with view to structuring a Shariah compliant blockchain-based Islamic finance transaction that would facilitate the attainment of Islamic finance objectives, in addition to eliminating the incidence of non-compliance and reputation risk to the Islamic finance industry as it is today and in time to come. Other objective include proffering suggestion based on findings of the chapter and as to needful actions thereof.

WHAT IS BLOCKCHAIN TECHNOLOGY?

A blockchain is a distributed or peer-to-peer[1] public ledger that consists of 'blocks' maintained by a distributed computers network which contain multiple verified transactions record without a central authority or third-party intermediary.[2] The blockchain comprises three essential elements as follows: a transaction, a transaction record and a system for verification and storage of the transaction. Open-source application generates the blocks and records information as to time and the manner the transaction occurs in sequence. Each block comprises a secured hash, generated while taking into account the index, timestamp, data inside the block and hash of the previous block. This manner of design renders a blockchain capable of auditing. Thus, after a block has been verified and added to the blockchain, any alteration to that block would produce a new hash which will be inconsistent with the hashes that precede and would be rejected. The block sequentially maintains data of all transactions that have occurred in the chain, hence the name blockchain. Specifically,

---

[1] A peer-to-peer, commonly written as P2P, is a description of a decentralised communication model via computer software that enables linkup of commercial and/or private users of the Internet to communicate or share resources with the same capabilities and any party can initiate a communication session.

[2] Darcy Allen, *Discovering and Developing the Blockchain Cryptoeconomy*, SSRN August 18, 2017, available at https://ssrn.com/abstract=2815255, accessed March 28, 2018.

blockchain is a database of irreversible time-stamped record of every transaction replicated on servers all over the world.[3]

Many people often confuse blockchain technology for cryptocurrencies such as bitcoins. What needs to be understood is that blockchain is the technology used in bitcoin and the technology is wider than the creation or use of bitcoins.[4] Thus, the blockchain technology is the basis of cryptocurrency such as bitcoin which is a distributed payment protocol.[5]

Also described as decentralised electronic public ledger, the blockchain keeps account of transactions sequentially and freely, enabling anybody to confirm and get to the information so kept. In short, blockchain can be referred to as a technology that generates a tamper-proof and authoritative record of what belongs to who and at what period of time.[6]

This technology could be used in any kind of transaction that involves value like goods, money and property. However, with respect to the creation of money via the blockchain, i.e. cryptocurrency, the shariah scholars are yet to unanimously decide the shariah compliance of it and the deliberations of the shariah scholars on this matter are on going. While some jurists sanction the legality or lawfulness of cryptocurrency, most others do not. Thus, the emergence of cryptocurrency is met by several *fatwas* (Islamic legal and religious rulings) prohibiting it in several Muslim countries.[7] Nevertheless, a *fatwa* was recently issued by Mufti Mohammad Abu Bakar

---

[3] G. W. Peters and E. Panayi, 'Understanding Modern Banking Ledgers Through Blockchain Technologies: Future of Transaction Processing and Smart Contracts on the Internet of Money', SSRN, available at https://papers.ssrn.com/sol3/Papers.cfm?abstract_id=2692487, accessed March 30, 2018.

[4] Satoshi Nakamoto, *Bitcoin: A Peer-to-Peer Electronic Cash System*, available at https://bitcoin.org/bitcoin.pdf, accessed March 14, 2018.

[5] See Christopher Dula and David LEE Kuo Chuen, 'Reshaping the Financial Order', in David Lee Kuo Chuen and Robert H. Deng (eds.), *Handbook of Blockchain, Digital Finance and Inclusion*, Vol. 1, Academic Press, London, 2017, p. 16. See also Hazik Mohd, *Blockchain Islamic in Finance*, available at https://www.linkedin.com/pulse/blockchain-islamic-finance-hazik-mohamed, accessed March 30, 2018.

[6] See Christian Catalini and Joshua S. Gans, *Some Simple Economics of the Blockchain*, MIT Sloan Research Paper No. 5191-16, SSRN, available at, https://ssrn.com/abstract=2874598, accessed March 20, 2018. See also Kevin D. Werbach, 'Trust, But Verify: Why the Blockchain Needs the Law', *Berkeley Technology Law Journal*, Vol. 31, No. 2, September 2017, available at https://papers.ssrn.com/sol3/papers.cfm?abstract_id=2844409, accessed March 20, 2018.

[7] Haamiz Ahmed, 'Is Bitcoin Halal or Haram?' *ProPakistani*, January 2, 2018, available at https://propakistani.pk/2018/01/02/bitcoin-halal-haram/, accessed March 14, 2018.

of Blossom Finance Indonesia that bitcoin qualifies as Islamic money and can be held and used as such by Muslims and in Islamic transactions.[8]

BLOCKCHAIN'S INTEGRATED SECURITY AND EMBEDDED TRUST SYSTEM

Blockchain is an innovatively secure technology that uses cryptography which involves complex mathematical algorithms to verify and secure data. Cryptography is the art of writing or solving codes. The decentralised network system used in it makes it impossible for hackers to hack into the system as there is no single point of failure system. The chain of information is secured as in a series of chain for which one requires huge computing power to alter or hack the data in the chain. Interestingly, the longer the blockchain becomes, the more secure the network becomes, accordingly, one cannot imagine the degree of efforts needed in order to hack a decentralised network comprising of thousands of computers. Ordinarily, a very huge computing energy is needed to 'hack' or modify data in the blocks. Ordinarily, a very huge computing energy is needed to 'hack' or modify data in the blocks. Therefore, while the chain expands, the amount of computing energy required to 'hack' them upsurges exponentially. This equally eliminates the risk of theft and fraud in blockchain. Additionally, it puts in place trust mechanism so that doing business transaction with people one does not know is not an issue.[9] In general, the blockchain process is by nature decentralised, transparent, immutable as well as auditable, and these are the properties of the technology behind blockchain. The diagram below illustrates the working of a blockchain transaction.

---

[8] The Fatwa was based on a similitude of qualities of money which according to the mufti are shared by bitcoin cryptocurrency as well as countries' stance on its legality. While some countries adopt a clear position that either allows or bans its usage, other countries are altogether silent about it. See Mufti Muhammad Abu-Bakar, *Shariah Analysis of Bitcoin, Cryptocurrency and Blockchain*, available at https://blossomfinance.com/bitcoin-working-paper, accessed April 5, 2017.

[9] D. Kevin Werbach, *Trust, But Verify: Why the Blockchain Needs the Law*, SSRN, available at https://ssrn.com/abstract=2844409, accessed April 3, 2018.

Blockchain's Applications, Uses and Potentials

The first system of record for business was a ledger captured on a clay tablet, and subsequently, the double-entry ledger was introduced to cater for and promote modern finance.[10] Ever since, ledgers have been digitised but with otherwise little change, capturing only a snapshot of a transaction at a moment in time that reflects only the information held by a single organisation. The working of blockchain is that once a transaction takes place, an asset is off one ledger and on to another person's ledger. Comparably, as a distributed ledger, blockchain shares information with and writes business transactions to an indestructible chain of perpetual sequence of records that is accessible by the parties involved in the transaction. In short, what blockchain technology does is that it moves the lens from information held by an individual owner to the cross-entity history of an asset or transaction.[11] Accordingly, it is important to understand that distributed ledgers can be shared and updated in near real time across a group of participants. Initially developed to address the problem of double spending in the cryptocurrency bitcoin,[12] the potentials of the technology were quickly discerned and its application is extended to variety of other applications beyond the original use for cryptocurrency.[13] From an operational angle, other advantages which the Islamic financial institutions can enjoy due to the usage of blockchain technology is that they can utilise decentralised data storages which are

---

[10] IBM Institute for Business Value, *Fast Forward: Rethinking Enterprises, Ecosystems and Economies with Blockchain*, June 2016, available at https://www.-01.ibm.com/common/ssi/cgi-bin/ssialias?htmlfid=GBE03757USEN, accessed March 14, 2018.

[11] Ibid.

[12] Satoshi Nakamoto, *Bitcoin: A Peer-to-Peer Electronic Cash System*, available at https://bitcoin.org/bitcoin.pdf, accessed March 14, 2018. NB: Satoshi Nakamoto is said to be the pseudo-name of the inventor of the blockchain that first published and introduced the idea with respect to the cryptocurrency '*Bitcoin*' in 2009. The major aim of the Bitcoin was to remedy what the author claimed to be the inherent weaknesses of the traditional payment model, being an intermediary-centred and trust-based model in processing electronic payment, by creating a system that needs neither an intermediary nor trust. It is in other words a decentralised 'trustless' electronic payment model.

[13] Campbell R. Harvey, *Cryptofinance*, SSRN, January 14, 2016, available at https://ssrn.com/abstract=2438299, accessed March 20, 2018. See also *How Can Blockchain Help Aadhaar Ensure Privacy & Transparency?* available at http://experiencesutra.com/insights/how-can-blockchain-help-aadhaar-ensure-privacy-and-transparency/, accessed March 20, 2018.

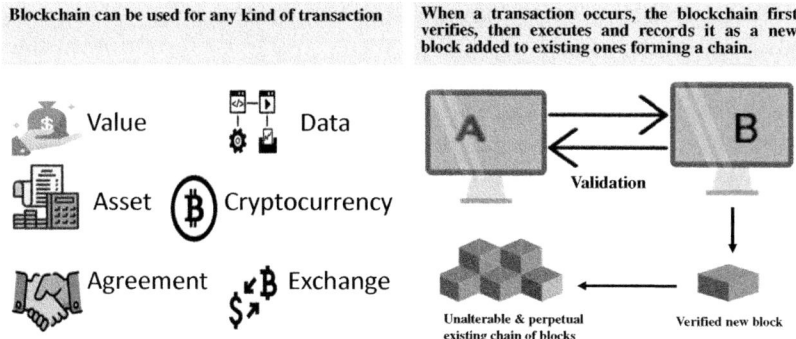

Fig. 6.1 Blockchain-based transactions (*Source* Author's own)

much secure and cost-efficient than the existing manual and centralised data storage used by most of the Islamic financial institutions. Almost all cloud storage services link to a centralised server and a centralised database which are susceptible to the risk of compromising the data from a single point of entry which forces the users to trust in the single provider.[14]

Several blockchain-based fintechs have been developed and made operational in the modern financing activities such as smart contract and other protocols for P2P lending and crowdfunding (Fig. 6.1).[15]

AUTOMATING SHARIAH GOVERNANCE AND COMPLIANCE IN BLOCKCHAIN TRANSACTIONS

The blockchain technology has so much powerful potential that hundreds of financial institutions, conventional and Islamic alike across non-Islamic and Islamic jurisdictions are jumping on board in pursuit of

---

[14] Blockchain Semantics Insights, *How Will Blockchain Revitalize Trade Finance?* available at https://www.blockchainsemantics.com/blog/revitalizing-trade-finance/, accessed March 30, 2018.

[15] Crowdfunding is about a kind of equity funding for an established tangible and lawful project which shares and limits risk among participants. See Paolo Fiore, *When Crowdfunding Is Sharia Compliant*, available at http://www.youris.com/Energy/Renewables/When-Crowdfunding-Is-Sharia-Compliant.kl, accessed March 20, 2018.

solutions in relation to it. With the advent of this technology, there is the possibility that financial services, payment system and every other category of money markets could be reinvented. There are reconfiguration possibilities within all industries in the economy whereby smart contracts would be employed for loan and intangible property like copyrights.[16] For Islamic finance, the potentials of the technology have raised one important issue, which is its Shariah governance, so that the transactions could be not only fair and transparent but Shariah compliant.[17]

In Islamic finance, it is indispensable that a fintech be Shariah compliant as in traditional practices. It is also a common knowledge that from a Shariah viewpoint, technology is generally treated as neutral phenomenon. However, the need to ascertain which fintech is vulnerable to the requirements of Shariah cannot be dispensed with. First and foremost, in order to address such concerns, it is pertinent to begin from the general rule of Shariah governing business dealings that every transaction is permitted unless there is express and clear authority that prohibits such a transaction. This rule of default permissibility for all transactions gives room for flexibility towards novel practices and other innovations in financial dealings. Accordingly, innovations in business transactions are regarded as permitted and gladly allowed. Therefore, fintech innovations would only be considered impermissible when there is a clear rule of Shariah as the authority that such innovations contradict.[18]

In this regard, the application of fintech would be made to abide by Shariah principles that stipulate the avoidance of certain prohibited aspects of business transactions. These prohibitions include interest or usury, gambling or speculation, fraud or cheating, harm and uncertainty among others, as in traditional practice of Islamic finance. Similarly, the practice of fintech-based transactions would be made to adhere to Shariah rules of contract that are to be observed in the transaction, including the pillars and conditions dictated by the Shariah. Additionally,

---

[16]R. M. Lacasse, et al., *Blockchain Technology—Arsenal for a Shariah-Compliant Financial Ecosystem?* 5th International Conference of Entrepreneurial Finance, CIFEMA 2017, Ibn Zohr University, Agadir, Morocco, December 4–5, 2017, p. 33 *et seq.* Also available at http://hdl.handle.net/10993/33529, accessed April 3, 2018.

[17]Hazik Mohammed, *Blockchain in Islamic Finance*, available at https://www.linkedin.com/pulse/blockchain-islamic-finance-hazik-mohamed, accessed March 28, 2018.

[18]Othman Abdullah, *Fintech and Shariah Governance for Islamic Finance*, available at https://islmfintech.com/fintech-and-Shariah-governance/, accessed March 29, 2018.

the application of fintech should be aimed at attaining Shariah objectives (maqasid al-Shariah) which include the realisation of benefits and the avoidance of difficulties and harms.[19]

The Making of Shariah Compliant Blockchain Structure

The blockchain provides a platform that makes possible not only the creation of cryptocurrency such as the bitcoin but also the recording of values involving currency and assets through its digitally decentralised ledger. As requirements of Shariah, the blockchain's inherent disclosure, transparency and enhancement of trust in transfers and exchange transactions can be considered particularly beneficial in that regard. The blockchain can serve in enforcing the rules of exchange in cash transactions for currency and/or lawful commodities.[20]

Along these lines, Shariah compliance can as well be assuredly programmed into the smart contract for any Islamic finance transaction. This can be automated or written into at the regulators' and all required parties' nodes that form part of the blockchain network. These nodes will then be enabled to validate transactions and append compliant blocks in the blockchain. In this manner, respective regulators (governmental and institutional), whose approval or certification is required for a particular smart contract-based transaction, can be part of the protocol that oversee and/or approve of any particular block to join the blockchain. Thus, any transaction that is not Shariah compliant in accordance with the protocols cannot be verified and would be absolutely rejected as unqualified to join the block.

[19] See Akram Laldin, 'Fintech and Shariah Governance', *Islamic Finance News (IFN)* Correspondence Reports, Vol. 14, No. 6, February 7, 2017. Also available at https://www.islamicfinancenews.com/fintech-and-Shariah-governance.html, accessed April 2, 2018.

[20] Mufti Muhammad Abu-Bakar, *Shariah Analysis of Bitcoin, Cryptocurrency and Blockchain*, available at https://blossomfinance.com/bitcoin-working-paper, accessed April 5, 2018.

P2P and Smart Contract Operations for Islamic Finance

A P2P refers to a network of computers wherein each computer and/ or device works as a server for the others in the network thereby enabling shared access to files and other resources without the intermediation of a central server. The P2P is a prominent fintech innovation that makes possible a P2P lending that features and incorporates the blockchain technology.[21] Primarily, and in the spirit of Shariah compliance, a Shariah compliant P2P finance establishes a group of businesses and investors, shares risks and channels resources into real economic activities that are beneficial to the group. For this purpose, the P2P is essentially designed to operate following the fundamental Islamic finance principles of profit and risk sharing instead of the model used by conventional finance which transfers risk for profit. In line with the principles of Shariah, money in Islamic finance must be used in a productive way, and to generate profit on money, it must be via legit and ethical business or investment that encompasses certain risk element.[22]

A smart contract protocol not only facilitates and verifies but enforces an agreement so that it dispenses with such requirement as notarisation and other technicalities (where applicable) for the perfection and enforceability of a legal document. This is so because the contract automatically executes itself once all terms and conditions embedded in its clauses are fulfilled. For instance, a smart contract drawn up to lease out property can be automated with the conditions being payment of rent and handing over of key (digital key that as well qualifies as lease document). Immediately, the tenant makes the due payment, and the contract authorises the transfer of the key to the leaseholder or tenant. The property-owner or landlord can neither stop the key from being instantly transferred to the tenant once payment is made, nor transfer same before payment of rent. With the contract recorded in public ledger and

---

[21] See Mohammed Abdullahi Ridza, *The Life and Law of Fintech*, Sweet & Maxwell Asia, Subang Jaya, Malaysia, 2017, p. 21 *et seq*. See https://en.bitcoinwiki.org/wiki/Peer-to-peer, accessed April 5, 2018, for illustration of P2P computer network in contrast to a client-server network.

[22] Beehive, *P2P and Islamic Finance*, https://www.beehive.ae/sharia-processing/, accessed April 10, 2018. See https://www.businessinsider.com/peer-to-peer-lending-how-digital-lending-marketplaces-are-disrupting-the-predominant-banking-model-2015-05/?IR=T, accessed April 5, 2018, for an illustration on how P2P lending network generally operates.

the anonymity of parties, the conditions of a smart contract are always met with certainty so that none of the parties can blame any other of wrongdoing.[23]

In effect, the smart contract protocol can be utilised to set up any computer operation that is condition-driven, so that transactions can only be possible after all required conditions for such transactions, including Shariah compliance, are accordingly satisfied. Assuredly then, the contract eliminates uncertainty and confusion arising from parties' default, as it takes care of execution and enforcement.[24] The concept of smart contracts can be used to run any condition-driven operation. Smart contracts take out the confusion and uncertainty from an agreement, because the enforcement is also taken care of by the program. This makes the underlying concept of smart contracts applicable to whole variety of businesses and operations.[25]

When blockchain technology is used in Islamic finance, the nature of the classical contracts used in Islamic finance also changes fully to the form of a *smart contract*.[26] Smart contracts are basically self-executing digital contracts in which the terms of the contract are electronically coded and will execute only if the conditions stipulated are met. A smart

---

[23] Anand Narayan, *A Brief Introduction to Smart Contracts and Their Endless Possibilities*, available at https://codebrahma.com/brief-intro-smart-contracts-endless-possibilities/, accessed April 10, 2018.

[24] Ibid.

[25] In essence, any sector from financial services and healthcare to administration and governance that aspires to do better with automated and extremely secure action based on certain conditions can immensely take advantage of smart contracts. See Trent J. MacDonald, et al, 'Blockchain and the Boundaries of Self-Organized Economies: Predictions for the Future of Banking', in Paulo Tasca, et al. (eds.) *Banking Beyond Banks and Money*, SSRN, available at https://ssrn.com/abstract=2749514, accessed March 28, 2018.

[26] Originally proposed by Nick Szabo in his work on digital currency in 1994, then a fanciful notion of what smart contract would be, even though at that time the existing economic and communication infrastructures was not sufficient enough to support its protocol. See Mark Giancaspro, 'Is a 'Smart Contract' Really a Smart Idea? Insights from a Legal Perspective', *Computer Law & Security Review*, Vol. 33, No. 6, December 2017, p. 825; Don Tapscott and Alex Tapscott, *Blockchain Revolution: How the Technology Behind Bitcoin Is Changing Money, Business and the World*, Penguin Random House, New York, 2016, p. 5; and Michael Gord, *Smart Contracts Described by Nick Szabo 20 Years Ago Now Becoming Reality*, April 26, 2016, available at https://bitcoinmagazine.com/articles/smart-contracts-described-by-nick-szabo-years-ago-now-becoming-reality-1461693751/, accessed March 27, 2017.

contract operates with inherent precision that aligns with recognition and execution of certain objectives of a contract including privity, verifiability, observability and enforceability. Moreover, smart contract enables parties to monitor each other's performance of the contract and verify if and when the contract has been carried out. It ensures that only the aspects required for the completion of the contract are shown to the parties. While being self-enforcing, it does away with any hindrance to guarantee the contract proceeds as scheduled according to rules and agreement.[27]

An Islamic finance transaction can be written in a smart contract format by the parties concerned. The smart contract protocol facilitates, verifies and/or enforces the negotiation or performance of a contract, enabling the execution of credible transaction short of any third-party intervention. Smart contract transactions are irreversible as well as trackable. The working of the smart contract has been extended onto property agreement and other products of physical nature, such as vehicles where, for instance, an algorithm could allow and/or revoke owner accessibility to digital vehicle keys if the owner in question fails to settle loan payment. Designated multi-signature protocols can be established for Islamic finance contract that ensure execution of the said contract only after the term thereto have been agreed to and signed with the parties' Shariah compliant digital keys.

The entire contractual process for an Islamic finance transaction can be automated in this manner. By automating the whole contractual process, the operations of Islamic financial institutions will be inherently streamlined and alleviated of administrative costs and legal complexities. Interestingly, smart contracts are easy to verify, immutable and highly secure, in addition to mitigating operational risks arising from settlement and counterparty risks in non-smart contracts.[28] In simple terms, it means that the number of human involvement required in the process will reduce making the IT governance system of the Islamic financial institutions stronger and reliable.

---

[27] Michael Gord, op cit.

[28] Aziz Zainuddin, *Blockchain in Islamic Finance*, available at https://infocus.wief.org/blockchain-in-islamic-finance/, accessed March 28, 2018. See also https://codebrahma.com/brief-intro-smart-contracts-endless-possibilities/, accessed April 8, 2018, for an illustrative operation of a blockchain smart contract.

REGULATORY OVERSIGHT FOR BLOCKCHAIN-BASED ISLAMIC FINANCING

The blockchain technology unbridles opportunities towards digital solution that is revolutionising fintech not only for business but also for governance, and accordingly, national governments are gradually developing keen interest in the technology.[29] This is equally true with respect to both conventional and Islamic finance businesses. For instance, Dubai as an international hub for Islamic finance has unveiled plan for its utilisation of blockchain in both public and private sectors aimed at making the country a global leader by 2020.[30] Malaysia is one Islamic finance jurisdictions where the blockchain technology manifests its presence and formal initiatives are taken to explore and tap into the resultant opportunities. Being a global key player in that regard, Malaysia is poised to be a viable test bed and suitable hub for the launch and take-off of Shariah compliant financial products by fintech companies in order to develop a fintech sector for the Islamic finance. In the same vein, the Bank Negara Malaysia (BNM), which is the Central Bank of Malaysia, and the Securities Commission (SC) of Malaysia have both issued guidelines to regulate the blockchain-based transactions within the ambit of extant finance and capital market laws. Meanwhile, the Malaysia Digital Economy Corp (MDEC),[31] a governmental agency for digitising the Malaysian economy, has its mandated updated and realigned in 2011 towards the blockchain-based innovations in addition to other

---

[29] See Philipp Paech, 'The Governance of Blockchain Financial Networks', *Modern Law Review*, Vol. 80, No. 6, 2017, p. 1073 *et seq*, also available at https://ssrn.com/abstract=2875487, accessed April 8, 2018. Pei Sai Fan, 'Singapore Approach to Develop and Regulate FinTech', in David Lee Kuo Chuen and Robert H. Deng (eds.), *Handbook of Blockchain, Digital Finance and Inclusion*, Vol. 1, Academic Press, London, 2018, p. 348.

[30] See D'Cunha S. Dutt, 'Dubai Sets Its Sights on Becoming the World's First Blockchain-Powered Government', *Forbes*, December 18, 2017, available at https://www.forbes.com/sites/supranadutt/2017/12/18/dubai-sets-sights-on-becoming-the-worlds-first-blockchain-powered-government/, accessed April 7, 2018. See also Zainuddin Aziz, *Blockchain in Islamic Finance*, available at https://infocus.wief.org/blockchain-in-islamic-finance/, accessed April 8, 2018.

[31] Established to help build a sustainable digital economy for Malaysia since 1996, MDEC aims to lead Malaysia become an integral part of the global digital revolution such as today championed by the blockchain technology. See Corporate Profile MDEC, *Championing Malaysia's Digital Economy*, available at https://www.mdec.my/about-mdec/corporate-profile, accessed April 8, 2018.

fintech-related dealings.[32] By and large, the BNM collaborates with the SC and MDEC to provide enabling infrastructure and conducive regulatory framework for a robust fintech landscape.[33]

Even though it is believed that strict regulation would tend to stifle blockchain's innovativeness and potentials in the finance realm, it is however inevitable in order to arrest its consequent disruption and maintain the existing harmony and order in the industry.[34] It is in recognition of this fact the BNM prepares the stage for the operations and development of innovative blockchain-based financial and blockchain-related transactions via a Sandbox and dedicated guidelines for that purpose. This is the Technology Regulatory Sandbox Framework 2016 (Framework) which is introduced to enable innovation of fintech to be deployed and tested in a live business environment, within specified parameters and time frames.[35] The Sandbox provides opportunity for the registered entities to conduct real business in a simulated environment while the BNM closely monitors their viability and possible compliance issues against regulatory standards and other peculiarities. It is noteworthy that the BNM regulates only products or services that come under its purview of regulated businesses under the relevant laws and regulations, so only such products and services come to test under the Sandbox.[36]

For peer-to-peer (P2P) lending and/or crowdfunding, which is the most utilised blockchain-based avenue in Islamic finance, the Malaysia Securities Commission has provided guidelines and regulations to that

---

[32] Samburaj Das, 'Malaysia Woos FinTech Developments for Shariah-Compliant Islamic Finance', *CCN FinTech News*, March 20, 2017, available at https://www.ccn.com/malaysia-woos-fintech-devs-Shariah-compliant-islamic-finance/, accessed April 8, 2018.

[33] See Punithaa Kylasapathy, et al, 'Unlocking Malaysia's Digital Future: Opportunities, Challenges and Policy Responses', *Bank Negara Malaysia Annual Report 2017*, available at http://www.bnm.gov.my/files/publication/ar/en/2017/ar2017_book.pdf, accessed April 8, 2018. See also Aznan bin Abdul Aziz, *Malaysia Is Fintech Ready*, Finnovasia KL 2017 Opening Address, available at http://www.bnm.gov.my/index.php?ch=en_speech&pg=en_speech&ac=721&lang=bm, accessed April 8, 2018.

[34] See Andreas Freund, 'Automated, Decentralized Trust: A Path to Financial Inclusion', in David Lee Kuo Chuen and Robert H. Deng (eds.), *Handbook of Blockchain, Digital Finance and Inclusion*, Vol. 1, Academic Press, London, 2018, p. 432 *et seq.*

[35] See Bank Negara Malaysia Circular BNM/RH/PD030-1, *Financial Technology Regulatory Sandbox Framework*, October 18, 2016, herein after referred to as the Framework.

[36] See Sect. 2.1 of the Framework.

effect, i.e. the Guidelines on Recognised Markets 2016,[37] which are welcomed as supportive of fintech development in the capital market and its related activities. After the SC announced the release of its regulatory framework for P2P financing, later that year it also announced the approval of six P2P operators licensed in Malaysia. This is an important milestone that enables entrepreneurs to start Malaysian-based fintech businesses.[38] These P2P financing entities expand the capacity of participating entrepreneurs and small businesses by pooling capital from investors in small sums via online digital platform. They offer a quick opportunity to get financing for such smaller businesses. The P2P framework is part of SC's ongoing effort to provide greater access to market-based financing through the application of innovative technology solutions.[39]

World over, fintech and blockchain-based transactions including P2P lending and crowdfunding have been making inroads into traditional Islamic finance. This development has resulted in an alliance, where eight Islamic crowdfunding platform operators from across the globe come together and form the Islamic Fintech Alliance (IFT Alliance).[40] It is an association of Islamic fintech entities undertaking blockchain-based activities, with objectives that include serving as a self-regulating standards-setting body for Islamic financial technology.[41]

---

[37] Securities Commission, Circular SC-GL/6-2015 (R1-2016), *Guidelines on Recognized Markets*, April 13, 2016.

[38] Othman Abdullahi, *Fintech and Islamic Finance*, available at https://islmfintech.com/fintech-and-islamic-finance/, accessed April 9, 2018.

[39] The Securities Commission Malaysia, *List of Registered Market Operators*, available at https://www.sc.com.my/digital/list_rmo/, accessed April 9, 2018.

[40] Launched on the April 1, 2016 in Kuala Lumpur, Malaysia, the founding members are BlossomFinance (USA/Indonesia), EasiUp (France), EthisCrowd (Singapore), Narwi (Qatar), FundingLab (Scotland/Palestine), KapitalBoost (Singapore), Launchgood (USA) and SkolaFund (Malaysia). See Othman Abdullahi, 'Major Fintech Achievements in Islamic Finance in 2016', *The Malaysian Reserve*, April 3, 2017, available at https://themalaysianreserve.com/2017/04/03/major-fintech-achievements-in-islamic-finance-in-2016/, accessed April 9, 2018.

[41] Other objectives of the Alliance are to broaden the reach of Islamic fintech by supporting network of innovators and to develop globally sustainable ecosystem by providing industry insights to regulators and stakeholders. See *About IFT Alliance*, available at http://islamicfintechalliance.com/, accessed April 9, 2018.

Utilising Shariah Compliant Blockchain Structure by Islamic Fintechs Around the World

Islamic fintech entities are joining the race towards digitalisation and automation of operations on blockchain-based platforms.

HADA DBank is the first digital bank to practically fuse blockchain technology with Islamic banking. Based in Kuala Lumpur, Malaysia, HADA DBank is a company working to place itself at the forefront of the new generation of financial banking systems. Using the traditional Islamic banking methodology of fair and transparent risk and responsibility sharing, the bank's operations are augmented by the technological innovation of blockchain.[42] HADA DBank derives certain advantages by using this technology in providing banking services. These include improved data integrity due to reduced potential for human error or fraud given the decentralised nature of the blockchain as well as increased transaction speed on real time. There is also reduced settlement risk due to speed and simplification of processes, cost reductions resulting from simplified back-office processes which require fewer personnel and less technology. Moreover, the absence of central point of failure improves the bank's data security and system resiliency, with reduced use of capital for reserves because decreased settlement times mean capital is not tied up for as long, if at all; while the opportunity to digitise sales transactions and contracts enables monitoring of delivery of related goods and assets.[43]

Similarly, Emirates Islamic is also championing in blockchain-based Islamic fintech. Emirates Islamic is one of the leading Islamic financial institutions based in UAE. The bank on June 11, 2017 announced that it will introduce blockchain technology into its cheques as a fraud prevention measure. Termed 'Cheque Chain', Emirates Islamic is the first Islamic bank in UAE to undertake this initiative to enhance security in the popular payment method. Emirates Islamic will issue new cheque

---

[42] The mission of this bank is to provide ethical and responsible banking services to everyone, especially the current "unbanked" population. The vision of this bank is to be the leading global blockchain and digital bank that emphasises ethics and responsibility through Islamic banking principles and services.

[43] About HADA Dbank, available at https://www.hada-dbank.com/, accessed March 29, 2018.

books carrying a unique quick response (QR) code on every leaf, along with a string of 20 random characters.[44]

Moreover, in May 2017, Al Rajhi Bank (ARB), the world's largest Islamic Bank, completed a secure, cross-border money transfer using Ripple blockchain technology.[45] This successful transaction marks the first time the technology has been used in Saudi Arabia. This was a money transfer transaction between Al Rajhi Bank's Head Offices in Riyadh and Jordan. Ripple has engineered a payment system like blockchain, which uses a shared ledger to process transactions. The network allows assets to move freely, directly and instantly therefore reducing time and cost of clearing, which makes the process less time-consuming and much cheaper.[46]

Equally, in February 2018, the Saudi Arabian Monetary Authority (SAMA), the Kingdom's central bank, has initiated a pilot program with Ripple to facilitate banks in the country to improve their payments infrastructure using xCurrent. SAMA is only the second central bank in the world, after Bank of England's successful proof of concept with Ripple last year, to implement blockchain technology to revolutionise payments system. Under this program, banks in Saudi Arabia will have access to the 100 plus financial institutions on RippleNet, thus enabling cheaper, faster and more transparent cross-border transactions.[47]

Likewise, in February 2018, the International Federation of Red Cross and Red Crescent Societies (IFRC) has developed an online

[44] Emirates Islamic, *Emirates Islamic Is First Islamic Bank to Integrate Blockchain Technology into Cheques*, June 11, 2017, available at https://www.emiratesislamic.ae/eng/latest-news/2017/june/news11062017/, accessed March 28, 2018.

[45] Ripple is a venture start-up headquartered in San Francisco, with several branches across the world. The company specialises in providing financial settlement solutions and is drawing significant interest from many in the banking industry because of its innovative approach to cross border money transfers.

[46] Ripple claims that transaction costs can go down by as much as 60% using the distributed ledger technology for retail remittance and commercial payments. See Zawya, 'Al Rajhi Bank Completes Transaction Using Blockchain Technology for the First Time in KSA', *Press Release*, May 14, 2017, available at https://www.zawya.com/mena/en/story/, accessed March 28, 2018.

[47] Team Ripple, *Ripple and Saudi Arabian Monetary Authority (SAMA) Offer Pilot Program for Saudi Banks*, February 14, 2018, available at https://ripple.com/ripple_press/ripple-and-saudi-arabian-monetary-authority-sama-offer-pilot-program-for-saudi-banks/, accessed March 28, 2018.

blockchain application which has trumped over 100 other project submissions to win the recognition of the leading Islamic finance multilateral development bank, i.e. the Islamic Development Bank (IDB). Developed by IFRC's global innovation team and AidTech, the blockchain application offers individuals and organisations the ability to track their contributions in highly complex humanitarian settings, providing transparency and laying a platform for increased trust between humanitarian organisations and the Islamic social financing world. IFRC was declared champion in the Fintech Islamic Finance Challenge organised by the IDB Group and IE Business School in Madrid. Islamic crowdfunding platform KapitalBoost, Shariah invoice financing peer-to-peer platform Invoice Wakalah and digital cash payment provider Teek Taka as well as big data analytics firm MyFinB were the finalists of the Fintech Islamic Finance Challenge.[48]

Furthermore, a Kuala Lumpur-based company HelloGold, the first tech start-up to gain Shariah compliance for its gold-trading platform in 2016, has added another feather in its cap: a Shariah compliant gold-backed cryptocurrency. Endorsed by Amanie Advisors, GOLDX is now a fully operational Shariah compliant Ethereum ERC20 token, backed by 99.99% investment-grade gold, the first in the world to own that distinction. GOLDX tokens are only issued according to the amount of gold physically held, and this information is publicly accessible and verified independently by its vaulting partner.[49]

Earlier in October 2017, the research arm of the IDB planned to use blockchain technology to develop Shariah compliant products, aiming to support financial inclusion efforts across its member countries. The Jeddah-based Islamic Research and Training Institute (IRTI) said it had signed an agreement with local firm Ateon and Belgium-based SettleMint, with the first stage to focus on a technical feasibility study. The agreement is the latest effort to combine blockchain technology

[48] IFRC, 'IFRC Blockchain Application Wins Global Islamic Finance Competition', *Press Release*, February 9, 2018, available at http://media.ifrc.org/ifrc/press-release/ifrc-block-chain-application-wins-global-islamic-finance-competition/, accessed March 28, 2018.

[49] Zawya, 'Fintech HelloGold Is World's First Shariah-Compliant Gold Platform', *Press Release*, December 6, 2016, available at https://www.zawya.com/mena/en/story/, accessed April 4, 2018. See also Bernardo Vizcaino, 'Malaysian Firm Adds Islamic Certification to Cryptocurrency', *Reuters News*, February 20, 2018, available at https://www.zawya.com/mena/en/story/Malaysian_firm_adds_Islamic_certification_to_crypto-currency/, accessed April 4, 2018.

to tap demand from Muslim investors, with firms from Indonesia to Canada having already received Shariah compliant certification for their products.[50]

TRANSACTION-SPECIFIC APPLICATION OF BLOCKCHAIN TECHNOLOGY IN ISLAMIC FINANCE

In 2016, a new prototype solution developed by Bank of America Merrill Lynch (BofAML), HSBC and the Infocomm Development Authority of Singapore (IDA) brings the paper-intensive letter of credit (LC) transactions onto the blockchain. The application enables exporters, importers and their respective banks to share information on a private distributed ledger (see steps and diagram below). The trade deal can then be executed automatically through a series of digital smart contracts.[51] The parties involved in the transaction can visualise data in real time on their devices and see the next actions to be performed.

Using blockchain technology to execute LCs can help streamline the manual processing of import/export documentation, improve security by reducing errors, making companies' working capital more predictable and increase convenience for all parties through mobile interaction. The seven steps to a blockchain-based LC transaction are as follows:

1. The importer creates an LC application for the importer bank to review and stores it on the blockchain.
2. The importer bank receives notification to review the LC and can approve or reject it based on the data provided. Once checked and approved, access is then provided to the exporter bank automatically for approval.

---

[50] Bernardo Vizcaino, 'Saudi Arabia's IDB Plans Blockchain-Based Financial Inclusion Product', *Reuters News*, October 20, 2018, available at https://www.reuters.com/article/us-islamic-finance-fintech/saudi-arabias-idb-plans-blockchain-based-financial-inclusion-product-idUSKBN1CP08W, accessed April 4, 2018.

[51] Luke Parker, 'Bank of America Merrill Lynch Explores Using a Blockchain for Trade Finance', *Brave Newcoin*, March 2, 2016, available at https://bravenewcoin.com/news/bank-of-america-merrill-lynch-explores-using-a-blockchain-for-trade-finance/, accessed April 4, 2018.

3. The exporter bank approves or rejects the LC. If approved, the exporter is able to view the LC requirements and is prompted to view through the application.
4. The exporter completes the shipment, adds invoice and export application data and attaches a photo image of any other required documents. Once validated, these documents are stored on the blockchain.
5. The documents are viewed by the exporter bank, which approves or rejects the application.
6. The importer bank reviews the data and images against the LC requirements, marking any discrepancies for review by the importer. When approved, the LC goes straight to completed status or is sent to the importer for settlement.
7. If required due to a discrepancy, the importer can review the export documents and approve or reject them.[52]

Figure 6.2 illustrates the operation of the LC in those seven steps.

Some of the prominent issues faced in the execution of LC are high costs and long time to execute. Expert estimation has put it that 50% of banks' costs for an LC arises from manual document handling and checking, which creates delays, errors and expense. The advantages of using blockchain in LC transaction is that it increases the speed of execution (less than 1 day), greatly reduced cost, reduced risk, currency fluctuations and value-added services like incremental payment.[53]

Illustration of smart contract operation to bridge the trade finance process into action (Fig. 6.3).

[52] Luke Parker, 'Bank of America Merrill Lynch, HSBC, and IDA Develop a Blockchain Prototype Solution for Trade Finance', *Brave NewCoin*, August 15, 2016, available at https://bravenewcoin.com/news/bank-of-america-merrill-lynch-hsbc-and-ida-develop-a-blockchain-prototype-solution-for-trade-finance, accessed April 13, 2018.

[53] Ibid.

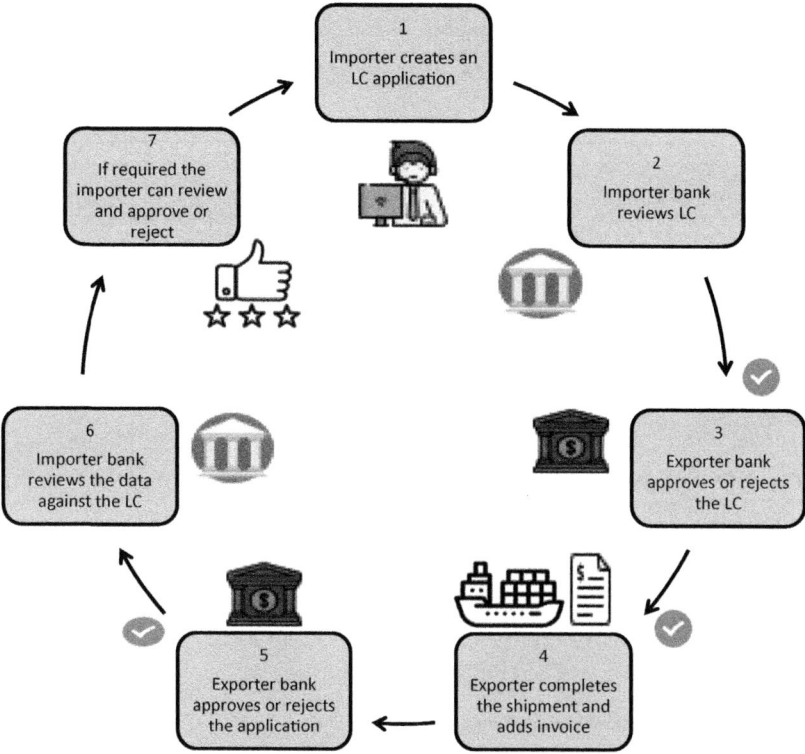

Fig. 6.2 Illustration of steps in the operation of LC (*Source* Author's own)

ISLAMIC TRADE FINANCE

Blockchain Musharakah Mutanaqisah

A smarter contract encapsulates the obligation to transfer rental proceeds and equity purchases to the bank with automated separation between rental and equity from monthly instalment. A smart contract enables the real-time transfer of share between bank and customer. Smart contract will diminish ownership of the bank to the customer if all the obligations is executed. Upon default, smart contract will execute banks to charge. With this mechanism, the benefits derived includes reduced settlement time and cost, reduced operational risk and automated processing in monthly instalment segregation, gradual purchase of shares and full ownership of asset at the end of contract.

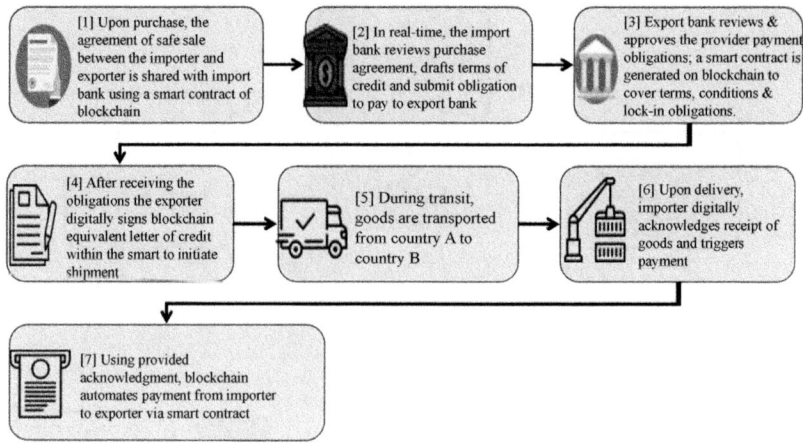

Fig. 6.3 Smart contract operation in trade finance process (*Source* Author's own)

Below is how Musharakah Mutanaqisah would be operating using smart contract in the future (Fig. 6.4).

COMMODITY MURABAHAH

1. Customer requests for financing via purchase of commodity (Master Commodity Murabahah Financing).
2. The bank arranger performs the financing in accordance with regulatory requirements.
3. Bank purchases commodity on spot basis from commodity broker 1.
4. Bank sells the commodity to customer on a deferred payment basis (cost+profit).
5. Customer authorises the bank as an agent.
6. The bank as agent sells the commodity to (commodity broker 2) on a spot basis.
7. Pay spot price.
8. Bank pays customer.
9. Customer pays sale price by instalment mode.[54]

---

[54]Amir Al-fatakh, *Financing: Commodity Murabaha*, Islamic Bankers Resource Centre, available at https://islamicbankers.me/islamic-banking-islamic-contracts/financing-commodity-murabaha-tawarruq/, accessed April 12, 2018.

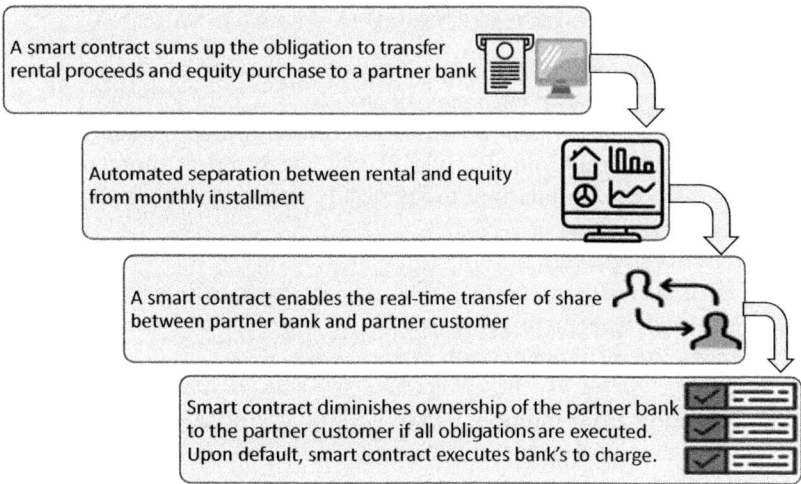

Fig. 6.4 Operation of Musharakah Mutanaqisah using smart contract (*Source* Author's own)

CHANGE WITH BLOCKCHAIN

1. Customer requests for financing via purchase of commodity (Master Commodity Murabahah Financing).
2. The bank arranger performs the financing in accordance with regulatory requirements.
3. Bank purchases commodity on spot basis from E-commodity market.
4. Bank sells the commodity to customer on a deferred payment basis (cost plus profit).
5. Customer sells the commodity on spot basis to E-commodity market.
6. E-commodity market pays spot price to the customer.
7. Customer pays sale price by instalment mode to Islamic bank via smart contract.[55]

---

[55] Rizal Mohd Nur, *Blockchain and Application in Islamic Finance,* available at https://www.slideshare.net/RizalMohdNor/blockchain-and-applications-in-islamic-finance, accessed April 12, 2018.

How Blockchain Reshapes Trade Financing

Trade financing, where financial institutions provide credit facilities in order to guarantee the exchange of goods, is a centuries-old industry that hasn't seen much change with the growth of global trade flows. In 2015 alone, the trade finance market was measured at more than $10 trillion USD. The problems in today's trade financing are summarised by Deloitte are as follows:

1. *Manual contract creation*: The import bank manually reviews the financial agreement provided by the importer and sends financials to the correspondent bank.
2. *Invoice factoring*: Exporters use invoices to achieve short-term financing from multiple banks, adding additional risk in the event the delivery of goods fails.
3. *Delayed timeline*: The shipment of goods is delayed due to multiple checks by intermediaries and numerous communication points.
4. *Manual AML review*: The export bank must manually conduct AML checks using the financials provided by the import bank.
5. *Multiple platforms*: Since each party across countries operates on different platforms, miscommunication is common and the propensity for fraud is high.
6. *Duplicative bills of lading*: Bills of lading are financed multiple times due to the inability of banks to verify their authenticity.
7. *Multiple versions of the truth*: As financials are sent from one entity to another, significant version control challenges exist as changes are made.
8. *Delayed payment*: Multiple intermediaries must verify that funds have been delivered to the importer as agreed prior to the disbursement of funds to the exporting bank.[56]

---

[56] Deloitte, *How Blockchain Can Reshape Trade Finance*, available at https://www2. deloitte.com/content/dam/Deloitte/global/Documents/grid/trade-finance-placemat. pdf, accessed March 20, 2018.

BLOCKCHAIN ADVANTAGES

In financial institutions, the transactions are currently recorded in multiple ledgers and each one captures at best a moment in time and reflects the information held by a single party. For instance, Bank ABC purchased or sold a mortgage where they will not record what happens next, what came before, or the role of others like partners, suppliers, consumers who are involved in the transaction and the recording of the transaction is prone to human error and vulnerable to tampering.[57] Use of blockchain technology distributed ledgers can be shared and updated in near real time across a group of participants. Every transaction becomes part of the permanent record and can be scrutinised by those that have permission and relevant information can be shared with others based on their roles and access privileges. As such, a shared ledger built on blockchain offers visibility, trust and permanence.[58] The advantages of blockchain are summarised below:

1. *Real-time review*: Financial documents linked and accessible through blockchain are reviewed and approved in real time, reducing the time it takes to initiate shipment.
2. *Transparent factoring*: Invoices accessed on blockchain provide a real-time and transparent view into subsequent short-term financing.
3. *Disintermediation*: Banks facilitating trade finance through blockchain do not require a trusted intermediary to assume risk, eliminating the need for correspondent banks.
4. *Reduced counterparty risk*: Bills of lading are tracked through blockchain, eliminating the potential for double spending.
5. *Decentralised contract execution*: As contract terms are met, status is updated on blockchain in real time, reducing the time and headcount required to monitor the delivery of goods.
6. *Proof of ownership*: The title available within blockchain provides transparency into the location and ownership of the goods.
7. *Automated settlement and reduced transaction fees*: Contract terms executed via smart contract eliminate the need for correspondent banks and additional transaction fees.
8. *Regulatory transparency*: Regulators are provided with a real-time view of essential documents to assist in enforcement and AML activities.[59]

---

[57] IBM, op cit. n. 10
[58] Ibid.
[59] Deloitte, op cit. n. 56 supra.

SHARIAH COMPLIANT SMART CONTRACT
FOR ISLAMIC CREDIT CARD

The application of fintech tools to an Islamic credit card lies in the fact that it is one of the popular Islamic financial products. Credit card payment is a popular method of payment compared with charge cards and debit cards in many jurisdictions. The credit card technology can be enhanced and advanced by integrating it within blockchain and smart contract to ensure more robust and effective Shariah compliance while using an Islamic credit card. Generally, three groups of Shariah compliant credit card arrangements have been identified:

1. A bank provides a line of credit to the cardholder and charges a monthly or yearly usage fee tied to the outstanding balance of the line of credit.
2. A customer is allowed to buy an item with a card, but the instant the card goes through, the bank purchases the item before selling it to the cardholder at a higher price.
3. A lease purchase agreement is where the bank holds title to the purchased item until the cardholder makes the final payment.[60]

Certain restrictions imposed by the Shariah on the card usage have distinguished conventional credit card users from Islamic ones. Islamic credit card users are not allowed to use them for the purchase of prohibited and non-Shariah compliant products and activities such as alcohol, pornography, gambling and piggery. At one extreme point, some Islamic banks restricted even the patronage of lawful services/products from stores that offer those prohibited services/products. However, some Islamic banks have relaxed such restrictions with respect to purchase of products of debatable prohibition such as tobacco or the purchase of lawful foods/drinks from restaurants or vending store that serves liquor.[61]

---

[60]Noor Suhaida Kasri, 'Shariah Compliance via Blockchain and Smart Contract—The Case for Islamic Credit Card', *Industry Insights*, July 18, 2017, available at https://journal.wahedinvest.com/Shariah-compliance-via-blockchain-and-smart-contract-the-case-for-islamic-credit-card/, accessed April 10, 2018.

[61]Nada Al Taher, 'Islamic Banks Allow Tobacco Purchase Now', *Gulf News*, August 6, 2014, available at http://gulfnews.com/news/uae/general/islamic-banks-allow-tobacco-purchase-now-1.1367888, accessed March 29, 2018.

Using blockchain smart contract can assist in implementing the right processes and procedures that ensure Islamic credit cards are barred from purchasing prohibited items in stores/vendors not recognised as Shariah compliant (e.g. bars, casinos) or stores that sell mixed items of halal and non-halal products. A separate blockchain on a data repository for tracking products can be established to inform on stores and their halal products for identification to the smart contract platform, so that Islamic credit cards cannot be used in purchasing prohibited items.

Findings and Recommendations

The blockchain is definitely a profound technology which that can be utilised to change the existing face of Islamic finance system to the better. For instance, Shariah governance of Islamic requires competent personnel which, depending on the size and sophistication of an institutions, has cost implications. However, the use of blockchain technology instead implies less human interference with the possibility of uniform Shariah compliance across the Islamic financial institutions that are automated for that purpose. Thus, it becomes easier to conduct Shariah audit and mitigate Shariah non-compliance risk with ease.

Equally, high level of IT governance in Islamic finance could be achieved via the use of blockchain technology that will eliminate *gharar* or uncertainty in Islamic finance transactions boosting the confidence of customers. This change might not be much evident to the eyes of the customers as the changes will be brought at the back end of Islamic financial institutions. Operations of Islamic finance will also change as transparency in the system and its processes will be achieved in a secure and cost-effective manner.

This will, however, impact on Shariah governance framework of Islamic financial institutions in the sense that the IT governance will become prominent part of Shariah risk management. Shariah risk management refers to a function that systematically identifies, measures, monitors and reports Shariah non-compliance risks to prevent any Shariah non-compliances.[62] Not only the documents prepared by the

---

[62] Paragraph 17.15, *Bank Negara Malaysia (BNM) Shariah Governance Framework for Islamic Financial Institutions*, available at http://www.bnm.gov.my/index.php?ch=57&pg=137&ac=645&bb=file, accessed April 20, 2018.

lawyers will be a concern of the Shariah advisory bodies but Shariah governance of smart contracts will also become a concern.

The emergence and adoption of blockchain technology for Islamic finance has certain implications for human capital development. Foremost is the need for IT professionals and to be educated in Islamic finance. This is to enable designing the appropriate protocols needed to accommodate peculiarities of Islamic finance. Secondly, universities and educational institutions offering IT courses will have to include Islamic finance as a portion of their syllabus in order to cater demand of more. It also implies that more IT professionals learned in Islamic finance, and other related professionals/expert who would want to study Islamic finance.[63]

Inversely, while blockchain technology reduces human participation which means less spending on operational cost, the technology requires more investment in IT. This investment might surpass what had been traditionally required to offset the operational cost in relation to personnel. Moreover, the cost of IT professionals is another cause for concern. The blockchain technology is a costly technology. It would cost the bank and financial institution more in order to structure a smart contract, perhaps more than the savings from operational cost due to reduced human participation.

Blockchain technology can be used using fiat money as well. However, to obtain the benefit of the technology in its best form, cryptocurrency plays an integral role. It is said that there is substantial risk in an exchange process with fiat money called "delivery versus payment", which is designed to ensure securities are only moved down the value chain at as close to the moment of payment as possible, minimising possible exposure to loss due to sudden changes in price.[64] A swift and

---

[63] The dearth of expert is generally worrisome reality in all Islamic finance jurisdiction. In Malaysia as at today, only one out of five graduates is of an IT-oriented background, who would then be expected to work for Islamic fintech. Even then, the requirement of Islamic finance education still needs be addressed. See Punithaa Kylasapathy et al., 'Unlocking Malaysia's Digital Future: Opportunities, Challenges and Policy Responses', *Bank Negara Malaysia Annual Report 2017*, available at http://www.bnm.gov.my/files/publication/ar/en/2017/ar2017_book.pdf, accessed April 8, 2018.

[64] M. D. Castillo *Is Blockchain Ready for Fiat? Why Banks See Big Promise in Crypto Cash?* September 6, 2017, available at https://www.coindesk.com/blockchain-ready-fiat-banks-see-big-promise-crypto-cash/1, accessed March 24, 2018.

effective delivery versus payment process is required for the effective use of blockchain technology in the transactions.

Hence, bitcoin will definitely be an integral part of blockchain technology usage in Islamic finance industry in future subject to Shariah approvals. Due to the usage of bitcoins or other cryptocurrencies, the most critical issue that will arise is lack of application of anti-money laundering and anti-terrorism financing rules including KYC requirements in the sale transactions that occur using cryptocurrencies. There will be no international cross-border transactions any more as unreported outflow of money will occur without restrictions. The whole world will become like one country where money transactions can be made without adhering to international rules.

At the moment it can be stated that if the law of the country are silent about trading of cryptocurrencies, then it is not prohibited to do such transactions in the country and also, if the country has not specifically legalised the use of it, then definitely there is no issue in using it in the transactions. Since Islamic financial institutions are regulated by the central banks, definitely an explicit guidance in the form of law or direction will be required from the central banks. Today countries like Japan have recognised cryptocurrency as a payment method while countries like the Philippines has recognised bitcoin exchanges as remittance companies. The biggest dilemma in this regard is the ongoing debate among the Shariah scholars on the Shariah compliance of bitcoins and other cryptocurrencies. In the case of Islamic financial institutions, it is not only the central banks that need to declare an explicit verdict on the matter, but the Shariah scholars also need to give their verdict on the permissibility of it.

However, the probing question here is that if the Islamic financial institutions switch to cryptocurrency, what will happen to the deposit-taking function of the banks? Will these institutions survive without the deposit taking functions and unless the whole economy/world start using cryptocurrencies, it is perceived that it might be impossible for the financial institutions to totally switch to cryptocurrencies and until then, it is contemplated that still the fiat money will play a vital role as the medium of exchange with or without blockchain technology integrated to the financial systems. But intermediaries like cryptocurrency exchanges might fasten the process of change.

CONSTRAINTS IN IMPLEMENTING BLOCKCHAIN

It is imperative to understand the constraints financial institutions will face in implementing blockchain technology. The most practical and up-to-date research found on this is the IBM report on blockchain[65] where it is stated that regulatory constraints, immature technology, lack of clear return on investment (ROI), insufficient skills, lack of executive buy-in and insufficient business case are the main constraints that can be faced in implementing blockchain by the financial institutions. In the report, it was highlighted that out of these challenges as per the outcome of the survey conducted by them the top three constraints identified are regulatory constraints, immature technology and lack of clear return on investment (ROI).

The blockchain industry is still in the early stages of development, and there are many kinds of limitations. Ideally, the blockchain industry would develop similarly to the cloud-computing model, for which standard infrastructure components—like connectivity, processing and storage systems—were defined and implemented very quickly at the beginning to allow the industry to focus on the higher level of developing value-added services instead of the core infrastructure. The current limitations are both internal and external and include those related to technical issues with the underlying technology, public perception and government regulation.[66]

Government and regulators have to reposition their focus in order to realise and benefit from the seeming potentialities of the blockchain technology. In particular, regulatory authorities will have to come up with appropriate smart contract guidelines. Most importantly, cyber laws and security laws need to be strengthened coupled with data protection laws. Contracts laws, both statutory and the common law (applicable in various jurisdictions) and consumer protection legislations will have to be amended to widen their application and scope. The judiciary and other

---

[65] IBM Institute for Business Value, *Leading the Pack in Blockchain Banking: Trailblazers Set the Pace*, September, 2016, available at https://www-01.ibm.com/common/ssi/cgi-bin/ssialias?htmlfid=GBP03467USEN, accessed March 14, 2018.

[66] Mohd Hazik, *The Blockchain and Islamic Finance*, December 7, 2016, available at https://www.linkedin.com/pulse/blockchain-islamic-finance-hazik-mohamed,   accessed April 12, 2018.

dispute resolution bodies need to be aware of how this technology works in the light of extant amended laws and they need to be prepared for the legal challenges resulting from this technology. Since the technology involves cross-border transaction, then there is need for special cyber tribunals or cyber courts of international status to adjudicate in matters that involve parties from different countries. Without this, the technology would not work and it cannot be sustained.

Conclusion

Islam generally welcomes innovation unless such innovation contradicts a clear Shariah provision. Blockchain technology is one such innovation that on its own does not contradict Shariah, rather it is aligned with Shariah. In simple terms, blockchain is important to Islamic finance as it allows all parties involved in a transaction to hold and make transactions in a completely transparent manner, irrespective of the fact that the parties involved are strangers to one another. The technology dispenses with the need for trust among parties as well as the formal intervention of neutral intermediaries. The potentials of blockchain's inherent trust and transparency develop prospect for regulating Islamic finance transactions with ease, in today's globalised economy. Blockchain takes care of the trust aspect while it renders transactions impersonal via smart contracts and cryptocurrencies. This greatly reduces transactions costs. So, blockchain technology incorporates Islamic values of transparency, equality, justice and trust into finance. Additionally, adopting the blockchain technology facilitates Islamic finance which acclimatises to the changing scene of contemporary economic and financial dealings.

With national governments and regulators opening up for the technology via pilot regulations for blockchain-based Islamic financing in some countries and plans for same in others, it signals a development in putting efforts towards blockchain mainstreaming. The technology is neutral and can be put to any use in accordance with its protocol. As such, workable Shariah compliant financing structures for blockchain transactions were conceived and illustrated. Several traditional financing transactions of Islamic finance and novel ones including trade financing, Musharakah Mutanaqisah, commodity murabahah, equity crowdfunding, any agreements (smart contract) and its performance between parties, can all be conveniently automated along those structures from initial stage to verifying, executing and recording all subsequent aspects of the transactional, thereby making it possible for the transactions to be digitally conducted in a retrievably permanent form.

Also, blockchain technology has positive impact on Islamic finance industry as it can enable Islamic finance transactions to be conducted in a reliable manner, paving way for regulators to merge and oversee Shariah governance as part of IT governance. With blockchain technology, space for IT governance in Shariah governance frameworks applicable to Islamic financial institutions will be created widening the scope and the functions of Shariah scholars sitting in Shariah advisory bodies of the IFIs. Using blockchain technology eliminates uncertainty, and commands to be stipulated in the smart contracts will be programmed by IT experts but endorsed by Shariah scholars. This means that application of the technology in Islamic finance industry will necessitate IT professionals to obtain Islamic finance education and Islamic scholars to obtain IT education. There is no doubt that the blockchain technology will definitely be integrated with Islamic finance as it is anticipated that more Islamic fintech would be implementing the technology in the near future.

Despite the fact that the blockchain technology presents tremendous benefits and opportunities for Islamic finance, it also faces and presents some challenges. The technology faces regulatory constraints (need for appropriate legislations), lack of expertise and skills among others. Again, the blockchain presents several technical and other challenges, which can only be overcome with time, result-oriented researches and decisive regulatory actions by governments and regulators towards peculiar issues resultant from the technology such as human capital impact, job displacement, money laundering and dispute resolution question.

REFERENCES

Akram Laldin. 'Fintech and Shariah Governance.' *Islamic Finance News (IFN)*, Correspondence Reports, Vol. 14, No. 6, February 7, 2017. Available at https://www.islamicfinancenews.com/fintech-and-shariah-governance.html. Accessed April 2, 2018.

Al Rajhi Bank. 'Al Rajhi Bank Completes Transaction Using Blockchain Technology for the first time in KSA', May 14, 2017. Available at https://www.alrajhibank.com.sa/en/media-centre/news/pages/blockchain.aspx. Accessed March 28, 2018.

Amir Al-fatakh. *Financing: Commodity Murabaha*. Islamic Bankers Resource Centre. Available at https://islamicbankers.me/islamic-banking-islamic-contracts/financing-commodity-murabaha-tawarruq/. Accessed April 12, 2018.

Anand Narayan. *A Brief Introduction to Smart Contracts and Their Endless Possibilities*. Available at https://codebrahma.com/brief-intro-smart-contracts-endless-possibilities/. Accessed April 10, 2018.

Andreas Freund. 'Automated, Decentralized Trust: A Path to Financial Inclusion.' In David Lee Kuo Chuen and Robert H. Deng (eds.), *Handbook of Blockchain, Digital Finance and Inclusion*, Vol. 1. Academic Press, London, 2018, pp. 431–450.

Aziz Zainuddin. *Blockchain in Islamic Finance*. Available at https://infocus.wief. org/blockchain-in-islamic-finance/. Accessed March 28, 2018.

Aznan bin Abdul Aziz. 'Malaysia Is Fintech Ready.' *Finnovasia KL 2017 Opening Address*. Available at http://www.bnm.gov.my/index.php?ch=en_speech&pg=en_speech&ac=721&lang=bm. Accessed April 8, 2018.

Bank Negara Malaysia. Circular BNM/RH/PD030-1. *Financial Technology Regulatory Sandbox Framework*, October 18, 2016.

Beehive. *P2P and Islamic Finance*. Available at https://www.beehive.ae/sharia-processing/. Accessed April 10, 2018.

Bernardo Vizcaino. 'Saudi Arabia's IDB Plans Blockchain-Based Financial Inclusion Product.' *Reuters News*, October 20, 2017. Available at https://www.reuters.com/article/us-islamic-finance-fintech/saudi-arabias-idb-plans-blockchain-based-financial-inclusion-product-idUSKBN1CP08W. Accessed April 4, 2018.

Bernardo Vizcaino. 'Malaysian Firm Adds Islamic Certification to Cryptocurrency.' *Reuters News*, February 20, 2018. Available at https://www.reuters.com/article/us-islamic-finance-cryptocurrencies/malaysian-firm-adds-islamic-certification-to-cryptocurrency-idUSKCN1G40K5. Accessed April 4, 2018.

Blockchain Semantics Insights. *How Will Blockchain Revitalize Trade Finance?* Available at https://www.blockchainsemantics.com/blog/revitalizing-trade-finance/. Accessed March 30, 2018.

Campbell R. Harvey. *Cryptofinance*. SSRN, January 14, 2016. Available at https://ssrn.com/abstract=2438299. Accessed March 20, 2018.

Christian Catalini, and Joshua S. Gans. *Some Simple Economics of the Blockchain*, MIT Sloan Research Paper No. 5191-16, SSRN, September 21, 2017. Available at https://ssrn.com/abstract=2874598. Accessed March 20, 2018.

Christopher Dula, and David LEE Kuo Chuen. 'Reshaping the Financial Order.' In David Lee Kuo Chuen and Robert H. Deng (eds.), *Handbook of Blockchain, Digital Finance and Inclusion*, Vol. 1. Academic Press, London, 2018, pp. 1–18.

Corporate Profile MDEC. *Championing Malaysia's Digital Economy*. Available at https://www.mdec.my/about-mdec/corporate-profile. Accessed April 8, 2018.

Darcy Allen, *Discovering and Developing the Blockchain Cryptoeconomy*. SSRN, August 18, 2017. Available at https://ssrn.com/abstract=2815255. Accessed March 28, 2018.

D'Cunha S. Dutt. 'Dubai Sets Its Sights on Becoming the World's First Blockchain-Powered Government.' *Forbes*, December 18, 2017. Available at https://www.forbes.com/sites/suparnadutt/2017/12/18/dubai-sets-sights-on-becoming the-worlds-first-blockchain-powered-government/. Accessed April 7, 2018.

Deloitte. *How Blockchain Can Reshape Trade Finance*. Available at https://www2.deloitte.com/content/dam/Deloitte/global/Documents/grid/trade-finance-placemat.pdf. Accessed April 14, 2018.

Deloitte Digital Commercial Bank. *Modernising Trade Finance*. Available at https://www2.deloitte.com/uk/en/pages/financial-services/solutions/modernising-trade-finance-in-commercial-banking.html. Accessed March 20, 2018.

D. Kevin Werbach. *Trust, But Verify: Why the Blockchain Needs the Law*. SSRN, September 28, 2016. Available at https://ssrn.com/abstract=2844409. Accessed April 3, 2018.

Don Tapscott, and Alex Tapscott. *Blockchain Revolution: How the Technology Behind Bitcoin Is Changing Money, Business and the World*. Penguin Random House, New York, 2016, p. 368.

Emirates Islamic. *Emirates Islamic Is First Islamic Bank to Integrate Blockchain Technology into Cheques*. June 11, 2017. Available at https://www.emiratesislamic.ae/eng/latest-news/2017/june/news11062017/. Accessed March 28, 2018.

G. W. Peters, and E. Panayi. 'Understanding Modern Banking Ledgers through Blockchain Technologies: Future of Transaction Processing and Smart Contracts on the Internet of Money.' SSRN, November 24, 2015. Available at https://papers.ssrn.com/sol3/Papers.cfm?abstract_id=2692487. Accessed March 30, 2018.

Haamiz Ahmed. 'Is Bitcoin Halal or Haram?' *ProPakistani*, January 2, 2018. Available at https://propakistani.pk/2018/01/02/bitcoin-halal-haram/. Accessed March 14, 2018.

HADA Dbank. *About HADA Dbank*. Available at https://www.hada-dbank.com/. Accessed March 29, 2018.

Hazik Mohammed. *Blockchain in Islamic Finance*. Available at https://www.linkedin.com/pulse/blockchain-islamic-finance-hazik-mohamed. Accessed March 28, 2018.

Hazik Mohd. *Blockchain Islamic in Finance.* Available at https://www.linkedin.com/pulse/blockchain-islamic-finance-hazik-mohamed. Accessed April 7, 2018.

IBM Institute for Business Value. *Fast Forward: Rethinking Enterprises, Ecosystems and Economies with Blockchain,* June 2016. Available at https://www-01.ibm.com/common/ssi/cgi-bin/ssialias?htmlfid=GBE03757USEN. Accessed March 14, 2018.

IBM Institute for Business Value. *Leading the Pack in Blockchain Banking: Trailblazers Set the Pace,* September 2016. Available at https://www-01.ibm.com/common/ssi/cgi-bin/ssialias?htmlfid=GBP03467USEN. Accessed March 14, 2018.

IFRC. 'IFRC Blockchain Application Wins Global Islamic Finance Competition.' *Press Release,* February 9, 2018. Available at http://media.ifrc.org/ifrc/press-release/ifrc-blockchain-application-wins-global-islamic-finance-competition/. Accessed March 28, 2018.

IFT Alliance. *About IFT Alliance.* Available at http://islamicfintechalliance.com/. Accessed April 9, 2018.

J. Tennenbaum. *Blockchain Practical Usage Around the World,* 2016. Available at https://www-01.ibm.com/events/wwe/grp/grp304.nsf/vLookupPDFs/Jeff%20Tennenbaum%20Presentation/$file/Jeff%20Tennenbaum%20Presentation.pdf. Accessed April 4, 2018.

Kevin D. Werbach. 'Trust, But Verify: Why the Blockchain Needs the Law.' *Berkeley Technology Law Journal,* Vol. 31, No. 2, September 2017, pp. 491–552. Available at https://papers.ssrn.com/sol3/papers.cfm?abstract_id=2844409. Accessed March 20, 2018.

Luke Parker. 'Bank of America Merrill Lynch Explores Using a Blockchain for Trade Finance.' *Brave NewCoin,* March 2, 2016. Available at https://bravenewcoin.com/news/bank-of-america-merrill-lynch-explores-using-a-blockchain-for-trade-finance/. Accessed April 4, 2018.

Luke Parker. 'Bank of America Merrill Lynch, HSBC, and IDA Develop a Blockchain Prototype Solution for Trade Finance.' *Brave NewCoin,* August 15, 2016. Available at https://bravenewcoin.com/news/bank-of-america-merrill-lynch-hsbc-and-ida-develop-a-blockchain-prototype-solution-for-trade-finance. Accessed April 13, 2018.

Mark Giancaspro. 'Is a "Smart Contract" Really a Smart Idea? Insights from a Legal Perspective.' *Computer Law & Security Review,* Vol. 33, No. 6, December 2017, pp. 825–835.

M. D. Castillo. *Is Blockchain Ready for Fiat? Why Banks See Big Promise in Crypto Cash?* September 6, 2017. Available at https://www.coindesk.com/blockchain-ready-fiat-banks-see-big-promise-crypto-cash. Accessed March 24, 2018.

Michael Gord. *Smart Contracts Described by Nick Szabo 20 Years Ago Now Becoming Reality*, April 26, 2016. Available at https://bitcoinmagazine. com/articles/smart-contracts-described-by-nick-szabo-years-ago-now-becoming-reality-1461693751/. Accessed March 27, 2017.

Mohammed Abdullahi Ridza. *The Life and Law of Fintech*. Sweet & Maxwell Asia, Subang Jaya, Malaysia, 2017, p. 21 *et seq*.

Mohd Hazik. *The Blockchain and Islamic Finance*, December 7, 2016. Available at https://www.linkedin.com/pulse/blockchain-islamic-finance-hazik-mohamed. Accessed April 12, 2018.

Mufti Muhammad Abu-Bakar. *Shariah Analysis of Bitcoin, Cryptocurrency and Blockchain*. Available at https://blossomfinance.com/bitcoin-working-paper. Accessed April 5, 2018.

Nada Al Taher. 'Islamic Banks Allow Tobacco Purchase Now.' *Gulf News*, August 6, 2014. Available at http://gulfnews.com/news/uae/general/islamic-banks-allow-tobacco-purchase-now-1.1367888. Accessed March 29, 2018.

Noor Suhaida Kasri. 'Shariah Compliance via Blockchain and Smart Contract— The Case for Islamic Credit Card.' *Industry Insights*, July 18, 2017. Available at https://journal.wahedinvest.com/Shariah-compliance-via-blockchain-and-smart-contract-the-case-for-islamic-credit-card/. Accessed April 10, 2018.

N. S. Kasri. 'Shariah Compliance via Blockchain and Smart Contract—The Case for Islamic Credit Card.' *Wahed Halal Investing Journal*, July 18, 2017. Available at https://journal.wahedinvest.com/Shariah-compliance-via-blockchain-and-smart-contract-the-case-for-islamic-credit-card/. Accessed April 18, 2018.

Othman Abdullah. *Fintech and Shariah Governance for Islamic Finance*. Available at https://islmfintech.com/fintech-and-Shariah-governance/. Accessed March 29, 2018.

Othman Abdullahi. *Fintech and Islamic Finance*. Available at https://islmfintech.com/fintech-and-islamic-finance/. Accessed April 9, 2018.

Othman Abdullahi. 'Major Fintech Achievements in Islamic Finance in 2016.' *The Malaysian Reserve*, April 3, 2017. Available at https://themalaysianreserve.com/2017/04/03/major-fintech-achievements-in-islamic-finance-in-2016/. Accessed April 9, 2018.

Paolo Fiore. *When Crowdfunding Is Sharia Compliant*. Available at http://www.youris.com/Energy/Renewables/When-Crowdfunding-Is-Sharia-Compliant.kl. Accessed March 20, 2018.

Pei Sai Fan. 'Singapore Approach to Develop and Regulate FinTech', in David Lee Kuo Chuen and Robert H. Deng (eds.), *Handbook of Blockchain, Digital Finance and Inclusion*, Vol. 1. Academic Press, London, 2018, pp. 347–357.

Philipp Paech. 'The Governance of Blockchain Financial Networks.' *Modern Law Review*, Vol. 80, No. 6, 2017, pp. 1073 *et seq.* Available at https://ssrn.com/abstract=2875487. Accessed April 8, 2018.

Punithaa Kylasapathy, et al. 'Unlocking Malaysia's Digital Future: Opportunities, Challenges and Policy Responses.' *Bank Negara Malaysia Annual Report 2017.* Available at http://www.bnm.gov.my/files/publication/ar/en/2017/ar2017_book.pdf. Accessed April 8, 2018.

Rizal Mohd Nur. *Blockchain and Application in Islamic Finance.* Available at https://www.slideshare.net/RizalMohdNor/blockchain-and-applications-in-islamic-finance. Accessed April 12, 2018.

R. M. Lacasse, et al. *Blockchain Technology—Arsenal for a Shariah-Compliant Financial Ecosystem?* 5th International Conference of Entrepreneurial Finance, CIFEMA 2017, Ibn Zohr University, Agadir, Morocco, December 4–5, 2017, p. 33 *et seq.* Available at http://hdl.handle.net/10993/33529. Accessed April 3, 2018.

R. M. Nor. *Blockchain Applications for the Islamic Financial and Capital Market Services Industry,* 2017. Available at https://www.slideshare.net/RizalMohdNor/blockchain-and-applications-in-islamic-finance.   Accessed April 14, 2018.

Samburaj Das. 'Malaysia Woos FinTech Developments for Shariah-Compliant Islamic Finance.' *CCN FinTech News,* March 20, 2017. Available at https://www.ccn.com/malaysia-woos-fintech-devs-Shariah-compliant-islamic-finance/. Accessed April 8, 2018.

Satoshi Nakamoto. *Bitcoin: A Peer-to-Peer Electronic Cash System.* Available at https://bitcoin.org/bitcoin.pdf. Accessed March 14, 2018.

Securities Commission Malaysia. *List of Registered Market Operators.* Available at https://www.sc.com.my/digital/list_rmo/. Accessed April 9, 2018.

Securities Commission Malaysia, Circular SC-GL/6-2015 (R1-2016). *Guidelines on Recognized Markets,* April 13, 2016.

S. L. Persio. 'Banks bring Blockchain Innovation to Letters of Credit.' *Global Trade Review,* August 10, 2016. Available at https://www.gtreview.com/news/asia/banks-blockchain-innovation-letters-of-credit/. Accessed April 4, 2018.

Team Ripple. *Ripple and Saudi Arabian Monetary Authority (SAMA) Offer Pilot Program for Saudi Banks,* February 14, 2018. Available at https://ripple.com/ripple_press/ripple-and-saudi-arabian-monetary-authority-sama-offer-pilot-program-for-saudi-banks/. Accessed March 28, 2018.

Trent J. MacDonald, Darcy Allen, and Jason Potts, et al. 'Blockchain and the Boundaries of Self-Organized Economies: Predictions for the Future of Banking.' In Paulo Tasca, et al. (eds.), *Banking Beyond Banks and Money.* SSRN. Available at https://ssrn.com/abstract=2749514. Accessed March 28, 2018.

Zainuddin Aziz. *Blockchain in Islamic Finance*. Available at https://infocus.wief. org/blockchain-in-islamic-finance/. Accessed April 8, 2018.

Zawya. 'Fintech Hellogold Is World's First Shariah-Compliant Gold Platform.' *Press Release*, December 6, 2016. Available at https://www.zawya.com/ mena/en/press-releases/story/Fintech_HelloGold_is_worlds_first_ Shariahcompliant_gold_platform-ZAWYA20161206085657/. Accessed April 4, 2018.

CHAPTER 7

Characterizing Cryptocurrencies and Why It Matters

Hylmun Izhar and Ahmet Suayb Gundogdu

Introduction

The unprecedented hype of cryptocurrency over the past few years coupled with an increasing prominence of digital economy should not go unnoticed. For sure, the rapid emergence of such phenomenon has considerably altered the landscape of financial transactions and the methods by which the global economy would grow. More importantly, it will potentially change the way economic agents interact in a great deal. Islamic finance as a growing and niche industry must timely respond to this. Various attempts have been made by different enthusiasts and advocates of Islamic finance to address this topical issue. One central question being constantly discussed is whether investing in cryptocurrency through blockchain technology is *Shari'ah* compliant. To be able to answer this question, the

H. Izhar (✉)
Islamic Research and Training Institute,
Islamic Development Bank Group, Jeddah, Saudi Arabia
e-mail: hizhar@isdb.org

H. Izhar · A. S. Gundogdu
Islamic Development Bank, Jeddah, Saudi Arabia

A. S. Gundogdu
e-mail: agundogdu@isdb.org

© The Author(s) 2019
M. M. Billah (ed.), *Halal Cryptocurrency Management*,
https://Doi.org/10.1007/978-3-030-10749-9_7

107

fundamental aspect to dig out is to ensure "the nature of cryptocurrency." Why it matters? Because this will determine whether an investment in cryptocurrency is justified from Shari'ah point of view. As many advocates of Islamic finance would unanimously agree, the structure by which a contractual agreement is assembled and the type of items being transacted can determine the validity and permissibility of any financial transactions. On this, *Shari'ah* through its abundant *fiqh* interpretations provides guiding principles and a variety of avenues for Shari'ah compliant financial activities. In case of currencies, such methodology would be misleading since what is discussed is not a transaction but medium of exchange to carry out transactions. Hence, the permissibility of cryptocurrencies should better be evaluated from the money creation process perspective in cryptocurrencies. With respect to investing in cryptocurrency, there hasn't been any undivided answer until now, but there are characteristically four opinions:

- Opinion 1: Cryptocurrency cannot be considered as *mal* (wealth); it is purely speculative; hence, it is not Shari'ah compliant
- Opinion 2: Cryptocurrency is money/currency
- Opinion 3: Cryptocurrency is an asset
- Opinion 4: Cryptocurrency is a security.

This study, therefore, is an attempt to investigate the possible DNA of cryptocurrency. The word "possible" is used deliberately since the analysis or opinion articulated in this article could in no way be considered as a verdict. Rather, it is an endeavor to further stimulate the discussion on this emerging topic and provide insight for Shari'ah scholars. The authoritative bodies to come up with a verdict, in the authors' opinion, would be OIC Islamic Fiqh Academy.

The analysis of this article is structured as follows: The second section following the introduction discusses briefly about cryptocurrencies, the third up to sixth section attempt to analyze whether cryptocurrencies could qualify as being wealth (*mal*), currency, asset, or security. The last section deliberates upon the finding of the possible new DNA of cryptocurrency and its potential interconnection with Islamic finance, followed by a conclusion.

Central Idea of Cryptocurrencies

Cryptocurrencies are digital or virtual currencies that are encrypted (secured) using cryptography. Cryptography refers to the use of encryption techniques to secure and verify the transfer of transactions. Bitcoin represents the first decentralized cryptocurrency, which is powered by a public ledger that records and validates all transactions chronologically, called the blockchain. Bitcoin transactions are carried out on trading platforms akin to forex trading and brokerage platforms (Pieters and Vivanco 2017).

Physical tokens have been and still being used as a means of payment (e.g., shells, gold coins, and bank notes). In such setting, a direct exchange of sellers' goods and buyers' tokens allows them to achieve an immediate and final settlement. This option is unavailable, however, when the two parties are not present in the same location, supposedly necessitating the usage of digital tokens. In such case, traditional banking system makes settlements by mere debit and credit of accounts. Since the system is based on long-lasting tradition in which accounts kept by regulated banks and central banks, the traditional system of settlement, which evolved over centuries, is much more robust. In a digital currency system, however, the means of payment are simply a string of bits. This poses a problem, as these strings of bits as any other digital record can easily be copied and reused for payment. Essentially, the digital token can be counterfeited by using it twice which is the so-called double-spending problem.

Cryptocurrencies such as Bitcoin go a step further and remove trusted third party, as proponents suppose unneeded. Instead, they rely on a decentralized network of (possibly anonymous) validators to maintain and update copies of the ledger. This necessitates that consensus between the validators is maintained about the correct record of transactions so that the users can be sure to receive and keep ownership of balances. But such a consensus ultimately requires that (i) users do not double spend the currency and (ii) that users can trust the validators to accurately update the ledger. Nevertheless, in a case of conflict there is no legal framework to protect the rights of investors living in different jurisdictions across several countries. This would make those invest their hard-earned money in cryptocurrencies vulnerable and open to deceit.

How do cryptocurrencies such as Bitcoin tackle these challenges? Trust in the currency is supposedly based on a blockchain which ensures the distributed verification, updating and storage of the record of transaction histories. This is done by forming a so-called blockchain. A block is a set of transactions that have been conducted between the users of the cryptocurrency. A chain is created from these blocks containing the history of past transactions that allows one to create a ledger where one can publicly verify the amount of balances or currency a user owns. Hence, a blockchain is like a book containing the ledger of all past transactions with a block being a new page recording all the current transactions. To ensure consensus but not legal right, validators compete for the right to update the chain with a new block. This competition can take various forms. In Bitcoin, it happens through a process called *mining*. Miners (i.e., transaction validators) compete to solve a computationally costly problem which is called proof of work (Franco 2014). The winner of this mining process has the right to update the chain with a new block. The consensus protocol prescribes then that the longest history will be accepted, again without any legal right, as the trusted record. The history of money, however, proved that trust and consensus cannot work until there is a legal order. Throughout the history, crooks have used emotional manipulation of trust to take advantage of vulnerable, yet, greedy people. More importantly, the way money is created is quite speculative (*Maysir*) and uncertain (*Gharar*) in cryptocurrencies. It is deceitful to call such casino computer way of operating as mining to convince people as if it is gold mining, and it is akin to traditional money. Casino machines also work based on such powerful computers with high capacity formula solving skills.

WHY CRYPTOCURRENCY IS DEEMED SPECULATIVE; IS IT A *MAL* (WEALTH) AFTER ALL?

It is key to understand the difference between money and commodity. The proponents of this view opine that cryptocurrencies, such as Bitcoins, are just numbers with digital entries on a cryptic blockchain. They have no intrinsic function. There is no real substance or underlying asset in money creation; it is just speculation on the fluctuation of numbers. This can result in cryptocurrencies being non-compliant and a form of *maysir* and prohibited speculation.

It is important to note that for something to be the subject of a contract, it must be *mutaqawwam*, Nazih Hammad, a contemporary jurist in his article in 2007 argues that the entire community of Islamic jurists—Shafi'ites, Malikites, Hanafites, and Hanbalites—are of the opinion that there are three elements of wealth. That is, three elements which, when present, will lead to the conclusion that the obligation has value and, from Shari'ah perspective, can be exchanged for a counter-value. Those three elements are: (1) that the obligation be an intended usufruct or contain the same; (2) that the usufruct has a monetary value in commercial practice or custom; and (3) that the usufruct be lawful from a Shari'ah perspective. Based on this proposition, although there is no issue in cryptocurrencies being *mutaqawwam*, it cannot be classified as *mal*, as inherently it does not have usufruct to be benefited by contracting parties. Its value can only materialize when it is cashed in using fiat money that backs it up.

Is Cryptocurrency a Currency?

In the literature of classic jurisprudence, what the modern society calls now as money was at that time termed as *nuqud* or *'umlah*. While *nuqud* refers to money being widely accepted by a large society, the specific meaning of *'umlah* is a type of currency that is only valid in a certain jurisdiction and may not be widely accepted.[1]

The principles of monetary economics theory on money suggest that anything to be considered as money or currency should fulfill the following primary functions: (1) unit of account, medium of exchange, and store of value. While at the outset, different types of cryptocurrency, such as Bitcoin and Ethereum, may fulfill these functions; such currency lacks of the fourth fundamental customary condition, namely being a legal tender issued by government or financial authority such as a central bank. This fourth condition coincidentally is also put forward by Muhammad Rawas Qal'ah Ji in his *"al Mu'amalat al-Maliyah al Mu'ashirah fi Dhau' al Fiqh wa al-Shar'iyyah"*.[2]

Interestingly, traditional jurists state that for anything to qualify as money or currency, it must have a *thamaniyyah* component that covers dual functions, namely an independent standard of value and unit of account. On this note, some argue that the current phenomenon of cryptocurrency demonstrates that it does not serve as an independent measure of value. Rather, it is the value of fiat currencies that is being used to determine the value of any form of cryptocurrency. Hence, cryptocurrency does not fulfill a *thamaniyyah* condition that requires a currency to have an independent reference of value.

[1] See a detailed discussion on this distinction by Hasan Mahmud al Shafii in *"al umlah wa Tarikhuha"* on page 197.

[2] See on page 23.

Is It an Asset?

An asset may be divided into fungible (*mithliyyat*) and non-fungibles (*qimiyyat*), and into movables and immovable. Asset is owned as either *'ayn* or *dayn*. *'Ayn* is a specific existing thing, considered as a unique object and not merely as a member of a certain category. *Dayn* is any property, not an *'ayn*, that a debtor owes, either now or in the future, or it can refer to such property only when due in the future. Some would argue that *mithliyyat* product possesses a certain degree of *thamaniyyah* component due to its nature in potentially creating debt (*dayn'*) when being transacted on a deferred method. This is a unique feature that *qimiyyat* product does not possess. Consequently, a subtle characterization of *mithliyyat* comes along, i.e., it cannot be leased-out since the nature of its material is perishable or consumable.

Having described what constitutes an asset, one would immediately notice that a profound feature of an asset is that it should possess an intrinsic value from which people can directly benefit. And cryptocurrency in any of its forms fails to fulfill this condition.

Can It Be Considered as a Security?

While no court or government agency has yet opined on whether cryptocurrency is a security, based on an analysis of case law applying the definition of "security" under the Securities Act in the USA, it appears that cryptocurrency is not a security. Let us take an example of Bitcoin; Bitcoin does not fall within the definition of any common type of security. In addition, Bitcoin does not appear to fall within the broad definition of "investment contract." A sale of Bitcoin is not an investment contract because a purchase of Bitcoin is not an investment in a common enterprise and purchasers should not expect to receive profits from their purchase based on the efforts of the seller. In a nutshell, a cryptocurrency transaction does not reflect an ownership right that can be enforced, over which future economic benefits may flow to the owner. From *fiqh muamalah* point of view, a technical detailed analysis in what constitutes financial securities, commercial paper and investment contracts, provided in AAOIFI Shari'ah Standards Nos. 16 and 17.

MONEY FROM THE THEORY OF ECONOMICS

The function of money as a medium of exchange is closely related to that of a standard of value. It is most likely that, as barter transactions grew more complicated, people formed the habit of assessing prices in terms of a standard article, and this standard also came to enjoy preferential treatment as a medium of exchange. Nowadays, there are some Muslim organizations which strongly recommend the implementation of gold standard. It seems that those organizations attempt to set up a coinization of gold money, rather than monetarization of gold money, which means using commodity money as implemented in the period of the Holy *Prophet Muhammad (saw)* and his companions (r). Monetarization of gold money, by which most of contemporary economists are now associated with, is defined as using gold standard in order to maintain equality between the value of the domestic monetary unit and a specified amount of gold.

This sort of money is defined as a medium of exchange which has a commodity value as distinct from the value which it has acquired by being generally acceptable in exchange for good and services. Its commodity value is that which it would have if it were not used as money. From the earliest time, gold and silver have served their major roles as a medium of exchange throughout the world. Dinar (gold money) is categorized as full bodied money, as well as dirham (silver money). On the other hand, some variants of gold standards which were used by UK and USA during 1879–1914 and 1925–1931 can be classified as a representative commodity money, instead of full bodied money, as gold coins and silver coins were not in circulation for transaction. From this explanation, we may differentiate between coinization and monetarization of gold; while coinization of gold standard refers to the use of full bodied money, monetarization of gold standard is attributed to the implementation of representative commodity money.

FIDUCIARY MONEY

Token Money

In the early development of bank, the goldsmith (officer in money changer) and bankers found it profitable to borrow commodity currency and to issue receipts which began to circulate as a means of payment and it was a profitable occupation (Zineldin 1990: 101). The goldsmiths began to pay interest for deposits of gold and silver coins, since it was profitable, either to melt down the coin or to sell it as bullion when its purchasing power as coin fell as well as to export it when its external value exceeded domestic value. The more the receipts of the goldsmiths circulated among their depositors, the more they were able to lend out part of the gold or silver which was deposited with them. This is the first example in English monetary history of token money resulting from the activities of financial institutions. The receipts for deposits, or bank notes, later were called tokens, as these were just simply papers, without having intrinsic value.

Fiat Money

The continued expansion of commerce and the scale of business soon made people think another type of money which is more efficient for large transactions. The idea of fiat money was actually coming up to overcome some difficulties in using full bodied money, such as liquidity in transaction, particularly when it comes to a huge amount of transactions. Even though it is harder to control the growth of money, as it easy to print/mint this type of money without bearing a high cost of production, however it will harm the economy when the growth of money is not absorbed by the equal amount of transaction in the real sector. Example of fiat money is the currency which is now widely used throughout the world.

Bank Money (Deposit Money)

Basically, bank money is not actually money. However, some economists call it quasi-money (near money), as it can be used for transaction. In the monetary theory, we may find bank money (deposit money) in the classification of base money (currency) as M0, Demand Deposit (M1), Time Deposit (M2). In this example, M1 and M2 can be classified as bank money.

BETTER THE DEVIL YOU KNOW THAN THE DEVIL YOU DON'T KNOW

Once the cryptocurrencies are accepted by governments for settlement of trade transactions and tax payment, they could be classified as money. However, this alone would not make them Shari'ah compliant. Neither present fiat currency should be deemed Shari'ah compliant. The issue of cryptocurrencies should be evaluated based on its money creation process. In this regard, some would argue that it is worse than fiat currency which is created through monetization of interest-based debt securities. However, unlike cryptocurrencies, both interest-based debt securities and legal dispute concerning settlement of monetary transactions are regulated based on legal tradition evolved throughout the centuries.

The prime example of this is Bitcoin. When we own Bitcoin, we do not own any claims on anything that belongs in the non-digital world. There is no collateral behind each Bitcoin, we cannot redeem them for an underlying asset, and it does not give us any right to claim anything against it. Yes, we may be able to use Bitcoin to purchase a cup of coffee, but the merchant accepts your Bitcoins at their own discretion since they have no legal obligation to take our Bitcoin and give us coffee. Bitcoin, therefore, is a soft token as it is confined to its own chain and has no rights outside the blockchain. Saying that, it is important to emphasize role of regulatory bodies in monetary transactions. Traditional settlement mechanism of banking sector by debit and credit entry is much more robust, with central bank surveillance, than blockchain. With the way current cryptocurrencies is structured right now coupled with the exuberance in investing in them, this novelty would worsen the debt creation culture and casino business of Wall Street that has already taken global economy hostage.

CONCLUSION

As the digital economy era is increasingly embraced by larger societies, what if cryptocurrencies are also gaining its momentum and eventually are accepted to become means of payment? Could we in the future consider cryptocurrencies as a currency; the answer is: It is possible of course. Nonetheless, its trading should be guided by the rules of *Sarf*. What about trading in cryptocurrencies with a main objective of solely taking advantage of their price differences? It is clearly tantamount to speculation, hence gambling.

So, what is the essence of a cryptocurrency? In our view, cryptocurrency is nothing but a token; it is created through a process called tokenization. So, essentially cryptocurrency is none other than a platform. Tokens have no representation of an asset, either physical or intangible, and are by definition confined to the chain in which they exist.

The prime example is Bitcoin. When we own Bitcoin, we do not own any claims on anything that belongs in the non-digital world. There is no collateral behind each Bitcoin, we cannot redeem them for an underlying asset, and it does not give us any rights to claim anything against it. We may be able to use Bitcoin to purchase a cup of coffee, but the merchant accepts your Bitcoins at their own discretion since they have no legal obligation to take our Bitcoin and give us coffee. Bitcoin, therefore, is a soft token as it is confined to its own chain and has no rights outside the block chain. As it is now, the *fiqh*-compliant twist would perhaps be to find a way to demonstrate that the values of cryptocurrencies represent the values of tangible assets, usufruct, or ownership over projects.

References

AAOIFI. (2015). '*Shariah Standards*'. Accounting and Auditing Organization for Islamic Financial Institutions.

Franco, P. (2014). *Understanding Bitcoin: Cryptography, Engineering and Economics*. West Sussex: Wiley.

Hammad, Nazih. (2007). Compensation for an Obligation to Sell Currency in the Future (Hedging). *Chicago Journal of International Law, 7*(2), 521–536.

Pieters, G., and Vivanco, S. (2017). Financial Regulations and Price Inconsistencies Across Bitcoin Markets. *Information Economics and Policy, 39*, 1–14.

Rawas, Muhammad Qal'ah Ji. (1999). *al-Mu'amalat al-Maliyah al-Mu'ashirah fi Dhau' al-Fiqh wa al-Syari'ah*. Beirut: Dar al-Nafa'is.

Zineldin, Mosad. (1990). *The Economics of Money and Banking: A Theoretical and Empirical Study of Islamic Interest-Free Banking*. Stockholm: Almqvist & Wicksell International.

PART III

Principles of Halal Cryptocurrency Management

CHAPTER 8

The Analysis of Cryptocurrency Based on *Maqasid al-Shari'ah*

Mohamed Cherif El Amri
and Mustafa Omar Mohammed

INTRODUCTION

The history of money is as old as the history of early creations on earth. According to al-Imam al-Ghazali (1901, vol. 4, pp. 97–98), Allah created gold and silver to be used as a medium of exchange and measure of values. This view was also supported by al-Maqrizi that people in ancient time and during his contemporary used gold and silver for trade and for remunerations (Allouche 1994). Money has been used as a medium of exchange, measure of other goods, standard for comparing commodity values, and store of purchasing power or value in general

M. C. E. Amri
Department of Islamic Economics and Finance,
Istanbul Sabahattin Zaim University, Istanbul, Turkey
e-mail: mohamed.amri@izu.edu.tr

M. O. Mohammed (✉)
Department of Economics and Centre for Islamic Economics,
Kulliyyah of Economics and Management Sciences,
International Islamic University Malaysia, Kuala Lumpur, Malaysia
e-mail: mustafa@iium.edu.my

© The Author(s) 2019   119
M. M. Billah (ed.), *Halal Cryptocurrency Management*,
https://doi.org/10.1007/978-3-030-10749-9_8

(Hasan 2015, p. 348). In history, money has been used in different forms ranging from precious metals to stones, shells, furs, animal skins, and tobacco (Sanusi 2002).

With the advent of the banking system, the concept of money evolved into paper money and of recent the electronic money. People now have to carry less physical money for their transactions. Instead, the financial system has revolutionized the way they deal with money. This coupled with the advancement of technology. People now rely on ATM machines, e-banking, mobile banking, credit cards, and e-wallets among others for their transactions. Recently, the global financial architecture has witnessed a drastic change in the structure of the financial relation, the digital finance—specifically the cryptocurrency revolution. Cryptocurrency is envisaged as the money of the future. It is accessed in the Internet independently and provides the individuals with personal freedom in the way they transact it because it is essentially not subject to any supervisory or regulatory authority.

There has been debate among Muslim scholars about the position of cryptocurrency in Islam particularly from Shari'ah perspective. Mufti Muhammad Abu-Bakar (2018) in a working paper provides views of the opponents and proponents of the cryptocurrency. The Mufti (2018) cites the opponents: the Grand Mufti of Egypt, the Turkish government, Fatwa Center of Palestine, and Shaykh Haitam from the UK who have declared cryptocurrency such as bitcoin unlawful on the grounds that it is not a legal tender, its issuer is unknown, it has no central authority backing it, it is highly speculative, and it can be easily used for illegal purposes such as money laundering. On the other hand, the Mufti (2018) cites the proponents: the Fatwa Center of South African Islamic seminar, Darul Uloom Zakariyya, which considers cryptocurrency lawful in the Shari'ah on the basis of legal maxim, "the basic rule is permissibility" and that cryptocurrency fulfills all the attributes of money. Other modern scholars who view cryptocurrency as Shari'ah compliant include Monzer Kahf (2018) although he acknowledges that the problems of loss of confidence and speculation could arise in bitcoin. Another proponent is Daud Bakar (Chairman of Shari'ah Advisory Council, the Central Bank of Malaysia). In this chapter, we have avoided being involved in the debate of halal (lawful) and haram (unlawful) of cryptocurrency. Instead, we have opted to analyze cryptocurrency based on Maqasid al-Shari'ah (the Objectives of Shari'ah). Hitherto, to the best knowledge of the author, there is hardly any work that has analyzed cryptocurrency based on al-Maqasid. Instead, there are two studies that have used al-Maqasid to analyze paper currency (Gapur et al. 2016) and money creation in the banking system (AlTwijry 2016). The most relevant study to this chapter is the work by Gapur Oziev and Magomet Yandiyev (2018), although the focus is on Shari'ah rulings rather than Maqasid.

This chapter is structured into five sections. The subsequent section two discusses cryptocurrency, its merits and demerits. Section three presents the concept of Maqasid al-Shari'ah and its relevance to wealth including money. The fourth section focuses on the analysis of crypto currency based on Maqasid al-Shari'ah. Section five concludes the paper and provides suggestions for future study.

Cryptocurrency, Its Merits and Demerits

The first cryptocurrency to capture the public imagination was bitcoin, launched in 2009 by an individual or group known under the pseudonym Satoshi Nakamoto (Investopedia Web site). Nakamoto designed and created 21 million bitcoins which could be accessed by solving mathematical algorithms in a process called "mining." Once mined, the bitcoin can be sold, used as payment, or saved for future investment. The word "crypto" refers to the encryption or cryptography that the instrument is built on and then added to a blockchain database. The "currency" here refers to the recognition of the instrument as a medium of exchange among its users (Mufti Muhammad Abu-Bakar 2018).

Gapur Oziev and Magomet Yandiyev (2018) provide three levels in which cryptocurrency operates: ownership of bitcoin, its emission, and solving mathematical algorithms. At the first level, parties in the transaction need to own the bitcoin and use them in the transactions. The client will need to download on the computer a special software program that can be used to open a wallet for storing bitcoins. Alternatively, the clients can also use fiat money to purchase bitcoins from cryptocurrency market and place them in the wallet. At the second level, the client uses a special software program that solves sophisticated mathematical equations generated by the bitcoin system. The user whose computer first solves the equation/puzzle (known as hash) gets a bitcoin as a reward. At the third level, the one who solved the equation/puzzle faster gets the right to execute transactions performed by bitcoins' holders at that particular time. The blockchain helps provide transparency and security in the form of private keys.

Gapur Oziev and Magomet Yandiyev (2018) illustrate the following regarding the transaction mechanism. When the user sells something and received bitcoins in the wallet, the record of the transaction is automatically sent to all computers connected to the bitcoin system, and all bitcoin owners will know that a certain owner of an electronic wallet with a certain number has acquired a certain amount of bitcoins from such a wallet under certain number. After some time, this person decides to buy something using his bitcoins. He instructs his wallet to transfer a certain sum of bitcoins to an address/wallet. His computer sends a request to all computers connected to the bitcoin system to confirm the validity of the transaction. The computers of other users check their records and send confirmation ascertaining the buyer: the electronic name/code of his wallet and the amount of bitcoins. At each level of confirmation and the amount of bitcoins transferred, all the computers in the system update the new record to the database.

The merits of the cryptocurrency lie in the decentralization of its emission that does not require a central regulatory and supervisory authority; there is competition in the primary distribution of bitcoins among users; the transactions are validated, disclosed, and transparent done with relative efficiency and speed. On the other hand, cryptocurrencies have their demerits. They are not asset-backed, it is impossible or difficult to recover bitcoins once they are lost or stolen funds, users remain anonymous, transactions are speculative and of late fraudulent, there is tax evasion, and bitcoins have failed to eliminate the social stratification.

MAQASID AL-SHARI'AH

The subject of Maqasid al-Shari'ah or Objectives of Shari'ah has tremendously gained prominence over the years. Several conferences are being held, and there are now volumes of literatures on al-Maqasid-related studies. The seminal stage of al-Maqasid theorization started with al-Juwayni (d.474H/1078A.D). His crude theory was later refined by his student, al-Ghazali (d.505H/1105A.D). Thereafter, al-Maqasid gradually evolved as an important independent branch of discipline. Subsequent leading scholars of al-Maqasid, succeeding al-Juwayni and al-Ghazali, include al-'Izz Ibn 'Abd salaam (d.660H/1260A.D), al-Qarafi (d.684H/1284A.D), Ibn Taymiyyah (d.728H/1328A.D), Ibn Qayyim al-Jawziyyah (d.751H/1351A.D), Najm al-Din al-Tufi (d.716H/1316A.D), and al-Shatibi (d.790H/1390A.D). Other prominent names include Ibn 'Ashur (d.1973), al-Raysuni (1992), and al-Imam Abu Zaharah (1997).

Muslim scholars from the advent of Islam were cognizant of the fact that the broad objectives of Maqasid al-Shari'ah are to promote Maslahah (welfare) and ward off Mafsadah (harm). However, the concepts of Maslahah and Mafsadah were not fully conceptualized into theories until the time of al-Juwayni who used the concept of Maslahah and Mafsadah to develop the preliminary theory of al-Maqasid. He categorized al-Maqasid into five levels: (1) Daruriyat (necessities), (2) al-Hajaat al-'Aammah (the public needs), (3) Mandubat (recommended), (4) Makrumat (moral behaviors), and (5) "what cannot be attributed to specific reasons"—difficult to determine. His ideas were, however, confined to legal matters such as the method of determining Shari'ah principles and rulings (Al-Juwayni, ed., Abdul Azim 1979).

As stated above, al-Juwayni's theory was later refined by his student, al-Ghazali. He categorized Maslahah into three: Daruriyat (necessities), Hajiyaat (complements), and Tahsiniyaat (embellishments). According to al-Ghazali, necessities are those elements without which the system of a nation will run into chaos. Complements are elements those that facilitate human lives. Meanwhile, embellishments are articles that are related to moral and ethical conducts. He further refined necessities into the preservation of five essential elements (al-Dharuriyat al-Khams), namely religion (al-Din), life (al-Nafs), intellect (al-Aql), progeny (al-Nasl), and wealth (al-Mal). These five essential elements are given priority according to this order. Attempts were made by several scholars to put al-Ghazali's theory into a framework as illustrated in Fig. 8.1.

Many Muslim scholars both past and present have extensively made use of al-Ghazali's theory in their works. Prominent scholars in the recent past who have greatly benefited from al-Ghazali's theory include Ibn 'Ashur, al-Shatibi, and Abu Zaharah. For example, Abu Zaharah (1997) extended al-Ghazali's theoretical framework to include justice and education. Modern scholars in the areas of economics and finance have also used al-Ghazali's framework as bases for their studies. For example, Chapra (2007) has used al-Ghazali's framework to develop a model of human development and well-being. Dusuki and Mokhtar (2010) have made use of al-Ghazali's framework to appraise sukuk issuance in the Islamic debt market. Larbani and Mustafa (2009) developed a decision-making tool based on al-Ghazali's framework for

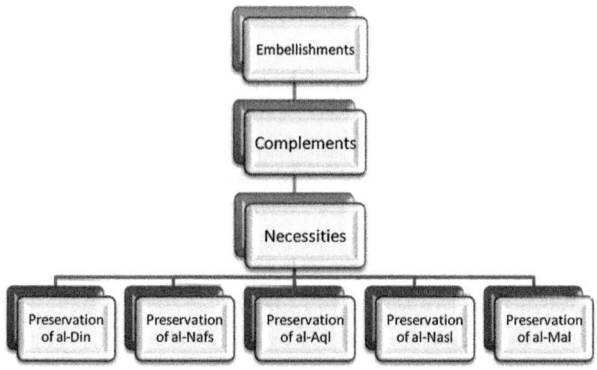

Fig. 8.1 Al-Ghazali's Maqasid theoretical framework (*Source* Author's own)

the managers of firms to use in allocating their investible resources to vital sectors of the economy. The discussion of al-Maqasid in this chapter is related to cryptocurrency. Hence, al-Maqasid will be discussed in the context of the preservation of al-Mal.

The meanings of the word al-Mal in the Quran vary relative to the different contexts in which they are used. Wealth in essence is "khayr" or something good (al-Quran, 2:215, and 2:272). Allah is the sole owner of al-Mal (wealth) and that people are entrusted as vicegerents (khulafa, singular khalifah) to utilize this wealth in a manner ordained by Allah (al-Quran, 57:7). In another instance, al-Mal is regarded as a test from Allah (al-Quran, 6:165) for man. The test is manifest in his struggles to earn it, and at the end of his achievements, he is also tested whether he is grateful of ungrateful to these bounties (al-Quran, 27:40). Al-Mal can be used to achieve the highest level of virtue (al-Quran, 2:261). The Quran reminds that al-Mal entails responsibility and accountability (al-Quran, 24:33, 57:7 and 4:6). In dealing with wealth, people are urged by the Quran to avoid negative elements such as hoarding, inequitable circulation of wealth, and its concentration in few hands (al-Quran, 9:34–35). The Quran has also urged people in their dealings to cooperate in matters of virtues and piety (5:2), avoid hardships (22:78), injustices (62:5), and ease means for one another (94:5–6). The Sunnah is another primary Shari'ah source that has explained al-Mal in detail with meanings similar to those provided by the Quran. The Prophet (saw) in several traditions or Sunnah has prohibited people from indulging into wasting wealth/property, hoarding, fraud, deceit, and injustice. Instead, they should promote mutual trust, transparency, disclosure, and compassion and kindness toward one another.

From the viewpoint of Muslim scholars, al-Mal in Arabic language broadly applies to anything valuable, which includes tangible and intangible properties (Al-Abbadi, 1988). Al-Shatibi (2004) defined al-Mal as, "Whatever is acquired legally, possessed, owned and the owner has exclusive authority to dispose the property." Al-Suyuti (1997), citing al-Shafi'i, considers wealth as "something valuable that can be exchanged and compensated for if damaged." Meanwhile, Muslim scholars of Maqasid al-Shari'ah define al-Mal largely in terms of its function and preservation. Some scholars, for instance, Auda (2008), propose a contextual shift in the use of the terminologies, from al-Juwayni's "protection" and later al-Ghazali's "preservation" to "development" and hence the development of al-Mal rather than its preservation. Wealth must be in circulation (*rawaj*), can transfer financial rights (*huquqmaliyyah*), is transparent (*wuduh*) in business dealings, can be preserved (*hifdh*) from corruption and misuse, is durable (*thabat*), and ensures fairness (*adl*) [Ibn 'Ashur (1998), Al-'Alam (1991)]. According to Ibn Ashur (2006), preservation of property denotes protecting the wealth of the community from destruction and misappropriation by others without counter values or compensation. Al-Raysuni (2006) cited al-Juwayni and al-Ghazali who regarded the preservation of al-Mal as its protection from thieves through severe punishments, and al-Shatibi is of the view that preservation of al-Mal is safeguarding it against injustice, deprivation such as of orphans, extravagance, envy, deceit in weight and measures, and corruption al-Raysuni (2006). Contemporary Muslim scholars, for example, Hassan and Mahlknecht (2011), Ng (2008), Dusuki and Bouheraoua (2011), and Chapra (2008) have expanded on the definition of al-Mal particularly its preservation to include protection of ownership rights, acquisition and development of property, investment, growth, transparency, justice, and circulation.

MAQASID AL-SHARI'AH AND CRYPTOCURRENCY

Based on the discussion on sections "Crypto Currency, Its Merits and Demerits" and "Maqasid al-Shari'ah" above, this section will analyze cryptocurrency based on Maqasid al-Shari'ah from five broad dimensions: justice, transparency and disclosure, wealth circulation, integrity and cooperation, and ease with no hardships.

Promotion of Justice as Opposed to Injustice

The objective of economic justice in financial transactions is reflected in the stability of the currency. The turbulence in its value and frequency in the price does not achieve economic justice in the transactions nor among the dealers. Therefore, it leads to injustice, which makes one affected by the price turmoil to feel that he is unjustly treated. This can be seen in the bitcoin where its value can fluctuate drastically.

Another manifestation of the absence of justice from this cryptocurrency transaction is that the amount of bitcoins is limited and does not exceed certain millions of units, which shows injustice. On the contrary, one of the conditions of the currency being traded is that it should not be limited because it is used as a store of value that can be readily used by other members of the society as price for goods and services. The limited number of bitcoins can be the direct cause of high fluctuation of the bitcoin price, where people compete to obtain it before it drained. The latter reason, limited amount, disqualifies cryptocurrencies from being traded because they lose the main feature of currency as medium of exchange, as there is no currency worldwide that is limited in number. In contrast, throughout the history people strive to increase wealth.

The absence of monetary authority or lack of intervention of a ruler is a clear manifestation of injustice and betrayal of the citizens. It is the right of the ruler and monetary authority to declare the issuance of currency and maintain the standard that people use in their transactions. Otherwise, if we allow the issuance of currency this way, such as cryptocurrency, we will see the issuances of many currencies and all will claim that their currency is the standard that must be relied upon for determining the prices of goods. This will cause turbulence in prices, lead to disputes, and result in injustices and many other problems that the rulers will fail to solve.

Ensuring Transparency and Disclosure

Enhancing transparency and disclosure means preventing ignorance, ambiguity, manipulation, deception, fraud, and error. The currency must be determined and should not be allowed to fluctuate, rise or fall quickly, as seen in these cryptocurrencies (except in the case of normal inflation over time). Determining national currency is the main conditions of validity of a currency to be used as a standard for the price of goods and services.Another issue is that the protocols used in the cryptocurrencies are exposed to errors, manipulation as well as fraud. "Wei Dai" said in 2011: "in my experience these kinds of protocols often have flaws that are not found until they happen."[1] In 2013, there was a technical error in the switching between the 7 and 8 version of the bitcoin mining protocol. Furthermore, there has also been a significant growth of electronic piracy after 2013 and stealing of many currencies from the bitcoin trading platforms (see: Theft and exchange shutdowns).

Ensuring Wealth Circulation as Opposed to Hoarding or Monopoly

One of the functions of currency is a medium exchange used for trading of goods and services which allows the real economy to grow and people to be motivated to participate in the real economic transactions such as agriculture, construction, and industry. It is noticeable in these currencies that they are traded through speculation, which is tantamount to gambling, something prohibited by the Shari'ah because it leads to eating others' money unjustly. Moreover, the Shari'ah has prohibited trading of currencies because they are treated as store of value not as a commodity.

Promotion of Integrity and Good Mutual Cooperation

The ruler of the state is responsible for the unity of his people, which is one of the Shari'ah objectives. Therefore, he's given the authority to issue currency that is used for valuing goods and services. Meanwhile, the issuers of the cryptocurrencies inadvertently declare that their purpose is to get rid of the authority of the ruler for various considerations that they claim.

A ruler from the Islamic perspective has the right to regulate the affairs of the people, to empower them to worship God, and to observe

---

[1] https://bitcointalk.org/index.php?topic=8602.5;wap2.

their religious and worldly interests, including providing them with sound judiciary institution, their security, the protection of their markets, and the preservation of family institutions through fair contracts and marriage. All these would take into account their public interests, improve them, and protect them from harms and at least minimize them. Promotion of public interest includes issuance of currency and putting in place policies and regulations for achieving such interest. Imam Ahmed said:

> It is not recommended that a currency be issued except for the ruler. And in another narration: It is not good to mint a currency from the mint except with the permission of the ruler. This is because if individuals are permitted to issue currency it'll cause instability. And the judge said: It is not allowed that currency be issued without the permission of the ruler as doing so will lead to the betrayal of the ruler.[2]

> Nawawi said: *"The judge Abu al-Tayeb said: it is not recommended for non-ruler to issue dirhams and dinars even if it is pure because the authority lies with the ruler and (if the non-ruler issues it) fraud and corruption may not be prevented."*
>
> Ibn al-Qayyim said: *"If the sultan (ruler) forbids the use of a currency, it is forbidden to use such a currency in a permissible transaction."* Therefore, the prohibition of non-ruler from issuing currency is to prevent fraud and corruption, as well as to prevent betrayal of the authority of the ruler in regulating the monetary policy of the state.

Easiness as Opposed to Hardship in Dealings

One of the characteristics of currency is its availability and easiness of getting access to it because it is a medium of exchange. Such easy access is not available in the cryptocurrencies due to its limited amount as well as the difficulty in its mining which requires special machines and training. The cost involved is not affordable by most of the people. All these lead to the hardship and instability in the life of the people, something that is against the Shari'ah objectives.

---

[2] محمد بن مفلح بن محمد المقدسي، الفروع، (بيروت: عالم الكتب، ط 4، 1985)، ج

CONCLUSION

From barter system, commodity money, metallic money, and fiat money, the world continues to increasingly embrace the digital currency coupled with advancement in technology. Cryptocurrencies are realities along with their merits and demerits. But for one thing, the debate about their Shari'ah compliance continues. The present chapter has set a new direction into the debate—analysis of cryptocurrency based on *Maqasid al-Shari'ah*. Future studies could use al-Ghazali's theory to identify the appropriate dimensions and elements that could be developed into *Maqasid* index to enhance the power of analysis provided in this study.

REFERENCES

Abu Zaharah, Muhammad. (1997). *Usul al-Fiqh*. Cairo: Dar al-Fikr al-'Arabi.
AIlal Al-Fasi. (n.d.). *Maqasid al-Shari'ah al-IslamiyyahWaMakarimuhaa*. Casablanca, Maktabah al-Wahdah al-'Arabiyyah.
Al-'Alam, Y. (1991). *Al-Maqasid al-'AmmahlilShariah*. Verginia: Al-Ma'had al-'AlamililFikr al-Islami. http://iefpedia.com/arab/wp-content/uploads/2009/09/العالم-حامد-يوسف-د.المقاصد-العامة-للشريعة-الإسلامية.pdf.
Al-Abbadi, A. S. (1988). Al-Fiqh al-Islamiwa al-Huquq al-Ma'nawiyyah. *MajallatMajma' Al-Fiqh al-Islami, 3*, 2465–2480.
Al-Ghazali, Abu Hamid. (1901). *Al-mustasfa min 'ilm al-usul* (1st Ed.). Egypt: Al-Matba'ah al-Amiriyyah.
Al-Ghazali, Abu Hamid. (n.d.). *al-Mustasfa*. Damascus: Dar al-Fikr.
Allouche, Adel. (1994). *Mamluk Economics—A Study and Translation of alMaqrizi'sighathah*. Salt Lake City: University of Utah Press.
Al-Juwayni, Abu al-Maali. (1979). *al-Burhan Fi Usul al-Fiqh* (ed. Abdul Azim al-Dib). Cairo: Dar al-Ansar.
Al-Raysuni, Ahmad. (1992). *Nazariyat al-Maqasid 'Inda al-Imam al-Shatibi*. Herndon: International Institute of Islamic Thought.
Al-Raysuni, Ahmad. (2006). *Imam Al-Shatibi's Theory of the Higher Objectives and Intents of Islamic Law*. Herndon, VA: International Institute of Islamic Thought.
Al-Shatibi, Abu Ishaq (2004). *Al-muwafaqat fi usul al-Shari'ah*. Dar al-Kutub al-'Ilmiyah, Beirut.
Al-Shatibi, Abu Ishaq. (n.d). *al-Muwafaqat* (ed. Abdallah Darraz). Beirut: Dar al-Ma'rifah.
Al-Suyuti, J. D. (1997). *Al-Ashbahwa al-Naza'er*. Riyadh: Maktabt Nizar Mustafa al-Baz.

AlTwijry, Othman Ibrahim A. (2016). *Shari'ah Perspective of Money Creation in Islamic Banking and the Need for MCF Model*. PhD dissertation, International Islamic University Malaysia, Kuala Lumpur.

Auda, Jasser. (2008). *Maqasid al-shariah as philosophy of Islamic law: A Systems Approach*. Herndon, VA: International Institute of Islamic Thought.

Chapra, M. Umer. (2007). *The Islamic Vision of Development in the Light of Maqasid al-Shari'ah* (Research Paper). Revised on 6 August 2007 and Published in 2008, p. 65. Available at http://www.irti.org.

Chapra, M. Umer. (2008). *The Islamic Vision of Development in the Light of maqasid al-Shari'ah* Jeddah: Islamic Research and Training Institute, Islamic Development Bank. Available at http://www.irti. org.../IDBDevelopments/.../The%20Islamic%20Vision%20of%20 Development%207.pdf.

Dusuki, A. W., and Bouheraoua, S. (2011). *The Framework of maqasid al-Shari'ah (Objectives of the Shari'ah) and Its Implications for Islamic Finance* (ISRA Research Paper No. 22/2011).

Dusuki, Asyraf W., and Mokhtar, Shabnam. (2010). *Critical Appraisal of Shari'ah Issues on Ownership in Asset-Based Sukuk as Implemented in the Islamic Debt Market* (Research Paper No. 8/2010). Kuala Lumpur: International Shari'ah Research Academy for Islamic Finance (ISRA), BNM.

Hassan, K., and Mahlknecht, M. (2011). *Islamic Capital Markets: Products and Strategies*. West Sussex: Wiley.

Hasan, Zubair. (2015). *Economics With Islamic Orientation*. Malaysia: Oxford FajarSdn. Bhd.

Ibn 'Ashur, M. al-Tahir. (1998). *Maqasid al-Shari'ah al-Islamiyyah* (ed. al-Misawi, Muhammad al-Tahir). Kuala Lumpur: al-Basa'ir.

Ibn 'Ashur, Muhammad al-Tahir. (2006). *Treatise on maqasid al-Shariah*. Herndon, VA: International Institute of Islamic Thought.

Investopedia. Cryptocurrency. Available at https://www.investopedia.com/ terms/c/cryptocurrency.asp#ixzz5JvLpifq8. Accessed on 29 June 2018.

Larbani, M., and Mustafa, M. (2009). A Decision Making Tools for the Allocation of Investible Resources Based on Al-Maqasid Al- Sharia Framework. *IIUM International Conference on Islamic Economics and the Economies of OIC Countries*. Istana Hotel, Kuala Lumpur, 28–29 April 2009.

Monzer Kahf. Fatwa on Bitcoin. Available at http://lightuponlight.com/blog/ fatwa-on-bitcoin-by-monzer-kahf/. Accessed on 29 June 2018.

Mufti Muhammad Abu-Bakar. (2018). Shariah Analysis of Bitcoin, Cryptocurrency and Blockchain. Available at https://blossomfinance.com/ bitcoin-working-paper.

Ng, B. K. (2008). *Maqasid al-Shariah—An Objective from a Prism of Wealth*. Available at http://legalpedia.wordpress.com/2009/02/01/maqasid-al-shariah-%E2%80%93-an-objective-from-a-prism-of-wealth/.

Oziev, Gapur, and Yandiyev, Magomet. (2018). Cryptocurrency from Shariah Perspective. Available at https://papers.ssrn.com/sol3/papers.cfm?abstract_id= 3101981.

Oziev, Gapur, Amafua, Mahfuth Khamis, Mohammed, Mustafa Omar, and Zaid, Muhammad Hafizi. (2016). Currency Exchange, Its Illah and Implications. *Journal of Islamic Finance*, 5(1),1–11.

Sanusi, Mahmood. (2002). *Proceedings of the 2002 International Conference on Stable and Just Global Monetary System* (ed. Meera, Ahamed Kameel). Kuala Lumpur: Research Centre, International Islamic University Malaysia.

CHAPTER 9

Fatawa Analysis of Bitcoin

Faraz Adam

INTRODUCTION

The world has witnessed several developments, innovations and advancements in all walks of life. From advancements in transport, communications, mobility, technology to advancements in the financial industry, the landscape of life has drastically changed over the past one hundred years. Islamic scholars have constantly engaged with these advances to understand them through the lens of Islamic law. Readers will find researchers and verdicts from Muslim jurists from across the world on developments in the recent past such as digital photography, air travel, paper money and limited liability companies. The financial world has witnessed a recent development which has left the world deliberating on its reality. The birth of Bitcoin has ignited research from across the world. Let alone Muslim scholars, conventional financial analysts and economists have been reflecting on the reality of this phenomenon. As a result, a number of *Fatawa* (verdicts) have been issued by scholars from across the world.

F. Adam (✉)
Amanah Finance Consultancy, Leicester, UK
e-mail: mfa@afinance.org
URL: http://www.afinance.org; http://www.darulfiqh.com

© The Author(s) 2019   133
M. M. Billah (ed.), *Halal Cryptocurrency Management*,
https://doi.org/10.1007/978-3-030-10749-9_9

Despite *Fatawa* on Bitcoin and cryptocurrencies circulating online, Muslim investors are still puzzled with regard to the ruling on investing in cryptocurrencies. This confusion is partly due to conflicting *Fatawa* and the fact that most *Fatawa* only focus on Bitcoin as opposed to the array of cryptocurrencies. Therefore, the purpose of this chapter is to analyze the *Fatawa* of three prominent scholars in the Islamic finance industry: Dr Ali al-Qurra Dagi, Dr Mohd Daud Bakar and Dr Abdus Sattar Abu Ghuddah. After presenting a summary of each *Fatwa*, an attempt is made to draw parallels on the key points raised in the *Fatawa*. The key themes are studied and challenged further to get a deeper understanding of the issues dominating the discussions. Before this analysis, it is pertinent to get an understanding of what a *Fatwa* is and understand some of the requirements needed to issue a *Fatwa*. The chapter is concluded with recommendations on how a coherent understanding of cryptocurrencies can materialize from a Shari'ah perspective.

What Is a Fatwa

The word *Fatwa*, which is also pronounced as *futya*, whose plural is *fatawa* and *fatawi*, means "response" to a question of any kind. In the technical sense, it means responding to a question about a ruling of Shari'ah. The word *Fatwa* and its linguistic roots have been used in the Qur'an in the general as well as the technical sense. For example, the technical meaning is to be found in the verses: "They ask your instruction concerning the women: Say: Allah instruct you about them," and "They ask you for a legal decision. Say: Allah directs about those who leave no descendants or ascendants as heirs."

Muftis or legal experts do not just respond to purely legal rules, rather, many of their answers are in response to queries regarding tenets of faith, mannerisms and general matters of religion. Many scholars assign a wide role to the Mufti or the expert who answers such questions. This is different to a *Qadhi* (judge) who does not render rulings about mannerisms or even worship. As with any profession and industry, not everyone is competent to comment and offer an opinion. Likewise, not everyone is competent to issue a *Fatwa* in Islamic finance. Competency is a result of rigorous legal education from within the tradition of Islamic jurisprudence, with a mastery of the schools of Islamic law, and training in the practical application of Islamic law. In addition to rigorous legal training in Islamic commercial law, a Mufti in Islamic finance must have a sound understanding of conventional finance and economics. In fact, the Shari'ah Governance Framework for Islamic Financial Institutions issued by Bank Negara Malaysia mentions:

> … the Shari'ah Committee members [at the institutional level] shall be appointed by the board upon the recommendation of its Nomination Committee. The number of Shari'ah Committee members to be appointed must not be less than five (5), the majority of whom must possess strong knowledge in Shari'ah and backed by the appropriate qualifications in that area.[1]

Before an opinion can be offered on Bitcoin, the Mufti must have a good understanding of the philosophy and economics behind Bitcoin, Blockchain, the operational dimension of Bitcoin as the very least requirements. The famous juristic principle states: "*al-Hukm ala shay' far'un an Tasawwurihi*"—Passing judgment on something is contingent and dependent on its prior conception. A multi-dimensional conception and understanding of Bitcoin is therefore necessary to ensure accuracy in the conclusion. Nevertheless, a *Fatwa* is a non-binding verdict of Islamic jurisprudence as opposed to a decree from a judge, which is binding.[2]

Role of Shari'ah Scholars

Shari'ah scholars play a vital role in contemporary Islamic finance and its operations. They are involved throughout the product structuring and development stage. Their involvement does not cease with the launch of the product; rather they are required to supervise, review and audit the practices. A Shari'ah advisor should possess the following criteria (Laldin and Furqani 2015):

- Must have mastery in *fiqh al-mu'amalat* (Islamic commercial law) and *Usul al-fiqh*
- Should have sufficient knowledge of the current Islamic and conventional finance practices

---

[1] Muhammad and Ali (2014).
[2] Usmani (2014).

- Should have deep understanding of Maqasid al-Shari'ah
- Must have the capability to derive legal rulings
- Should have sufficient understanding of the issue and problem posed
- Should have the attributes of boldness, trustworthiness and dynamism
- Should have good reputation and good Islamic character.

The resolution No. 104 (7/11) issued by the OIC Fiqh Academy gave several recommendations to Muftis and Shari'ah scholars in respect to their Fatwas. The resolution emphasized the importance of the research methodology in *Fatawa* to be backed by valid Shari'ah principles. Scholars were encouraged to take into consideration the resolutions and recommendations of Fiqh academies, in an endeavor to regulate, coordinate and unify *Fatawa* in the Muslim world. The resolution highlighted the need to restrict who can issue *Fatwa* by arguing that the Mufti should be one who is well known for his scholarship, knowledge, righteousness and fear of Allah, the Almighty. In the same resolution, Shari'ah scholars are advised to:

- Abide by evidence from Qur'an, Sunnah, *Ijma'* (consensus of the Muslim Ummah), *Qiyas* (analogy) and other evidence from *Shari'ah,* in addition to abiding by the rules of *Takhrij* (looking for evidence) and those of *Istinbat* (deducing of law).
- Pay attention to priorities in bringing about good and staving off evil.
- Take into consideration the real, material world, the customs and changes of environments and circumstances which do not clash with any of the fundamentals of *Shari'ah.*
- Go along with the circumstances of the progress of civilization which combine both genuine interest and compliance with the rules of *Shari'ah.*

The Fatawa

In an interview with Al Jazeera in late 2017, Shaykh Dr Ali al-Qurra Dagi pressed that at present, he did not consider it to be permissible to purchase and transact with Bitcoin and cryptocurrencies. However, cryptocurrencies do have the potential to be Shari'ah compliant he proposed (Al Jazeera 2017). He presented three possible ways by which Bitcoin and other cryptocurrencies can be Shari'ah compliant and save the investors from huge financial losses. The first solution he proposed was the existence of a regulatory body and framework. He argued that everything in Islam has a system and framework within which it operates. For anything to be acceptable, it will require some framework and regulation. He proposed that a country can adopt a cryptocurrency as its primary or secondary currency. Another idea he suggested to bring cryptocurrencies under regulation was for a network of banks to issue cryptocurrency. This would bring some oversight and regulation to cryptocurrencies. A third proposal he offered was for the incorporation of a joint stock company where the developers and the investors have co-ownership in a cryptocurrency.

In the discussion, Dr Ali argued that cryptocurrencies are not currencies at present, even though they are called "currencies." This argument alludes to the Islamic legal maxim: "In contracts, effect is given to the objectives and meanings, not to the words and phrases" (al-Zuhayli 1985). This principle highlights that the substance of a contract and meanings are considered, not merely the terms and words utilized. Thus, using the word "currencies" for cryptos is of no relevance in jurisprudential analysis. A Shari'ah scholar must analyze the underlying substance, nature and operations of cryptocurrencies regardless of what it is commonly called among the people.

In support of his dismissal of cryptocurrencies not being currencies, he reasoned that cryptocurrencies do not function like currencies nor do they possess currency traits. The first trait he discussed was medium of exchange. A medium of exchange is an item that buyers give to sellers when they want to purchase goods and services. A medium of exchange is anything that is readily acceptable as payment; It is something that people hold because they plan to swap it for something else, rather than because they want the good itself (Mankiw 2009). He argued that cryptocurrencies do not serve as a medium of exchange nor are they readily accepted among people as payment. The second trait he discussed was "store of value." A store of value is an item that people can use to transfer purchasing power from the present to the future. In other words, it is something that is expected to retain its value in a reasonably predictable way over time. Gold or silver that was mined hundreds of years ago would still be valuable today. But perishable food would quickly become worthless as it goes bad. Hence, gold or silver are good stores of value, but perishable food much less so (Mankiw 2009). Dr Ali asserted that cryptocurrencies are not a store of value. The third trait he referred to was "standard of deferred payment." Money serves as a standard of payment contracted to be made at some future date. It facilitates borrowing and lending activities (Mankiw 2009). He argued that cryptocurrencies do not serve this function either. He asserted that cryptocurrencies do not have these traits or functions due to the absence of regulation to govern and mold their function.

If cryptocurrencies are not currencies according to his research, would they be considered as assets? He dismissed the notion of cryptocurrencies being "crypto-assets." The reason why they failed as assets was the lack of "intrinsic value" in cryptocurrencies he argues. Thus, at present, he concludes that due to the lack of regulatory oversight, it is not permissible to transact in Bitcoin.

The second *Fatwa* is that of the current chairman of the Shari'ah Advisory Council, Dr Mohd Daud Bakar. He recently delivered a lecture on blockchain and cryptocurrencies (Pikri 2018). Interestingly, Dr Bakar's views focused more on blockchain as opposed to just cryptocurrencies. He expressed his belief in this phenomenon by stating; "I am a man of Shari'ah, and I see ways to preserve Shari'ah within digital currencies, especially because digital currencies are a phenomenon that will happen, whether we like it or not." He highlighted that blockchain facilitates not only exchanges, but also remittances. This would reduce time and costs for customers. Unlike others who are skeptical of Bitcoin and focused on negative repercussions, Dr Bakar argued that Blockchain and cryptocurrencies could combat money laundering. Blockchain can help ensure that the identity linked to monies is kept on record. To demonstrate how money laundering can be reduced on the Blockchain, he gave the following example: "*If we pay Zakat though Bitcoin—if this is allowed by Fatwa—then we can see exactly how the money is spent. Another example is BR1M allowances. We can observe exactly where the money is spent, whether in schoolbooks and etc.*"

In reference to Zakat on the blockchain, he believed that such a Zakat system can help with accountability. Zakat payers would be able to trace their Zakat payments and see the impact it has. In respect to the practical implementation and use of cryptocurrencies, he suggested that Malaysia can turn a cryptocurrency into a local currency. This would bring regulation and oversight.

In regard to the varying *Fatawa* issued on cryptocurrencies, he argued: "*Ulama* (scholars) today consider it as *Haram* (unlawful) because it is *Gharar* (uncertain). But in my humble opinion, they misunderstand the difference between uncertainty and risk." Dr Bakar argues that risk is not a sufficient reason to declare Bitcoin as unlawful. He states that from a *Fatwa* standpoint, a government can declare something unlawful, however, from a pure Shari'ah perspective, it cannot be said that something is *Haram* because there is risk. Interestingly, he made a reference to fiat currencies and drew a parallel on the underpinning philosophy: "*Digital currency was created based on a feeling of trust or peer-to-peer. Meanwhile, fiat money is also based on trust.*"

The third Fatwa under consideration is that of Dr Abdus Sattar Abu Ghuddah. He recently published a short treatise analyzing cryptocurrencies from the lens of Shari'ah. He discounts Bitcoin from possessing the necessary traits and functions of cryptocurrencies with similar arguments to Dr Ali. He enumerates the following four characteristics of currencies: unit of account, widespread medium of exchange, store of value and being considered as a currency by official bodies and authorities. A unit of account is the yardstick people use to post prices and record debts. It is the thing that goods and services are priced in terms of, such as on menus, contracts or price labels. In modern economies, the unit of account is usually a currency, for example, the pound in the UK, but it could be a type of good instead. In the past, items would often be priced in terms of something very common, such as staple foods ("bushels of wheat") or farm animals (Mankiw 2009). Since Bitcoin is not commonly used to price goods or services, Dr Abdus Sattar argues that it fails to be a unit of account. Another argument he raises is that a currency must have widespread use as a medium of exchange to be a currency, whereas Bitcoin is used only in certain networks and places. A third characteristic he raises is "store of value." He disputes Bitcoin being a store of value due to its volatility. The fourth characteristic highlighted is the recognition of an official body or authority. After dismissing Bitcoin as currency, he argues that it can neither be considered as commodity (*sil'ah*). He reasons that an asset or commodity is something from which benefit is derived. The asset itself gives utility and benefit to the owner. However, Bitcoin has no such benefit in and of itself nor use.

Dr Abdus Sattar says that any Shari'ah ruling on cryptocurrencies depends on: an intricate understanding and perception of cryptocurrencies, an awareness of the laws related to money and currency and the authority and power of the governing bodies. In concluding his position, he suggests that there are two premises to prevent the current use of cryptocurrencies: It is the right of the government and the central banks—in respect to monetary policy—to maintain what is beneficial for the masses, and in most countries, the authorities have either banned the use of cryptocurrencies or have not supported the use of them. His second argument is based on the principles of the "prohibition of inflicting harm and reciprocating harm" in Shari'ah as well as principles of "excessive and unnecessary risk taking" and the "squandering of wealth." He argues that trading in cryptocurrencies has all these features. Hence, at present, he discourages all transactions and dealings with cryptocurrencies.

The Key Themes of the Fatawa

After analyzing the *Fatawa*, we can separate the points of contention into two: intrinsic issues and extrinsic issues. Intrinsic issues refer to the nature of Bitcoin, operations and characteristics. Extrinsic issues refer to issues such as authority over monetary affairs, risk and harm to people. This division is alluded to by Dr Ali al-Qurrah Dagi who proposes that Bitcoin can be a currency if it is adopted by the government. This shows that intrinsically, Bitcoin can qualify as a currency, however, there are extrinsic issues preventing that transformation. Dr Bakar shares a similar argument demonstrating that Bitcoin and other cryptocurrencies can be nationalized and used as a means of exchange. These points of contentions are analyzed to get a deeper understanding of the issues raised. The *Fatawa* revolve around the following themes: the authority of the government in respect to monetary policy, the characteristics of money, *Gharar*, risk and harm.

The Nature of Bitcoin

All three *Fatawa* consider Bitcoin to be an entity with potential to be currency. The recognition of Bitcoin as an entity and as *Mal* (property) is crucial to the discussion. For anything to be a valid consideration or counter-exchange, it must be *Mal and Mutaqawwim* (legal value in

Shari'ah) (al-Kasani 1986). For anything to be considered as *Mal*, it must have desirability and storability. Bitcoin possesses features which gives it desirability. For example, the blockchain technology behind Bitcoin, the replacement of trusted party intermediations with the proof-of-work protocol, decentralization, limited supply and borderless payments with less transactional fees all make Bitcoin desirable. This has resulted in a demand for Bitcoin. In respect to storability, Bitcoins are encoded within the blockchain and are entries on a public ledger. Your ownership is reflected by your Bitcoin address being credited with a balance. Considering that Bitcoins are merely digits and entries on a public ledger, there is no evidence or premise indicating to them being unlawful. Hence, Bitcoins have *Taqawwum*. Hence, it can be argued that Bitcoin is something which has existence; it is *Mal* with *Taqawwum*.

The Issue of Authority and Governance

All the *Fatawa* raise the argument of government authority. Dr Abdus Sattar Abu Ghuddah explicitly states that setting monetary policy and determining currency is a core function and role of the government. He mentions that historical Islamic governments had a minting house called *Dar al-Darb* (House of Minting). In those times, anyone who had gold or silver could not coin the metals into currency on their own accord. The authorities would mint the metals in a particular form. Such practices are underpinned with the Islamic juristic principle of *Maslahah* (public interest and benefit) he argues, which is best served by giving the authorities this function. Thus, he concludes that it is the government alone who has the authority to introduce a currency. Any unofficial currency cannot be deemed currency even though it may be used as a currency.

Dr Abdus Sattar highlights a key point in this entire discourse by stating that this issue is underpinned by the principle of *Maslahah*. Islam advocates the preservation of the wealth of people. Thus, any system which destroys the wealth of people and puts it at severe risk fails to comply with the Maqasid al-Shari'ah. For this *Maslahah* to be realized, the following question needs answering: is it necessary for a human system in the form of a government to have oversight of currency or is an automated, digital, programmed system sufficient as it fulfils the same function? To answer this question, it is pertinent to look at the development of currency in Islamic history and to gauge the scholarly writings of classical legal experts. Until the caliphate of Abdul Malik ibn

Marwan, the Islamic government did not control the currency nor its coinage. The Islamic government did not have a "Royal Mint," however, "Umar ibn al-Khattab" (May Allah be pleased with him) did introduce some measures to stabilize the alloy, content and weight of silver coins. In the year 74 A.H, the government of Abdul Malik ibn Marwan centralized monetary governance and introduced an Islamic dirham (al-Buhuti 2015). Minting houses were established, taking control of money circulation, quality and purity of currencies (Zarra-Nezhad 2004). Thus, in the first generation of Islam, currency regulation was not a core function of the government. This supports the philosophy of *Maslahah*.

The legal experts have discussed in their legal writings the process by which a currency is developed. The Hanafi jurists argue that customary usage (*Ta'amul*) can establish currency just as coinage and minting from the government established currency (Efindi). The Hanafi jurists reasoned that anything minted and centralized would give a known benchmark and a known point of reference, thus, creating ease in the markets and facilitating transactions. The Shafi'i jurists state that it is disliked for other than the government to mint coins and currency as it was the role of the government and there is always a risk of counterfeiting, forgery and corruption (Nawawi). They argued that a governing body would be most effective in preventing malpractice. The Hanbali jurists are explicit in stating that it is not permissible for the sultan to ban the currency commonly used by people as it will cause financial harm to the people, unless they are recompensed proportionately in the new currency without a fee (al-Ruhaibani 1994). Considering the benefit and harm for the masses, Imam al-Suyuti also states that it is disliked for the government to withdraw or nullify a currency commonly used among people (al-Suyuti 2004). Imam al-Buhuti says that the reason why the government should take control of minting is to benefit the people and to make it easy for them in their transactions and affairs (al-Buhuti 2015). From the above precedents, it is clear that a governing body was favored as it is in the interests of the people to have an authoritative body preventing fraud, corruption and monetary malpractices. The government and ruling authority would have been the most efficient and instrumental in achieving these ideals in the medieval era. However, the Hanafi writings are interesting as they do not discard the common usage of people as a factor to create currency. In fact, they give the same weighting to common usage of people to that of government institutionalization of currency. This further supports the notion of *Maslahah*. Whatever is in the interests of the people in a manner that brings benefits and wards off harm is acceptable. Furthermore, the Qur'an and Sunnah have not defined currency, instead, they have left it to the understanding of the people and custom of the people as mentioned by Imam Ibn Taymiyyah (1995). This is a common feature for those aspects of law which are fluid, dynamic and adjustable. Considering the above arguments, Shaykh Abdullah al-Mani explicitly argues that determining a currency is not restricted to government policy. He states: "Currency is whatever is agreed upon, whether by government authority or public practice" (Mani 1984). Thus, it is reasonable to conclude that a currency can be determined by public practice. If a decentralized system can provide benefits similar to that of a centralized system, a medium of exchange can become money through public practice and widespread acceptance. However, the government would still have the right to restrict other currencies if it was in the interest of the people, as mentioned by Dr Bakar. The government is there to benefit the people and work in their best interests.

The Characteristics of Currency and Bitcoin

Dr Ali al-Qurra Dagi analyzes Bitcoin in respect to the core functions of money and concludes that Bitcoin does not possess these functions. Dr Abdul Sattar discredits Bitcoin from possessing any of the features money has. Although Bitcoin does not function as a unit of account in legal jurisdictions and neither is it a national means of exchange, it may be argued that within an ecosystem, it plays these functions. In fact, due to the borderless nature of Bitcoin, an atomized network of users has surfaced. One may argue that it is within this borderless ecosystem that Bitcoin is being used as a medium of exchange to some extent and as a unit of account. In terms of being a store of value, Bitcoin surely suffers from volatility. However, the notion of being a store of value is something in respect to money. Currency on the other hand is something which has no intrinsic value. While money stores intrinsic value within itself, fiat currency possesses buying power bestowed upon it by the government. If we consider the case of fiat currencies, a number of currencies have had their values wiped off as a result of inflation and hyperinflation, yet they were still considered to be functional currencies. Does a currency require intrinsic value or utility? According to Islamic economics, a currency does not need to possess any utility besides being a medium of exchange. Money has no intrinsic utility; it is only a medium of exchange (Usmani 1998). Thus, it seems that a currency does not have to be a "store of value." Where is the value then derived from if it has no intrinsic value? What would make people trade, transact and desire in a currency which has no intrinsic value or worth? Similar to fiat currencies, it seems that Bitcoin entertains extrinsic value. While fiat currencies acquire value due to being a legal tender and a trusted means of exchange, Bitcoin acquires value due to the blockchain technology, anonymity, the replacement of trusted party intermediations with the proof-of-work protocol, borderless payments with less transactional fees and the notion and craze over an innovative monetary system.

Another angle to consider whether Bitcoin is currency is to consider the very purpose it has been created to serve. Bitcoin was created to serve as a peer-to-peer payment system. It can be argued that Bitcoin was launched as a medium of exchange. The blockchain provides a system for this currency. The fact that people are using them as investments does not negate their currency feature. At present, Bitcoins can be a medium of exchange in a transaction. The people have assigned a "value" to Bitcoin due to which they purchase, sell, accept and exchange Bitcoin. Indeed, the value can be manipulated, exploited and speculated, however, these are external issues which require regulation and control.

Risk Taking

An argument raised against Bitcoin is the risk profile of Bitcoin. Is every risk prohibited? Ibn Taymiyyah states that there is no authentic evidence in the Shari'ah that requires the prohibition of every risk; in fact, it is known that Allah Almighty and His Messenger did not prohibit every risk nor everything of uncertain gain or loss or delivery. There is no authentic Shari'ah evidence that requires the prohibition of all these types, neither a text nor an analogy. What is prohibited of these types is that which involves acquiring the property of others illegitimately. The Shari'ah's reason for prohibiting [a transaction] is the illegitimate acquisition of others' property, and it is prohibited to acquire others' property illegitimately even in the absence of risk (Ibn Taymiyya 1995). Risk, in and of itself, is not prohibited. In fact, the presence of risk is a fundamental element to profit from a venture.

The Islamic legal maxims state: "[The right to] profit [from something] goes with responsibility [for it]." Another maxim states: "Liability is an obligation accompanying gain" (al-Kasani 1986).

Investing in high-risk investments such as shares in a Shari'ah compliant start-up company cannot be deemed impermissible even though there is exposure to high risk. The volatility of such an investment will not impact the inherent compliance of the assets and transaction. Undeniably, trading, investments and gambling are all regarded as speculative risks. However, there are clear differences between gambling, trade and investments which highlight the difference in risk. Trading and investing are positive-sum games while gambling is a zero-sum game. Positive-sum games are where the parties gain together or lose together. In a partnership, partners mutually gain or mutually lose if the venture fails. In zero-sum games, one party gains at the expense of another. Considering Bitcoin transactions, Bitcoin is exchanged for a counter-exchange where both parties anticipate gain from their acquired asset. It is never guaranteed that one party will surely lose. Thus, Bitcoin transactions are positive-sum games as both transacting parties anticipate gain. Therefore, Bitcoin exchanges cannot be likened to *Maysir* and *Qimar* (gambling) due to the inherent difference between positive-sum and zero-sum games.

Another argument raised is the concept of *Gharar*. Although *Gharar* is a broad concept, not every risk is *Gharar*. *Gharar* revolves around the uncertainty, deception or gross ambiguity at the point of sale in respect to the subject matter, price or in delivery of the asset or payment (Awqaf Kuwait 2004). The future price movement of an asset does not fall under the purview of *Gharar*. The fluctuating future value of a Shari'ah compliant asset or commodity will not render the transaction void at present. Of course, when it is highly predictable and probable that the asset is on the verge of collapsing or being banned, purchasing such an asset would be discouraged. However, on the balance of probabilities, such information in respect to Bitcoin is mere speculation. Indeed, speculation which brings imbalance in a person's life is discouraged altogether. If a person brings harm to himself or his dependents due to his lack of moderation and risk appetite, such actions will be blameworthy and reproachable. Again, this would be an extrinsic issue in respect to cryptocurrencies and not an intrinsic issue. Such a problem can be addressed by reminding investors of their obligations and duties to themselves and others.

RECOMMANDATIONS

On most contemporary issues, conflicting *Fatawa* is inevitable. The very nature of a *Fatwa* makes it something subjective as it is based on the Mufti's understanding and interpretation of a phenomenon. Nevertheless, such *Fatawa* are always welcomed and encouraged as they add to the body of knowledge. Every article, research and *Fatwa* helps develop ideas and arguments. These small efforts bring motion and move us toward the truth. In all such contemporary matters, the most decisive and thorough conclusion is reached via *Ijtihad Jama'i* (collective *Ijtihad*). This is where a group of experts come together to deliberate all angles in any given issue. The experts include Shari'ah scholars, economists, accountants, lawyers, bankers, financial analysts and professionals from whichever industry is pertinent to the matter under deliberation.

This type of *Ijtihad* is essential in Islamic finance due to the complexity of contemporary issues, making it difficult for an individual to grasp comprehensively. What makes collective *Ijtihad* even more important is that such conclusions will impact Muslims collectively. Hence, resolutions issued by international fatwa councils, standard setting bodies and regulatory bodies are the most effective in these matters such as Islamic Fiqh Academy of Organisation of Islamic Countries, Islamic Fiqh Academy of Muslim World League, Accounting and Auditing Organisation of Islamic Financial Institutions (AAOIFI), Shari'ah Advisory Council of Central Bank of Malaysia (SAC of BNM) and Shari'ah Advisory Council of Securities Commission Malaysia. The collective *Ijtihad* process elevates these opinions to majority opinions in the industry. Thus, a *Fatwa* or resolution is required from these bodies to get clarity in the industry.

REFERENCES

al-Buhuti. (2015). *Sharh Muntaha al-Iradat.* Beirut: Ar Risalah al Alamiyyah.

Al Jazeera. (2017). *YouTube.* Consulté le, April 16, 2018, sur YouTube, https://www.youtube.com/watch?v=VJXuO7vc_CQ.

al-Kasani. (1986). *Bada'i al-Sana'i.* Beirut: Dar al-Kutub al-ilmiyyah.

al-Ruhaibani. (1994). *Matalib Uli al-Nuha.* al-Maktab al-Islami.

al-Suyuti. (2004). *al-Hawi lil al-Fatawi.* Beirut: Dar al-Fikr.

al-Zuhayli, W. (1985). *al-Fiqh al-Islami wa Adillatuhu.* Damascus: Dar al-Fikr.

Awqaf Kuwait. (2004). *al-Mawsu'ah al-Fiqhiyyah al-Kuwaitiyyah* (3rd ed.). Kuwait: Awqaf.

Efindi. *Majma' al-Anhur.* Beirut: Dar al-Kutub.

Ibn Taymiyya. (1995). *Majmu' al-Fatawa*. al-Madinah: Majma al-Malik Fahd.

Laldin, M., & Furqani, H. (2015). Shari'ah Scholars, Ijtihad and Decision Making in Islamic Finance. *Journal of Islamic Business and Management, 5* (1), 37–50.

Mani, A. (1984). *Paper Money: Its Reality, History, Value and Legal Ruling.*

Mankiw, N. (2009). *Principles of Macroeconomics* (5th ed.). Mason, OH: South-Western Cengage Learning.

Muhammad, M., & Ali, M. (2014). Who Can Exercise Ijtihad in Islamic Financial Matters. *ISRA Bloomberg Bulletin.*

Pikri, E. (2018). *Is Cryptocurrency Haram? The Chairmain of BNM's Shari'ah Advisory Council Says No.* Consulté le April 16, 2018, sur Vulcanpost: https://vulcanpost.com/632153/haram-cryptocurrency-syariah-advisory-council/.

Usmani, M. T. (1998). *An Introduction to Islamic Finance.* Karachi.

Usmani, M. (2014). *Usul al-Ifta wa Adabuhu.* Damascus: Dar al-Qalam.

Zarra-Nezhad, M. (2004). *A Brief History of Money in Islam and Estimating the Value of Dirham an Dinar.* Ahvaz: Shahid Chamran University.

CHAPTER 10

Shari'ah Code of Ethics in Cryptocurrency

Mohd Ma'sum Billah
and Mohammed Fawzi Aminu Amadu

INTRODUCTION

The Cryptocurrency, an innovative type of digital currency that is created through cryptography and stored within a block chain using encryption technology, is currently taking the world of finance by storm with the different Cryptocurrency types having a market capitalization of about $422,752,572,307.00.[1] The use of these coins is going global[2] however for many different reasons there have been mixed reaction to

---

[1] Cryptocurrency Market Capitalizations, https://coinmarketcap.com.

[2] "Islam and Cryptocurrency, Halal or Not Halal?" Al Jazeera, https://www.aljazeera.com/news/2018/04/islam-cryptocurrency-halal-halal-180408145004684.html.

M. M. Billah (✉)
Finance, Insurance, Fintech and Investment, Islamic Economics Institute, King Abdul Aziz University, Jeddah, Kingdom of Saudi Arabia
URL: http://www.drmasumbillah.blogspot.com

M. F. A. Amadu
Islamic Finance and Business Development, Accra, Ghana
e-mail: mfawzi@gmambassadors.com

© The Author(s) 2019   149
M. M. Billah (ed.), *Halal Cryptocurrency Management*,
https://doi.org/10.1007/978-3-030-10749-9_10

the use of Cryptocurrencies with some religious authorities[3] and governments[4] expressing their disapproval of its use. It is these disapprovals and other reasons that have been echoed around the globe that necessitates that ethical considerations be looked into with regard to the novel concept of Cryptocurrency. With a fifth of the world being Muslim, the Islamic view of the status of Cryptocurrency—whether its use is *Halal* (permitted) or Haram (forbidden)—is very important. Ethics is at the very basis of Islam for the *Qur'an* states:

> You are the best of people evolved for mankind given that you command what is good and forbid what evil and you believe in Allah.[5]

Thus, it is important that ethical issues arising from the activities of Cryptocurrency are analyzed with concern.

LITERATURE REVIEW

Cryptocurrency is increasingly the topic of discussion in many circles and due to this, there exists a lot of information on it and its derivatives. There are research papers, magazine and newspaper articles and even many videos that present various information relating to Cryptocurrency. From the Islamic perspective and with regard to the use of Cryptocurrency, the existing discourse around it has been about it being permissible (*Halal*) or forbidden (*Haram*). Given that the Islamic Finance industry is growing very fast and becoming a global phenomenon,[6] matters of Islamic ethical considerations are of paramount importance in the acceptability of any of the Cryptocurrencies that are being offered to consumers. Norton Rose Fulbright (2013) identified, Sharing—profit, loss and risk, no unfair gain, no speculation, no uncertainty, no investment that are not in the public interest and no hoarding of money as being among the core values of Islamic economy in the contemporary era.

---

[3] Ashok, India, BitCoin? Top Imam Says Bitcoin Forbidden Under Islam, Compares It to Gambling, https://www.ibtimes.co.uk/bitcoin-fatwa-top-imam-says-cryptocurrency-forbidden-under-islam-compares-it-gambling-1653529.

[4] Thailand First Country to Ban Digital Currency Bitcoin, http://investvine.com/thailand-first-country-to-ban-digital-currency-bitcoin/.

[5] *Qur'an* 3:110.

[6] Lukonga, Inutu, Islamic Finance, Consumer Finance and Financial Stability.

AN OVERVIEW OF CRYPTOCURRENCY

Cryptocurrency is a phenomenon that leverages technology and combines it with the mathematical science of cryptography to create a digital currency that can be used for financial transactions around the globe. There are many versions of Cryptocurrency being offered just as there are many differing fiat currencies around the world. Bitcoin is the most popular of these currencies similar to how the Dollar among fiat currencies.[7] This overview will be using the Bitcoin model.

Bitcoin in this case is the currency that is created using cryptographic science that uses a public key and a private key along with a system of mining that ensures transactions are properly categorized and registered in a database known as a Block-chain. The block-chain creates publicly available ledger within which Bitcoin transactions are stored and then shared across the peer-to-peer Bitcoin system; this ledger ensures that Bitcoins are properly tracked to avoid duplicated use of Bitcoins.[8] Bitcoins just like other digital currencies are traded. The system on mining alluded to earlier is the process where some entities known as miners process transaction requests and when these requests are completed and approved, they are entered into the blockchain to formally register the transaction. The miners are paid[9] a fraction of the value of the Bitcoin transaction for their work. The process of getting a result from mining is based on guesswork[10] with any of the miners.

ETHICAL CONSIDERATION

As calling to good and forbidding what is evil in central to the Islamic ethos[11]; and as this is the means to everlasting success it is of utmost importance that the use of Cryptocurrency be viewed through the lens of the Islamic law (Shari'ah) to understand how it can be used. Also the importance of ethics within the Islamic understanding us clarified by the

[7] D'Alfonso, Alexander, Langer, Peter, and Vandelis, Zintis (2016) "The Future of Cryptocurrency: An Investor's Comparison of Bitcoin and Ethereum."

[8] Mufti Abu-Bakr, Mohammed (2017) "Shari'ah Analysis of Bitcoin, Cryptocurrency and Blockchain."

[9] Acheson, Noelle (2018) "How Bitcoin Mining Works."

[10] Ibid.

[11] *al-Qur'an* 3:104.

statement of the Prophet Muhammad (Peace Be Upon Him) when he states that:

I have been sent for the purpose of perfecting good morals.[12]

There is no doubt that there are unique features of Cryptocurrency that facilitate ease for its users and facilitating ease for mankind is what *Allah (swt)* desires for mankind.[13] The desire for ease notwithstanding, it is necessary that moral rules be followed in delivering such ease.

Protection of wealth features prominently in the five objectives of *Shari'ah* and so the issue of Cryptocurrency which is being offered as a store of wealth is worth analyzing in light of Islamic ethical considerations and especially the core ethical values that were earlier mentioned, i.e., Sharing—profit, loss and risk, no unfair gain, no speculation, no uncertainty, no investment that are not in the public interest and no hoarding of money. Before delving into the discussion of Cryptocurrency in light of the core ethical values identified, a key feature of Cryptocurrency—lack of central regulation—must the discussed in light of the Islamic concept of obeying those in authority. The Qur'an commands the believers:

O you who have believed, obey Allah and obey the Messenger and those in authority among you...[14]

By virtue of this divine ruling, there is a need to situate the use of Cryptocurrency within the broader understanding of those in authority and this can mean and includes government. In most countries, the central bank or a similar entity is the only one that is allowed to issue currency,[15] in light of this the recent announcements by some governments[16]

---

[12] *Al-Muwatta* 1614.

[13] *al-Qur'an* 4:28.

[14] *al-Qur'an* 4:59.

[15] Uzair, Mohammed (1982) "Central Banking Operations in an Interest Free Banking System."

[16] Mufti Abu-Bakr, Mohammed (2017) "Shari'ah Analysis of Bitcoin, Cryptocurrency and Blockchain," p. 16.

that they are banning the use of Cryptocurrency raises many issues for the use of such a currency. For one, how acceptable is the use of Cryptocurrency for a person whose government has banned the use of the currency? What is the impact of such a ban on the risk of holding such a currency and how should this be treated vis-a-vis the concept of *Garar* (uncertainty)?

On the flip side of this consideration is the *Shari'ah* maxim that custom may be recognized as law[17] as well as the Prophet Muhammad's teaching that:

> Muslims must abide by their agreements insofar as these agreements do not make what is legal, forbidden and what is forbidden, legal.[18]

In light of these rules from the *Shari'ah*, the case can be made for the acceptability of Cryptocurrency based on its current global acceptance—and this is significant. The sheer size of the market capitalization of Cryptocurrency along of how many people and entities have agreed to recognize Bitcoin makes it difficult to ignore its potential as currency (albeit novel). In this regard and within the *Shari'ah* context, it would be necessary to determine the relative weight to be given to the issue of approval by those in authority in the various countries where Bitcoin is banned vrs the the international acceptability of Bitcoin which would qualify it under custom—for it is becoming acceptable globally to use it as a medium of exchange. This analysis would be complicated by the fact that some authorities (countries) accept the use of Bitcoin while others do not. Furthermore, the use of the Internet makes this discussion a little more complex as the Internet has no real jurisdiction and thus consideration would have to be given to the fact that no single jurisdiction rules the Internet and so the question would be if country level ban can be justifiably transaction applied to an online transaction that operates with a system that has no jurisdiction (actually a touted feature of Bitcoin).

---

[17] Ghani, Hafiz Abdul (2011) "Urf-o-Adah (Custom and Usage) as a Source of Islamic Law," p. 183.

[18] *al-Tirmidhi* 1272.

Shari'ah Principles Under Which the Bitcoin Should Be Analyzed

Excessive Risk (Garar)

Excessive Risk or *Garar* is an important ethical concept in Islam, it is forbidden (*haram*) to undertake a transaction that involves *Garar*. It refers to any issue that, causes uncertainty to exist in a transaction based on either the object of trade itself or matters related to it in the transaction process, i.e., hidden information, price, quality, etc.[19] With regard to the risk inherent in the use of Bitcoin, there are a number of issues that need to be discussed. First and foremost is the risk to the user given in the case where government (authority) bans the use of Cryptocurrency. What would be the possible impact to the wealth of the owners of these Cryptocurrency, these issue and potential action of governments to ensure the ban they have placed on Cryptocurrency are in the early days yet and serious consideration need to be given to its potential ramification. Secondly, there is the issue of the peer-to-peer network that forms the system creating and managing the Cryptocurrency. The dangers in the online work are myriad—from the Distributed Denial of Service, which is a cyberattack where a server is intentionally bombarded with too much requests to deal with and hence fails to be responsive.[20] It is noteworthy though that recent advances in blockchain technology where users across networks rent out their services to create the power needed to compute and create blockchains may be the answer to solving the Distributed Denial of Service attacks.

Due to lack of a central regulator, some risks associated with traditional transactions are higher with Cryptocurrency, as there is no regulator, what happens in a blockchain cannot be resolved as it is with regulated transactions.[21] Some of these issues are, spoofing payment information and phishing, hacking a payment gateway,[22] user address error,[23] loss of

---

[19] Akhter Uddin, Mohammed (2015) "Principles of Islamic Finance, Riba, Gharar and Maysir," p. 4.

[20] Jenkinson, Gareth (2017) "How DDOS Attacks Affects Bitcoin Exchanges."

[21] Malanov, Alexey (2017) "Problems and Risks of Cryptocurrencies."

[22] Ibid.

[23] Ibid.

a wallet file,[24] insecure initial coin offering (ICO)[25] and spoofing of a user address.[26] Combined, these issues total risk factors must be analyzed in terms of the concept of *Garar* to determine whether the weighted risk of using Cryptocurrency in light of these potential risk is excessive or not.

Gambling

Gambling (*Maysir*) relates to all games of chance where outcome cannot be predetermined. The Qur'an categorically condemns gambling when it says:

> They ask you about wine and gambling. Say, "In them is great sin and [yet, some] benefit for people. But their sin is greater than their benefit." And they ask you what they should spend. Say, "The excess [beyond needs]." Thus Allah makes clear to you the verses [of revelation] that you might give thought.[27]

The *Qur'an* further states that:

> O you who have believed, indeed, intoxicants, gambling, [sacrificing on] stone alters [to other than Allah], and divining arrows are but defilement from the work of Satan, so avoid it that you may be successful.[28]

> Satan only wants to cause between you animosity and hatred through intoxicants and gambling and to avert you from the remembrance of Allah and from prayer. So will you not desist?[29]

This categorical condemnation of gambling is the basis[30] for which some scholars have ruled against the use of Cryptocurrency since the process of mining in order to create a transaction register in the blockchain involves a process akin to mining.

---

[24] Ibid.

[25] Ibid.

[26] Ibid.

[27] *al-Qur'an* 2:219.

[28] *al-Qur'an* 5:91.

[29] *al-Qur'an* 5:92.

[30] Mufti Abu-Bakr, Mohammed (2017) "Shari'ah Analysis of Bitcoin, Cryptocurrency and Blockchain," p. 17.

The data mining process by the miners in the Cryptocurrency system invests a lot of money and resources in running computer programs that aim to solve as much cryptic code as possible in the transaction blocks in order to create a successful registry by creating Bitcoins and be paid a share of the Bitcoin value of the transaction completed.[31]

The process of creating the block-chain through mining is one of the most critical matters that need to be reviewed in order for Cryptocurrency to be to gain Shari'ah approval for the process clearly has characteristics of gambling and unfair business practice. There is no exact science to determine who can decipher the cryptic code, it is a clear game of chance by those who have invested in the resources to run the codes that attempt to decipher the cryptic code and thus succeed in solving the puzzle and be paid a commission of the value of the Bitcoin transaction. Solving by chance is an instance of gambling and this clearly is a case of the gambling that is condemned by the *Qur'an* as shown by the verses quoted above. Furthermore, this mining process also goes against other ethical considerations of Islam among these, the *Qur'an* states:

> Give full measure and do not be of those who cause loss. And weigh with an even balance.[32]

> And give full measure when you measure, and weigh with an even balance. That is the best [way] and best in result.[33]

> Woe to those who give less [than due], Who, when they take a measure from people, take in full. But if they give by measure or by weight to them, they cause loss. Do they not think that they will be resurrected, For a tremendous Day - The Day when mankind will stand before the Lord of the worlds?[34]

In light of the above verses and with regard to gambling which always leads to some losing while others gain, the mining that causes loss as people are encouraged to invest money and resources with the hope of

---

[31] Marjan, Mohammed (2017) "Shari'ah Analysis of Cryptocurrency, Bitcoin," Presented at the Shari'ah Fintech Forum (SFF), Hilton Hotel, Petaling Jaya.

[32] *al-Qur'an* 26:181–182.

[33] *Qur'an* 17:35.

[34] *Qur'an* 83:1–6.

making returns, but these returns are based on speculation and chance, thus in the end many investors in mining do not get rewarded for the effort and money the invested that facilitates the very survival of the system upon which the creation of Bitcoins is based, the peer-to-peer network. Now given the strong wording of the *Qur'an* as regards creating loss and not giving what is due, it is of a necessity that scholars would question the suitability of this aspect of Cryptocurrency while considering whether it is acceptable from an Islamic perspective. One may say that the miners acquiesced to participate knowing very well that they may not be successful, but then that is the essence of the *Qur'anic* injunction against gambling, to preserve wealth and not to risk it in a process through which one can unfairly lose that wealth.

Monopoly

Monopoly is another issue that Islam preaches against, the prophet of Islam preached against various forms of monopoly.[35] The issue of monopoly is has cropped up because as the value of Bitcoin continues to increase thereby making mining a very lucrative business, some very powerful and wealthy entities are investing considerable amount of money into powerful and expensive computers that are increasingly muscling out smaller players in the industry.[36] This issue on monopoly is linked to risk, gambling and unfair practices. With regard to risk, strong firms that control the most powerful machines can skew the success rate in their favor and such power, industry experts say can lead these companies to determine the future of Bitcoin.[37] These concerns need to be investigated critically as the wealth of a considerable number of people is currently invested in Cryptocurrency and any unfair practices can lead to the destruction of the wealth of people and families. As the protection on wealth and the protection of public interest are key among the ethical concerns that Islam cares about, this issue will factor into scholarly discussions on the use of Cryptocurrency.

---

[35] Ali Sulaiman, M. A. B., Hisam, Mohammed W., and Sanyal, Shouvik (2014) "Ethical Business Practices in Islam," SMS VARANASI, vol. VI, no. 2, p. 24.

[36] Roberts, Jeff John (2017) "Does Bitcoin Have a Mining Monopoly Problem?" *Fortune*, http://fortune.com/2017/08/25/bitcoin-mining/.

[37] Ibid.

Another aspect of the issue of monopoly is that, it should be analyzed it the two technical matters of the total amount of Bitcoins that can be created and control of how quickly the monies are created. Does the systems' control of these factors amount to a monopoly within the context of the system and does this feed create an artificial strength for the value of Bitcoin in terms of demand and supply? Some business transactions will continue forever, why does the currency have a finite life?

Green Tech—Public Good

Another important matter that needs be considered within the ethical framework of Islam and with regard to Cryptocurrency is the issue of environmental friendliness of managing Cryptocurrency. The environment is for all of humanity and now more than ever humanity has a need to protect the environment. This very reason among others is the reason why ethical finance is gaining popularity around the work, and there is no wonder that Islamic Finance forms one of the three sectors of ethical finance.[38]

Issues related to the general public good and thus protection of the environment is of utmost importance within the Islamic Ethical Framework. In Islam, it is taught that *Allah (swt)* created the world and all the creatures in it with their functions based on an intricate balance,[39] and man must strive to keep this balance. It is in this regard that the concerns about the enormous power need to manage Bitcoin, one that is estimated to soon equal the amount of energy consumed by the USA,[40] must be taken seriously.

China, which uses coal power plants, being the home of significant Bitcoin mining,[41] it is not difficult to understand why there is a need to worry about the consequences of such power consumption—it will have a direct correlation with the use of coal which is dangerous for the environment. The cost of Bitcoin mining to the environment and by

---

[38] Thomson Reuters Responsible Finance Report (2015) The Emerging Convergence of SRI, ESG and Islamic Finance.

[39] Izzi deen, Mawil Y. (2005) "Islamic Environmental Ethics, Law, and Society."

[40] Shane, Daniel (2017) "Bitcoin Boom May Be a Disaster for the Environment," http://money.cnn.com/2017/12/07/technology/bitcoin-energy-environment/index.html.

[41] Ibid.

extension to worldwide public safety must be considered and worked on to ensure that there are not disproportionate adverse effect to the environment because of the power consumption needed to manage Cryptocurrency.

Corruption

Another important matter that needs be considered within the ethical framework of Islam and with regard to Cryptocurrency is the issue that the lack of regulation and government control or oversight has made Cryptocurrency a means for corrupt people to easily facilitate their practices and thus leading to an increase in socially harmful practices.[42] That some research estimate that almost half of all Bitcoin transactions are related to illegal activity is very worrying and thus a critical look at the accuracy of such reports and attendant action, should the report prove to be is needed. Given that the crimes being mentioned as being facilitated through Cryptocurrency are very serious crimes to society, Islamic ethical considerations would not look favorably at Cryptocurrency. Crimes such as such as hacks, money laundering and the trading of drugs and illegal pornography[43] are among the crimes that Cryptocurrency is being used to aid and such being the case, if proven, the case for Cryptocurrency as an unregulated currency would suffer because of the weight of crime to the value proposition of digital currency.

CURRENT STATUS

Despite the growth of Cryptocurrency is significant, there are many factors at play that need to settle before a proper trend for the digital currencies that are being introduced can be properly assessed, at least from the ethical perspective. Within the *Shari'ah* sphere, there is no doubt there a lot of work needs to be done before a clear direction for status of Cryptocurrency as we know it will be arrived at. At the moment, both governments and religious bodies have given

---

[42] Sulleyman, Aatif (2018) "Bitcoin Price Is so High Because Criminals Are Using It for Illegal Trades, Research Suggests," *Independent*, https://www.independent.co.uk/life-style/gadgets-and-tech/news/bitcoin-price-fall-criminals-blockchain-anonymous-cryptocurrency-zcash-monero-dash-a8174716.html.

[43] Ibid.

contradictory positions on the use of Cryptocurrency. As mentioned earlier some governments, just like some clerics have banned the use of Cryptocurrency, while other governments and clerics have approved the use of the currencies.

Cryptocurrencies, as we are using them now, can be said to be a new phenomenon and thus there is the need for time to properly study it and thus come out with more accurate positions on its use or otherwise from the Islamic perspective. The technological complexity involved in the creation and management of Cryptocurrencies are not easy matters to be understood by *Shari'ah* experts[44] as their expertise will generally not include complicated computer technologies and how they work. Of course, *Shari'ah* experts can seek the help of computer technology experts to help them understand the issues related to the creation and management of cryptocurrencies. It is telling that major religious bodies like the Islamic *Fiqh* Academy are among those are yet to make a pronouncement on the matter of Cryptocurrencies.

THE WAY FORWARD

One of the criticisms of Cryptocurrencies is that they have no intrinsic value[45] and this is a potential value from an Islamic perspective. There were in the past efforts at creating e-payment systems that met Islamic requirement of being linked to assets with intrinsic value.[46] Recent efforts are being made to create Cryptocurrencies that are more in line with Islamic Ethical Framework. Once such effort is by OneGram in the United Arab Emirates.[47] OneGram ties it Cryptocurrency to physical gold and by that means ensures that the intrinsic value of its Cryptocurrency. Laudable us that may be, there are more weighty issues to be dealt with, without which the effort would not make much of a difference.

---

[44]Business and Economy (2018) Al Jazeera, "Islam and Cryptocurrency, Halal or Not Halal?"

[45]Marjan, Mohammed (2017) "Shari'ah Analysis of Cryptocurrency, Bitcoin," Presented at the Shari'ah Fintech Forum (SFF), Hilton Hotel, Petaling Jaya.

[46]e-dinar.com.

[47]Business and Economy (2018) Al Jazeera, "Islam and Cryptocurrency, Halal or Not Halal?"

The first of these weighty issues is that of gambling, this is very much condemned by the *Qur'an* and so there is the need for the Islamic Finance industry to look into the matter and have the religious scholars give a strong ruling on whether the mining process is considered gambling that should be avoided or otherwise. This issue is at the core of acceptability of Cryptocurrency as if the mining process is deemed to be gambling, then there it would be difficult to accept the current form of the Cryptocurrency as being in conformity with Islamic Ethics and thus Islamic law. The issues of authority (not necessarily central authority), but governments and their position on the use of otherwise of Cryptocurrency, must also be tackled. Government action can cause a lot of problems to users of the currency and insofar as a proper consensus that gives confidence to the consumer is not reached, the acceptability of Cryptocurrency from the point of view of Islamic Ethics will suffer some credibility.

RECOMMENDATIONS

The main recommendation from the research done is that there must be significant effort by reputable Islamic scholars and institutions to put more effort into analyzing the issues relating to Islamic ethical concerns of using Cryptocurrency with an aim to giving clarity on those matters so that they can ease the decision by Muslims and ethically minded people on how to use or not to use Cryptocurrency.

There are many gray areas and issues that need prioritization to help get some clarity. For example in the case of central authority vis-a-vis custom, the fact the many people and entities around the world are now accustomed to trading Cryptocurrency. Does the general acceptability without central control outweigh the need for central control or vice versa?

CONCLUSION

Cryptocurrency is gaining currency and clearly have some benefits, benefits that include ease of transacting business that is in line with Islamic ethics as *Allah (swt)* desires ease for HIS creation. But there are many issues that have led to contradictory rulings by *Shari'a* scholars and thus leaves ethical consumers confused. The issues that are causing confusion must be ironed out so that the Cryptocurrency industry's status within the Islamic Ethical Framework would be appropriately situated. Is it *Halal* or *Haram*? The Islamic Finance industry has a duty to perform in working to develop systems that ease the life of people and thus fulfill Islamic financial ethics and delivers well to the people.

REFERENCES

Acheson, Noelle (2018) "How Bitcoin Mining Works."

Akhter Uddin, Mohammed (2015) "Principles of Islamic Finance, Riba, Gharar and Maysir." p. 4.

Ali Sulaiman, M. A. B., Hisam, Mohammed W., and Sanyal, Shouvik (2014) "Ethical Business Practices in Islam." SMS VARANASI, vol. VI, no. 2, p. 24.

Al Muwatta 1614.

al-Qur'an 3:110.

Ashok, India, BitCoin? Top Imam Says Bitcoin Forbidden Under Islam, Compares It to Gambling. https://www.ibtimes.co.uk/bitcoin-fatwa-top-imam-says-cryptocurrency-forbidden-under-islam-compares-it-gambling-1653529.

Business and Economy (2018) Al Jazeera, "Islam and Cryptocurrency, Halal or Not Halal?"

Cryptocurrency Market Capitalizations. https://coinmarketcap.com.

D'Alfonso, Alexander, Langer, Peter, and Vandelis, Zintis (2016) "The Future of Cryptocurrency: An Investor's Comparison of Bitcoin and Ethereum."

e-dinar.com.

Ghani, Hafiz Abdul (2011) "Urf-o-Adah (Custom and Usage) as a Source of Islamic Law." p. 183.

"Islam and Cryptocurrency, Halal or Not Halal?" Al Jazeera. https://www.aljazeera.com/news/2018/04/islam-cryptocurrency-halal-halal-180408145004684.html.

Izzi deen, Mawil Y. (2005) "Islamic Environmental Ethics, Law, and Society."

Jenkinson, Gareth (2017) "How DDOS Attacks Affects Bitcoin Exchanges."

Malanov, Alexey (2017) "Problems and Risks of Cryptocurrencies."

Marjan, Mohammed (2017) "Shari'ah Analysis of Cryptocurrency, Bitcoin." Presented at the Shari'ah Fintech Forum (SFF), Hilton Hotel, Petaling Jaya.

Mufti Abu-Bakr, Mohammed (2017a) "Shari'ah Analysis of Bitcoin, Cryptocurrency and Blockchain."

Mufti Abu-Bakr, Mohammed (2017b) "Shari'ah Analysis of Bitcoin, Cryptocurrency and Blockchain." p. 16.

Mufti Abu-Bakr, Mohammed (2017c) "Shari'ah Analysis of Bitcoin, Cryptocurrency and Blockchain." p. 17.

Roberts, Jeff John (2017) "Does Bitcoin Have a Mining Monopoly Problem?" *Fortune*. http://fortune.com/2017/08/25/bitcoin-mining/.

Shane, Daniel (2017) "Bitcoin Boom May Be a Disaster for the Environment." http://money.cnn.com/2017/12/07/technology/bitcoin-energy-environment/index.html.

Sulleyman, Aatif (2018) "Bitcoin Price Is so High Because Criminals Are Using It for Illegal Trades, Research Suggests." *Independent*. https://www.independent.co.uk/life-style/gadgets-and-tech/news/bitcoin-price-fall-criminals-blockchain-anonymous-cryptocurrency-zcash-monero-dash-a8174716.html.

Thailand First Country to Ban Digital Currency Bitcoin. http://investvine.com/thailand-first-country-to-ban-digital-currency-bitcoin/.

Thomson Reuters Responsible Finance Report (2015) "The Emerging Convergence of SRI, ESG and Islamic Finance."

Tirmidhi Hadith 1272.

Uzair, Mohammed (1982) "Central Banking Operations in an Interest Free Banking System."

CHAPTER 11

Standard *Shari'ah* Regulatory Frameworks of Cryptocurrency

Mohd Ma'sum Billah, Asma Hakimah Ab Halim and Aminurasyed Mahpop

The Position of Cryptocurrency in the *Shari'ah*

Scholars have mixed views on the validity of cryptocurrency in the *Shari'ah*. Among them, one establishes the basis of comparison with the application of minted coins based on custom *('Urf)*. Mufti Faraz viewed that, "minted coins served no other purpose but as a medium of exchange from inception due to the custom *('Urf)* being implemented and imposed by the government. In such an instance, the natural process of usage *(ta'amul)* and forming a habit is fast tracked by legislation."[1] Whether the same rule can be applied to cryptocurrency? He critically

---

[1] Faraz Adam, Bitcoin: Shari'ah Compliant? Available at http://darulfiqh.com/wp-content/uploads/2017/08/Research-Paper-on-Bitcoin-Mufti-Faraz-Adam.pdf. Accessed on 10 March 2018, p. 17.

M. M. Billah (✉)
Finance, Insurance, Fintech and Investment, Islamic Economics Institute, King Abdul Aziz University, Jeddah, Kingdom of Saudi Arabia
URL: http://www.drmasumbillah.blogspot.com

A. H. A. Halim · A. Mahpop
Faculty of Law, Universiti Kebangsaan Malaysia, Bangi Selangor, Malaysia

© The Author(s) 2019
M. M. Billah (ed.), *Halal Cryptocurrency Management*,
https://doi.org/10.1007/978-3-030-10749-9_11

165

reasoned that "cryptocurrencies would not fit into the classical types of money."[2] His view is based on the different types of money identified, which should comprise of natural money (*thaman khilqi*) such as gold and silver, and artificial and customary money (*al-thamanurfi*).[3] *Al-Thamanurfi* is divided into two: The first one is the commodity money which has intrinsic value but cannot be used for other functions, and this type of money also does not have "*intrinsic monetary value (thamani-yyah)*." The second one is fiat money and also "has no intrinsic monetary value and cannot function more except being a medium of exchange."[4]

He further argued that "cryptocurrencies would not fit into classical types of money due to non-existence of natural money (*thamankhilqi*) nor customary money (*thaman 'urfi*)."[5] Therefore, they are not qualified as natural money (*thamankhilqi*) because the cryptocurrencies "do not possess intrinsic monetary value (*thamaniyyah*)."[6] He reasoned as such:

> Cryptocurrencies are merely digits. Cryptocurrencies are not commodity money because they do not have any intrinsic value, whereas commodity money has intrinsic value and serves an alternative function besides being a medium of exchange...cryptocurrencies do not have an 'Ayn (origin)[7] and nor are they ever sought for image and corpus.[8]

Another researcher[9] analyzed in the aspect of *Maqasid* (objectives), that is, the purpose of *Shari'ah* to preserve the rights of people specifically in the preservation of wealth.[10] Deliberating the consequence of using this medium of exchange in the transaction, he justified that this transaction

---

[2] Faraz Adam, p. 45.

[3] *Al-Thaman 'urfi* means artificial and customary money—Mufti Faraz, p. 12.

[4] Faraz Adam, p. 45.

[5] Ibid.

[6] Ibid.

[7] 'Ayn means corpus- Mufti Faraz, p. 45

[8] What Does 'Nor Are They Ever Sought for Image and Corpus Mean?—Cryptocurrencies Are Merely Digits: Faraz Adam, p. 45

[9] Luqman Nurhisam is a postgraduate student at Universitas Islam Negeri Sunan Kalijaga Yogyakarta, Indonesia.

[10] Luqman Nurhisam, Bitcoin Dalam Kacamata Hukum Islam, *Ar-Raniry: International Journal of Islamic Studies*, vol. 4, no. 1, Juni 2017, 184

could harm the contracting parties due to the aspect of uncertainties and creation of money without clear supervision. He views that the responsibility to create currency is under the authority of government. This is the aspect of *Maslahah* (public interest) in the economy system that should be preserved in a country. In addition, this medium of exchange also is not produced by the regulators; for example, in Indonesia, the Circulation by the Bank of Indonesia (No:16/06/Dkom) stated that bitcoin is not recognized as circulated money in the country."[11]

Based on these views, it is evidenced that for the cryptocurrency to be regarded as legal and *halal* by complying the aspect of *Maslahah* (public interest), it should be recognized by the authority, issued by the authority, and should also be regulated to avoid harmful consequences in the society. The issue of cryptocurrency as "virtual currency" should be addressed as it becomes the means to facilitate the transaction in the contemporary world. The approaches by selected countries will be discussed.

REGULATORY FRAMEWORKS OF CRYPTOCURRENCY

Hassan and Yusoff define the regulatory frameworks as:

> the collection of important rules, standards, processes, and institutions, which defines the marketplace within which an industry operates. It involves the application of rules that acts as a guide to the acceptable standards of conduct within the area being regulated. The purpose of the regulatory framework is to protect the consumer, to ensure fair restrictions on competition, to maintain appropriate standards of conduct …, and to provide sufficient redress mechanisms for unhealthy conduct.[12]

How cryptocurrency can be regulated depends on the nature of transaction in the countries. Therefore, it is pertinent to analyze how different countries deal with this issue, and what are the legal and regulatory frameworks governing this subject.

---

[11] Luqman Nurhisam, Bitcoin Dalam Kacamata Hukum Islam, *Ar-Raniry: International Journal of Islamic Studies*, vol. 4, no. 1, Juni 2017, 183.

[12] R. Hassan and A. Yusoff, 'The Outlook of the Malaysian Islamic Capital Market' (2009) 3 MLJ cxvii; [2009] 3 MLJA 117.

MALAYSIA

In Malaysia, the law that addressing the issue of cryptocurrency is stated in Policy Document on Cryptocurrency titled Anti-Money Laundering and Counter Financing of Terrorism (AML/CFT)-Digital Currencies (Sector 6).

> This document is applicable to reporting institutions carrying on the following activities as listed in Paragraph 25 of the First Schedule to the AMLA: (a) activities carried out by any person who provides any or any combination of the following services: (i) exchanging digital currency for money; (ii) exchanging money for digital currency; or (iii) exchanging one digital currency for another digital currency, whether in the course of carrying on a digital currency exchange business or otherwise.[13]

This clause indicates that Malaysia regards the transaction in digital currency as risky transaction as it might involve in legal activities. This Policy Document is based on the definition made by the Financial Action Task Force (FATF) in the released report entitled "Virtual Currencies- Key definitions and Potential AM/CFT Risks."[14] The issuance of this Policy, however, does not indicate that the bank recognized this transaction. This is reiterated by the bank in the Policy Document as follows:

> ...digital currencies are not recognised as legal tender in Malaysia. Members of the public are therefore advised to undertake the necessary due diligence and assessment of risks involved in dealing in digital currencies or with entities providing services associated with digital currencies.[15]

Malaysia promotes a significant transparency in dealing with digital currencies in order to "protect the integrity of the financial system and strengthen incentives to prevent their abuse of illegal activities."[16] Therefore, it is clearly stated in the Policy Document that,

> any person offering services to exchange digital currencies either from or to fiat money, or from or to another digital currency is subject to

[13]http://www.bnm.gov.my/index.php?ch=57&pg=538&ac=680&bb=file.
[14]Para 1.2 of Policy Document.
[15]Para 1.6 of Policy Document.
[16]Para 1.4 of Policy Document.

obligations under the Anti-Money Laundering, Anti-Terrorism Financing and Proceeds of Unlawful Activities Act 2001 (AMLA) as a reporting institution pursuant to First Schedule of AMLA.[17]

The Policy Document further provides:

> This document is applicable to reporting institutions carrying on the following activities as listed in Paragraph 25 of the First Schedule to the AMLA:
>
> (a) Activities carried out by any person who provides any or any combination of the following services:
>
> (i) Exchanging digital currency for money;
> (ii) Exchanging money for digital currency; or
> (iii) Exchanging one digital currency for another digital currency,
>
> Whether in the course of carrying on a digital currency exchange business or otherwise.[18]

Despite the list provided in the types of services in digital currencies, the bank emphasized:

> Nothing in this document shall be taken to indicate the Bank's licensing, authorization, endorsement or validation of digital currencies or any entities involved in providing services associated with digital currencies.[19]

It is further stated in the Policy Document that:

> Accordingly, dealings in digital currencies are not covered by prudential and market conduct requirements applicable to licensed and authorised activities, or by establishment avenues for redress in the event of complaints or losses and damages incurred by parties dealing in digital currencies.[20]

---

[17] Para 1.5 of Policy Document.
[18] Para 4.1 of Policy Document.
[19] Ibid.
[20] Para 1.7 of Policy Document.

JAPAN

Japan reaction to the issue of digital currencies is based on the MtGox Failure and the Financial Action Task Force (FATF) Guidance in 2015. The recommendation made for all virtual currency (VC) exchangers be registered or licensed and be under the same scrutiny as financial institutions. Amendments made to the "Act on Settlement of Funds" and the "Act on Prevention of Transfer of Criminal Proceeds" (together with the ancillary amendments to the relevant orders for enforcement, cabinet office ordinances, etc., the *Virtual Currency Act* or the "Act" hereunder) came into effect on 1 April 2017 (the "Effective Date").[21]

Therefore, virtual currency is recognized through the issuance of the Law on Guidance Note on the Japanese Virtual Currency Legislation. The legislation also highlights the need for registration. The law defines the virtual currency and the types of business involved. This Guidance provides the definition of virtual currency in two types:

> The type 1 VC: financial value (recorded by way of electronic means in the electronic devices etc., excluding and fiat currency/currencies (of Japan or otherwise) and assets denominated in any such fiat currency, which may be used to pay the price in exchange for the goods purchased or rent or the services received to/against unspecified person/persons for such goods or services received to/against unspecified person/persons for such goods or services and which may e purchased from and/or sold to the unspecified person/persons;

> The type II VC: Financial value recorded by way of electronic means in the electronic devices etc., excluding any fiat currency/currencies (of Japan or otherwise) and assets denominated in any such fiat currency, which may be exchanged, as against unspecified person/persons, with any such financial value as set out in paragraph (i) above and which may be transferred via electronic data processing system.[22]

---

[21] Guidance Note on the Japanese Virtual Currency Legislation and Overview on Registration Requirement Thereunder. Available at http://www.so-law.jp/wp-content/uploads/2017/07/Japanese_VC_Act_and_Registration-Overview_170704.pdf. Accessed on 30 March 2018.

[22] Ibid.

While the virtual currency business includes:

> Under the VC Act, the virtual currency exchange business (the "VC Exchange Business") means any of the following acts carried out as a business:
>
> (i) Sale and purchase of VC (i.e. exchange between VC and a fiat currency), or exchange a VC to another VC;
> (ii) An intermediary, brokerage or agency service for the acts described in above (i); and
> (iii) Management (custody) of a fiat currency or VC on behalf of the users/recipient in relation to the acts described in above (i) and (ii).[23]

Regulator's attitude in Japan is friendly to VC exchange as the government wants to promote Fintech and new businesses. Series of discussions between Japan Financial Services Authority with VC Exchanges produced positive impact with the set up of the Act and the surrounding regulations that could facilitate the transaction in VC.

CANADA

In Canada, the acceptance to digital currency transaction is depending on the types and level of transaction. The Canadian Securities Administration, for example, recognized cryptocurrencies offered by organizations conducting business within Canada or Canadian investors as securities or derivatives for the purpose of the Canadian regulatory framework.[24] However, the characteristic of each cryptocurrency needs to be reviewed. The cryptocurrency "most likely to be considered a security" if the "cryptocurrency is tied intrinsically to a business, or involves an investment contract."[25] In the case of cryptocurrency "is traded on

---

[23] Ibid.

[24] David Ramm, Jack Shawdon, and Philip Stone, A Guide to International Regulation of Cryptocurrencies. Available at https://www.morganlewis.com/-/media/files/publication/outside-publication/article/2018/law360_a-guide-to-international-regulation-of-cryptocurrencies_30jan18.ashx?la=en&hash=253F0508F41AE9B2731A3F24EDB0B-1BF92454C16. Accessed on 30 March 2018, p. 3.

[25] Ibid.

an exchange active in Canada, the exchange may be considered an alternative trading system. This transaction need to seek recognition by the Canadian regulator."[26]

In banking practices, Financial Consumer Agency of Canada stated that digital currencies are not legal tender in Canada. They are based on the definition of legal tender in *The Currency Act* as banknotes issued by the Bank of Canada under the Bank of Canada Act, and coins issued under the *Royal Canadian Mint Act*. Therefore, digital currencies are not supported by any government or central authority such as the Bank of Canada.[27]

GERMAN

The German Financial Services Authority "BaFin" recognized cryptocurrencies as financial instruments; however, it opined that "the act of merely using cryptocurrencies as cash or deposit money does not require authorization."[28] In addition, BaFin has also confirmed that;

"A service provider or supplier may receive payment for goods / services in a cryptocurrency without carrying out banking business or financial services."[29] In the case where "the activities could constitute or are similar enough to broking services," the authorization is still a requirement.[30] There are other several transactions also require authorization such as "where a mining pool offers shares in proceeds, or additionally provides services for the creation/maintenance of a market, authorization may be required."[31] In addition, "the European Securities and Markets Authority (ESMA) issued a statement on Nov. 13, 2017, reminding companies

---

[26] Ibid.

[27] Digital Currency. Available at https://www.canada.ca/en/financial-consumer-agency/services/payment/digital-currency.html. Accessed on 30 March 2018.

[28] David Ramm, Jack Shawdon, and Philip Stone, A Guide to International Regulation of Cryptocurrencies. Available at https://www.morganlewis.com/-/media/files/publication/outside-publication/article/2018/law360_a-guide-to-international-regulation-of-cryptocurrencies_30jan18.ashx?la=en&hash=253F0508F41AE-9B2731A3F24EDB0B1BF92454C16. Accessed on 30 March 2018, p. 3.

[29] Ibid.

[30] Ibid.

[31] Ibid.

considering an ICO to have regard for applicable regulatory requirements. ESMA confirmed that cryptocurrencies may constitute financial instruments or securities, and companies will need to analyze the features of the cryptocurrency and the structure of the ICO to determine whether key legislation applies, such as: the Prospectus Directive, Markets in Financial Instruments Directive and the Alternative Investment Fund Managers Directive."[32]

United Kingdom

UK government take monitoring approach to cryptocurrency. As stated in the *Her Majesty's Revenue and Customs* Internal Manuals:

HMRC will continue to monitor the current and developing uses of cryptocurrencies and the block-chain technology that underpins them. Guidance may need to be amended to reflect these developments or changes in the regulatory environment in which cryptocurrencies operate. As cryptocurrencies are not recognized national currencies, transactions in which they function as consideration given or received are 'barter transactions'. There is guidance on barter transactions at CG78310: this guidance is written in terms of non-sterling currency but is applicable to cryptocurrencies.[33]

This approach is taken based on the understanding of the transaction of cryptocurrencies that;

generally operate via a peer to peer networks and independent of any central authority or bank, where all functions such as issue (creation), transaction processing and verification are managed collectively by this network.[34]

The legal and regulatory status of cryptocurrency is still ongoing as this transaction is evolving. In the perspective of taxation, the law will analyze the operation of each cryptocurrency as each of it;

---

[32] Ibid.

[33] Introduction and Computation: Chargeable Assets: Intangible Assets: Cryptocurrencies. https://www.gov.uk/hmrc-internal-manuals/capital-gains-manual/cg12100. Accessed on 30 March 2018.

[34] Ibid.

"operates according to a pre-defined and collectively agreed set of rules. As such each case will need to be considered on the basis of its own individual facts and circumstances. The relevant legislation and case law will be applied to determine the correct tax treatment."[35] *For example;* "Where the nature of the cryptocurrency means they are dealt in without identifying the particular unit of currency being sold then they should be pooled as per TCGA92/S104(3)(ii). If TCGA92/S104(3)(ii) applies then the holder of the cryptocurrency will have a single pooled asset for Capital Gains Tax purposes that will increase or decrease with each acquisition, part disposal or disposal."[36]

UNITED ARAB EMIRATES

A corporate legal expert Arjun Kharpal observed that the approach made by regulators in Abu Dhabi in addressing the issue of cryptocurrency whereby, they; "*are beginning to regulate initial coin offerings (ICOs) — the rapidly growing way that cryptocurrency start-ups are raising money — but have warned of the "many risks" involved.*"[37]

In line with this effort, for the first time, Abu Dhabi's *Financial Services Regulatory Authority* (FSRA) released guidelines on ICOs and virtual currencies. Based on the guidelines; "*companies wishing to execute an ICO must approach the FSRA to see whether it will fall under the body's regulation. Companies will also have to publish a prospectus, just like a firm would for an initial public offering (IPO) on the stock market. Any market intermediaries, or secondary market operators dealing with ICOs must be approved by the FSRA.*"[38]

Notwithstanding, all ICO may be regulated for example;

"if a token is issued as part of an ICO may not constitute an "offer of securities, therefore, it will remain unregulated.[39] In this situation, the investors should beware before committing money."[40] The risk of fraud and

---

[35] Ibid.

[36] Ibid.

[37] Arjun Kharpal, Abu Dhabi Regulates ICOs for Cryptocurrency Funding. Available at https://www.cnbc.com/2017/10/09/abu-dhabi-regulates-icos-for-cryptocurrency-company-funding.html. Accessed on 30 March 2018.

[38] Ibid.

[39] Ibid.

[40] Ibid.

loss of capital is therefore significantly higher for example in the case where the "issuer promises extremely high investment returns that are disproportionately high relative to those generally available in the market."[41]

It is submitted that in fact the chapter of Cryptocurrencies in Abu Dhabi is seen as commodities, but not as a currency, and thus, they remain unregulated.[42]

HALAL CRYPTOCURRENCY—POSSIBLE RECOMMENDATIONS

The producer of the cryptocurrency should be from the sovereign authority, government, or central bank. The inventor of a cryptocurrency shall be known to avoid any element that likely to lead to higher risk or fraud with uncertainty (*Garar*). Therefore, the approach made by Malaysia regulator in promoting transparency is one of the best approaches that could be adopted in preparing the *Shari'ah* regulatory framework of cryptocurrency. The aspect of transparency for reporting institutions includes the declaration to the bank. Section 7.1 provides the requirement for reporting institutions covered under Paragraph 4.1 of the Policy Document to declare its details to the Bank.[43] The adoption of risk-based application is also necessary in addressing the issue related to risk. In the Policy Document, there are three types of risk available.[44] The first risk is the risk assessment, whereby the reporting institutions must take appropriate steps to identify, asses, and understand their risk in relation to their customers, countries, or geographical areas and products, services. The second one is risk control and mitigation. These are the requirements for financial institutions to have policies, controls, and procedures to manage and mitigate money laundering risks that have been identified. The third one is risk profiling whereby the requirement of reporting institutions to conduct risk profiling on their customers. Silva suggested having;

> A solid compliance program, by adopting a compliance policy, due diligence of major customers, elaboration of forms such as know your

---

[41] Ibid.
[42] Ibid.
[43] Para 7.1 of the Policy Document.
[44] Para 8.0 of the Policy Document.

customer and reporting of information by the companies involved especially the companies that act as intermediaries in the transactions.[45]

CONCLUSION

In the rapid growth of cryptocurrency in the contemporary economic environment, several jurisdictions take diversified approaches in dealing with digitally designed cryptocurrency. There are jurisdictions that may apply defense mechanisms by introducing the law that could protect the involvement in the cryptocurrency platform; among them is Malaysia. Some jurisdictions strengthen their laws to facilitate this crypto-based cyberspace transaction. However, the issue of strengthening legal infrastructure of cryptocurrency is significant to ensure the investors in particular as well as the countries who venture in these platforms are protected under the law, and mitigate the risk of loss. A *Halal* cryptocurrency model is no exception; thus, it shall be a prerequisite for its operation to ensure that the establishment and operation of a cryptocurrency platform under the *Shari'ah* principles are regulated and duly guided by applicable laws, *Shari'ah* standard, objectives, manuals, policies, and guidelines within the *Maqasid al-Shari'ah*, which shall be closely monitored, screened through, and duly approved by a qualified *Shari'ah Advisory Board*.

REFERENCES

Arjun Kharpal. Abu Dhabi Regulates ICOs for Cryptocurrency Funding—But Warns of 'Many Risks'. Available at https://www.cnbc.com/2017/10/09/abu-dhabi-regulates-icos-for-cryptocurrency-company-funding.html. Accessed on 30 March 2018.

David Ramm, Jack Shawdon, and Philip Stone. A Guide to International Regulation of Cryptocurrencies. Available at https://www.morganlewis.com/-/media/files/publication/outside-publication/article/2018/law360_a-guide-to-international-regulation-of-cryptocurrencies_30jan18.ashx?la=en&hash=253F0508F41AE9B2731A3F24EDB0B1BF92454C16. Accessed on 30 March 2018.

---

[45] Doles Silva, Cryptocurrencies and International Regulation. Available at https://www.uncitral.org/pdf/english/congress/Papers_for_Congress/29-DOLES_SILVA-Cryptocurrencies_and_International_Regulation.pdf. Accessed on 30 March 2018.

Digital Currency. Available at https://www.canada.ca/en/financial-consumer-agency/services/payment/digital-currency.html. Accessed on 30 March 2018.

Digital Currency from Financial Consumer Agency of Canada. Available at https://www.canada.ca/en/financial-consumer-agency/services/payment/digital-currency.html. Accessed on 30 March 2018.

Doles Silva. Cryptocurrencies and International Regulation. Available at https://www.uncitral.org/pdf/english/congress/Papers_for_Congress/29-DOLES_SILVA-Cryptocurrencies_and_International_Regulation.pdf. Accessed on 30 March 2018.

Guidance Note on the Japanese Virtual Currency Legislation and Overview on Registration Requirement Thereunder. Available at http://www.so-law.jp/wp-content/uploads/2017/07/Japanese_VC_Act_and_Registration-Overview_170704.pdf. Accessed on 30 March 2018.

Faraz Adam. Bitcoin: Shariah Compliant? Available at http://darulfiqh.com/wp-content/uploads/2017/08/Research-Paper-on-Bitcoin-Mufti-Faraz-Adam.pdf. Accessed on 10 March 2018.

Introduction and Computation: Chargeable Assets: Intangible assets: Cryptocurrencies. Available at https://www.gov.uk/hmrc-internal-manuals/capital-gains-manual/cg12100. Accessed on 30 March 2018.

Luqman Nurhisam. Bitcoin Dalam Kacamata Hukum Islam. *Ar-Raniry: International Journal of Islamic Studies*, vol. 4, no. 1, Juni 2017, 184.

New Payment Products and Systems: Mitigating the Risk of Finance's New Wild West. Available at https://application-production.cdn.ranenetwork.com/blog/wp-content/uploads/2016/02/24102341/GIC_NewPaymentProducts_TL_1013.ashx_.pdf. Accessed on 30 April 2018.

Revenue and Customs Brief 9. (2014). Bitcoin and Other Cryptocurrencies. Available at https://www.gov.uk/government/publications/revenue-and-customs-brief-9-2014-bitcoin-and-other-cryptocurrencies/revenue-and-customs-brief-9-2014-bitcoin-and-other-cryptocurrencies. Accessed on 30 March 2018.

CHAPTER 12

Existing Regulatory Frameworks of Cryptocurrency and the *Shari'ah* Alternative

Nafis Alam and Abdolhossein (Pejman) Zameni

Introduction

The financial system across the globe is going through a massive transformation from the traditional mode to the advanced use of technology and rapid financial innovation. The advent of buzzwords such as Financial Technology (FinTech) and cryptocurrency has changed the way we transact money and fulfill our financial needs. FinTech and digital currency such as Bitcoin and other altcoins have changed the financial landscape and have affected masses including Muslims. Given that, Islam as a religion treats money and banking from a different perspective where users and providers of the financial services have to adhere to

N. Alam (✉) · A. Zameni
Henley Business School,
University of Reading Malaysia, Iskandar Puteri, Malaysia
e-mail: n.alam@henley.edu.my

A. Zameni
e-mail: a.zameni@henley.edu.my

© The Author(s) 2019
M. M. Billah (ed.), *Halal Cryptocurrency Management*,
https://doi.org/10.1007/978-3-030-10749-9_12

the Islamic principles (Shari'ah), it is important to assess the impact of financial innovation from Shari'ah perspective. According to the study of *Pew Research Center* which is undertaken by Lipka and Hackett (2017), as of 2015, followers of Islam religion constitute 24.1% of the world's population or about 1.8 billion and expected to grow to nearly 3 billion by 2060. Since the Muslim population is and will be one of the largest future investor and spenders in physical and financial assets, it is imperative that any financial innovation such as cryptocurrency should adhere to the Shari'ah principles to have a legitimate and Islamic mode of payment and exchange.

Since the focus of the book is to delve deep into the halal cryptocurrency regulatory framework, this chapter will explore more how the existing regulatory framework of cryptocurrency is perceived in Islamic countries and what are the Shari'ah perspectives on the cryptocurrencies. The focus of the chapter is to look into the existing regulatory framework on cryptocurrencies among Muslim-dominated countries, it is important to highlight its geographical dispersion. As per the report by Desilver and Masci (2017), Muslims make up a majority of the population in 49 countries around the world. Sixty-two percentage of Muslims are living in Asia-Pacific region, with Indonesia having the largest number of Muslim population, of about 209 million (13% of the world's Muslims population) and India is in the second rank with 176 million Muslim population, which is just 14.4% of its overall population. Looking at the distribution of Muslim population from regional perspective, the highest concentration of Muslim is in the Middle East-North Africa (MENA) region which is roughly about 341 million (93% of total population), 30% in sub-Saharan Africa and 24% in the Asia-Pacific region (Desilver and Masci 2017). Table 12.1, shows the percentage of Muslim population in different countries by Pew Research Center.[1] As it is seen, the highest concentration of Muslim is mostly in MENA countries.

Table 12.1 categorizes the percentage of the Muslim population from a regional perspective. It is evident that majority of Muslims are from MENA and Central Asia (Table 12.2).

---

[1] http://www.pewresearch.org/download-datasets/.

Table 12.1 Percentage of Muslim population in different countries

>90%	>90%	>90%	>90%	>90%	>80%	>70%	>50%
Afghanistan	Niger	Mali	Turkmenistan	Tajikistan	Cocos Islands	Bahrain	Albania
Algeria	Pakistan	Mauritania	Uzbekistan	Tunisia	Guinea	Kazakhstan	Bosnia-Herzegovina
Azerbaijan	Palestinian Territories	Mayotte	Western Sahara	Turkey	Indonesia	Kuwait	Brunei
Bangladesh	Saudi Arabia	Morocco	Jordan	Gambia	Kyrgyzstan	Qatar	Burkina Faso
Comoros	Senegal	Yemen	Kosovo	Iran	Oman	Sierra Leone	Chad
Djibouti	Somalia	Maldives	Libya	Iraq	Syria	UAE	Lebanon
Egypt	Sudan						

Source Authors view

Table 12.2   Percentage of Muslim population by continent/region

>90%	>80%	>40%	>30%	>20%
Middle East-North Africa (MENA)	Central Asia	Africa	South Asia	Asia
			Sub-Saharan Africa	

Source Authors view

EXISTING REGULATORY FRAMEWORKS OF CRYPTOCURRENCY

Recently, cryptocurrencies and its legality as a form of money have sparked a heated debate in the financial world. Cryptocurrency is a form of digital money that is designed to be secure and, in many cases, anonymous. It is a currency associated with the Internet that uses cryptography, the process of converting legible information into a set of codes, to track purchases and transfers. Cryptography is used to secure the transactions and to control the creation of new *coins*. The first cryptocurrency to be created was Bitcoin back in 2009. Today there are over 1500 different types of cryptocurrencies, often referred to as Altcoins.

Regarding the cryptocurrencies, Bitcoin is one of the digital currencies among many others which have pioneered a new approach to tracking financial transactions. The underlying technology of digital currencies is called blockchain. Blockchain can record every transaction made in that currency in identical copies of a digital ledger that is shared among the currency's users (Trautman 2016). The essential difference between Bitcoin and earlier currencies is that Bitcoins can be owned by any individual, without permission from any bank or government (Yeoh 2017). This section tries to provide some overview and insight into existing regulatory frameworks on cryptocurrency, especially Bitcoin.

When we talk about the legal status of cryptocurrencies, our focus is on the most commonly used and traded Crypto Bitcoin. The legality of Bitcoin varies significantly from country to country. Some countries outrightly have banned the Bitcoin and announced it as illegal such as India, Indonesia, and Nepal. On the other hand, there are countries that have not banned it but don't have any view on it such as many European Union nations. The third category includes the countries that have accepted the Bitcoin and started explicitly trade with it such as Venezuela and Zimbabwe. It can be seen that acceptance or rejection of Bitcoin cannot be considered as a global acceptance and the usage varies

Table 12.3 Countries with highest relative potential for Bitcoin adoption

Ranking	Country (standardized)
1	Argentina
2	Venezuela, RB
3	Zimbabwe
4	Malawi
5	United States
6	Belarus
7	Nigeria
8	Congo, Dem. Rep.
9	Iceland
10	Iran, Islamic Rep.

Source Adopted from Hileman (2016)

according to the legal status as per the financial regulators of the countries. Some countries categorized cryptocurrencies differently and put it in different categories of money or medium of exchange and thus the applied regulation will differ as per the definition by the regulators. It is important to mention that there is a difference between virtual currency and electronic money, even though they are both offered in digital form. The major difference between the two is that electronic money is a digital form of a country's legal tender currency backed and issued by a central authority, while virtual currencies such as cryptocurrencies are not backed by any legal tender currency or central authority.

Along with the various uses of the cryptos, Bitcoin Market Potential Index (BMPI), consisting of the following ten countries having the "countries with highest relative potential for Bitcoin adoption" has been created (Hileman 2016) (Table 12.3).

Table 12.4 illustrates the list of countries with their legal stance toward cryptocurrency. As it is seen, some of the countries have accepted the cryptocurrency but some not yet, or announced it as an illegal mode of exchange.

The European Union (EU) does not have a definite legislation about the Bitcoin as a currency, but EU has mentioned that VAT/GST is not imposed on the conversion of traditional (fiat) currency to Bitcoin and vice versa. However, if Bitcoin is used to buy goods and services, the VAT/GST and other taxes like income tax still are applied to those transactions (The Law Library of Congress 2014).

In 2016, the European Commission received a proposal from The European Parliament to set up a task force to monitor virtual currencies

Table 12.4 List of countries with their legal stance toward cryptocurrency

Countries/Union	Legal	Countries/Union	Legal	Countries/Union	Legal	Countries/Union	Legal	Countries/Union	Illegal
EU	Y	South Korea	Y	Mexico	Y	Iceland	Y	**Algeria**	Y
Argentina	Y	Spain	Y	Morocco	Y	Hong Kong	Y	Bangladesh	Y
Australia	Y	Sweden	Y	Netherlands	Y	Hungary	Y	Bolivia	Y
Austria	Y	Switzerland	Y	New Zealand	Y	Saudi Arabia	Y	Cambodia	Y
Belgium	Y	Taiwan	Y	Japan	Y	Singapore	Y	Ecuador	Y
Bosnia and Herzegovina	Y	Thailand	Y	Jordan	Y	Germany	Y	India	Y
Brazil	Y	Trinidad and Tobago	Y	Kyrgyzstan	Y	Greece	Y	Indonesia	Y
Bulgaria	Y	Turkey	Y	Nicaragua	Y	Slovenia	Y	Macedonia	Y
Canada	Y	UAE	Y	Malaysia	Y	South Africa	Y	Nepal	Y
Chile	Y	UK	Y	Malta	Y	Romania	Y	Namibia	Y
Denmark	Y	Ukraine	Y	Italy	Y	Russia	Y	Pakistan	Y
Colombia	Y	US	Y	Jamaica	Y	Finland	Y	Iran	Y
Costa Rica	Y	Vietnam	Y	Lebanon	Y	France	Y	China	Y
Croatia	Y	Zimbabwe	Y	Lithuania	Y	Israel	Y		
Cyprus	Y	Nigeria	Y	Luxembourg	Y	Slovakia	Y		
Czech Republic	Y	Norway	Y	Estonia	Y	Poland	Y		
		Philippines	Y	Ireland	Y	Portugal	Y		

Source Authors view

in order to stop money laundering, and terrorism (News European Parliament 2016). Moreover, the European Commission also submitted a parallel proposal intended to prevent tax evasion practices by some countries and people as revealed in the Panama Papers (del Castillo 2016). European Union, in 2017, publicized that the proposal will involve cryptocurrency exchanges and cryptocurrency wallets to recognize doubtful movements (Coleman 2017). Interestingly, in March 2018, Andrea Enria, the chief executive of the European Banking Authority, with the view of not putting too much restriction on FinTech and financial innovation, proposed that we would be obtaining better results if we prevent banks and financial institutions from trading the digital currencies rather than imposing regulation on cryptocurrencies (Binham 2018).

In the following paragraphs, we will highlight the existing legal framework for the cryptocurrencies in different countries. The discussion is more concentrated on Islamic countries or countries with the significant Muslim population in addition to countries with significant economic status. This will give us a clear view of how Muslim countries perceive the usage of virtual currencies and what role does the regulator play in determining the legality from The Shari'ah perspective.

Algeria, in order to prevent the drug trafficking, tax evasion, and money laundering, intends to ban the usage of virtual currency in the new finance law 2018 (Zitouni 2017), which beforehand it was legal. Based on Article 117: "The purchase, sale, use, and holding of the so-called virtual currency is prohibited. The virtual currency is the one used by Internet users through the web. It is characterized by the absence of physical support such as coins, banknotes, payments by check or bank cards," according to Article 113 of the PLF 2018 which stipulates: "Any violation of this provision is punished in accordance with the laws and regulations in force" (Zitouni 2017; Ethani 2017).

The Central Bank of **Nigeria** (CBN), as of January 2017, has banned all Nigerian banks from all transactions in virtual currencies like Bitcoin, Onecoin, and ripples (Opeyemi 2017). Later, the CBN clarified that as they don't own the Bitcoin and blockchain, same as no one owns the Internet, and they can't regulate it.

Recently in September 2017, Bank of Namibia has passed a circular to advise their banks that bank transactions in Bitcoin and other virtual currencies have been banned and cannot be accepted as means of payment for goods and services in Namibia (Bank of Namibia 2017).

In case of Indonesia, Bank Indonesia (BI) effective 1 January 2018, has banned the cryptocurrency as a legal means of payment for Indonesian. On the other hand, Indonesian are allowed to trade, mine, and hold the cryptocurrencies (Erwida Maulia 2017). With the new regulation, Indonesia has joined the bandwagon of countries like China and India that has banned Bitcoin and cryptocurrencies. Deputy Governor of the central bank of Indonesia Sugeng mentioned, the bank would keep studying and monitoring the use and potential risks of cryptocurrencies in Indonesia and might issue further regulations later. He also added, "the central bank was very supportive of financial technology but wanted to make sure it would not pose any harm to the country's financial stability." For now, "If anyone dares to receive or use virtual currencies like Bitcoin as [a payment tool], then BI will not bear responsibility," another official said, referring to the central bank (Erwida Maulia 2017).

Following Indonesia, **Namibia, Pakistan**, and some other country, India has also banned the cryptocurrency. Arun Jaitley, Finance Minister, on his budget speech on 1 February 2018, mentioned that government does its best to stop the usage of Bitcoin and other altcoins in India, home to one of the largest Bitcoin traders in the world, one out of every 10 Bitcoin transactions in the world (Anand 2018). But instead, India's government encourages the usage of blockchain technology in payment systems. According to Ragunathan (malaysiadigest.com 2017), blockchain technology is a Bitcoin verification mechanism to verify the cryptocurrency transaction, "When I send one Bitcoin to you, the blockchain will verify the transaction to ensure that it is a genuine account."

The Inland Revenue Board (IRB) of Malaysia on 19 January 2018 announced that all cryptocurrency traders are obliged to keep all the records for audit purposes and reveal any transactions from cryptocurrency trading when requested. In addition, IRB mentioned that cryptocurrency is not regulated in Malaysia yet, but all traders still subject to Malaysian income tax law.[2] It means that Bitcoin in Malaysia is not considered as illegal, but it cannot be used as a legal tender/currency to pay for things.

On the other hand, North American countries like Canada, USA, and **Mexico** have a quite clear stand and regulations pertaining to the

---

[2] https://www.thestar.com.my/tech/tech-news/2018/01/19/irb-cryptocurrency-not-regulated-but-traders-still-subject-to-malaysian-income-tax/#8lG6acOmbTUCg-7mC.99.

usage and legality of the Bitcoin (Sandra Appel 2014; IRS 2014). In these three countries, usage of the Bitcoin is legal. The Revenue Agency of Canada in November 2013 announced that Bitcoin payments should be treated as barter transactions. The Canadian federal government in the year 2014 (Openparliemnt.ca 2014) declared that they intend to regulate Bitcoin through its anti-money laundering and counter-terrorist financing legislation.

The largest number of cryptocurrency traders, Bitcoin ATMs, and trading volumes is in the USA, while there are a various stances regarding the legality of cryptocurrency in different states. For example, Texas, Kansas, Tennessee, South Carolina, and Montana are the friendliest according to state regulation, whereas New York, New Hampshire, Connecticut, Hawaii, Georgia, North Carolina, Washington, and New Mexico have regulations not favorable to virtual currency. The other 37 states/territories are gray areas currently.

In the case of **Mexico**, Mexico made it legal as of 2017, and it is going to be regulated under the FinTech law. The Mexican government has not stopped the usage of alternative digital currencies completely but instead, regulators are trying to introduce their own form of Bitcoin and their own blockchain specific to Mexico.

If we focus on the Middle Eastern countries, regulators in **Israel, Saudi Arabia, Jordan**, and Lebanon have not announced the usage of Bitcoin or any cryptocurrency illegal, but have issued a warning discouraging the usage of cryptocurrencies (Knutsen 2014; Obeidat 2014). Israel's government categorized the cryptocurrency as one type of property and capital gains tax is imposed on traders and miners (Wolf 2014). Saudi Arabian Monetary Authority (SAMA) in July 2017 have warned people of using cryptocurrency as it is high risk and also mentioned that dealers of the cryptocurrency will not have any protection or rights.[3] In addition, there is a Bitcoin ATM in the city of Jubail.[4]

Central Bank of **Lebanon** issued a Bitcoin warning in 2013 announcing that due to the increasing number of risks related to cryptocurrency issuance and use of "e-money" is prohibited under a decree issued in 2000. The warning prohibited the use of Bitcoin by financial

---

[3] https://english.alarabiya.net/.
[4] https://coinatmradar.com/country/187/bitcoin-atm-saudi-arabia/.

institutions in the country but left the situation for private citizens unclear (Knutsen 2014).

Turkey does not consider the Bitcoin as electronic money as it has a high volatility and price swing, consequently, it is not regulated (BDDK 2013; The Law Library of Congress 2014).

Iran as another country in the Middle East does not have a clear regulation on Bitcoin. Central Bank of Iran has announced that cryptocurrency trading is illegal but there is no mandate to stop you from Bitcoin trading. Apparently, the Iranian Central Bank has adopted a "wait-and-see" policy toward cryptocurrencies.[5]

For the **United Arab Emirates**, the usage of cryptocurrencies is applicable to some approved institutions. RA DMCC a Dubai-based gold trader located in the free zone received the government-issued license on 13 February 2018, which allows it to trade in crypto-commodities and offers unparalleled full market value insurance on such investments, but the license is applicable for proprietary trading in crypto-commodities only.[6]

The Kyrgyz Republic announced that Bitcoin is considered a commodity (AKIpress.com 2018), not a security or currency under the laws and may be legally mined, bought, sold, and traded on a local commodity exchange,[7] but the usage of Bitcoin as a currency within the country is prohibited.

East Asian countries like China, **Hong Kong**, **Japan**, South Korea, and Taiwan have not announced the Bitcoin as an illegal currency. In particular, **Hong Kong** does not have any stance regarding the Bitcoin, but existing laws (such as the Organized and Serious Crimes Ordinance) provide sanctions against unlawful acts involving Bitcoins, such as fraud or money laundering.[8]

However, **Japan** has eradicated the consumption tax on Bitcoin trading on 1 April 2017, when it formally acknowledged Bitcoin as a legal tender/means of payment (Parker 2017a, b). In addition, Japan removed the likelihood of double taxation on trading of Bitcoins. In fact, the city of Hirosaki has officially accepted Bitcoin donations with the

---

[5] https://coiniran.com/en/.

[6] https://www.dmcc.ae/news/worlds-first-deep-cold-storage-crypto-commodities-launched-regal-assets-dubai.

[7] http://en.kyrgyzbusiness.com/blockchain-en/.

[8] http://www.info.gov.hk/gia/general/201401/08/P201401080357.htm.

purpose of attracting international tourists and financing local projects (Parker 2017a).

In **China**, the regulation prohibits financial firm and private sectors from trading the Bitcoin (Leng 2018). Additionally, China has banned mining of Bitcoin and other ICOs and has been coming hard on the Chinese crypto miners. In this regard, Jia and Xiaojin (2018) noted in their article that Bitcoin miners should make an orderly exit from China because they have consumed huge amounts of resources and stoked speculation of virtual currencies.

Interestingly, Bitcoin legality in South American countries is disputable. For example, **Argentina, Brazil,**[9] **Chile**, and **Colombia** have not announced usage of the Bitcoin illegal, but they mentioned, it is not regulated (The Law Library of Congress 2014), whereas Bolivia and Ecuador have issued a ban on Bitcoin and other digital currencies (Cuthbertson 2014).

Australia on 1 July 2017 has officially announced that it will consider the Bitcoin just like money and it will no longer be subject to double taxation (Suberg 2017).

SHARI'AH PERSPECTIVE ON CRYPTOCURRENCY

When it comes to Shari'ah standpoint on the legality of cryptocurrencies, there is no consensus among the Islamic finance experts or Shari'ah scholars. If we have to take an unbiased stance on the matter, it is well articulated by Evans (2016)[10] in his paper that Bitcoin incorporates the principles of Maslaha (social benefits of positive externalities) and mutual risk-sharing. The virtual currency provides an opportunity for the unbanked population to transact in the global marketplace without going through the banking system. Many Islamic scholars will not agree with the reasoning of *maslaha* if they have to base on the true definition of currency as per Shari'ah principles. As per Shari'ah injunctions, any form of currency needs to have an intrinsic value. The value of a currency must be backed up by an asset or tied to a commodity of actual value and can also be shown by the difficulty of attaining it. To be accepted as a form of currency, Shari'ah also requires a currency to be tangible or to

[9] http://www.bcb.gov.br/pre/normativos/busca/normativo.asp?numero=31379& tipo=Comunicado&data=16/11/2017.

[10] http://jibfnet.com/journals/jibf/Vol_3_No_1_June_2015/1.pdf.

have an evidence of existence. If we focus on the Shari'ah rulings on the money, Imam Ibn Taymiyyah (d. 728 H) stated that the physical body of money is never the objective of acquiring money; rather, it is the counter-exchange which is the objective and benefit of money. He further emphasized that "When currencies and money are inter-traded with the intention of investment and profit, it opposes the very purpose of money."

Some of the established Islamic institutions which have a responsibility to pass on Fatwas (Islamic rulings) on matters pertaining to Shari'ah permissibility has a clear judgment on the permissibility of the cryptocurrency. For instance, Grand Mufti of Egypt has declared that cryptocurrency is Haram (not permissible as per Shari'ah).[11] The ruling was based on the fact that Bitcoin is primarily used for causing harm to individuals, groups, and institutions and it is being directly used to fund terrorist activities.

Even the Kuwaiti government categorically passed the fatwa that cryptocurrency is impermissible and it is not a legal form of currency.[12] Even a renowned Shari'ah scholar Dr. Haitham al-Haddad who is a jurist and serves as a judge for the Islamic Council of Europe has spoken against the Bitcoin.[13] Turkish Directorate of Religious Affairs also noted that buying and selling virtual currencies is not compatible with The Islamic religion.[14]

Among all the negative discussion about the permissibility of cryptocurrency in Islamic finance, there is a very recent positive development. An Indonesian FinTech start-up Blossom Finance that uses cryptocurrency to help Muslims with Islamic financial law has published a study that concludes Bitcoin does qualify as a Islamic money.[15] Another renowned Shari'ah Scholar who is also the Chairman of the Shari'ah Advisory Council of the Central bank of Malaysia, Mohd Daud also disagrees that cryptocurrencies are Haram under Shari'ah law due to its fluctuating value. His assertions are based on the reason that both fiat

[11] http://www.bbc.com/news/world-middle-east-42541270.

[12] https://www.zawya.com/mena/en/story/Kuwait_issues_fatwas_against_Bitcoin_trading-SNG_107796937/.

[13] https://www.islam21c.com/islamic-law/fatwa-bitcoin-cryptocurrencies/.

[14] http://www.euronews.com/2017/11/28/bitcoin-is-not-compatible-with-islam-turkeys-religious-authorities-say.

[15] https://blossomfinance.com/is-bitcoin-halal-Shari'ah-analysis-of-bitcoin-cryptocurrency-and-blockchain.

money and cryptocurrency are based on trust. The value of fiat money internationally also fluctuates yet they are not considered Haram even if there is a risk.

In between the debate, some institutions are launching their own Shari'ah compatible version of cryptocurrency. Onegram coin (https://onegram.org/) is one such cryptocurrency. It is the first cryptocurrency which is backed by gold and also compatible with Shari'ah rulings in the form of money.

Even though there is no clear consensus on Shari'ah applicability of cryptocurrency, there is a growing usage of blockchain technology in Shari'ah-complaint activities. For instance, in Indonesia, microfinance start-up Blossom Finance uses Bitcoin to transfer crowd-sourced investments to small- and medium-sized enterprises in need of capital. In addition to the cost-saving factor, Blossom finance is built on the halal risk-sharing factor since it is crowd sourced and profits are shared through investment ratios. Canada-Based Gold Money was certified Halal during early 2017 for its gold-based financial services. It utilizes blockchain technology to facilitate its financial transactions. While Malaysian company HelloGold also utilizes blockchain technology in its Shari'ah-compliant gold trading platform to minimize costs and reduce processing delays.

To conclude, yet there is not a consensus over acceptance, rejection, or even regulating the cryptocurrency globally. Few countries, like Japan and South Korea, already have started the acceptance and usage of the digital currencies in their daily transactions, while some countries like Indonesia, India, Nepal, Bangladesh, and Pakistan banned it. Some countries argue that imposing regulations on cryptocurrency and FinTech will demotivate and discourage the inevitable revolution and development of the technology in the financial sector, instead, we could impose some regulations on banks and financial institutions not to buy and sell altcoins until it reaches to its maturity and stability.

On the other hand, this new type of currency has created an enjoyable atmosphere for terrorists, tax evaders, and money launderers, which is pretty worrying. But, one of the solution to the hot and current financial situation that the whole world is encountering that majority of countries and financial regulatory authorities should start to monitor the suspicious financial activities by imposing the Know Your Customer rule on their customers by asking them to reveal their identity, which on the other hand, it would be against the spirit of the cryptocurrencies.

It means, on both sides, regulators and customers should give up on something in order to find an optimum solution which would benefit everyone. With all these arguments against cryptocurrencies, the only thing that all countries are supportive of is the development of blockchain as a beneficial platform for legitimate financial usage.

References

AKIpress.com (2018). *New Report on Legal Status of Blockchain Commerce in the Kyrgyz Republic Released*. AKIpress News Agency. Available at https://akipress.com/news:604488/. Accessed 17 April 2018.

Anand, Nupur. (2018). Budget 2018 Busts Bitcoin: Arun Jaitley Has Just Killed India's Cryptocurrency Party. *Quartz*. Available at https://qz.com/1195316/budget-2018-busts-bitcoin-arun-jaitley-has-just-killed-in-dias-cryptocurrency-party/. Accessed 1 April 2018.

Bank of Namibia, C. of E. (2017). *Position on Distributed Ledger Technologies and Virtual Currencies in Namibia*. Bank of Namibia. Available at https://www.bon.com.na/CMSTemplates/Bon/Files/bon.com.na/c6/c6e59534-4bc8-4730-a091-eaffa172d2e9.pdf. Accessed 14 November 2017.

BDDK. (2013). Press Release.

Binham. (2018). EU Body Strikes Back at Cryptocurrency Regulation. *Financial Times*. Available at https://www.ft.com/content/bc48eafc-2301-11e8-ae48-60d3531b7d11. Accessed 12 April 2018.

Coleman, Lester. (2017). The European Union Wants to Identify Bitcoin Users. *Cryptocoins News*. Available at https://www.cryptocoinsnews.com/the-european-union-wants-to-identify-bitcoin-users/. Accessed 14 November 2017.

Cuthbertson, Anthony. (2014). Cryptocurrency Round-Up: Bolivian Bitcoin Ban, iOS Apps & Dogecoin at McDonald's. *International Business Times*. Available at http://www.ibtimes.co.uk/cryptocurrency-round-bolivian-bitcoin-ban-ios-apps-dogecoin-mcdonalds-1453453. Accessed 14 November 2017.

del Castillo, Michael. (2016). European Union Adopts Tighter Bitcoin Controls Amid Terrorism Crackdown. *CoinDesk. Coincides*. Available at https://www.coindesk.com/european-union-proposes-tighter-bitcoin-controls-panama-papers-response/. Accessed 14 November 2017.

Desilver, Drew, & Masci, David. (2017). *World Muslim Population More Widespread Than You Might Think*. Pew Research Center Report. Available at http://www.pewresearch.org/fact-tank/2017/01/31/worlds-muslim-population-more-widespread-than-you-might-think/. Accessed 10 April 2018.

Erwida Maulia, N. (2017). Bank Indonesia Declares Bitcoin Payment Illegal. *Nikkei Asian Review*. Available at https://asia.nikkei.com/Politics-Economy/Economy/Bank-Indonesia-declares-bitcoin-payment-illegal. Accessed 13 April 2018.

Ethani, Rabie. (2017). 'S O M M A I R E'. *Journal Officiel La, 76*(2). Available at https://www.joradp.dz/FTP/jo-francais/2017/F2017076.pdf. Accessed 12 April 2018.

Hileman, G. (2016). The Bitcoin Market Potential Index. In *International Conference on Financial Cryptography and Data Security*. Berlin, Heidelberg: Springer, pp. 92–93. https://doi.org/10.1007/978-3-662-48051-9_7.

IRS. (2014). *IRS Virtual Currency Guidance*. Internal Revenue Service. Available at https://www.irs.gov/newsroom/irs-virtual-currency-guidance. Accessed 14 November 2017.

Jia, C., & Xiaojin, R. (2018). PBOC Gets Tougher on Bitcoin—Chinadaily.com. cn. *ChinaDaily*. Available at http://www.chinadaily.com.cn/a/201801/05/WS5a4eb4cba31008cf16da527c.html. Accessed 18 April 2018.

Knutsen, E. (2014). Despite Warnings, Bitcoin Gains Toehold in Region. *The Daily Star Lebanon*. Available at http://www.dailystar.com.lb/Business/Lebanon/2014/Feb-24/248247-despite-warnings-bitcoin-gains-toehold-in-region.ashx. Accessed 1 April 2018.

Leng, S. (2018). Beijing Bans Bitcoin, but When Did It All Go Wrong for Cryptocurrencies in China? *South China Morning Post*. Available at http://www.scmp.com/news/china/economy/article/2132119/beijing-bans-bit-coin-when-did-it-all-go-wrong-cryptocurrencies. Accessed 18 April 2018.

Lipka, Michael, & Hackett, Conrad. (2017). *Why Muslims are the World's Fastest-Growing Religious Group*. Pew Research Center. Available at http://www.pewresearch.org/fact-tank/2017/04/06/why-muslims-are-the-worlds-fastest-growing-religious-group/. Accessed 9 April 2018.

Malaysiadigest.com. (2017). *Thinking of Investing In Bitcoins? Read This First*. malaysiadigest.com. Available at http://www.malaysiandigest.com/front-page/282-main-tile/681290-thinking-of-investing-in-bitcoins-read-this-first.html. Accessed 16 April 2018.

News European Parliament. (2016). *MEPs Call for Virtual Currency Watchdog to Combat Money Laundering and Terrorism*. News European Parliament. Available at http://www.europarl.europa.eu/news/en/press-room/20160524IPR28821/meps-call-for-virtual-currency-watch-dog-to-combat-money-laundering-and-terrorism. Accessed 14 November 2017.

Obeidat, O. (2014). Central Bank Warns Against Using Bitcoin. *The Jordan Times*. Available at http://www.jordantimes.com/news/local/central-bank-warns-against-using-bitcoin. Accessed 17 April 2018.

Openparliemnt.ca. (2014). *Bill C-31 (Historical)*. Openparliemnt.ca. Available at https://openparliament.ca/bills/41-2/C-31/. Accessed 16 April 2018.

Opeyemi, Adeola. (2017). *Central Bank of Nigeria Bans Transaction in Bitcoins, Onecoin, Others* ▷ *NAIJ.COM*. Naija.ng. Available at https://www.naija.

ng/1083244-central-bank-nigeria-bans-transaction-bitcoins-onecoin-others. html#1083244. Accessed 14 November 2017.

Parker, Luke. (2017a). *Bitcoin Regulation Overhaul in Japan. Brave New Coin.* Digital Currency Insights. Available at https://bravenewcoin.com/news/bit-coin-regulation-overhaul-in-japan/. Accessed 14 November 2017.

Parker, Luke. (2017b). *Local Government Using Bitcoin to Promote Tourism in Japan. Brave New Coin.* Digital Currency Insights. Available at https://bravenewcoin.com/news/local-government-using-bitcoin-to-promote-tour-ism-in-japan/. Accessed 14 November 2017.

Sandra Appel, M. (2014). *Can You Take a Security Interest in Bitcoin?—Finance and Banking—Canada, Monday, Connecting Knowledge & People.* Available at http://www.mondaq.com/canada/x/313572/securitization+structured+-finance/Can+You+Take+A+Security++Interest+In+Bitcoin. Accessed 14 November 2017.

Suberg, William. (2017). *Bitcoin to Become 'Just Like Money' in Australia July 1.* The Cointelegraph, Future of Money. Available at https://cointelegraph.com/news/bitcoin-to-become-just-like-money-in-australia-july-1. Accessed 15 November 2017.

The Law Library of Congress. (2014). *Bitcoin Survey.* The Law Library of Congress, Global Legal Research Center. Available at http://www.loc.gov/law/help/bitcoin-survey/. Accessed 14 November 2017.

Trautman, L. J. (2016). Is Disruptive Blockchain Technology the Future of Financial Services? *The Consumer Finance Law Quarterly Report,* 232. Available at https://ssrn.com/abstract=2786186.

Wolf, D. (2014). *Bitcoin Israel—Q & A.* Dave Wolf & Co. Law Offices. Available at http://www.lawfirmwolf.com/bitcoin-israel-law. Accessed 1 April 2018.

Yeoh, P. (2017). Regulatory Issues in Blockchain Technology. *Journal of Financial Regulation and Compliance,* 25(2). https://doi.org/10.1108/JFRC-08-2016-0068.

Zitouni, Aymen. (2017). PLF 2018: Algeria Wants to Ban Bitcoin and Other Crypto-Currencies. *Maghreb Emergent.* Available at https://www.huffpost-maghreb.com/2017/10/26/algerie-interdiction-bitc_n_18384452.html. Accessed 1 April 2018.

CHAPTER 13

Regulatory and *Shari'ah* Framework of Cryptocurrency

*Rusni Hassan, Nadiyah Syahira Nordin
and Rizal Mohd Nor*

INTRODUCTION

Cryptocurrency has been seen to create a new phenomenon to the landscape of financial services industry. It has gained traction in attracting all relevant players in the industry to delve deeper into the issue. Preceding bitcoin as the inaugural prevalent product, cryptocurrency has been utilized as the medium of payment in various sectors. Since then, cryptocurrency become up-to-the-minute phenomena in the financial services industry. To many, the scheme seemed to exhibit many potential benefits including greater speed of payment and efficiency particularly

R. Hassan (✉) · N. S. Nordin
IIUM Institute of Islamic Banking and Finance (IIiBF),
Kuala Lumpur, Malaysia
e-mail: hrusni@iium.edu.my

R. M. Nor
Kulliyyah of Information and Communication Technology (KICT),
International Islamic University Malaysia (IIUM), Kuala Lumpur, Malaysia

© The Author(s) 2019   195
M. M. Billah (ed.), *Halal Cryptocurrency Management*,
https://doi.org/10.1007/978-3-030-10749-9_13

cross-borders and thus serves as the best choice to ultimately promote financial inclusion using online platform.[1]

Cryptocurrency, being one of the types of virtual currency, is a privately owned system that mainly offers to facilitate peer-to-peer exchange system bypassing traditional financial institutions' services and clearing houses. The penetration has also been pervasive in Islamic finance landscape. It is apparent through the introduction of Blossom Finance in Indonesia that used cryptocurrency (bitcoin), as the currency of the capital in *Mudarabah* structure of micro-financing that they facilitated.[2]

Since cryptocurrency is a new phenomenon in the financial system, the world's financial regulators are seemed to be indecisive on their approach towards cryptocurrency and digital currencies. There is widespread concern about the digital currency system's possible impact on national currencies, its potential for criminal misuse and the implications of its use for taxation. Many countries are still unconvinced that digital currencies or cryptocurrencies are to be accorded the status as a legal tender.

Similarly, how cryptocurrency is perceived in Shari'ah perspective has not been widely discussed. Whether cryptocurrency satisfies the core principles of Shari'ah and legal tender status is among the main issues argued by many scholars. This is evidenced by the contemporary views of Muslim scholars on this matter. Using the *fatwa* as the basis of the discussion, this research examines the Shari'ah perspective of cryptocurrency and highlights the issues and concerns. This is followed by the discussion on the regulatory framework on cryptocurrency in selected countries.

Regulatory Framework on Cryptocurrency

There have been few regulatory responses regarding virtual currency. This denotes a new milestone for this emerging phenomenon that has caught regulators' attention to put forth cryptocurrency as one of their

---

[1] Quoc Khanh Nguyen, "Blockchain—A Financial Technology for Future Sustainable Development", *3rd International Conference on Green Technology and Sustainable Development*, 2016: 51.

[2] Jamie Redman, "Bitcoin Brings '100% Mathematical Certainty' to Comply with Islamic Law", *The Coin Telegraph*, https://cointelegraph.com/news/bitcoin-brings-100-mathematical-certainty-to-comply-with-islamic-law (accessed January 12, 2017).

regulatory concerns. This discussion highlights the regulatory framework of selected countries that are considered as active participants in cryptocurrency dealings and have officially made a statement of their position regarding cryptocurrency.

Malaysia

The Central Bank of Malaysia (CBM) does not impose a blanket ban approach on cryptocurrency, viewing that it would otherwise stifle innovation and creativity. The concern is much amplified from the perspective of Anti-Money Laundering and Counter Financing of Terrorism Act (AML/CFT). CBM has issued a Policy Document (PD) of AML/CFT—Digital Currencies (Sector 6) 2016 to address risks associated with digital currencies. The PD in a nutshell sets out minimum requirement and standard of reporting that has to be observed to improve transparency of activities related to digital currencies. In the PD, there is no explicit provision concerning cryptocurrency per se, but rather provides a broader regulatory guidance on digital currency exchanges for avoidance of anti-money laundering and terrorism financing (AM/TF). The PD provides that "any person offering services to exchange digital currencies either to fiat money or to another digital currency and vice versa will be subject to obligations on AM/TF". This includes the obligation to establish a policy on AM/TF which includes the duty of the person (or institution) to report any suspicious transactions, to conduct customer due diligence, to appoint compliance officer and other measures necessary to combat AM/TF.

CBM has also issued Financial Technology (Fintech) Regulatory Sandbox Framework in an effort to provide a regulatory environment conducive for the deployment of Fintech. Acknowledging the importance of cryptocurrency which is the bred of Fintech, as more adaptable to the new technological shift and new payment system mechanism, denotes the importance of regulation in this aspect. Not only the Fintech or cryptocurrency companies need to get approval from CBM to operate their business, the companies must also prove that their products and services are useful, functional and compatible with laws and regulations; the companies have sufficient resources and expertise to mitigate and control potential risks; and the companies are led and managed by persons with credibility and integrity.

The two regulations issued demonstrate CBM's trajectory in regulatory approach towards cryptocurrency and Fintech in general, in ensuring that its operations and activities do not disrupt sound financial and business practices; promote fair treatment of consumers; and promote safety, reliability and efficiency of financial systems. It is also interesting to note that the regulation also emphasis innovative solutions offered by digital currencies for Islamic financial services must be consistent with prevailing Shari'ah principles.

Canada

Governor General of Canada gave his royal assent[3] to Bill C-31 that includes amendments to Canada Proceeds of Crime (Money Laundering) and Terrorist Financing Act.[4] This will treat (any form of) virtual currency as money service business for the purpose of its Anti-Money Laundering Law. The immediate implication of the law is that companies in Canada dealing with virtual currencies and companies outside Canada dealing directly with person or entities in Canada have to register with Financial Transaction and Report Analysis Centre of Canada (FINTRAC).[5]

The Financial Consumer Agency of Canada does not recognize cryptocurrency as legal tender and declares that the central authority does not legally support the digital currency, nor the financial institutions manage the oversight of the digital currency businesses. It is also clearly pronounced by the government that digital currency/cryptocurrency is not exempted from Canadian tax obligation and thus rendering it subject to Income Tax Act.

---

[3] Royal assent is the final step required for parliamentary bill to become law.

[4] See Division 19 of Bill C-31: Money Laundering and Terrorist Financing, Amendment for Proceeds of Crime (Money Laundering) and Terrorist Financing Act, (2006), c. 12, s. 3(1), http://www.parl.ca/DocumentViewer/en/41-2/bill/C-31/royal-assent/page-344#37.

[5] Jasper Hamill, Canadian Regulators Welcome US Bitcoin Refugees with Open Arms, REGISTER (May 20, 2013), http://www.theregister.co.uk/2013/05/20/canada_welcomes_bitcoin_traders_fintrac_letter/.

European Union (EU)

European Union has not calibrated specific regulation for virtual currency as a currency, because they view that virtual currency is more suitable to be an investment vehicle rather than a currency, due to its high volatility.[6] However, it is notable that Council of European Union has proposed an amendment to the definition of virtual currency in the 4th Anti-Money Laundering Directive (4AMLD), which is later been suggested to issue as a separate Directive that will establish in the form of the 5th Anti-Money Laundering Directive (5AMLD). Apart from that, European Central Bank (ECB) has published two reports in 2012 and 2015, stating that ECB does not recognize virtual currency as a legal tender.[7]

On December 13, 2013, the European Banking Authority (EBA), the regulatory agency of the EU responsible for advising EU institutions on banking, e-money regulation and payments, issued a warning on the dangers associated with transactions, such as buying, holding or trading virtual currencies. The EBA pointed out that since the bitcoin is not regulated, consumers are not protected and are at risk of losing their money and that consumers may still be liable for taxes when using virtual currencies.[8]

Australia

Australian Taxation Office has issued a guidance paper on taxation treatment of cryptocurrencies specifically on bitcoin. The supply of bitcoin is regarded as an asset for capital gains tax (CGT) and not for goods and services tax (GST) purposes.[9]

Apart from that, Australia has also introduced new guideline (effective 3 April 2018) that incorporates requirement for cryptocurrency exchanges and service providers to register their business and to furnish

---

[6] European Central Bank, *Virtual Currency Schemes* (Brussel: ECB, 2015), 23.

[7] Ibid.

[8] Press Release, European Banking Authority, EBA Warns Consumers on Virtual Currencies (December 13, 2013), http://www.eba.europa.eu/-/eba-warns-consumers-on-virtual-currencies.

[9] Australian Government (AUSTRAC), "Digital Currency Exchange Providers: Register Online with AUSTRAC", http://www.austrac.gov.au/news/digital-currency-exchange-providers-register-online-austrac (accessed April 16, 2018).

the necessary reporting related to arising suspicion of money laundering activity. Track records of 7 years are expected for the businesses to retain their credibility and to showcase a trail of good performance.

United States of America (USA)

In USA, the Internal Revenue Service (IRS) has issued Virtual Currency Guidance stating that virtual currency shall be treated as property for US federal tax purposes.[10] Further, the US Anti-Money Laundering Agency known as FinCEN (Financial Crimes Enforcement Network)[11] suggests that activities that are classified as Money Services Businesses (MSB)[12] and Money Transmission Businesses (MTB) should be applied equally to both real currency and virtual currency. Following that, FinCEN has published guidance that further defines the parties who are considered performing MSB are the administrator or exchanger of virtual currency and money transmitter that are bound to FinCEN regulation.

The Commodity Futures Trading Commission (CFTC) appears to be at the forefront in making the clarion call to market players on its mandate to regulate cryptocurrency trading, especially in derivatives market.[13] In 2018, it appears to be the first regulator to allow for trading

---

[10] See *The Internal Revenue Service's Virtual Currency Guideline*, https://www.irs.gov/uac/newsroom/irs-virtual-currency-guidance.

[11] FinCEN function is to safeguard the US financial system from illicit use and combat money laundering and promote national security through the collection, analysis and dissemination of financial intelligence and strategic use of financial authorities. FinCEN exercises regulatory functions primarily under the Currency and Financial Transactions Reporting Act of 1970, as amended by Title III of the USA PATRIOT Act of 2001 and other legislation, which legislative framework is commonly referred to as the "Bank Secrecy Act" (BSA). See https://www.fincen.gov/.

[12] Money Services Businesses (MSB) as defined in US Bank Secrecy Act Regulation—Definitions and Other Regulations Relating to Money Service Businesses is "A person wherever located doing business, whether or not on a regular basis or as an organized or licensed business concern, wholly or in substantial part within the United States, in one or more of the capacities listed in paragraphs (ff)(1) through (ff)(7) of this section. This includes but is not limited to maintenance of any agent, agency, branch, or office within the United States", https://www.law.cornell.edu/cfr/text/31/1010.100 and https://www.gpo.gov/fdsys/pkg/FR-2011-07-21/pdf/2011-18309.pdf.

[13] Matthew Kluchenek, "Bitcoin and Cryptocurrencies: Welcome to Your Regulator", *Harvard Business Law Review*, 2016: 1–2.

of cryptocurrency derivatives.[14] This sends a signal to the global market that cryptocurrency can be recognized as the new asset class for investment purposes. The CFTC would ensure that it is at the best interest of consumer protection that such allowance is taken place. Conversational dialogue is continuously conducted with relevant cryptocurrency exchanges involved to maintain a certain threshold of quality market conduct for derivatives businesses. USA does not have a dedicated provision or regulation concerning cryptocurrency, rather it is much dependable on the regulatory agencies governing the sector/activities.

Japan

Japan made an amendment of Payment Services Act effective June 2017 that includes the virtual currency exchanges regulation.[15] The amendment allows for virtual currency business to register to Financial Services Agency for the purpose of licensing.[16] Japan is seen to take an extra prudential measure in regulating virtual currency activities because of the experience from Mt Gox collapse in 2014.[17] Apart from that, as for the tax treatment, consumption tax on cryptocurrency such as bitcoin is now exempted according to Fund Settlement Law and replaced with taxable capital gains tax (CGT) as, in this case is bitcoin, is viewed

---

[14] Robert Schimdt, "Bitcoin-Futures Regulator Clears Employees to Trade Crypto Coins", *Bloomberg News*, https://www.bloomberg.com/news/articles/2018-02-28/bitcoin-futures-regulator-clears-employees-to-trade-crypto-coins (accessed May 3, 2018).

[15] Yuri Suzuki and Ryosuke Oue, "Fintech Legislation in Japan", *Global Banking and Financial Policy Review*, 2016.

[16] Sayuri Umeda, *Japan: Bitcoin to be Regulated*, http://www.loc.gov/law/foreign-news/article/japan-bitcoin-to-be-regulated/ (accessed July 21, 2017).

[17] Mt. Gox is a bitcoin currency exchange based in Tokyo. It is one of the various unregulated cryptocurrency exchanges existing in the cryptocurrency ecosystem. The collapse of Mt. Gox in 2014 was preceded with several suspicious trading activities that were leaked from the data dump that shows Mt. Gox transaction history that caused the bitcoin rate during that time experienced a high spike in price due to the fraudulent transaction. In early 2014, Mt. Gox folded because of insolvency. Mt. Gox collapse is an example of how manipulation triggers volatility in bitcoin price that later can actually backfire the actor of the fraudulent activities (Neil Gandal, JT. Hamrick, Tyler Moore and Tali Oberman, *"Price Manipulation in Bitcoin Ecosystem"*, Workshop on the Economics of Information Security [WEIS], 2016).

as being an asset-like.[18] Japan is said to be a positive precedent in Asia region in coming out with an official statement and calibration of regulation in regards to cryptocurrency.

Apart from that, due to the heightened heist and theft risks that cryptocurrency exchanges may be exposed to, Japan is now exploring to set up the self-regulatory body of the individual cryptocurrency exchanges to bolster public confidence and trust. The clampdown that had taken place in few cryptocurrency exchanges in Japan had prompted them to become one of the first few countries to introduce licensing requirements for cryptocurrency exchanges. The introduction of licensing requirement is an important regulatory milestone because it enables the regulator to address money laundering and terrorism financing risk,[19] as it requires for identification of the contracting parties. Consumer's right and protection would also be better preserved when the licensing requirement is implemented to safeguard any moral hazard involving cryptocurrency transaction.

South Korea

South Korea cryptocurrency practice is a bit peculiar in nature, whereby cryptocurrency exchanges sat within banks in form of virtual bank accounts. In January 2018, the Financial Services Commission of South Korea introduces new cryptocurrency regulation that primarily highlights the compliance with AML Act and Know Your Customer (KYC) policy.[20]

Under the ambit of the new regulation, the Government aims to reduce the avenues of cryptocurrency being used for illicit activities and businesses, as well as price manipulation and speculation. It also only allows for cryptocurrency trading from real-name bank account from a real account, rather than just manipulating the bank platform.

---

[18] Kevin Helms, "Japan Declares Sale of Bitcoin Exempt from Consumption Tax", *Bitcoin News*, https://news.bitcoin.com/japan-sale-bitcoin-exempt-consumption-tax/ (accessed July 21, 2017).

[19] Takashi Nakazaki and Ken Kawai, "Development of Legal Framework for Virtual Currency in Japan", *Anderson Mori & Tomotsune Law*, 2016: 2.

[20] Chrisjan Pauw, "South Korea and Crypto Regulation: Explained", *Coin Telegraph*, February 6, 2018, https://cointelegraph.com/explained/south-korea-and-crypto-regulations-explained (accessed April 16, 2018).

This new imposition is also aimed to minimize AML and tax evasion risks, which are the initial concerns of what prompted the calibration of the regulation.

United Kingdom (UK)

The Financial Conduct Authority (FCA) does not have a regulatory scope over cryptocurrency. As such, there is no guideline issued concerning cryptocurrency/virtual currency, making it as a clearly unregulated market in the UK.[21]

Although there is no clear guideline or regulation crafted to address regulatory measure on cryptocurrency, the FCA has issued a series of Consumer Warning to alert people on risks associated with cryptocurrency dealings. Recently, a Consumer Warning on Initial Coins Offerings (ICO) was published,[22] mainly highlighting the unregulated nature of ICO poses consumer to a higher exposure of scam and fraud.

In addition to that, similarly in other jurisdiction, regulatory concern is prompted to address the risk of money laundering and terrorism financing. The UK Treasury did state in a press statement that they are mulling over to bring virtual currency exchange platform within the AML and Counter-Terrorist Financing regulation.[23]

From the development in regulatory responses of countries across the globe, three observations can be derived. Firstly, most countries are not recognizing cryptocurrency as a currency holding the legal tender, instead perceiving it as a property or financial asset that comes along with tax consequences. Secondly, it is apparent that regulators approach in recognizing cryptocurrencies as property or financial asset that attracts taxable capital gain is actually one way to regulate cryptocurrency dealings. Thirdly, notwithstanding the associated risks surrounding

---

[21] Edward Robinson, "U.K. Starts Cryptocurrency Inquiry as Lawmakers Weigh Regulation", *Bloomberg News*, February 22, 2018, https://www.bloomberg.com/news/articles/2018-02-22/u-k-starts-cryptocurrency-inquiry-as-lawmakers-weigh-regulation (accessed May 2, 2018).

[22] See UK Financial Conduct Authority's Consumer Warning on ICO and Other Issuance, https://www.fca.org.uk/news/statements/initial-coin-offerings.

[23] Shafi Mussadique, "UK Government Plans Bitcoin Crackdown Amid Money Laundering Concern", *The Independent (UK)*, December 4, 2017, https://www.independent.co.uk/news/business/news/uk-bitcoin-regulation-money-laundering-crytocurrency-european-union-eu-a8090791.html (accessed May 1, 2018).

cryptocurrency ecosystem, regulators are attempting to promulgate regulation without stifling innovation happening around the financial landscape. For example, registration of operators and licensing requirement is introduced instead of outright declaration on illegality of cryptocurrency. Apart from that, the regulatory guidance that most of the countries have issued are more for combating money-laundering that may be implicated in cryptocurrency activities.

SHARI'AH FRAMEWORK ON CRYPTOCURRENCY

Cryptocurrency does not only penetrate the conventional financial system but also the Islamic financial system. If the questions of the financial stability and legal tender status are among the issues of concern in the financial system, another additional issue that needs to be reconciled for Islamic financial system is the Shari'ah compliant status of such currency. Shari'ah analysis needs to be made on the features of cryptocurrency before it can be allowed to be used and traded. There is hardly any conclusive deliberation on this matter either in the form of fatwa issued by the scholars or standard issued by Islamic authority on this matter. Relying on the fatwa preliminarily issued by the scholars' cryptocurrency, the following discussion analyses the features of cryptocurrency and its validation process to examine its status from Shari'ah perspective.

Fatwa on Cryptocurrency

There are a few *fatwa* issued in regards to cryptocurrency and its validity from Shari'ah aspects.

Firstly, National Fatwa Council of Malaysia has issued statement on bitcoin.[24] The Council views that bitcoin is not suitable to be used as a currency because it is vulnerable to high volatility and fluctuation as well as the speculation that affects its price. Bitcoin or cryptocurrency, is a virtual currency exchanged in a virtual platform and thus may have an issue of possession (*qabdh*) which is required in the transactions. If

---

[24] Majlis Fatwa Kebangsaan, Hukum Penggunaan Bitcoin Sebagai Medium untuk Bermuamalat, *e-fatwa Majlis Fatwa Kebangsaan,* April 2, 2014, https://web. archive.org/web/20150122215500/http:/www.e-fatwa.gov.my/blog/hukum-penggunaan-bitcoin-sebagai-medium-untuk-bermuamalat.

cryptocurrency was to be treated as currency, it has to satisfy the require-ment of currency exchange (*ahkam sarf*).

Secondly, Monzer Kahf has concerns on the manipulation in the price of cryptocurrency[25] given the fact that there is no authority governing it. From Shari'ah perspective, cryptocurrency is permissible for exchange and traded if the transaction satisfies the rule of spot delivery in dealing with currency. However, there should be no speculation in obtaining and disposing the coins.

Third, the Council of Scholars in Syabakah Islamiyah Fatwa, Qatar also has issued fatwa on cryptocurrency stating that[26]:

> Virtual currency is a currency in a virtual form and not in the form of paper money or commodity. So exchanging virtual currency with other currency is considered a currency exchange transaction (sarf). And currency exchange transaction (sarf) requires spot delivery and at par exchange if it involves the same denominator. If it is different denominator, it requires spot delivery without the requirement of at par exchange.

Fourth, Sheikh Dr. Abdul Sattar Abu Ghuddah[27] is of the view that currency issuance and dealing is the centralized prerogative and mandate of the government (*wali al-amr*). Secondly, the harm (*darar*) associated with cryptocurrency may render it to impermissibility because it may ensue more detrimental repercussion at national and individual level. This is to ensure consumer protection and financial stability soundness, which cryptocurrency ecosystem would not be able to preserve.

Based on the *fatwa* and statements given regarding cryptocurrency, it is apparent that scholars are giving their opinion on the basis that cryptocurrency is a form of currency thus attaching the rule of dealing in *sarf* to it. As such the rules on possession (*qabd*),[28] spot delivery and exchange; and speculation (*taghrir*) are to be carefully considered.

---

[25] See Monzer Kahf, *Fatwa*, http://monzer.kahf.com/index.html.

[26] See Fatwa Syabakah Islamiyah, No. 251170, http://fatwa.islamweb.net/fatwa/index.php?page=showfatwa&Option=FatwaId&Id=251170.

[27] Abdul Sattar Abu Ghuddah, *al-Nuqud al-Raqamiyah al-Ru'yah al-Syar'iyyah wal Athar al-Iqtisodiyah* (Doha, 2018), 24–25.

[28] There are two types of possessions recognized in Shari'ah that are real possession (*qabd haqiqi*) and constructive possession (*qabd hukmi*). *Qabd hukmi* is defined as taking possession in physical form or when the buyer is observed taking goods sold to him. On the other hand, *qabd hukmi* is a legal possession that refers to taking possession implicitly or

Shari'ah Analysis on Cryptocurrency

In understanding cryptocurrency from Shari'ah perspective, it is instrumental to determine what is currency from Shari'ah standpoint and what function it entails.

Ibn Abidin views that currency must have a store of value and that it is being transacted and exchanged regardless of the economic condition that affects the value of the currency.[29] If it involves an exchange of currency against another currency, it should adhere to the rule of *ribawi* items, whereby the exchange should be on spot basis and of the same weight. This view is similar to Ibn Qudamah that mentioned currency in Shari'ah perspective should be treated carefully to not be susceptible to the practice of *riba*.[30]

Al-Ghazali[31] is of the opinion that a currency should incorporate the function of being medium of exchange and measure of value. He emphasizes that the essential characteristic of money is not desired because of the money; rather it is desired because of the function it performs. To be accepted as the medium of exchange, currency must have a certain measure of value recognized by the people doing the transactions with it.

Ibn Taymiyah echoes this view[32] stating that currency serves two main functions, which are to measure the value of goods and to be paid in exchange for different type and quantities of goods.[33] A currency is fundamentally the price (*thaman*) that is meant to be the measurement of an object of value (*mi'yar al-amwal*), through which qualities of the object (*maqadir al-amwal*) can be known.

---

not in physical form (Asyraf Wajdi Dusuki, Status of Ownership [*qabdh*] in Islamic Sale Contract, *Global Perspective on Islamic Banking and Insurance*, 175 [2010]: 22–23).

[29] Ibn Abidin, *Darr Al-Mukhtar wa Hasyiyah Ibn Abidin* (Beirut: Dar Al-Fikr, 1992), 534.

[30] Ibn Qudamah, *Al-Mughni li Ibnu Qudamah* (Cairo: Maktab Al-Kaherah, 1968), 39.

[31] Al-Ghazali, *Kitab Al-Shukr Ihya' Ulumuddin* (Beirut: Dar Al-Ma'rifah, n.d.), 90.

[32] Ibn Taymiyah, *Majmu' Fatawa*, ed. Abdul Rahman Ibn Muhammad (Madinah: Majma' Al-Malik Al-Fahd li Tiba'ah, 1995), 250.

[33] Abdul Azim Islahi, "An Analytical Study on Al-Ghazali's Thought on Money and Interest", *Munich Personal RePEc Archive*, 2001.

According to Taqi Uthmani,[34] a currency should satisfy two major prerequisites. Firstly, it should be used as a medium of payment and accepted as tools for settlement of debts. When that is being accepted to circulate within an economy, it can be considered as commonly acceptable currency (*awraq athmanan 'urufiyyah*). Secondly, it should also be legally recognized as a currency in one's jurisdiction (*'umlah qanuniyah*). The value of currency is derived from the recognition of the regulatory authority, thus creating public confidence to use it as medium of payment.

Apart from that, it is the responsibility of the government or the authority to guarantee the supply of the money and oversee the fluctuating value of the currency that will directly affect the purchasing power of the currency to unit of goods and services. Al-Ghazali underlines the alarming danger if the production is not wisely governed because it may lead to undesirable inflation that harms the purchasing power of the currency and the value that the currency entails. These phenomena accentuate the importance of the legal recognition and control from the monetary authority. Legal cognizance on the currency mitigates the erosion of the value, providing standardized currency to be used as the medium of payment, and thus benefits the *ummah*.

Supporting this view, Monzer Kahf stated[35] that regulatory intervention is instrumental in order to regulate inflation and deflation that may influence the purchasing value of the currency.

From the above discussion, there are four prerequisites that can be extracted to be the constituency of currency in Shari'ah perspective. Those are (i) currency is to perform the function as the medium of exchange for trading goods and services (ii) currency is to have a store of value; (iii) currency is to be commonly accepted as the currency circulating within a community; and (iv) currency is to be recognized as legal tender in a jurisdiction.

The technological landscape now allows people to trade goods and services using cryptocurrency for payment and commercial transaction purposes. It serves as a new platform that has become popular and

---

[34] Taqi Uthmani, *Buhuth fi Qadhaya Fiqh Muasorah* (Damsyik: Dar Al-Qalam, 2003), 157.

[35] Monzer Kahf, *The Islamic Economy: An Analytical Study of the Functioning of the Islamic Economic System* (Canada, 1978).

acceptable. This displays public trust and confidence on its reliability to secure their payment and to retain its value. Not only it is utilized for commercial purposes, but also it has become an alternative mode of saving and investment, depending on risks associated with it. This indicates that cryptocurrency could store wealth and value that the coin possesses. Further, the reliability of cryptocurrency to be the medium of exchange also implies the ability of storing value because it can be used to measure the value of goods and debt in relation to time.

Cryptocurrency is transacted and exchanged within a virtual community of network that together using the common currency for exchange. Users of cryptocurrency are required to enter the network by signing up as the new participant without the need for further identification details. From this perspective, cryptocurrency seems to fulfil the prerequisite of being commonly acceptable within a community within the context of `uruf practiced because every participants signing up in the network is utilizing the common currency for exchange and trading.

On the prerequisites of currency stated by the fatwas, the feature of cryptocurrency satisfies the requirement of medium of exchange in a sense that the validating protocol allows users to use cryptocurrency as means of payment between transacting parties within a virtual community network. The coins are satisfied to set off payment and measuring value of goods traded or exchanged. Cryptocurrency also qualifies as a currency having store of value as the stringent validating mechanism allows users to retain the value of currency and its value would appreciate and depreciate similar like other acceptable currencies. The fluctuation of value can be benefited through acquiring and disposing coins for value. Cryptocurrency is also commonly acceptable within the virtual community network that uses the common currency for exchange.

Shari'ah Analysis on Cryptocurrency Architecture and Algorithm

Cryptocurrency is a type of virtual currencies that is designed to incorporate and exchange digital information through a cryptography process.[36] The default architecture of cryptocurrency comprises of the validating

---

[36]Cryptography is a process of converting ordinary plain text and syntax into unintelligible text and vice versa, which is what to be known synonymous to encryption and decryption (Lathan and Watkins LLP, *Cryptocurrency: A Primer* [New York, 2015]).

system, mathematical algorithm and coin supply protocol that differ from one cryptocurrency developer from another. The following discussion provides a brief discourse on these aspects to determine the Shari'ah permissibility on cryptocurrency.

Validating System

Validating system is the method used to validate transaction performed across the network using cryptocurrency. Validating methods chosen will determine how the network will reach consensus for transaction validation and thus will be appended as the new block into the blockchain. Notwithstanding the methods adopted by the cryptocurrency developer whether it is Proof-of-Stake (POS),[37] Proof-of-Work (POW)[38] or Proof-of-Retrievability (POR),[39] there will be some time lapse needed for the network to reach consensus and validate the transaction for the coin transferred can be acquired or possessed at the receiver's end. For instance, cryptocurrency with POW validating method would rely on the miners' speed and computational capability to solve the hash algorithm. Normally it takes 10 minutes in bitcoin operational structure for miners to solve the mathematical problem,[40] and it could be stretched longer as time progresses due to the intensified complexity of the function. It is to note that the transacting parties have actually concluded the transaction; it is just the protocol of the system to verify the transaction to ensure security and authenticity of the transaction made.

---

[37] *Proof of Stake*: A mining concept that states that a person's ability to mine or validate blocks is according to how many coins he holds. The more coins he holds, the more mining power he is entitled to. Hence, the 'stake' he has in the mining power.

[38] *Proof of Work*: The original mining concept in Bitcoin system. It relies on the miners' effort to compete against one another to complete transaction and get rewarded. The main working principle is a complex mathematical puzzle, hence the 'work' needed to solve the puzzle.

[39] *Proof of Retrievability*: It is a protocol, which enables clients to retrieve 'files' from an 'archive', which ensures an accompanying digital signature can be checked accordingly to confirm authenticity of a transaction.

[40] Jason Teutsch, Sanjay Jain and Prateek Saxena, "When Cryptocurrencies Mine Their Own Business", *Financial Cryptography and Data Security* (2016): 499–514.

This currency exchange mode is important to be examined in view of the Shari'ah requirement of spot basis transaction in currency exchange (*bai' sarf*).[41] The scholars have allowed 3 days (T+2) settlement period of foreign currency exchanges, recognizing that transaction as being "spot transaction". The T+2 is deemed as spot although the delivery and settlement is delayed from the day the contract is being concluded, because the 48-hour period is the time needed for transaction confirmation.[42] The permissibility of the T+2 transactions can be seen in the resolution of Shari'ah Advisory Council (SAC) of Central Bank of Malaysia where it stated that:

> The SAC, in its 38th meeting dated 28 August 2003, has resolved that the delivery and settlement of a spot foreign exchange transaction based on T+2 is permissible.[43]

In the case of cryptocurrency, it would take less than three days so it bears no issue as far as the spot transaction requirement is concerned.

Another Shari'ah requirement for all types of transactions including currency transaction is that the parties must have possession (*qabd*) of the asset/currency. In the transaction performed using cryptocurrency, constructive possession takes place and thus it poses no Shari'ah issue. Once the transaction is validated and added into the block, the coins received by the user that is stored in their digital wallet can be exchanged and cleared at clearing houses. For example, clearing houses for bitcoin provide services to exchange bitcoin into any currency according to the market rate. Therefore, there is confirmed possession of the currency when it is stored in the respective users' digital wallet. As for exchange involving commodity, the commodity could also be possessed and delivered to the users pursuant to the exchange been made. In this context,

---

[41] In transaction involving currency with same denomination, it shall be in an equal amount and there shall not be deferment in delivery of one or both counter values (AAOIFI Shari'ah Standard, *Dealing with Currencies*, Standard No. 2/1/2 and No. 2/1/3).

[42] Bahroddin Badri, "*Qabd* (Possession): An Overview", *Bloomberg Finance*, June, 2015.

[43] Bank Negara Malaysia, *Shari'ah Resolutions in Islamic Finance* (Kuala Lumpur: BNM, 2010), 138.

cryptocurrency is in fact the medium of exchange across the virtual network for the acquisition of identified commodity or asset.

Mathematical Algorithm

Mathematical algorithm is very much connected to the validating system, which determines the digital security of the transaction using cryptocurrency. It signifies the mathematical procedure for data calculation and processing. Processing data, speed of blocks adding and coins release are determined by the mathematical algorithm being applied. The mathematical algorithm is the factor that can ensure the reliability of the cryptocurrency system. The incorporation of hash function that could not be reverse engineered and the blockchain concept that makes the information hardly to be altered and modified renders the system to be secured and accountable.

Some cryptocurrencies such as bitcoin, peercoin and namecoin use SHA-256 as the mathematical algorithm. SHA-256 is a cryptographic hash algorithm that generates fixed length of 256-bit hash value. This ensures the security of the information in the transaction and for the purpose of validation and verification, because hash value, once it is being encrypted to generate a digest (output), it is not irreversible and is not revocable into the same hash algorithm even when the hash function mechanics is known.

Monzer Kahf has expressed his concern that when the public confidence of virtual currency collapses, the accounting or settlement system of it crumbles because cryptocurrency relies on the network to keep it continuously operating. However, the mechanics of the mathematical algorithm used in cryptocurrency seems to refute the concern it defines the reliability and security of the system. Therefore, it renders cryptocurrency to be accepted and public confidence is stored towards it, thus addressing the concern on the depletion of public confidence when the system crumbles and becomes unreliable.

Coin Supply

There are three categories of cryptocurrency coins supply; which are fixed number of supply, flexible number of supply and premined coins supply. Fixed number of supply entails a finite and limited supply of coins that could be mined in the system (example: bitcoin). Flexible number of supply, on the other hand, does not fix a hard limit on its supply but rather it is designed to eventually attain an annual inflation rate of 1%. Therefore, the mining of the coin is flexible and adjusted according to achieve the desired rate (example: Peercoin).[44] Premined coins supply is a readily mined coin that will be further distributed according to the schedule until it reached the maximum cap of the supply (example: Aureus).[45]

In the context of coin supply and production, there are few Shari'ah issues that may come along and require further attention.

Coin supply or production in cryptocurrency is done through the mining process that involves the real investment of computational power and energy by the miners. Miners solve the POW puzzle to be appended on the chain, which signifies the computational effort that has been invested (Teutsch, Jain and Saxena 2016). Mining is a process of generating new coins, thus it reflects the physical endeavour and power involved in the process. The computational effort also implicitly embodies the amount of watts and energy required to solve the hash problem. The quantum of watts and energy required is the item that brings value to cryptocurrency within the context of its coins production, because it involves the real resources of computers and power.

Therefore, it is observed that the computational energy represented by the power and watts needed are the intangible value in cryptocurrency coins production. The miners would be compensated because the coins generated through the hash problem solved are represented by a real and valid assets and investment. Mining activity is considered as a venture that the miners chose to participate resulted to more assets to be produced and circulated within the network. Mining activities ensure the maintenance of the network.

From Shari'ah perspective, authority for money production resides with the monetary authority or the government. The requirement is set to prevent future harm when the permission is given to anyone in unregulated manner and thus leading to price instability. Having one central authority to produce money that is used as medium of payment is part of attaining *maslahah*. The role of the authority to guarantee the value of the currency and its supply is instrumental as far as the

---

[44] European Central Bank, *Virtual Currency Schemes*, 11.

[45] See Aureus official website, http://aureus.cc.

money/currency production is concerned. Without such guarantee, the currency ceases to function as the medium of payment and as the tool to establish and extinguish debt, because there is no inherent value in the currency anymore. Without aforementioned role or function of the regulator, it would create a greater harm instead of positive effects. For instance, unregulated supply of money can affect the value of money, and unsupervised market forces result in volatile price fluctuation. Therefore, although any form of money is permissible to function as a currency for medium of exchange, the existence of the imminent harm would deflect the foundation of permissibility given.

The cryptocurrency supply or production is hard to regulate because the network is self-regulated in a way that it is not centrally administered. For example, a severe depletion in bitcoin price occurred during Mt. Gox collapse, which results in the users' huge chunk of loss.[46] The greatest lesson from the colossal collapse is the decentralized nature of cryptocurrency that made it possible for anyone to enter the market without central administration on the quantum of supply and demand interaction. Apart from that, the collapse also proved that although the technology is reliable and secured, the absence of regulatory measure has resulted in the loss of people's money in the Mt. Gox exchange, which has eventually cause the diminishing of the bitcoin price.

Shari'ah Analysis on Legal Tender

Legal tender is a tender of payment that by virtue of the law, it could not be rejected in a settlement of debt denominated in the same currency.[47] It is an object confers the right to user to use it as the medium of payment, exchanges and discharge of contract with the other transacting parties.[48] Legal tender is essentially the legal foundation of the monetary system which is accorded based on each jurisdiction of the country. The currency in the country that is accorded the legal tender status is thus the "lawful money" in the country.

---

[46] Gandal, Hamrick, Moore and Oberman, "Price Manipulation in Bitcoin Ecosystem", 4–5.

[47] Nick McBride, "Payment and Concept of Legal Tender", *Reserve Bank of New Zealand*, 70 (2007).

[48] Dror Goldberg, "Legal Tender", *Bar-Ilan University Working Paper*, 2009.

Having the legal tender title would make the cryptocurrency not only a legal currency of the country but also it is consistent with market movement and volatility, simply because there would be an authority oversees the fluctuation and maintain the currency value in order to avoid harmful depreciation in its value. Without such recognition, cryptocurrency ceases to fulfil the prerequisite of performing the function of legal currency, and thus upsetting the confidence of the public.

Having possessed all the attributes explained above, contemporary scholars, however, are concerned about the absence of cryptocurrency's status as a legal tender. Sheikh Taqi Uthmani and Monzer Kahf emphasized on the need of government or monetary authority's recognition of the cryptocurrency to regulate the fluctuating value of the currency; evade the inflation and deflation risk that may harm the value of the currency and the underlying purchasing power it holds. That is the *maslahah* that cryptocurrency failed to achieve by not having the legal tender status.

The public confidence could not be instilled only through showcasing a reliable and secure network system; it comprises also the price stability of the currency because that affects the value that currency holds. Despite the ability to offer a reliable virtual network of cryptocurrency exchange and fulfilling the three prerequisites of currency (medium of exchange, store of value, commonly acceptable), cryptocurrency still pose considerable risk in terms of the high volatility of its price.

The Shari'ah approved currency should originate from the authority of the government so the necessary regulatory and prudential measure can be taken to ensure its stability and thus serve its purpose for the community. This is what is meant by the real *maslahah*.

Conclusion

Cryptocurrency seems to satisfy the prerequisites of currency from Shari'ah perspective except the legal tender status. From the deliberation made, it seems that legal tender stands out to be the most important prerequisite for currency to be recognized from Shari'ah standpoint. Having the legal tender title would make the cryptocurrency practice consistent with market's movement and volatility, because there would be an authority oversees the fluctuation and maintain the currency value in order to avoid harmful depreciation of its value. The cryptocurrency that performs as the means of payment without legal tender status accorded to it may pose considerable risk for the regulators, users and economic ambience as a whole. This is congruent to the contemporary scholars' view that emphasizes the importance of having the legal recognition for the currency used as the medium of exchange and means of payment. This study observes that cryptocurrency features in the context of its default architecture capturing the validating mechanism, mathematical algorithm and coins supply fulfil the prerequisite of currency from Shari'ah perspective. However, the issue that is brewing still is the absence of legal tender status in cryptocurrency that may pose risk and problem in the eyes of Shari'ah.

Both the validating mechanism and mathematical algorithm that serve as the default architecture of cryptocurrency could offer security and reliability to the virtual community or users of cryptocurrency, but cryptocurrency is still vulnerable to the external market factor that would affect the price value of the coins being exchanged. Despite the stringent cryptocurrency architecture that would supply coins to its users through mining protocol being employed, the value of cryptocurrency is still prone to high volatility due to the absence of regulatory measure taken to control the price of the currency. With such fragility, it seems that cryptocurrency does not satisfy the prime prerequisite of currency that has been highlighted by fatwa of the scholars.

Echoing the contemporary scholars view on the importance of legal tender on top of the currency being accepted as the medium of exchange and can store value, this study agrees that cryptocurrency features comply the prerequisites of currency recognized in Shari'ah standpoint. It is however found in the absence of legal tender title, the three initial prerequisites would cease to function because of the considerable risk that may surface when there is no regulatory measure.

References

AAOIFI Shari'ah Standard, *Dealing with Currencies*, Standard No. 2/1/2 and No. 2/1/3.

Abdul Azim Islahi, "An Analytical Study on Al-Ghazali's Thought on Money and Interest", *Munich Personal RePEc Archive*, 2001.

Abdul Sattar Abu Ghuddah, *al-Nuqud al-Raqamiyah al-Ru'yah al-Syar'iyyah wal Athar al-Iqtisodiyah* (Doha, 2018), 24–25.

Al-Ghazali, *Kitab Al-Shukr Ihya' Ulumuddin* (Beirut: Dar Al-Ma'rifah, n.d.), 90.

Asyraf Wajdi Dusuki, Status of Ownership (*qabdh*) in Islamic Sale Contract, *Global Perspective on Islamic Banking and Insurance*, 175 (2010): 22–23.

Aureus official website, http://aureus.cc.

Australian Government (AUSTRAC), "Digital Currency Exchange Providers: Register Online with AUSTRAC", http://www.austrac.gov.au/news/digital-currency-exchange-providers-register-online-austrac (accessed April 16, 2018).

Bahroddin Badri, "*Qabd* (Possession): An Overview", *Bloomberg Finance*, June, 2015.

Bank Negara Malaysia, *Shari'ah Resolutions in Islamic Finance* (Kuala Lumpur: BNM, 2010), 138.

Chrisjan Pauw, "South Korea and Crypto Regulation: Explained", *Coin Telegraph*, February 6, 2018, https://cointelegraph.com/explained/south-korea-and-crypto-regulations-explained (accessed April 16, 2018).

Division 19 of Bill C-31: Money Laundering and Terrorist Financing, Amendment for Proceeds of Crime (Money Laundering) and Terrorist Financing Act, (2006), c. 12, s. 3(1), http://www.parl.ca/DocumentViewer/en/41-2/bill/C-31/royal-assent/page-344#37.

Dror Goldberg, "Legal Tender", *Bar-Ilan University Working Paper*, 2009.

Edward Robinson, "U.K. Starts Cryptocurrency Inquiry as Lawmakers Weigh Regulation", *Bloomberg News*, February 22, 2018, https://www.bloomberg.com/news/articles/2018-02-22/u-k-starts-cryptocurrency-inquiry-as-lawmakers-weigh-regulation (accessed May 2, 2018).

European Central Bank, *Virtual Currency Schemes*, 11.

European Central Bank, *Virtual Currency Schemes* (Brussel: ECB, 2015), 23.

Fatwa Syabakah Islamiyah, No. 251170, http://fatwa.islamweb.net/fatwa/index.php?page=showfatwa&Option=FatwaId&Id=251170.

Gandal, Hamrick, Moore and Oberman, "Price Manipulation in Bitcoin Ecosystem", 4–5.

https://www.ato.gov.au/General/Gen/Tax-treatment-of-crypto-currencies-in-Australia—specifically-bitcoin/.

https://www.fincen.gov/.

https://www.law.cornell.edu/cfr/text/31/1010.100 and https://www.gpo.gov/fdsys/pkg/FR-2011-07-21/pdf/2011-18309.pdf.

Ibn Abidin, *Darr Al-Mukhtar wa Hasyiyah Ibn Abidin* (Beirut: Dar Al-Fikr, 1992), 534.

Ibn Qudamah, *Al-Mughni li Ibnu Qudamah* (Cairo: Maktab Al-Kaherah, 1968), 39.

Ibn Taymiyah, *Majmu' Fatawa*, ed. Abdul Rahman Ibn Muhammad (Madinah: Majma' Al-Malik Al-Fahd li Tiba'ah, 1995), 250.

Jamie Redman, "Bitcoin Brings '100% Mathematical Certainty' to Comply with Islamic Law", *The Coin Telegraph*, https://cointelegraph.com/news/bitcoin-brings-100-mathematical-certainty-to-comply-with-islamic-law (accessed January 12, 2017).

Jason Teutsch, Sanjay Jain and Prateek Saxena, "When Cryptocurrencies Mine Their Own Business", *Financial Cryptography and Data Security* (2016): 499–514.

Jasper Hamill, Canadian Regulators Welcome US Bitcoin Refugees with Open Arms, REGISTER (May 20, 2013), http://www.theregister.co.uk/2013/05/20/canada_welcomes_bitcoin_traders_fintrac_letter/.

Kevin Helms, "Japan Declares Sale of Bitcoin Exempt from Consumption Tax", *Bitcoin News*, https://news.bitcoin.com/japan-sale-bitcoin-exempt-consumption-tax/ (accessed July 21, 2017).

Lathan and Watkins LLP, *Cryptocurrency: A Primer* (New York, 2015).

Majlis Fatwa Kebangsaan, Hukum Penggunaan Bitcoin Sebagai Medium untuk Bermuamalat, *e-fatwa Majlis Fatwa Kebangsaan* (April 2, 2014), https://web.archive.org/web/20150122215500/http:/www.e-fatwa.gov.my/blog/hukum-penggunaan-bitcoin-sebagai-medium-untuk-bermuamalat.

Matthew Kluchenek, "Bitcoin and Cryptocurrencies: Welcome to Your Regulator", *Harvard Business Law Review*, 2016: 1–2.

Monzer Kahf, *Fatwa*, http://monzer.kahf.com/index.html.

Monzer Kahf, *The Islamic Economy: An Analytical Study of the Functioning of the Islamic Economic System* (Canada, 1978).

Neil Gandal, JT. Hamrick, Tyler Moore and Tali Oberman, "Price Manipulation in Bitcoin Ecosystem", *Workshop on the Economics of Information Security (WEIS)*, 2016.

Nick McBride, "Payment and Concept of Legal Tender", *Reserve Bank of New Zealand*, 70 (2007).

Press Release, European Banking Authority, EBA Warns Consumers on Virtual Currencies (December 13, 2013), http://www.eba.europa.eu/-/eba-warns-consumers-on-virtual-currencies.

Quoc Khanh Nguyen, "Blockchain—A Financial Technology for Future Sustainable Development", *3rd International Conference on Green Technology and Sustainable Development*, 2016: 51.

Robert Schimdt, "Bitcoin-Futures Regulator Clears Employees to Trade Crypto Coins", *Bloomberg News*, https://www.bloomberg.com/news/articles/2018-02-28/bitcoin-futures-regulator-clears-employees-to-trade-crypto-coins (accessed May 3, 2018).

Sayuri Umeda, *Japan: Bitcoin to be Regulated*, http://www.loc.gov/law/foreign-news/article/japan-bitcoin-to-be-regulated/ (accessed July 21, 2017).

Shafi Mussadique, "UK Government Plans Bitcoin Crackdown Amid Money Laundering Concern", *The Independent (UK)*, December 4, 2017, https://www.independent.co.uk/news/business/news/uk-bitcoin-regulation-money-laundering-crytocurrency-european-union-eu-a8090791.html (accessed May 1, 2018).

Takashi Nakazaki and Ken Kawai, "Development of Legal Framework for Virtual Currency in Japan", *Anderson Mori & Tomotsune Law*, 2016: 2.

Taqi Uthmani, *Buhuth fi Qadhaya Fiqh Muasorah* (Damsyik: Dar Al-Qalam, 2003), 157.

The Internal Revenue Service's Virtual Currency Guideline, https://www.irs.gov/uac/newsroom/irs-virtual-currency-guidance.

UK Financial Conduct Authority's Consumer Warning on ICO and Other Issuance, https://www.fca.org.uk/news/statements/initial-coin-offerings.

Yuri Suzuki and Ryosuke Oue, "Fintech Legislation in Japan", *Global Banking and Financial Policy Review*, 2016.

PART IV

Empiricality of Halal Cryptocurrency Management

CHAPTER 14

Halal Cryptocurrency: Its Establishment and Operational Mechanisms

Mohd Ma'Sum Billah

INTRODUCTION

The brainchild idea with every strategic and business model of *Halal* Cryptocurrency Management was first discovered and initiated with intellectual discussions, writings and designations by some academia, researchers, scholars, industrialists and software professionals sometimes in early 2017. The idea has been shared among the interested ones, presented in forums and written in periodicals and promoted in the social media. Subsequently, some initiated to establish a *Shari'ah* compliant Cryptocurrency model with global operation. A *Shari'ah* compliant Cryptocurrency is a digital currency platform initiated by cryptography and operated based on a block-chain technology. Its objective, operational mechanisms, technicalities, culture and all activities shall be in total compliance with the *Shari'ah* principles (*Halal* standard), which shall regularly be referred to and screened through by a *Shari'ah* board before one's operation takes place. It shall be treated as a commercial entity, offering Cryptocurrency globally based on *Halal* standard (*Shari'ah* compliance)

M. M. Billah (✉)
Finance, Insurance, Fintech and Investment, Islamic Economics Institute, King Abdul Aziz University, Jeddah, Kingdom of Saudi Arabia
URL: http://www.drmasumbillah.blogspot.com

© The Author(s) 2019
M. M. Billah (ed.), *Halal Cryptocurrency Management*,
https://doi.org/10.1007/978-3-030-10749-9_14

221

within the *Maqasid al-Shari'ah*. For a *Halal* Cryptocurrency, it is among the prerequisites to ensure that the entity and its total operations are backed by a valued asset. In other word, a *Halal* Cryptocurrency shall be on asset-back operation within the ambit of *Shari'ah*.

OBJECTIVES

Among the objectives of a *Halal* Cryptocurrency are:

- Offering and managing *Halal* Cryptocurrency with the rules of *Shari'ah* compliance.
- To create a legitimate income opportunity for all mankind (regardless of one's religion, race, status, gender, color or nationality) within the *Maqasid al-Shari'ah*.
- To create a micro-investment platform for all mankind with holistic approach of universal character (regardless of one's religion, race, status, gender, colour or nationality) through *Halal* Cryptocurrency Management.
- To create an economic well-being for all mankind through *Halal* Cryptocurrency platform based on the holistic principles of mutual cooperation and solidarity.
- To care about the poor and helpless ones by segregating a part of the income over the *Halal* Cryptocurrency operation within the divine principles of humanity.

GOVERNING PRINCIPLES

The governing principles of a *Halal* Cryptocurrency are as follows:

- All levels of products and services of a *Halal* Cryptocurrency Management shall be designed, regulated and operated in accordance with the principles of *Shari'ah*.
- All activities, policies, technicalities and mechanisms of a *Halal* Cryptocurrency Management shall be in conformity with the *Halal* standard and within the *Maqasid al-Shari'ah*.
- All activities, policies, technicalities, mechanisms, products and services of a *Halal* Cryptocurrency shall be closely monitored, screened and approved by the *Shari'ah* Advisory Board (SAB) of a *Halal* Cryptocurrency Management to ensure every *Shari'ah* compliance is strictly observed.

- The *Halal* Cryptocurrency Management's Board of Advisors (BOA) shall also play a vital role to advise the company, to ensure its policies, products and services are in conformity with the *Shari'ah* principles within the *Maqasid al-Shari'ah*.
- A *Halal* Cryptocurrency Management shall also strictly observe and duly comply with other applicable national or international laws and policies.

ETHICAL PRINCIPLES

Among the ethical principles of a *Halal* Cryptocurrency Management are:

- All levels of decision makers, advisors, operators and facilitators of a *Halal* Cryptocurrency Management shall observe the principles of *Shari'ah* (*Halal* standard) in their activities with relation to a *Halal* Cryptocurrency Management in view of *Maqasid Al-Shari'ah*.
- Anyone involves in a *Halal* Cryptocurrency Management directly or indirectly shall observe the divine principles of honesty, transparency, rights and obligations while strictly opposing and avoiding the unlawful culture or unethical gain at the expense of others.
- None of the parties involved in a *Halal* Cryptocurrency Management directly or indirectly shall be allowed to practice undue influence, misrepresentation, duress, malpractices, falsehood, manipulation, selfishness, deceit and/or other unethical action.

MODEL AND STRUCTURE

A *Halal* Cryptocurrency Management shall be based on the following model and structure:

- A *Halal* Cryptocurrency Management is a digital currency model based on the principles of *Shari'ah* (*Halal* standard).
- The total operation of a *Halal* Cryptocurrency Management is a *Shari'ah* compliant hybrid model.
- It evolves as both an asset-back and also an asset-base operation within the *Shari'ah* frameworks.
- The company is backed by a valued asset, while its products and services (business operations) are based on asset (valued coins/tokens).

- A *Halal* Cryptocurrency Management's total operation is facilitated by *Shari'ah* justified instruments and divine principles, like *al-Mudarabah* (co-partnership), *al-Musharakah* (partnership or joint-venture), *al-Wakalah* (agency with commission), *al-Wadiyah* (deposit), *al-Ju'alah* (reward or service charge), *al-Amanah* (trust), *al-Ijarah* (charge), *al-Tabarru'at* (donation) and *al-Zakat* (alms).
- The structure of a *Halal* Cryptocurrency Management is thus, it is a *Halal* hybrid platform of Cryptocurrency backed by a valued asset and, facilitated and dully operated mainly based on the *Shari'ah* principles of *al-Musharakah* and others (shared profit) and *al-Wakalah* (agency with service charge).
- A *Halal* Cryptocurrency operation shall be based on "Issuer Coin or Token" by trading platform by decentralized direct (one-to-one) buying and selling (*Bai' wa al-Shira'*).
- A *Halal* Cryptocurrency Management can also be operated through exchange platform based on a *Shari'ah* hybrid mechanism, facilitated by the doctrines of *al-Shuftaza* (exchange), *al-Hewalah* (transfer), *al-Kafalah* (custodianship), *al-Amanah* (trust), *al-Wakalah* (agency by commission), *al-Ju'alah* (reward for services) and *al-Ujrah* (service charge) within the *Shari'ah* frameworks.

OPERATIONAL MECHANISM

The operational mechanisms of a *Halal* Cryptocurrency Management are as follows:

- The operation adapts its prime operational tool based on valued coin or token offering through the issuance of the initial coin offering (ICO) justified and duly screened through by the general principles of *Shari'ah* and divine ethical standard.
- The offered coins or tokens through the ICO may also be effectively transacted (buying-selling) further in the secondary market within the *Shari'ah* ambit.
- A *Halal* Cryptocurrency Management may also provide a platform for the international *Waqf* cooperation and contribution through Cryptocurrency.

TECHNOLOGICAL MODEL

- The products and services under a *Halal* Cryptocurrency Management (*Halal* Cryptocurrency in coins or tokens) shall be operated based on a *Shari'ah* screened block-chain technology.
- The block-chain technology is cyberspace platform provider with a reliable block-chain solution to systemize, manage, operate and function all activities of a *Halal* Cryptocurrency Management within the *Maqasid al-Shari'ah*.
- The block-chain technology for a *Halal* Cryptocurrency Management is closely monitored by the *Shari'ah* experts to ensure all technological supports for a *Halal* Cryptocurrency platform are with *Shari'ah* compliance (*Halal* standard).

SCOPE AND LIMITATIONS

Among the scope and limitations of a *Halal* Cryptocurrency Management are:

- A *Halal* Cryptocurrency Management shall be operated within the principles of *Maqasid al-Shari'ah*.
- All its policies, activities, structures, systems, products and services shall be in conformity with the *Shari'ah* principles.
- The culture shall generally be, in compliance with the divine ethical standards and *Halal* principles.

PRODUCTS AND SERVICES

Among the products and services of a *Halal* Cryptocurrency Management are:

- *Halal* Cryptocurrency with valued coins/tokens.
- *Waqf* management through Cryptocurrency.
- Investment through *Halal* Cryptocurrency.
- Trading platform through *Halal* Cryptocurrency.
- Humanitarian concern through *Halal* Cryptocurrency Management.
- Global *Tabarru'at* (Charity) Foundation through *Halal* Cryptocurrency Management.

BACKING ASSET

The company, its products and services shall be backed by valued assets as a backing asset. Thus, a certified proof of product (POP) shall be prerequisite to ensure that, the total operation of a *Halal* Cryptocurrency Management is backed by commercially valued asset. Backing asset for a *Halal* Cryptocurrency Management and its operation refers to a certified POP carrying the commercial value of a legitimate asset, product, property, intellectual property, IT, solution, program and/or others recognized by the Shari'ah principles. The POP shall carry the value at least the equivalent of the ICO. For a valid operation of a *Halal* Cryptocurrency, the backing asset is prerequisite to ensure that the total products and services or business activities of the entity are an asset-backed operation. The backing asset shall only be treated as the backing asset of the company, its activities, products and services. The backing asset is just for the purpose of supporting and facilitating the company's capacity.

DECISION MAKERS

The decision making in a *Halal* Cryptocurrency Management shall be empowered to the following authorities:

- Board of Directors (General Decision).
- SAB (Shari'ah Compliance, Screening and Approval).
- In-house Advisor or Consultant (Technical advice).
- BOA (Overall advice).

SHARI'AH ADVISORY BOARD

The SAB of a *Halal* Cryptocurrency Management shall comprise of qualified *Shari'ah* scholars including *Mufti*, *Shari'ah* judge, *Shari'ah* lawyer, Islamic finance expert, Islamic finance researcher, *Shari'ah* scholars in Cryptocurrency and others.

Among the functions of the SAB are:

- To advise, supervise, monitor and approve a *Halal* Cryptocurrency Management and all its policies, systems, activities, operations and mechanisms to ensure the company and its operation are generally compliance with the *Shari'ah* principles.

- The SAB shall also screen and approve all activities of a *Halal* Cryptocurrency Management to ensure all are compliant with the *Shari'ah* principles (*Halal* standard).
- The SAB shall also contribute to a *Halal* Cryptocurrency Management in training its employees and also the public as per required with *Shari'ah* compliant Cryptocurrency model.

BOARD OF ADVISORS

The BOA of a *Halal* Cryptocurrency Management may comprise of renowned scholars including academia, financial experts, business operators and other key people in the Islamic financial industry.

Among the functions of the BOA are:

- To advise the *Halal* Cryptocurrency Management to ensure that the company is moving forward dynamically within the *Maqasid al-Shari'ah*.
- The BOA shall also contribute to a *Halal* Cryptocurrency Management in training its employees and also the public as per required with *Shari'ah* compliant Cryptocurrency model.

THE MANAGEMENT

A *Halal* Cryptocurrency Management shall be managed by a qualified management team by complying the business dynamism, quality management and smart strategies within the holistic spirit of *Shari'ah* ethical principles. The management team shall be headed by a well experienced with corporate personality and Islamic finance expert Managing Director or Chief Executive Director.

THE PUBLIC STATEMENT

In every operation of *Shari'ah* compliant Cryptocurrency, it is recommended to make a public statement through social media, soft-launching or organizing a summit prior to the actual operation takes place by ICO or initial product offering (IPO) or initial token offering (ITO). Thus, a model of a public statement may be as follows:

A *Halal* Cryptocurrency Management is a *Shari'ah* compliant Cryptocurrency. It is backed by a valued asset with legal authentic proof of property (POP). Its establishment, policies, management, operation, activities and general culture are compliant to the spirit of *Halal* standard and within the *Maqasid al-Shari'ah*.

Its block-chain technology, ledger system and operational mechanisms are designed as a *Halal* hybrid model based on the *Shari'ah* doctrines of *Silsalat al-Katl, al-Ta'awun, al-Musharakah, al-Bai wa al-Shira', al-Wakalah, al-Fudhuli, al-Ju'alah* and *al-Tabarru'at*.

The total activities of *Halal* Cryptocurrency Management are generally screened through by Islamic finance and *Halal* Cryptocurrency expert, supervised by a SAB comprising of a team of renowned *Shari'ah* scholars and further advised by a Board of Advisers (BoA) comprising of a group of academia, economists and industrialists, to ensure the activities and operation of *Halal* Cryptocurrency Management are compliance with the spirit of *Halal* standard.

Among the prime objectives of a *Halal* Cryptocurrency Management are: to create an economic and entrepreneurial opportunities for all mankind (particularly those of with less fortunate), embracing with the universal character (regardless of one's religion, color, status, gender or nationality) and within the holistic spirit of *Maqasid al-Shari'ah*.

It is also the strict policy of a *Halal* Cryptocurrency Management with a special provision to segregate part of all levels of its income for the humanitarian causes within the broad principles of *Zakat* and *al-Tabarru'at*.

THE WHITE PAPER: INTRODUCTION TO *HALAL* COIN

The Halal *COIN*

It is a *Shari'ah* compliant (*Halal*) Cryptocurrency Management platform with global prospect. Its block-chain system, technology, model, objective, operational mechanisms, technicalities, culture and all activities shall be in total compliance with the *Shari'ah* principles (*Halal* standard), which shall regularly be advised by the company's BOA, screened through by the company's in-house adviser prior to the approval by the SAB of the company and thereafter shall be operated or executed globally.

Emerging of Block-Chain

The Cryptocurrency through the block-chain technology is a cyberspace economic revolution in the twenty-first century. Numerous players are in the market globally to offer Cryptocurrency platforms but with many shortcomings like lack of regulatory supports, poor strategic planning, uncertainty and mostly with no backing asset, but only on virtual assumption. Whereas a *Halal* model of Cryptocurrency is a *Shari'ah* compliant Cryptocurrency model is timely to fill the gap of the ongoing shortcomings in the Cryptocurrency market. The *Halal* Cryptocurrency model is thus, backed by a valued asset (POP), operated based on valued assets (coins), transactions are based on *Shari'ah* instruments of *al-Musharakah*, *al-Wakalah*, *al-Ju'alah*, *al-Tabarru'at* and so on, concerns about humanitarian well-being, regulated by the standard *Shari'ah* principles, oppose to uncertainty in any component and liberty in enjoying with legitimate (*Halal*) investment return. Thus, in the *Halal* Cryptocurrency model has the greater opportunity to attract the global Cryptocurrency market with sustainable existence in the emergence of block-chain technology.

Background of Halal COIN

The idea of a *Halal* Cryptocurrency model was initiated with strategic structure in early 2007 on how a *Halal* Cryptocurrency model can be developed and duly operated globally with a unique model to meet the contemporary demand as to Cryptocurrency operation with *Halal* standard within the *Maqasid al-Shari'ah*. It was initiated with grassroots ideas, strategies, mechanisms and structures. It has been continued by sharing in different occasions and countries around the world both in Muslim and non-Muslim environments outreaching through social media in particular. To strengthen the idea further, this book project on *Halal* Cryptocurrency Management undertaken has been by focusing on numerous specialized issues as among the pioneering and leading works on *Halal* Cryptocurrency model in the contemporary world of Cryptocurrency.

How Halal COIN Could Help to Solve Some Problem

The prime objective of a *Halal* Cryptocurrency model is to create an enterprising and entrepreneuring based community across the world through *Halal* Cryptocurrency Management and participation globally.

This may ultimately fight the poverties, jobless, domestic economic crisis and world eco-catastrophe. A *Halal* Cryptocurrency Management is with universal character welcoming, encouraging and benefiting to all mankind regardless of one's religion, race, status, gender, color or even nationality. The operation does not concern only money making, but part of its income (2.5%) is mandatorily deductible as *Zakat* for the charitable causes. Furthermore, all gross income in every transaction, account, management, activities, income and services may be encouraged to be subjected a reasonable deduction as *al-Tabarru'at* (charity) for the humanitarian causes within the *Maqasid al-Shari'ah*.

The Meaning of Halal COIN

Halal COIN refers to *Halal* Cryptocurrency model, to be operated based on the *Shari'ah* principles. It is a coin or token-based offering and activated by transactions based on *Shari'ah* trading mechanisms through *Halal* screened block-chain technology.

HALAL COIN BRANDING AND DEFINITION

The basic features of *Halal* Cryptocurrency model is that it shall be operated based on the *Halal* standard (compliant with the *Shari'ah* principles) closely supervised by a world-class SAB, advised by team of scholars as a BOA and further monitored and screened through in-house *Shari'ah* expert. The management of *Halal* Cryptocurrency Management is to abide by the standard *Shari'ah* guidelines and ethical standard. All investors (token holders) are protected by transparent transactions and are formalized based on the *Shari'ah* doctrine of *al-Musharakah* (partnership), *al-Jualah* (service charge) and *al-Wakalah* (agency).

Halal *COIN Structural Analysis*

A *Halal* Cryptocurrency Management shall be based on the following model and structure:

- The model shall be based on the principles of *Shari'ah* (*Halal* standard).
- The total operation shall be based on a *Shari'ah* compliant hybrid model.

- It evolves as both an asset-backed and also an asset-based operation within the *Shari'ah* frameworks.
- The company is backed by a valued asset, while its products and services (business operations) are based on asset (valued coins or tokens).
- The total operation is facilitated by *Shari'ah* justified instruments and divine principles. Among those doctrines are: *al-Mudarabah* (co-partnership), *al-Musharakah* (partnership or joint-venture), *al-Wakalah* (agency with commission), *al-Wadiyah* (deposit), *al-Ju'alah* (reward or service charge), *al-Amanah* (trust), *al-Ijarah* (charge), *al-Tabarru'at* (donation) and *al-Zakat* (alms or compulsory tax).
- The structure of the model is thus, it is a *Halal* hybrid platform of Cryptocurrency backed by valued asset and, facilitated and dully operated mainly based on the *Shari'ah* principles within *Maqasid al-Shari'ah*.
- The operation shall be based on "Issuer Coin or Token", but exceptionally, it can be based on exchange platform subject to strict *Shari'ah* ethical guidelines.
  A *Halal* Cryptocurrency operation shall primarily be based on "Issuer Coin or Token" by trading platform, a decentralized direct (one-to-one) buying and selling (*Bai' wa al-Shira'*). However, it may exceptionally be operated through exchange platform based on a *Shari'ah* hybrid mechanism, facilitated by the doctrines of *al-Shuftaza* (exchange), *al-Hewalah* (transfer), *al-Kafalah* (custodianship), *al-Amanah* (trust), *al-Wakalah* (agency by commission), *al-Ju'alah* (reward for services) and *al-Ujrah* (service charge) within the *Shari'ah* frameworks.

APPLICATION OF A *HALAL* CRYPTOCURRENCY

Financial Assets Exchange (Backing Asset)

The company, its products and services are strictly backed by a valued asset as a backing asset. Backing asset for a *Halal* Cryptocurrency Management and its operation refers to certified POP with an approved value equivalent to the value of the ICO at least.

Pass-Up Plan

Total Volume

Total volume with ICO may rationally be recommended not to exceed: 1,000,000,000 coins, or tokens with roaring value may not exceed USD 1.00.00 each. Thus, total value with all phases of the ICO may not exceed USD 1,000,000,000.00.

Launch Time

At a convenient time only after the following confirmations:

- Registration of the company.
- Documentations (Manual, Policies, Guidelines, Standards, Planning and Strategies).
- Complete tested model through block-chain technology.
- System of operation.
- Management team.
- Equipped office.
- Shari'ah Advisory Board.
- Board of Advisors.
- Technical Advisor.
- Web site.
- White paper and public statement.
- Bank Accounts.
- Summit.
- Soft-launching.
- Initial coin offering.

Digital Asset Ratio

Total value of the offered coins or tokens.

Halal *Cryptocurrency Appreciation Logic*

No competitive model of *Halal* Cryptocurrency has been launched yet. Huge demand globally, but no supply (available model), yet thus it's timely for the *Halal* Cryptocurrency to grab the global market with utmost appreciation.

PROJECT PROGRESS AND TEAM

The project of *Halal* Cryptocurrency model is ready in hand with all modeling, strategic and structural solutions, required documentations, backing asset, decision makers, advisory panel, supervisory panel, marketing teams, audit (compliance), procedure, mechanisms, technological supports, logistic supports and management team with almost preparation. Thus, various teams are as follows:

- Board of Directors.
- Shari'ah Advisory Board.
- Board of Advisors.
- Technical Advisors.
- Management Team.

OPERATION

A *Halal* Cryptocurrency Management may maintain its operating office in any offshore or in any other suitable location. It may maintain its corporate offices or branches in different locations or jurisdictions, as may time to time be decided by the Board of Directors.

MARKET

A *Halal* Cryptocurrency Management shall be in liberty to create its marketplace across the cyber world within the legitimate frameworks, but within the spirit of *Maqasid al-Shari'ah*. The customers and investors are not limited, but open to anyone regardless of one's religion, race, status, gender or nationality.

ACCOUNTS

A *Halal* Cryptocurrency Management may maintain the following accounts

- Customer's or Investor's Account (coin holders).
- Board of Directors' accounts.
- Company's Management Account.
- *Waqf* Cooperation Account.
- Humanitarian Account.
- *Tabarru'at* (Charity) Account.

SIGNIFICANT RESULTS

Among the significant results of a *Halal* Cryptocurrency operation are:

- To create an atmosphere for all mankind to participate with investment opportunities through *Halal* Cryptocurrency within the *Maqasid al-Shari'ah*.
- To help everyone generally and particularly those who are poor and less income group to create an economic opportunity by participating in the *Halal* Cryptocurrency Management.
- To create a global awareness among all with an encouragement to enjoy with entrepreneuring and enterprising opportunities through *Halal* Cryptocurrency Management.
- To create an economic empowerment with basic rights for all mankind through *Halal* Cryptocurrency Management.

HUMANITARIAN CONCERN THROUGH *TABARRU'AT*

A *Halal* Cryptocurrency Management may aim at creating a *Tabarru'at* (Charity) fund through the partial contribution from the income to care and concern about those who are poor, helpless, destitute, orphans and other underprivileged ones in any society to meet their basic needs and natural rights of well-beings within the holistic spirit of *Maqasid al-Shari'ah*.

CONCLUSION

In the contemporary digital space, there are numerous type of Cryptocurrency operated, but with no standard system, operational mechanisms non-compliance to the legal requirements. This may be a negative phenomenon to the participants in the Cryptocurrency and also to the system in general. For a sustainable existence of Cryptocurrency, it shall observe and maintain from its establishment till its effective operation all legal requirements. A *Halal* Cryptocurrency model is in no exception, which shall be recognized only by its existence with legal and *Shari'ah* compliance in its establishment, system, operation and code of ethics.

CHAPTER 15

Case Study of Bitcoin and Its *Halal* Dimension

Farrukh Habib and Salami Saheed Adekunle

INTRODUCTION

Crypto-asset is a form of digital or electronic asset, which was introduced with the inception of Bitcoin in 2009. The authors' own definition of crypto-asset is that '*it is a digital representation of value that uses cryptographic encryption technique.*' Before delving into the main discussion, it is crucial to mention at the very beginning of this chapter that according to the authors, the term 'cryptocurrency' is a misnomer and a nomenclature which is used inappropriately. It has been made clearer in another chapter of this book that neither all types of crypto-assets are 'currencies,' nor 'cryptocurrencies' are the only type of crypto-assets. Actually, cryptocurrencies are a subset of crypto-assets, while there are many other types of crypto-assets. The only reason for the popularity of the term 'cryptocurrency' for all types of crypto-assets is that the first crypto-asset, Bitcoin, and other early-stage crypto-assets,

F. Habib (✉)
International Shari'ah Research Academy
for Islamic Finance (ISRA), Kuala Lumpur, Malaysia

S. S. Adekunle
International Centre for Education
in Islamic Finance (INCEIF), Kuala Lumpur, Malaysia

© The Author(s) 2019
M. M. Billah (ed.), *Halal Cryptocurrency Management*,
https://doi.org/10.1007/978-3-030-10749-9_15

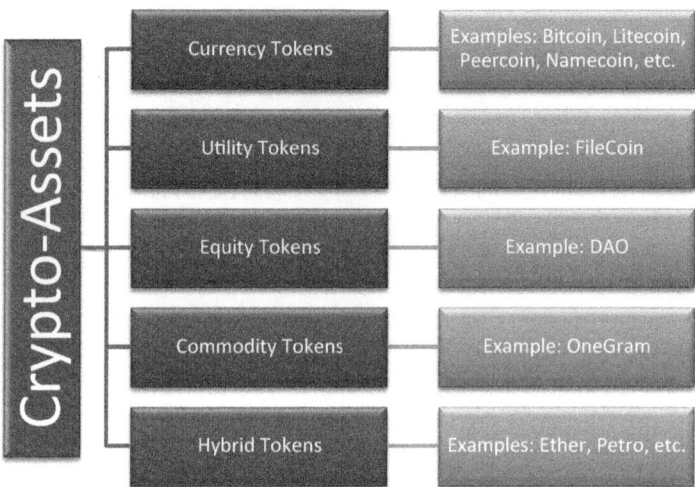

Fig. 15.1 Types of crypto-assets (*Source* Author's own)

Namecoin, Litecoin, Peercoin, and others, were created as currency tokens. However, most of the crypto-assets are hybrid, having features of currency, as well as other types of asset, and hence making it difficult to draw a clear line of distinction, but the classification is still useful in acquiring a better understanding and presenting the discussion in a less confusing manner. Therefore, an accurate classification of crypto-assets, along with the Bitcoin, is given in Fig. 15.1.

Therefore, unlike the general trend, in this chapter, the term 'cryptocurrency' is only used for the currency tokens and not for all types of crypto-assets. For the general class, the term 'crypto-assets' is preferred and used throughout the chapter, which is technically and logically more appropriate and less confusing for such type of asset class.

Generally, the introduction of Internet, e-commerce, mobile network, and smart devices has greatly contributed in changing the shape of monetary and financial services. However, the inception of Bitcoin, and other crypto-assets, has been among the greatest influencers and strongest catalyst for disruption. Although the crypto-asset class, like Bitcoin, is still at its infancy stage, experts have already regarded its impact and effect as the beginning of a new technological revolution, particularly relevant to the financial services sector.

Money has a history of transformation through several items: shells, wheels, beads, and even cows. Broadly from commodity, money is made of a substance that had its own value such as gold and silver coins through representative money which is a certificate, a debt receipt, or digital token, exchangeable for the underlying commodity to fiat currency which does not have intrinsic usage or benefit and does not represent an underlying asset in a vault somewhere; money has recorded significant transformation. Today, digital money in the form of virtual currency as represented by Bitcoin and other currency tokens is another significant milestone in money transformation. While the value of fiat money comes from being recognized as legal tender by the government of the issuing country which then leads to its acceptance by the people, Bitcoin's value emanates from the recognition of stakeholders in the participating community. In other words, it is derived from general people's trust in the system and the economic principle of demand and supply.

Bitcoin has been mainstreaming gradually in the major financial discourse and multi-billion-dollar financial technology industry away from its obscure origin as a monetary experiment of a small group of techno-libertarians. It is being accepted in a growing number of online and offline stores as a form of payment. This increasing acceptability of Bitcoin has gravitated the interest of many financial stakeholders to this virtual currency. There are growing need and calls by and on policy makers for a well-analyzed and robust Shari'ah and regulatory positions for this almost USD 500 billion industry. Islamic economists and finance practitioners are also expectedly concerned about the Shari'ah perspective of this new asset class. Thus, this chapter seeks to and presents an analysis on the case study of Bitcoin and its halal dimension. While doing so, it hopes to offer a significant contribution in this direction.

HISTORICAL AND RECENT DEVELOPMENTS

A cryptocurrency is developed using cryptography which is the technique of encrypting information, or transactions in the case of cryptocurrencies, for the sake of its secured exchange, and algorithms designed to solve difficult computational problems as the proof-of-work. The underlying technology of cryptocurrencies, crypto-assets in general, is referred to as blockchain. It is the technology of digital distributed ledger, where information is saved in the form of blocks with the help of cryptographic security (Wyk 2013).

There are presently over 1442 cryptocurrencies which could be broadly classified into Bitcoin and alternative coins, or altcoins in short (Coinmarketcap.com 2018). According to this classification, every crypto-asset, other than bitcoins, is called altcoin. As of December 2017, there were over 16.78 million bitcoins in circulation with a total market value of USD 158 billion (Higgins 2017).

Following the global financial crisis, in 2008, Satoshi Nakamoto, a pseudonym, introduced the idea of digital peer-to-peer (P2P) payment system in the form of Bitcoin and suggested reducing the intermediary role of financial institutions in the financial transactions. The system was introduced as an alternative to building trust among the parties of a transaction at a distributed network while maintaining their anonymity and that too without having a third party to establish that trust (Nakamoto 2008). Just after initiating the idea, Satoshi Nakamoto also developed the system and uploaded it as an open source program in 2009.

Altcoins are the alternative crypto-assets launched after the success of Bitcoin. They are projected as better substitutes to Bitcoin by trying to target any perceived limitations of Bitcoin and develop newer versions with competitive advantages. They include Litecoin (LTC, launched in 2011), Ethereum (ETH, launched in 2015), Zcash (ZEC, launched in 2016), Dash (originally known as Darkcoin, launched in 2014), Ripple (XRP, launched in 2012), Monero (XMR, launched in 2014), and many others (Bajpai 2017).

Policy decisions of nations toward Bitcoin are multifarious, while some are friendly such as Estonia, the USA, Denmark, Japan, Sweden South Korea, the Netherlands, Finland, Canada, UK, and Australia (Scott 2016). Some adopt ban on Bitcoin, such include Bangladesh, Bolivia, China, Ecuador, Iceland, India, Russia, Sweden, Thailand, Vietnam (Smart 2015), while others remain indecisive. Examples of such nations include Malaysia (De 2017). In many of these states, the journey of their regulatory development on Bitcoin has been long and in some cases still continuous. Japan, for instance, approved a law regulating virtual currencies on May 25, 2016, which was promulgated on June 3, 2016. The law was enacted and came into effect on April 1, 2017. On September 30, 2017, the Financial Services Agency (FSA) of Japan granted its first license for digital currency exchanges to 11 companies. On April 1, 2017, it enacted a new law authorizing the use of digital currency as a method of payment, essentially granting it the same legal status as any other currency. The law follows months of debate which ultimately brought Bitcoin exchanges under anti-money laundering (AML) and know-your-customer (KYC) rules, and resulted in the categorization of Bitcoin as a kind of payment instrument.

BITCOIN EXPLAINED

Crypto-assets got to financial limelight since 2008 just toward the end of the global financial crisis, and the first was Bitcoin in 2009 developed by Satoshi Nakamoto (the pseudonym publishing the initial white paper about Bitcoin). Bitcoin is a concept of an encrypted virtual currency using the blockchain protocol to perform financial transactions. In the aftermath of the financial crises in 2008, Bitcoin was developed as an alternative to traditional currencies (Deloitte 2015).

In a strict sense, the definition of Bitcoin can be given as:

> Bitcoin is a collection of concepts and technologies that form the basis of a digital money ecosystem. (Antonopoulos 2015, p. 1)

Another definition is given as:

> Bitcoin is a decentralized digital currency. (Franco 2015, p. 3)

The meaning of decentralized is that Bitcoin is neither controlled by central authority nor issued, endorsed, or regulated by any central bank. Instead, bitcoins are created through a computational process known as mining. The blockchain technology behind it tracks and records data across a digital ledger, which is distributed on a network made up of participating parties. The distributed ledger system means that instead of data being kept only by two counterparties or in a central repository, it is verified and stored across hundreds or thousands of computers across the globe (Deloitte 2015).

In other words, Bitcoin, the system,[1] exists in the form of copies of a distributed digital ledger containing all the transactions of Bitcoin that are

---

[1] Throughout this chapter, the term 'Bitcoin' with capital 'B' refers to the system or the blockchain ledger itself which is only one, and hence, it is not correct to use this term in plural form with an 's'. On the other hand, the term with small 'b' or in plural form with an 's' is used for the currency units generated by the system in the form of digital tokens.

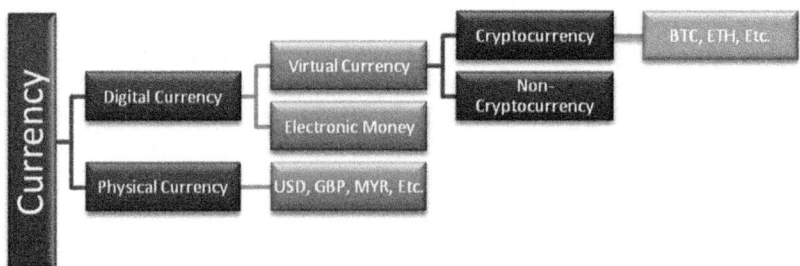

Fig. 15.2 Taxonomy of Bitcoin as a currency (*Source* Author's own)

stored and updated through the nodes that communicate with each other over the Internet. The copies contain—that are updated continuously—the record of every transaction that has been completed within the system since its inception, creating an immutable history (Nakamoto 2008).

Bitcoin—as a leading cryptocurrency—is a decentralized currency as it is not tied to any country. This means that Bitcoin is not under the control of any central bank and nor can it be minted by a centralized authority. Bitcoin does not rely on any centralized clearinghouse or third party to verify money supply and transaction. Rather, it is built on a decentralized network of computers toward the singular purpose of validating and clearing transactions on the Bitcoin Network. The distributed and decentralized network allows each individual user (miner) to verify the validity of individual transactions and the system, as a whole, through the cryptographic protocols. All these data are stored by each miner on a distributed ledger known as the blockchain. Blockchain—a distributed ledger—is stored locally on the computer hard drive of every miner running a full version of the Bitcoin software (Kaye Scholer 2016).

It is also important to understand the categorization of Bitcoin in the context of currency. Therefore, Fig. 15.2 summarizes the taxonomy of Bitcoin as a currency.

According to Fig. 15.2, the currency or money can be divided into: (1) physical currency and (2) digital currency. Physical currency is what is available in the form of paper notes or bills issued by a national government as a legal tender. Examples of such currency are US dollar bill, a note of Malaysian ringgit, etc. On the other hand, digital currency does not have any physical form, because it is stored, seen and transferred through electronic system. This can be divided into: (1) electronic money and (2) virtual currency. Electronic money is simply a digital representation of the physical currency. Therefore, it is centralized, issued by a government, has the status of legal tender, and pegged and represented in the same units as physical currency. The example of electronic money is the balance in a bank account shown in an online system. If someone has deposited USD 10,000 in a bank account, the same amount is represented in the online account system. If the depositor withdraws USD 3000 from the account, the online system will then show only USD 7000 as the account balance.

The second form of digital currency is virtual currency which is, unlike electronic money, not issued by a government; hence, it is not a legal tender. It may not be pegged or represented in the same unit as physical currency. This category can be further classified into: (1) non-cryptocurrency and (2) cryptocurrency. Non-cryptocurrency, as the name suggests, does not use cryptographic technique for encryption, and they are not particularly created as a 'currency' in a strict sense. Their usage is limited to a certain organization, specific service, or discount. Examples of such currency are: credits of an online gaming community; loyalty points of a specific company which can be used for special discounts or to purchase special gifts; air miles which are offered to a frequently flying member by an airline company; and many others.

Lastly, it is the cryptocurrencies which can be issued and used as a medium of exchange, as well as a representation of certain type of digital asset.

CURRENT RESOLUTIONS AND *FATWAS* ON BITCOIN: A CRITICAL ANALYSIS

Shari'ah opinions are diverse on Bitcoin. Some Islamic legal verdicts hold impermissibility of Bitcoin based on its volatility and intangibility among other reasons. Some scholars either consider it permissible while others are indecisive. Even among Shari'ah scholars holding the position of impermissibility, some isolate Bitcoin while others generalize it to encompass other crypto-assets. Few of these opinions are presented here.

Scholars Who Are Against Bitcoin

- Turkey's Directorate of Religious Affairs (Diyanet), which is the top state organization dealing with religious matters, has ruled that digital currency, Bitcoin, is not appropriate according to Islam.

The directorate's head said: "the purchase and selling of digital currencies is not appropriate according to [Islamic] religion at this point due to the fact that they are open to speculation in terms of value and they can easily be used mostly in illegal deeds such as money laundering. They are also far from state auditing and supervision" (Hurriyet Daily News 2017).

- Egypt's Dar Al Iftaa (the office of the Grand Mufti of Egypt) issued a Fatwa (Islamic ruling) that deems Bitcoin as forbidden by Islam. "Bitcoin could be harmful to the country's social and economic security", Dar Al Iftaa said, stressing that the currency could break through the national security and central financial system. The Egyptian Grand Mufti's Counsellor, Magdy Ashour, said that the currency "is used directly to fund terrorists" explaining that its transactions threaten major damage to the economy. Moreover, the system has no set rules, which is considered as a contract annulment in Islam, that is why it is forbidden, Ashour added (Middle East Monitor 2018).

- Dar al-Ifta, the Supreme Fatwa Council of Palestine, holds that Bitcoin is not a price because it is against the foundation of being a price. At the same time, it cannot be considered a commodity because bitcoin does not satisfy any desire in humans from consumption perspective. So, its essence can be explained as: it is an electronic program which is used as a tool to get rich. It sometimes takes the function of currency in some places and in some countries. Thus, mining of bitcoins is also prohibited, because it consists of grave uncertainty (*gharar*) and entails the essence of gambling (qimar). It is similarly not permissible to buy and sell bitcoins because until now it is a currency with unknown issuer with no guarantor. It is also too much volatile and risky and prone to attack on its keys. It similarly gives a great space to hardship, fraud and deception (Dar Al-Ifta'Al-Falasteeniyya 2017).

Scholars Who Are in Favor of Bitcoin

Mohd Daud Bakar, a prominent Shari'ah scholar in Malaysia, offers the following arguments in favor of bitcoin:

- The presumption of Shari'ah on new issues and realities is permissibility until and unless there is sufficient evidence to prove otherwise. This permissibility should be extended to digital currencies (crypto-assets) such as bitcoin, Ethereum, etc.

- Digital currencies, in their current forms are the most secured form of currencies, even much more than some printed monies in circulation. This is due to high level algorithm coding and enhanced security which makes digital currencies un-hackable and uncompromised.
- Speculation constitutes a major pivot upon which many prohibit cryptocurrencies, however, this argument is questionable because mere existence of speculation may not provide sufficient ground for impermissibility, unless it is proved to be manipulative and unjust.
- There should be a differentiation between *gharar* (uncertainty) and *khatar* (risk). While the former is prohibited element in the Islamic law, the latter is required to justify liability and profit. Both cannot be simply equated to each other. Hence, huge risk due to price volatility and fluctuation in value may not inevitably mean the presence of *gharar* in Bitcoin.
- Due to the fact that Bitcoin is not a legal tender, this has become one of the main reasons of its impermissibility, according to various Shari'ah scholars. However, this is an administrative issue, not a Shari'ah issue. It may be a concern for a state or national government, but it is not a basic Shari'ah requirement for a currency (Bakar 2018).

Moreover, from the views of the opponents of Bitcoin, it can easily be observed that most of the arguments are based on misunderstanding and limited knowledge of its technical aspects. In addition, some bias can also be seen in those fatwas due to political and governmental pressure. Due to this, it is crucial to objectively analyze the halal dimensions of Bitcoin from purely Islamic jurisprudential perspective. In view of that, the next section discusses the topic in light of principles of classical Islamic jurisprudence.

Islamic Legal Criterion for Mal and Bitcoin

It has been established in another chapter of this book that crypto-assets can be considered as mal (property or asset). Furthermore, Shari'ah recognizes intangible assets as mal as well. If all the prohibitive elements are avoided, crypto-assets can also become mal mutaqawwam (legit or valid asset). Similarly, being a type of crypto-asset, this can be also true for Bitcoin. However, it is pertinent to specifically discuss whether Bitcoin qualifies as mal mutaqawwam and whether it is a currency or commodity. Hence, the discussion also delves into the legal criterion of money and currency in Shari'ah focusing on the nature of Bitcoin.

Is Bitcoin Mal?

According to the famous Arabic dictionary 'Lisan Al Arab,' the literal meanings of mal is something which can be possessed (Ibn Manzur 1975). However, Islamic jurists differ in defining mal from the fiqh perspective. Hanafi scholars define mal in a different manner. Ibn Abidin (1992), a Hanafi scholar, states:

> The meaning of 'mal' is [something which] the [human] nature inclines towards [due to its worth], and its [physical] storage is possible for the time of necessity. The worth [of something] is established by people's worth [by having them considering it as worthy] either all of them or few of them [consider its value]. Meanwhile legitimacy [of something] is established by its value and its permissibility to benefit from it in Shari'ah. Hence, whatever is permissible [to benefit from in Shari'ah] without any commercial value is not mal, e.g. a single grain of wheat; and whatever is valuable without permissibility of usage is not a legit asset, e.g. wine; if both the elements [commercial value and permissibility] are absent [in something], then both cannot be established [to prove it as mal], e.g. blood.[2]

The main features of mal are: (1) ownership can be established on it; (2) it can be possessed; (3) it can be stored; and (4) it can be used at the time of necessity. It is clear from the earlier explanation of Bitcoin that a bitcoin can be easily stored in digital or electronic devices through a special computer programs called 'e-wallet,' 'bitcoin-wallet,' or 'crypto-wallet.' Bitcoins exist in the form of unique and separate digital tokens or units on the blockchain; in this way, they are distinguishable among each other. Through private key of the wallet, ownership can be established—as well as, they can be spent or transferred with it at the time of necessity.

[2] Ibn Abidin (1992, vol. 4, p. 501).

Therefore, it can be said that all these main features of mal are present in Bitcoin.

In addition, it is also noticed that mal should have commercial value in order to be considered as worthy, and it should not fundamentally contain any impermissible element, in order to be mutaqawwam (legit asset). If these two conditions are met, it can be considered as mal by the non-Hanafi scholars and mal mutaqawwam by Hanafi jurists.

From the above definition, it is observed that Hanafi jurists put a condition of being commercially valuable or worthy to be considered as mal. However, mal then can be divided into mutaqawwam, which means valid or legit asset from Shari'ah perspective too. In other words, if Shari'ah allows people to benefit from or use it, then it is mutaqawwam. For example, a car, a house, an apple, etc., are types of mal mutaqawwam. On the contrary, if something has value among people, but Shari'ah does not permit to use it or benefit from it, then it is called mal ghayr-mutaqawwam (invalid asset). For example, wine is a valuable asset, however Muslims are not allowed to use it or benefit from it in any way, and hence, it is mal ghayr-mutaqawwam for them. Nevertheless, it is crucial to note that in Shari'ah, mal ghayr-mutaqawwam is usually something which is intrinsically impermissible. In other words, that thing is either prohibited itself due to its nature or fundamentally contains an element which is prohibited. However, something does not become mal ghayr-mutaqawwam due to external factors. For example, if someone steals an apple, it is not permissible for the thief to consume it, not because the apple is mal ghayr-mutaqawwam, it is still mal mutaqawwam, but because it was acquired by illegal means.

Contrary to the Hanafi jurists, the majority of scholars opine that mal refers to everything which has value and be compensated if it is destroyed (Al-Zuhayli 2010). For example, Al-Suyuti (1983) quotes the definition of mal from Imam Shafi that mal refers to something which has value, is used as consideration in trade, must be compensated for if destroyed, and that people do not behave as if it is a valueless thing. For non-Hanafi scholars, there is no distinction between mal mutaqawwam and ghayr-mutaqawwam. For them, the permissibility of usage of something or benefitting from it is a fundamental element of value itself. If Shari'ah does not allow to use something, it cannot be considered as mal at all.

To establish the commercial value of a bitcoin, its value in terms of fiat money can be considered. According to Coinmarketcap.com (2018), one bitcoin is worth USD 9359, on May 10, 2018. It means that people who demand it or suppliers (the buyers and the sellers) are ready to pay or accept USD 9359 as the price for a bitcoin. Moreover, currently, bitcoin can be used to buy presents with gift cards, via Gyft or e-Gifter. It can be used to pay for flights and hotels, through Expedia, CheapAir, and Surf Air. Microsoft accepts bitcoin in its app stores, where the products offered like movies, games, and app-based services can be downloaded. Some musicians (Bjork, Imogen Heap) let their customers download their music in exchange for bitcoins. Additionally, Overstock was one of the first big retailers to start accepting bitcoin, back in 2014. Sharps Pixley, APMEX, and JM Bullion let their customers exchange bitcoin for bullion gold. Some fast food restaurants, like KFC Canada, Subway, PizzaForCoins, also accept bitcoin as a mode of payment. Several private and public universities in the USA, as well as a couple of New York preschools accept bitcoin. Some legal and accounting firms also accept payment for their services in the bitcoin. Some charities or crowdfunding sites, such as Bit Hope, BitGive, or Fidelity Charitable, accept bitcoins for fund transfer (Acheson 2018).

According to Spendbitcoins.com (2018), over 100,000 merchants around the world accept bitcoin as a mode of payment as on May 10, 2018. Those merchants offer a huge and diverse set of goods and services in exchange of bitcoins. All these data demonstrate that bitcoins do have commercial value. One can still argue that only few people accept and perceive the commercial value of bitcoins, but this argument does not hold weight. Because as mentioned in the definition of Ibn Abidin (1992) earlier, even few people's acceptance is sufficient to establish commercial value of bitcoins.

As for the taqawwum or permissibility of usage and benefits, it can be said that bitcoins are unique digits generated through a computer program as a result of mining, which consists of validating and endorsing the transactions, and keeping the ledger secured and updated. The miners compete with each other in completing the blocks containing records of transactions first, because whoever completes the block faster than others gets the reward in the form of newly generated bitcoins, as well as the fees of the transactions within that block. Once all the bitcoins are mined, the miners would still receive incentive in the form of transaction fee. Therefore, the main features of Bitcoin, the process of issuance and distribution, the blockchain platform, the equipment and resources required to mine bitcoins do not consist of any element which is fundamentally impermissible in Shari'ah. One of the Islamic legal maxims supports this analogy as:

الْأَصْلُ فِي الْأَشْيَاءِ الْإِبَاحَةُ حَتَّى يَدُلُّ الدَّلِيلُ عَلَى التَّحْرِيمِ

The original principle in [Shari'ah ruling of] things [or transactions] is permissibility, unless evidence [from the Shari'ah sources] proofs its impermissibility. (Al-Suyuti 1983, p. 60)

Damad Affandi (n.d.), a Hanafi scholar, explains in his famous book, 'majma al-anhar,' the approach of Islamic jurists as:

Note that the original principle in all the things, except private parts, is permissibility, because Allah taala said: 'it is He who created for you all that the earth contains' (Al-Baqarah, 29); and he said: 'O people, eat permissible good things out of what lies in the earth' (Al-Baqarah, 168). And the impermissibility can only be established with either general textual evidence or narration. So, when proofs pointing towards impermissibility are not found, the things remain permissible.[3]

Based on this discussion, it can be said that it is generally allowed to use and benefit from bitcoins as mal from Shari'ah perspective. Hence, Bitcoin can be considered as mal mutaqawwam for Hanafi jurists and simply mal for majority of the jurists.

Is Intangibility a Shari'ah Issue for Bitcoin?

Bitcoins are a form of digital asset; they are intangible. They do not have corporeal form (ayn); therefore, one may argue that it is not Shari'ah compliant due to nonexistence. This argument is flawed, because there is a huge difference between nonexistent thing and intangible thing. Electricity and mobile air time are also intangible form of asset, but it does not mean that they do not exist. Similarly, bitcoins do exist on the blockchain platform. They can be created, stored, transferred, owned, possessed, spent and destroyed; that is why, it can be said that they have existence. However, the question is whether Shari'ah recognizes intangible assets as valid or not. The answer is that *Shari'ah* recognizes

---

[3] Damad Affandi (n.d., vol. 3, p. 568).

intangible assets as mal mutaqawwam. Internationally recognized contemporary Shari'ah authorities, like Islamic Fiqh Academy of the Organization of Islamic Cooperation (OIC) and Accounting and Auditing Organization of Islamic Financial Institutions (AAOIFI), have also resolved that intangible or virtual assets are property of inherent monetary value that entitles them to legal protection and that any violations of property rights associated with them are punishable (IDB & IFA, 2000, Resolution No. 43 (5/5); AAOIFI, 2012, Article No. 3/3/3/1). Subsequently, the exchange of electricity and air time is valid. In the same vein, intangibility does not affect the ruling of bitcoins.

ISLAMIC LEGAL CRITERIA OF MONEY AND BITCOIN

According to Investopedia.com (2018), money is an official legal tender issued by a state government which is circulated as medium of exchange. Generally, it consists of notes and coins. Consequently, upon this traditional concept, many economists have narrowed the perception of money to only the widely popular fiat money issued by national governments. Nevertheless, from Shari'ah perspective, all these characteristics may not be required, making the perception about money wider.

From economic perspective, money has three main functions, such as: (1) store of value, it should provide stability to the value for future use; (2) medium of exchange, it should be widely accepted for exchanging goods and services; and (3) unit of account, it should serve as a measure of value of other goods and services. The third function as unit of account cannot be established for a money, unless it is a stable store of value and a widely used medium of exchange. In other words, the first two conditions are prerequisite for the third one.

In order to perform these three main functions, and to become good money, money should have various characteristics. For example, it should be: durable, so it is easily storable; portable, so it can be easily transferred or transported anywhere; divisible, so all types of transactions in small denomination can be easily performed; uniform, so it can be easily replaceable with the same unit of money; limited in supply, so it can avoid inflationary effect; hard to counterfeit, so it can avoid fraud; valuable, so it can be exchanged for other valuable goods and services; widely acceptable, so transactions can be performed with it anywhere; and legal tender, so the counterparty can be forced to accept it which gives trust to the money.

In the case of Bitcoin, it is observed that it has all the attributes of good money, except that it is not a legal tender, and it has not yet acquired wide acceptance by general people. Nevertheless, it is too early to expect that Bitcoin should acquire such level of wider acceptance.

Definition of Money in Islamic Law

According to Al-Mausuah Al-Fiqhiyyah (2007), in literal terms, money is a currency made of gold, silver, or any other thing which is dealt in as currency. Technically, money can be anything which is used as a medium of exchange whether it is gold, silver, petal, skin, or paper, if it gets general acceptability among people. According to Turkamani (1988), money refers to anything which is widely acceptable as a medium of exchange and store of value in Shari'ah; it does not matter what is the nature and form of that thing. It goes without saying that the element used as medium of exchange should be Shari'ah compliant. In other words, as a basic requirement, it has to be mal mutaqawwam.

Shaykh Taqi Usmani (2015), a contemporary Hanafi jurist, says that money refers to something which has following three attributes:

- Medium of exchange;
- Unit of account; and
- Store of value.

These definitions of Islamic scholars are very similar to what economists say with regard to the definition of money and what common people understand. For instance, Merriam-Webster dictionary defines money as: '*something generally accepted as a medium* of exchange, a measure of value, or a means of payment' (Merriam-Webster 2018). It may be summarized based on these definitions that money is something which has the following attributes:

- Medium of exchange;
- Accepted as a mean of payment;
- Store of value; and
- Unit of account.

Bitcoin, as stated earlier, has been created to be a medium of exchange or a mean of payment (Nakamoto 2008). In fact, this is the only purpose or intrinsic usage or benefit of Bitcoin, as it cannot be used for any other purpose. This is actually the fundamental criteria for money. Ibn Taymiyyah (1995) writes:

> Dirhams and dinars are not intended per se, they are a tool to acquire other things. That is why, they become price [or money, in an exchange transaction], unlike all other [types of] assets [like goods and services] as the purpose [of acquiring them] is to derive benefit from themselves.[4]

Moreover, the exponential growth in the acceptance level of Bitcoin as a mode of payment by various market participants also support this feature. As for the features of store of value and unit of account, it is too early to expect Bitcoin to have such attributes.

Differences Between Money and Commodity

It is pertinent to discuss the differences between money and commodity here, because money is not equivalent to commodity according to Shari'ah. Shari'ah emphasizes to treat money just for its basic purpose, i.e., as medium of exchange and measure of value. Ibn Taymiyyah (1995) explains that dirhams and dinars (gold and silver coins) have no intrinsic use and purpose, but they are created just to be used as a medium of exchange. The same explanation is given by Ibn Qayyim (1973) that money is not desired for itself, but rather it is created to facilitate the trade of goods. So, if money itself is treated as a good or commodity, this would lead to destruction. Hence, it is subject to Shari'ah rules of exchange (*sarf*) and interest (*riba*).

On the other hand, commodities or goods warrant a different set of Shari'ah rules and criteria, because they have intrinsic use and purpose. Shaykh Usmani (2015) deliberates the differences between money and commodity in a conclusive manner by explaining the following three fundamental differences between money and commodity:

- Money has neither an intrinsic usage, nor it is capable of directly fulfilling needs of human beings, such as eating, drinking and

---

[4]Ibn Taymiyyah (1995, vol. 19, p. 252).

wearing etc. On the contrary, the commodity has an intrinsic usage, and can be utilized directly without the need of exchanging it with something else.

- The commodities may have different qualities and attributes. But money has no quality except it is a medium of exchange and measure of value. That is why, all the units of money have same value and equal to each other. There is no difference between dirty note of USD 100 and a new note of USD 100.
- A particular commodity can be specified in an exchange transaction by stipulation. For example, if someone purchases a particular car, the seller has to deliver that particular car; he cannot change it with another car. Contrary to this, money cannot be specified in a transaction of exchange by stipulation. For example, it does not matter if a buyer shows a particular note of USD 100 to the seller, and then pays with another note of USD 100.

With this understanding, it can be argued that Bitcoin seems to fulfill the criteria of money, rather than commodity. However, it is pivotal to understand that if Bitcoin is money or currency, which type of money it is?

Types of Money in Shari'ah

The Islamic jurists classify money into mainly two types: (1) natural money and (2) customary money.

Natural Money

According to the scholars, gold and silver are natural money, because these metals have served the purpose of a medium of exchange throughout human history. Their monetary value is naturally understood by human beings. Therefore, it is perceived that their value has not been established through artificial means. In fact, many scholars hold that their value intrinsically exists regardless of their form. Due to such status, the famous jurist, Imam al-Ghazali (2004), says that Allah the Almighty created gold and silver to be circulated among people and become standards of measurement for different assets or other goods and services. They are the means to acquire all other assets. They are precious and valuable in the eyes of people, but not desired for their own sake; but rather to be used as a mean to obtaining other assets.

Customary Money

Customary money refers to the money which receives the status of money due to custom and acceptability of people. It is originally not meant to serve the purpose of money, but people accept it widely as a medium of exchange. Commodities other than gold and silver used as money are common forms of customary money. The customary money does not intrinsically have the quality of money (thamaniyyah); rather, such feature is assigned to it through artificial factors. Customary money can be further divided into two types: (1) commodity money and (2) fiat money.

Commodity money is used as medium of exchange, but this feature is not natural. In other words, it does not have thamaniyyah by default. However, it has other intrinsic usage or benefits. Thus, it can be used for other purposes. Fiat money, on the other hand, refers to a currency neither has thamaniyyah by default, nor it has any intrinsic usage or benefit. The reason for such money to have value is due to an artificial factor. For example, national currencies are backed by governments, and counterparties are bound by law to accept such currencies in their specific jurisdictions by virtue of the status of legal tender.

With this understanding, it can be argued that Bitcoin is a customary money. It has some resemblance with the natural money in the sense that it can only be used as a medium of exchange, and it does not have any other benefit. But due to the fact that its value has been established by the custom of the people, it is more appropriately a customary money. If people stop perceiving that bitcoins have value, they would become useless numbers and mere digits stored on a blockchain platform.

Conclusion

A famous Islamic legal maxim is stated as:

> Changes in ijtihad-based rulings due to changed circumstances should not be objected to.[5]

Latest advancements in technology have posed many challenges to Islamic scholars in seeking Shari'ah opinions for unprecedented cases.

---

[5] Al-Ghazzi (2003, vol. 8, p. 1100).

Things get changed, due to different dynamics and unique circumstances; subsequently, their Shari'ah rulings that are based on ijtihad also keep changing in order to accommodate their altered characteristics. Riding on the same waves of evolution, money has transformed from gold, silver, and commodities to digital money and cryptocurrencies. However, the most important thing is to analyze the exact nature and fiqhi characterization of cryptocurrencies without entertaining any confusion in light of the fundamental Shari'ah principles. This is the main key to understand this advanced phenomenon and find its Shari'ah solutions.

Based on the discussion, presented in this chapter, it can be argued that Bitcoin qualifies for mal mutaqawwam. Furthermore, it can be categorized as customary money. Subsequently, in dealing with Bitcoin, Shari'ah rules of currency exchange and interest (riba) should be strictly adhered to.

References

Acheson, N. (2018). *What Can You Buy with Bitcoin?* Accessed on 10 May 2018: https://www.coindesk.com/information/what-can-you-buy-with-bitcoins/.

Al-Ghazali, M. (2004). *Ihya Uloom Al-Deen.* Beirut, Lebanon: Dar Al-Marefah.

Al-Ghazzi, M. S. (2003). *Mausuah Al-Qawaid Al-Fiqhiyyah.* Beirut, Lebanon: Muassasah Al-Risalah.

Al-Suyuti, I. (1983). *Al-ashbah Wa Al-nazair Fi Qawa'id Wa Furu'Fiqh Al-shafi'iyah.* Beirut, Lebanon: Dar Al-Hadith.

Al-Zuhayli, W. (2010). *Fiqih Al-Islami Wa Adillatuh.* Damascus, Syria: Dar Al-Fikr Al-Islami Gema Insani.

Antonopoulos, A. M. (2015). *Mastering Bitcoin.* Sebastopol, CA: O'Reilly Media, Inc.

Bajpai, P. (2017). *The 6 Most Important Cryptocurrencies Other Than Bitcoin.* Accessed on 9 May 2018: https://www.investopedia.com/tech/most-important-cryptocurrencies-other-than-bitcoin/.

Bakar. M. D. (2018). Shari'ah and Financial Technology: Alignment or Rejection? *Malaysian Business,* February 2018 edition.

Coinmarketcap.com. (2018). Accessed on 17 January 2018: https://coinmarketcap.com/.

Damad Affandi, A. R. S. (n.d.). *Majma Al-Anhar.* Beirut, Lebanon: Dar Ihya Al-Turath Al-Arabi.

Dar Al-Ifta'Al-Falasteeniyya. (2017). *Ruling of Dealing in Electronic Currency Named Bitcoin and Its Mining*. Fatwa1/158, Number 297/2017/16, Issued on 14 December 2017. Accessed on 10 May 2018: http://www.darifta.org/majles2014/showfile/show.php?id=307.

De, N. (2017). *Malaysia's Central Bank Releases Draft Rules for Cryptocurrency Exchanges*. Accessed on 9 May 2018: https://www.coindesk.com/malaysias-central-bank-releases-draft-rules-cryptocurrency-exchanges/.

Deloitte. (2015). *Blockchain: Disrupting the Financial Services Industry?* Ireland: Deloitte & Touche House.

Estevao, P. (2018). *The Bitcoin Transaction Life Cycle*. Accessed on 6 February 2019: https://imgur.com/a/BCvZr.

Franco, P. (2015). *Understanding Bitcoin*. Chichester, UK: Wiley.

Higgins, S. (2017). *$300 Billion: Bitcoin Price Boosts Crypto Market Value to Record High*. Accessed on 9 May 2018: https://www.coindesk.com/300-billion-bitcoin-price-boosts-crypto-market-value-record-high/.

Hurriyet Daily News. (2017). *Turkey's Top Religious Body Declares Bitcoin 'Inappropriate'*. Ankara, Turkey: Hurriyet Daily News, 29 November 2017, 12:38:00. Accessed on 10 May 2018: http://www.hurriyetdailynews.com/turkeys-top-religious-body-declares-bitcoin-inappropriate-123243.

Ibn Abidin, M. (1992). *Radd Al-Muhtar Ala Durr Al-Mukhtar*. Beirut, Lebanon: Dar Al-Fikr.

Ibn Manzur, Y. A. D. M. (1975). *Lisan Al-Arab*. Beirut, Lebanon: Al Dar al-Misriyya Li-l-ta'lif wa-l-tarhim.

Ibn Qayyim, M. (1973). *Ilam Al-Muaqqeen An Rabb Al-Alameen*. Beirut, Lebanon: Dar Al-Kotob Al-Ilmiyyah.

Ibn Taymiyyah, A. (1995). *Majmu Al-Fatawa*. Medina, Saudi Arabia: King Fahd Complex for the Printing of the Holy Qur'an.

Investopedia.com. (2018). *Money*. Accessed on 10 May 2018: https://www.investopedia.com/terms/m/money.asp.

Kaye Scholer. (2016). *An Introduction to Bitcoin and Blockchain Technology*. Washington, USA: Arnold & Porter Kaye Scholer LLP.

Merriam-Webster. (2018). *Money*. Accessed on 10 May 2018: https://www.merriam-webster.com/dictionary/money?utm_campaign=sd&utm_medium=serp&utm_source=jsonld.

Middle East Monitor. (2018). *Egypt Says 'Bitcoin' Currency Is Prohibited by Islam*. Egypt: Middle East Monitor, 2 January 2018, 09:22:00. Accessed on 10 May 2018: https://www.middleeastmonitor.com/20180102-egypt-says-bitcoin-currency-is-prohibited-by-islam/.

Nakamoto, S. (2008). *Bitcoin: A Peer-to-Peer Electronic Cash System*. Retrieved from: https://bitcoin.org/: https://bitcoin.org/en/bitcoin-paper.

Scott, A. (2016). *These Are the World's Top 10 Bitcoin-Friendly Countries*. Accessed on 9 May 2018: https://news.bitcoin.com/worlds-top-10-bitcoin-friendly-countries/.

Smart, E. (2015). *Top 10 Countries in Which Bitcoin Is Banned.* Accessed on 9 May 2018: https://www.ccn.com/top-10-countries-bitcoin-banned/.

Spendbitcoins.com. (2018). Accessed on 10 May 2018: http://spendbitcoins.com/.

Turkamani, A. K. (1988). *Al-Syasah Al-Naqdiyah Wa Al-Masrafiyah Fi Al-Islam.* Oman: Muassasah Al-Risalah.

Usmani, M. T. (2015). *Fiqh al-Buyu.* Damascus, Syria: Dar al-Qalam.

Wyk, G. V. (2013). *The Idiot's Guide to Bitcoin.* Chaos Publications.

PART V

Social Financing Through Halal Cryptocurrency Management

CHAPTER 16

Islamic Social Financing Through Cryptocurrency

Houssem eddine Bedoui and Aroua Robbana

INTRODUCTION

The dawn of private social cryptocurrencies has proved that it is still feasible to issue and create a cryptocurrency for specific social causes. However, it would be more relevant at that the national regulator would issue this new cryptocurrency for social projects to serve the Sustainable Development Goals (Sdgs). The descriptive chapter defines in the first section the definitions of digital finance and the cryptocurrency. The cryptocurrency is then a digital encrypted currency powered by an open public ledger platform named blockchain.

The chapters displayed the two sub-categories of cryptocurrencies (coins and tokens). The second section of the chapter focuses on the link between digital finance and social finance. It gives the potentiality and

Disclaimer The views and opinions expressed in this chapter are those of the authors and do not necessarily reflect the official policy or position of their institutions.

H. e. Bedoui (✉)
Islamic Development Bank (IsDB), Jeddah, Saudi Arabia

A. Robbana
International Islamic University Malaysia (IIUM), Gombak, Malaysia

© The Author(s) 2019   259
M. M. Billah (ed.), *Halal Cryptocurrency Management*,
https://doi.org/10.1007/978-3-030-10749-9_16

the opportunities creating in linking both finances together to work on "digital social finance". It gives as well the connections between the SDGs and social finance and how through digitizations SDGs can be achieved.

Finally, the chapter provides an update on the required framework for a central bank to issue its social cryptocurrency. The first requirement is the regulator perspective where it displays the different monetary policy challenges. The second requirement is the *Shari'ah* compliance one by displaying the update on the different conditions to guarantee the compliance of the issuance.

DIGITAL FINANCE

McKinsey Global Institute (2016)[1] defines digital finance as any financial services delivered over digital infrastructure (mobile and Internet). This broad definition includes:

i. All financial services (payments, savings accounts, credit, insurance, etc.).
ii. All users (individuals at all income levels, enterprises of all sizes, and government and nongovernment entities at all levels, etc.).
iii. All financial services providers (banks, payment providers, other financial institutions, telecoms companies, financial technology [fintech] start-ups, retailers, etc.).

Hence, digital currencies (cryptocurrencies) area core component of digital finance. They rely on blockchain technology. Blockchain records transactions made in identical copies of a digital "shared" ledger among users.

> A shared ledger is essentially a database that keeps track of who owns a financial, physical or electronic asset: a diamond, a unit of currency, or items inside a shipping container. (Walport 2016)

Blockchain technology has gained rapid interest because of its decentralized nature and its strong security properties (Wright and De Filippi 2015).

---

[1] Manyika et al. (2016).

However, blockchains are not restricted to decentralized cryptocurrencies; it can also be applied to other innovative ideas such as smart contracts, payment solutions and trade finance (Wood, n.d.).

With the emergence of blockchain technique and cryptocurrency, the mass emergence of new terms led to misunderstanding and misuse of them. Some names are regarded as a cryptocurrency, their meaning and usage overlap considerably and are often taken for granted and used interchangeably, despite their differences. In order to adjust the miss-concept, these names to be used throughout this chapter are briefly defined below. However, first, let us recall a brief definition of a cryptocurrency.

The Committee on Payments and Market Infrastructures (CPMI)[2] acknowledged three critical characteristics of cryptocurrencies:

i. *Assets*: These assets "have some monetary characteristics (such as being used as a means of payment), but are not typically issued in or connected to a sovereign currency, are not a liability of any entity and are not backed by any authority".

ii. *Electronic*: "The second key aspect is the way in which these digital currencies are transferred, typically via a built-in distributed ledger. This aspect can be viewed as the genuinely innovative element within digital currency schemes".

iii. *Peer-to-peer*: "The third aspect is the variety of third-party institutions, almost exclusively non-banks, which have been active in developing and operating digital currency and distributed ledger mechanisms" (CPMI 2015).

Bech and Garratt (2017)[3] represented in the form of a Venn diagram with the intersection of these above-mentioned characteristics. Whereas, the commodity money is the intersection of only "Assets" and "Peer-to-peer" characteristics.

Hence, a cryptocurrency is a digital encrypted currency powered by an open public ledger platform called Blockchain. Under cryptocurrency, there are mainly two sub-categories: coins and tokens.

---

[2] CPMI (2015).
[3] Bech and Garratt (2017).

Coins

Coins, alternative cryptocurrency coins, crypto-coins are often used interchangeably to refer to a digital equivalent of "money" created using cryptography techniques. Coins are mainly two types, one which presents a hard fork of Bitcoin such as *Namecoin, Litecoin, Bitcoin cash, Bitcoin Gold* and *Auroracoin*. They are merely built using Bitcoin original protocol with some changes to its underlying codes. Hence, they are considered as derivatives of Bitcoin with a different set of features. As for the second type of coins, they are mainly created using their own independent blockchain protocols like Ethereum, Ripple, Waves and Counterparty.

Tokens

While coins are only a mean of payment, tokens have broader functionality thanks to their sophisticated programming features. In simpler terms, besides being a mean of payment within a particular project's ecosystem, a token is considered as a unit of value created by a particular entity in order to present any particular asset or utility such as granting a right, buying a company's share and even buying a ticket to a concert. Tokens can perform several functions, and as Richard Olsen, co-founder and CEO of Lykke (Bitcoin, FX, and Digital Assets Trading application) said:

> There won't be millions of tokens. There will be millions of kinds of tokens.[4]

Unlike, coins which need a native platform to exist and operate, tokens can be hosted on some blockchain protocols which use smart contract such as Ethereum which provides a standard known as ERC20 helping tokens issuance (Fig. 16.1).

Are Cryptocurrencies Money?

Ali et al. (2014)[5] presented the three historical purposes and features of money (physical and digital). The first purpose of money is to be a *store of value*. Hence, with money, users can buy goods and services from

---

[4] Siegel (2017).
[5] Ali et al. (2014, p. 279).

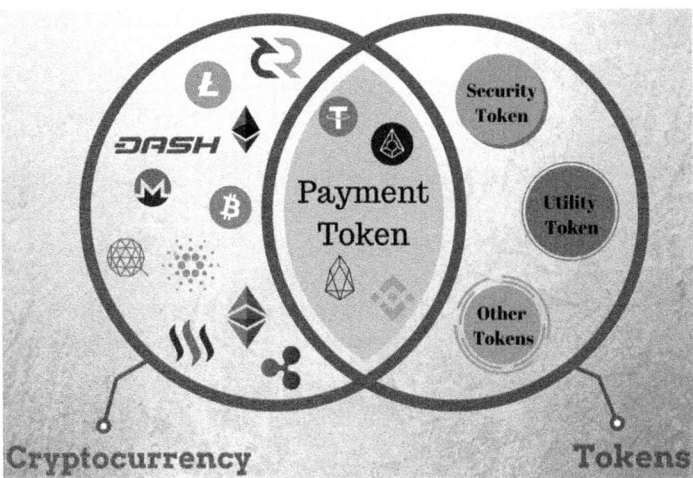

Fig. 16.1 Differences between tokens and cryptocurrencies (*Source* Authors' own)

today to some future date. The money then helps in transferring "purchasing power". Second, money played the role of a medium of exchange historically to make payments. Third, money serves as a *unit of account* that helps in measuring the value of any item for sale. In theory, Ali et al. (2014)[6] showed that cryptocurrencies could be considered money. They satisfy the three roles of money mentioned above. They showed that cryptocurrencies all three purposes for only a small public globally.

DIGITAL SOCIAL FINANCE

Social Finance and SDGs

Social finance is a wide-ranging type of finance that carries financial and social returns together. It comprises many forms of funding and investments. For instance, social enterprise lending, impact investing, social impact bond, green finance, microfinance/micro funds, community investing. Moreover, financial inclusion is an essential category of social and sustainable finance. The World Bank defined financial inclusion as

---

[6]Ali et al. (2014, p. 279).

"the proportion of individuals and firms that use financial services" (World Bank 2013, p. 1).

Financial inclusion and social finance have been identified as an enabler for eleven of the other seventeen 2030 SDGs (UNSGSA 2016, pp. 6–7).

- *SDG-1* (UNDP 2018a): on ending poverty in all its forms everywhere by 2030. Financial inclusion is vital for poverty reduction. Significant evidence shows that the poor benefit from principal payments, savings and insurance services.
- *SDG-2* (UNDP 2018b): by alleviating the perils of hunger, achieving food security and improved nutrition and promoting sustainable agriculture.
- *SDG-3* (UNDP 2018c): on ensuring healthy lives and improving well-being for all at all ages.
- *SDG-4* (UNDP 2018d): by guaranteeing inclusive and equitable quality education and promote lifelong learning opportunities for all.
- *SDG-5* (UNDP 2018e): on achieving gender equality and empowering all women and girls.
- *SDG-6* (UNDP 2018f): by ensuring availability and sustainable management of water and sanitation for all.
- *SDG-7* (UNDP 2018g): on securing access to affordable, reliable, sustainable and modern energy for all.
- *SDG-8* (UNDP 2018h): on promoting a sustained, inclusive and sustainable economic growth, approving full and productive employment and decent work for all.
- *SDG-9* (UNDP 2018i): on building a resilient infrastructure, promoting inclusive and sustainable industrialization and fostering innovation.
- *SDG-10* (UNDP 2018j): on reducing inequality within and among countries.
- *SDG-16* (UNDP 2018k): on endorsing peaceful and inclusive societies for sustainable development, providing access to justice for all and building effective, accountable and inclusive institutions at all levels.

Sustainable finance and particularly financial inclusion became a topic of great interest for regulators, policymakers and other market stakeholders. Indeed, many of the worlds' poor would benefit from financial services but cannot access them due to market failures or inadequate public policies.

The augmented awareness of social finance reflects an increasing real-ization of its potentially transformative power to accelerate social development goals gains. Social finance provides individuals and firms with greater access to resources to meet their primary needs, such as investing in education, energy, water quality, sanitization quality and capitalizing on business opportunities. Indeed, McKinsey Global Institute (2016)[7] confirms that social finance and financial inclusion can support the accomplishment of development goals.

Digital Social Finance

McKinsey Global Institute (2016)[8] also noted that digital finance alone could benefit 1.6 billions of people by inspiring an inclusive growth that increases $3.7 trillion to the GDP of emerging economies by 2025, which represents an increase of 6% against a business-as-usual scenario. The report highlighted three essential building blocks to achieve the targets mentioned above. First, it is needed to have a comprehensive digital infrastructure which allows having extensive connectivity and dynamic digital payments infrastructure. The second required block is to have active financial services whereby a market promotes a stable financial system, and innovation is nurtured and adopted by markets. The third building block is that people would prefer innovative products to present alternatives and where new digital products offer a real advantage in cost and utility for users.

The World Bank's Global Financial Development Report 2014 confirmed that digital finance would help the social finance. Innovative technologies including mobile payments, financial technologies (fintech) make it easier and cheaper for people to use financial services.

> The impact of new technologies can be amplified by the private sector's adoption of business models that complement technology platforms (as is the case with banking correspondents). To harness the promise of new technologies, regulators need to allow competing financial service providers and consumers to take advantage of technological innovations. (World Bank 2013)

---

[7] Manyika et al. (2016).
[8] Manyika et al. (2016).

McKinsey Global Institute (2016)[9] presented the three principal channels of digital finance that can boost GDP. First, electronic payments improve the productivity of financial and non-financial organizations. Digital finance saves time by empowering people and allows them to work more. Finally, a more comprehensive financial inclusion empowers formal financial system to capture more savings in the economy, extend more credits and increase investments.

Digital Social Finance and SDGs

It was showed that digital social finance has continuing effects on economic growth and living standards of nations. First, it helps in endorsing innovation. Electronic payments boost the emergence of new business models and new start-ups and new financial products and services (P2P lending, crowdfunding, micropayment for the poor, etc.). This helps in more entrepreneurship opportunities and more job creation. Moreover, these electronic payments enable better transparency which helps governments to reduce and to condense more the informal economies. Also, electronic payments became more and more common. More electronic transactions are taking place which increases market liquidity. Besides, social digital finance helps in raising the quality and quantity of basic needs (health, hygiene, energy and education) which de facto permits the upgrading of human capital. Finally, electronic payments could decrease the inefficiencies of the current payment flow by reducing leakage and by transaction costs. McKinsey Global Institute (2016)[10] showed that electronic payments could reduce the leakage in government spending by $110 billion a year in emerging economies.

When it comes to the highlighted eleven SDGs above, digital social finance contributes to achieving them as such.

- *SDG-1—No poverty*: given the reduced leakage, more government aids reach needy people....
- *SDG-2—Zero hunger*: with the Internet of things (IoT) and artificial intelligence (AI), farming is getting digitized, and sharecroppers invest better during planting periods and optimize their

---

[9] Manyika et al. (2016).
[10] Manyika et al. (2016).

consumption between harvests. Moreover, with reduced leakage, food aid reaches the poor.

- *SDG-3—Good health and well-being*: the decreased leakage of government spending on health will de facto improve government health spending.
- *SDG-4—Quality education*: the government spending on education will reduce through electronic payment. Hence, this leakage savings help in paying teachers and improves their productivity and reduce their absenteeism.
- *SDG-5—Gender equality*: Digital financier moved women's physical barriers to have a banking account. This empowers them and gives them more control over their finances.
- *SDG-6—Clean water and sanitation*: some cryptocurrencies emerged this SDG (Clean Water Coin[11]) which helps in providing clean water and sanitation.
- *SDG-7—Affordable and clean energy*: Mobile *Pay As You Go* (PAYG) schemes helps the energy customers to take control using their mobiles of their energy spending. This endorses more energy saving and boosts access to clean and renewable energy. Better targeted subsidies increase the use of energy.
- *SDG-8—Decent work and economic growth*: as explained earlier, electronic payments raise the pool of savings. Big data help reducing risks by having access to data history of lenders.
- *SDG-9—Industry, innovation, and infrastructure*: As explained earlier, digital finance empowers the entrepreneurship ecosystems worldwide by developing new business models, start-ups and products….
- *SDG-10—Reduced inequalities*: Transparency inherent to digital finance helps government aids to be accessible as fraud and theft are reduced. Moreover, financial inclusion benefits more a wide range of poor communities reducing then inequalities.
- *SDG-16—Peace, justice and strong communities*: Digital finance transparency enables better monitoring of corruption (The Law Library of Congress 2018).

---

[11] "CleanWaterCoin (WATER) Price, Charts, Market Cap, and Other Metrics | CoinMarketCap," n.d.; "Clean Water Coin | Cryptocurrency Altcoin | A Crypto Charity," n.d.

SOCIAL CRYPTOCURRENCY

The purpose now is to explore the opportunity of creating an Islamic social cryptocurrency. The cryptocurrency phenomena become central to most social-economic innovations and companies developed through blockchain technology. There are emergent efforts to create governmental and private cryptocurrencies. For instance, some cooperative and collaborative enterprises made efforts to create their cryptocurrencies (De Filippi 2015).

Theses social cryptocurrencies can be either on their coin or token format. Tokenization is an aspect of blockchain technology that is enabling the effective transfer of value across the Internet. The fluidity and liquidity created by this concept help to connect products and services while defying the restrictions of location and continually breaking the barriers of compatibility. Tokenization will empower for instance some private sector business to issue their tokens as an integral part of the platform operations.

On another hand, social finance has seen the emergence as well of *social coins*. Few digital currency projects have started which create their own "charity coins" to support specific nonprofits or charity work. The *Clean Water Coin*[12] was explicitly created to help fund the work of the nonprofit organization Charity: Water. The initiative lets a community participate in helping in social purposes, for instance here, providing clean water. Hence, they will create campaigns and raise funds for purposely clean water projects. Moreover, *Faircoin*,[13] issued by *Fair Coop*, is an initiative started by Spanish activist Enric Duran Giralt.[14] The purpose is to launch *Faircoin* as a global cryptocurrency for transfers among the global cooperative network (Scott 2016).

Creating a social cryptocurrency at a national level can be done through the regulator (here the central bank). Hence, the regulator will issue the cryptocurrency and manage the monetary policy and financial

---

[12] "CleanWaterCoin (WATER) Price, Charts, Market Cap, and Other Metrics | CoinMarketCap," n.d.; "Clean Water Coin | Cryptocurrency Altcoin | A Crypto Charity," n.d.

[13] König (2015).

[14] Enric Duran Giralt also known as Robin Banks or the Robin Hood of the Banks is a Catalan anti-capitalist activist ("Nace Fair.coop, la cooperativa que combate el capitalismo desde dentro," n.d.).

stability. Some central banks have started to consider issuing their cryptocurrencies named by Bank for International Settlements (2018)[15] *central bank digital currency* (CBDC). This idea is not an original idea since James Tobin in 1985[16] already mentioned the numerous trends that would motivate central banks to issue their own CBDC (central bank cryptocurrency/national cryptocurrencies).

These trends include (BIS Bank for International Settlements 2018):

i. increasing awareness of technological innovations for financial services;
ii. the rise of new entrants into electronic payments and intermediation;
iii. diminishing the use of cash in some countries; and
iv. the emergence of private money (private digital tokens).

Regulation of Cryptocurrency

The issuance of anew national social cryptocurrency urges the central bank to anticipate an appropriate methodology that includes quantitative and qualitative analysis. This methodology evaluates among others the stress testing that includes backing either by gold, silver or a basket of commodities (that contains gold and silver) (Abdullah and Mohd Nor 2018).

Bank for International Settlements (2018)[17] emphasized the potential effect of national cryptocurrencies in three core central banking areas:

• payments;
• monetary policy implementation; and
• financial stability.

According to the Bank for International Settlements (2018), CBDC is still not a well-defined term. It may be confusing since it may refer to various concepts. Nevertheless, it is intended to be an innovative form of central banks money with its three roles (a unit of account, a medium of

---

[15] BIS Bank for International Settlements (2018).
[16] Tobin (1985).
[17] BIS Bank for International Settlements (2018).

exchange and a store of value). However, this form is not that innovative for commercial entities. "*Central banks provide digital money in the form of reserves or settlement account balances held by commercial banks and certain other financial institutions at the central bank*" (BIS 2018).

This fusion of innovative and existing forms of central bank money makes thought-provoking to exactly outline what a CBDC is.

ACBDC is a digital form of central bank money that is different from balances in traditional reserve or settlement accounts. (BIS 2018)

Bech and Garratt (2017) noticed that a CBDC is a combination of four fundamental properties:

– *issuer* (central bank or other);
– *form* (digital or physical);
– *accessibility* (widely or restricted); and
– *technology* (token-based or account-based).

Table 16.1 displays a comparison of the differences between existing central bank money and CBDC.

Table 16.1   Key design features of central bank money

	Existing central bank money		Central bank digital currencies		
	Cash	Reserves and settlement balances	General purpose		Wholesale only token
			Token	Accounts	
24/7 availability	✓	✗	✓	(✓)	(✓)
Anonymity vis-á-vis central bank	✓	✗	(✓)	✗	(✓)
Peer-to-peer transfer	✓	✗	(✓)	✗	(✓)
Interest-bearing	✗	(✓)	(✓)	(✓)	(✓)
Limits or caps	✗	✗	(✓)	(✓)	(✓)

✓ = existing or likely feature (✓) = possible feature, ✗ = not typical or possible feature

Islamic Cryptocurrency

Oziev and Yandiev (2017) in their work entitled "Cryptocurrency from *Shari'ah* Perspective" showed the relevant eleven requirements of money and its circulation to be *Shari'ah* compliant:

i. "the process of money emission, its supply, and withdrawal from the market should be free from Riba;
ii. money can be made of any material (metal, wood, plastic, etc.);
iii. the money emitter and the monetary regulator may be two different entities/organizations;
iv. the money emitter is a risk-free institution;
v. the money emitter should not enter into transactions with financial institutions aimed at obtaining income;
vi. it is not forbidden to use the currency/money of other countries;
vii. money does not necessarily have to be backed by real assets;
viii. money must be emitted in a sufficient quantity to serve the needs of the economy;
ix. no prohibitions and or restrictions on monetary transactions, as well as exchange and transfer of money (not clear);
x. money and monetary circulation should facilitate the life of the people;
xi. ownership right of a person over money should be transparent" (Oziev and Yandiev 2017).

Regarding the first and seventh point highlighted by Oziev and Yandiev, Alzubaidi and Abdullah (2017) concluded that "*Islam recognized commodities with intrinsic physical value only to be considered as money*" (Alzubaidi and Abdullah 2017). Moreover, they have identified that there is still an issue with an Islamic cryptocurrency that does not have an intrinsic value compared to *commodity money* (gold and silver).

They have resolved as well, that are the blockchain is a technique consisting of computational and mathematical applications, and it does not have intrinsically prohibited elements. On the contrary, blockchain empowering transparency it removes prohibited *Gharar* elements from transactions.

Besides, one key challenge appears from the condition 3 is that the currency issuer should be different from the regulator which is the case here given the regulator (Central Bank) will be the one in charge of the currency issuance. To conclude with a positive note, it is not prohibited from an Islamic perspective to use the currency of other countries. Hence, the issuer could be a supranational or a Multi Development Bank (MDB) that issue series of cryptocurrency (or one cryptocurrency per project).

CONCLUSION

In this descriptive chapter, we presented the theoretical feasibility of a (supra-) national cryptocurrency issuance. The new issuance can be channelled towards social finance and financial inclusion purposes. Where a nation will select strategic social projects to which it will direct the new issuance of the cryptocurrency. Indeed, we have identified the different definitions of the cryptocurrency, and we agreed on the BIS definition that concerns a central bank currency named CBDC. As to whether a central bank should issue a cryptocurrency and assessed related monetary and financial issues in doing so. Given central banks oversee regulatory aspects of such issuance and managing the monetary and financial stability, we have displayed the differences between a comparison between digital and physical issuances. Finally, the chapter concluded by endorsing the idea of an issuance that does not limit itself to only geographical borders where MDBs still can issue Islamic social cryptocurrencies for SDGs projects.

REFERENCES

Abdullah, A., and Mohd Nor, R., 2018. A Framework for the Development of a National Crypto-Currency. *International Journal of Economics and Finance* 10, 14. https://doi.org/10.5539/ijef.v10n9p14.

Ali, R., Barrdear, J., Clews, R., and Southgate, J., 2014. The Economics of Digital Currencies.

Alzubaidi, I.B., and Abdullah, A., 2017. Developing a Digital Currency from an Islamic Perspective: Case of Blockchain Technology. *International Business Research* 10. https://doi.org/10.5539/ibr.v10n11p79.

Bech, M.L., and Garratt, R., 2017. Central Bank Cryptocurrencies.

BIS Bank for International Settlements, 2018. Central Bank Digital Currencies.

Clean Water Coin | Cryptocurrency Altcoin | A Crypto Charity (WWW Document), n.d. http://www.cleanwatercoin.org/. Accessed October 22, 2018.

CleanWaterCoin (WATER) Price, Charts, Market Cap, and Other Metrics | CoinMarketCap (WWW Document), n.d. https://coinmarketcap.com/currencies/cleanwatercoin/. Accessed October 22, 2018.

CPMI, 2015. Digital Currencies.

De Filippi, P. (Ed.), 2015. Translating Commons-Based Peer Production Values into Metrics: Toward Commons-Based Cryptocurrencies. In *Handbook of Digital Currency: Bitcoin, Innovation, Financial Instruments, and Big Data.* Elsevier/AP, Amsterdam.

König, T., 2015. White Paper of Faircoin.

Manyika, J., Lund, S., Singer, M., White, O., and Berry, C., 2016. *Digital Finance for All: Powering Inclusive Growth in Emerging Economics.* McKinsey Global Institute.

Nace Fair.coop, la cooperativa que combate el capitalismo desde dentro (WWW Document), n.d. https://www.publico.es/internacional/nace-fair-coop-cooperativa-combate.html. Accessed October 24, 2018.

Oziev, G., and Yandiev, M., 2017. Cryptocurrency from Shari'ah Perspective (SSRN Scholarly Paper No. ID 3101981). Social Science Research Network, Rochester, NY.

Scott, B., 2016. How Can Cryptocurrency and Blockchain Technology Play a Role in Building Social and Solidarity Finance? United Nations Research Institute for Social Development UNRISD (UNRISD Workshop 25).

Siegel, D., 2017. The Token Handbook (WWW Document). Hacker Noon. https://hackernoon.com/the-token-handbook-a80244a6aacb. Accessed October 22, 2018.

The Law Library of Congress, 2018. Regulation of Cryptocurrency in Selected Jurisdictions 75.

Tobin, J., 1985. Financial Innovation and Deregulation in Perspective. Cowles Found.Pap.

UNDP, 2018a. Goal 1: End Poverty in All Its Forms Everywhere. United Nations Sustainable Development.

UNDP, 2018b. Goal 2: Zero Hunger. United Nations Sustainable Development.

UNDP, 2018c. Goal 3: Good Health and Well-Being. United Nations Sustainable Development.

UNDP, 2018d. Goal 4: Quality Education. United Nations Sustainable Development.

UNDP, 2018e. Goal 5: Water and Sanitation. United Nations Sustainable Development.

UNDP, 2018f. Goal 6: Clean Water and Sanitation. United Nations Sustainable Development.

UNDP, 2018g. Goal 7: Affordable and Clean Energy. United Nations Sustainable Development.

UNDP, 2018h. Goal 8: Decent Work and Economic Growth. United Nations Sustainable Development.

UNDP, 2018i. Goal 9: Industries, Innovation and Infrastructure. United Nations Sustainable Development.

UNDP, 2018j. Goal 10: Reduce Inequality Within and Among Countries. United Nations Sustainable Development.

UNDP, 2018k. Goal 16: Peace, Justice and Strong Institutions. United Nations Sustainable Development.

UNSGSA, 2016. UNSGSA Annual Report 2016. UN Secretary-General's Special Advocate for Inclusive Finance for Development (UNSGSA).

Walport, M., 2016. Distributed Ledger Technology: Beyond Block Chain 88.

Wood, D.G., n.d. Ethereum: A Secure Decentralised Generalised Transaction Ledger 32.

World Bank, 2013. *Global Financial Development Report 2014: Financial Inclusion.* The World Bank. https://doi.org/10.1596/978-0-8213-9985-9.

Wright, A., and De Filippi, P., 2015. Decentralized Blockchain Technology and the Rise of Lex Cryptographia. *SSRN Electronic Journal.* https://doi.org/10.2139/ssrn.2580664.

CHAPTER 17

Zakat Standard Framework of *Halal* Cryptocurrency

Irfan Syauqi Beik, Mohammad Soleh Nurzaman and Aisha Putrina Sari

Introduction

The evolution of money begins with the use of valuable commodities such as gold and silver, fiat money, and digital money as the latest. The money that once can only be used directly, peer to peer, is now also growing with technological advances, especially the Internet. According to Bakar et al. (2017), transaction over Internet relies almost exclusively on financial institutions serving as trusted third parties to process. The third parties are also playing role to minimize fraud activities. On the other hand, the presence of financial institutions leads to greater cost because there is an additional fee to be paid. From the reasons above, blockchain arises. Developed by Nakamoto (2008),

I. S. Beik (✉) · M. S. Nurzaman · A. P. Sari
Center of Strategic Studies, The National Board of Zakat (BAZNAS),
The Republic of Indonesia, Central Jakarta, Indonesia
e-mail: irfan.beik@puskasbaznas.com

I. S. Beik
Department of Islamic Economics,
Bogor Agricultural University, Bogor, Indonesia

© The Author(s) 2019
M. M. Billah (ed.), *Halal Cryptocurrency Management*,
https://doi.org/10.1007/978-3-030-10749-9_17

275

mechanism in blockchain allowing an elimination of the role of third parties (Papadopoulos 2015). Leon et al. (2017) explain that a blockchain as a method of recording digital information data by means of a logbook which has the following features namely ordered, incremental, verifiable, and digital.

Cryptocurrency is one of the results from blockchain technology. It makes payment system more transparent and secure (Al Zubaidi and Abdullah 2017). Therefore, the holders of a crypto money have the accurate duplicate of the blockchain and thus enabling the visibility of all transactions to the system's users. This particular condition removes asymmetric information in which characterized by the traditional financial system. Even though cryptocurrency already acknowledged by some countries (e.g., USA and Japan) as a currency, controversy still arises. Papadopoulos (2015) asserts that cryptocurrency is not money in a proper definition. Furthermore, he defines cryptocurrency as convertible digital currencies or digital equivalent of cash. Similar to that, Bohme et al. (2015) convey that Bitcoin, the first and the biggest cryptocurrency, represents a payment platform instead of as a currency.

Unfortunately, only few literatures discuss about cryptocurrency from Shari'ah perspective. The feasibility of using cryptocurrency in Islamic financial transactions is still questionable because it is not clear whether cryptocurrency can be defined as a currency or as an asset or wealth. The former needs cryptocurrency to comply with Shari'ah rules while the latter leads to issue in zakat. In order to fulfill the gap, this research attempts to elaborate Shari'ah perspective of cryptocurrency and its use in payment of zakat. First, we will discuss about zakat payment and blockchain, second, about wealth in Islamic perspective, third, cryptocurrency and standard zakat, and the last is conclusion.

Zakat and Blockchain

Zakat is one of the instruments for the distribution of property among Muslim as the properties reach certain quantity (*nishab*) and time (*haul*). It prevents the wealth concentrated only in a few people (Yusoff and Densumite 2012). According to QS At Taubah: 60, zakat given to specified beneficiaries (*ashnaf*) or *mustahiq* namely the poor, the needy, the administrator of zakat (*amil*), new Muslim (*muallaf*), the slaves (*riqab*), the debtors for their needs (*gharimin*), in the cause of Allah (*Fi sabilillah*), and travelers for Allah's sake (*Ibnu sabil*). The ashnaf mentioned above are mostly people who do not have the purchasing power to fulfill their needs; whereas, there is a minimum requirement to be fulfilled for living. As zakat is very important, Caliph Abu Bakr and other companions declare war to every Muslims who reluctant to pay zakat. In that era, zakat paid through the state (*khilafah*). But nowadays, there are several ways for Muslims to pay zakat, directly to the ashnaf or through the institution of zakat, while the latter gives advantages more.

Some of the advantages of paying zakat through institutions are that collected money can be distributed properly to the *ashnaf* because they already have a *mustahiq* database. It will minimize the overlap over *mustahiq* and extent the outreach. In addition, zakat institutions already have programs in accordance with the ability of the *mustahiq* if the zakat is channeled productively. Although many Muslim countries have either state zakat institutions or institutions recognized by the state, the acquisition of zakat received is still less than its potential. One of the reasons was about the trust of zakat payer to the zakat institutions (Zainal et al. 2016). The question that arises is, if the payment of zakat through zakat institutions is constrained by the issue of trust, can mechanism of blockchain be the answer?

A blockchain is invented from blocks of data that are linked through a sequenced cryptographic chain with hashes contains three main elements namely block data, chaining-hash, and block-hash (Leon et al. 2017). By using blockchain, both parties can have transactions without using third parties so it will reduce the cost (Papadopoulos 2015). Blockchain technology brings together Islamic values (trust, justice, equality, and efficiency) in finance that formulate and uphold the spirit of Islamic finance. This is in line with the expectations of all stakeholders of Islamic finance. Blockchain's records of transactions cannot be manipulated or altered. Hence, it fulfills the *Shari'ah* compliance aspects of Islamic finance.

Designing blockchain mechanism to zakat is highly possible since it can be used not only for commercial but also for other purposes. The zakat payers (*muzakki*) simply pay zakat through the application of blockchain. In such applications, zakat institutions offer the programs they have planned. As *muzakki* already choose one of the zakat institutions and pay their zakat, then the funds of the transaction will be recorded in the blockchain ledger. Therefore, every transaction becomes transparent and accessible to everyone within the network. Every transaction in the blockchain is permanent and will be distributed in a wide network. It prevents the zakat institutions to misuse the zakat fund.

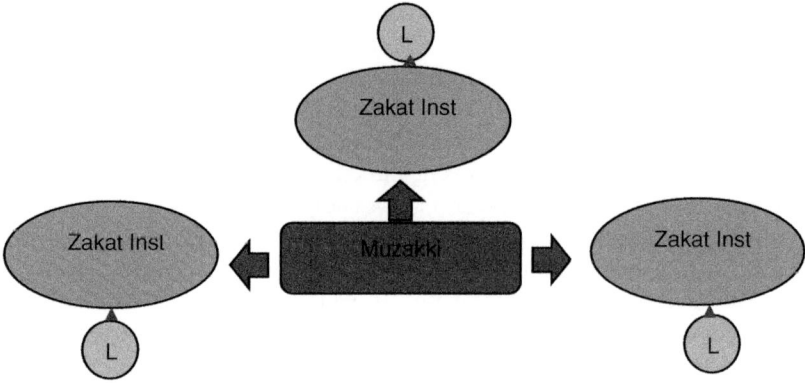

Fig. 17.1   Blockchain in Zakat (*Source* Author's own)

Not only because the network will verify the activities but also because the *muzakki* can supervise it directly. Figure 17.1 depicts the illustration of zakat payment via blockchain mechanism.

Issues surrounding the zakat payment and the solutions are provided in Table 17.1.

Wealth in Islamic Perspective

Shari'ah recognizes wealth ownership (*maal*). However, human beings are merely receiving the mandate (*amanah*) to have the wealth from Allah. According to the early scholars of Islamic economics, Allah is the supreme owner of things while human beings ownership is relative (Hosseini 1988). This is in accordance Quran on Surah Al Baqarah verse 29 that "*He who created for you all of that which is on the earth*" and affirmed on Surah Yunus verse 55 that "*Unquestionably, to Allah belongs whatever is in the heavens and the earth. Unquestionably, the promise of Allah is truth, but most of them do not know.*"

Shari'ah perspective about wealth is neither disregard like a zuhud nor exaggerate like the materialist (Qardhawi 2004). The implication of the perspectives is that Shari'ah views wealth as a means and not a purpose in life (Az-Zuhaili 2011). Wealth in the hands of Muslims can be used to perform worship such as paying zakat and hajj. In addition, the treasures can also be used for the benefit of Islam, such as building a place of worship, helping the disaster in Muslims region, and so forth.

Table 17.1 Issues and solutions on zakat and blockchain

Issues	Solution
Governance	The Global Solution Networks (GSN) framework to blockchain governance: 1. Platform Ecosystems 2. Application Ecosystems 3. Overall Blockchain System Since blockchain has a robust governance framework, it may solve the governance issues on zakat
Efficiency	Blockchain might be harnessed to enhance the efficiency of zakat collection and distribution. For example, zakat may be calculated and monitored using smart apps
Impact on socio-economic development	Collaborate with private sectors to untapped the wealth of potential donors/muzakki
Trust	The advent of blockchain technology provides another means by which muzakki can monitor zakat payment and ensure that beneficiaries receive what has been allocated to them: – In this age of ever-increasing connectivity, technology can also be used to link donors in wealthy Muslim nations to those in need in poverty-stricken or conflict-torn areas, in a more structured and transparent manner – Laws and regulations, along with innovative products and methods, cannot alone guarantee the effective revival of the institutions of zakat. We need a softer element, upon which the long-term sustainability and viability of waqf ultimately depends. And the softer element is trust or amanah, which can be achieved through blockchain
Poor management	Blockchain can improve the management of zakat with its unedited and immortal database which could be accessed by everyone who uses the technology

In short, the term *maal* described as something that possessed by someone. But, there were some different opinions about *maal*. We can see some of definitions about *maal* from the four imams as depicted in Table 17.2.

From the Imam Hanafi point of view, according to Turner (2006), we can conclude that wealth in his perspective is something that can be stored. This implies good which has no physical form, or goods with physical form but cannot be stored such as food cannot be considered as wealth. Imam Hanafi perspectives are quite different from others imams who pay attention more to the intrinsic value of the wealth.

Table 17.2 Definitions of *Maal* according to four Imams modified from Turner (2006)

Madzhab	Definition of Maal	Point of view
Hanafi	Something that is desirable, present physically and can be stored	The goods itself
Maliki	Something which possession is exercised and the owner is exempted from anxiety of expropriation by others	Ownership
Shafii	Anything that comes with benefit	The importance of value
Hanbalis	Something that accrued in benefit and able to be utilized in normal instance	The principle of usability and benefit

On the other hand, various definitions and perspectives of the four imams give contemporary Muslims to define *maal* for objects that during their life are not yet existed by referring to some of the definition above. One object that currently exists and not yet defined as wealth in Shari'ah perspective is cryptocurrency. From the summary depicted in Table 17.3, we can see whether cryptocurrency is a wealth or not based on four imams definitions.

From Table 17.3, we can see that only on the criteria of wealth mentioned by Imam Hanafi that cannot be fulfilled by cryptocurrency. Meanwhile, if it refers to the criteria of wealth based on Imam Maliki, Imam Shafii and Imam Hambali then it can be concluded that cryptocurrency can be considered as a wealth. When Muslims choose to consider cryptocurrency as a wealth, then there will be zakat implications related to it. Since zakat is obligatory for every Muslims, we will discuss about cryptocurrency and zakat standard in the next section.

Cryptocurrency and Zakat Standard

While *nishab* of gold is 20-dinar, zakat on silver should be paid with *nishab* of 200 dirham. This refers to a famous hadits narrated by Ahmad and Abu Dawud in which the Prophet Muhammad SAW said:

> When you possess two hundred dirhams and one year passes on them, five dirhams are payable. Nothing is incumbent on you, that is, on gold, till it reaches twenty dinars. When you possess twenty dinars and one year passes on them, half a dinar is payable. Whatever exceeds, that will be reckoned properly.

Table 17.3   Cryptocurrency and the criteria of *Maal* according to four imams

Madzhab	*Definitions*	*Cryptocurrency*		
		Yes/No	*Explanation*	
Hanafi	Desirable	Yes	Promising, as a currency (for some countries, it is legal for transactions) and for investment (due to its increasing value)	
	Physical form	No	No physical form, only in cryptograph using algorithm. But it has a value, can be stored and can be exchanged to some local currencies such as USD	
	Can be stored	Yes	Every cryptocurrency owners have an account and wallet as a storage	
Maliki	Can be owned	Yes	Every cryptocurrency owner's records in the blockchain	
	Safe	Yes	Every transaction uses cryptocurrency recorded permanently and verified by the networks. In short, it can minimize the misuses. Although it can be stolen by hackers, it is clear that every property owned by society exposed by that kind of risk	
Shafii	Benefit	Yes	It can be used for any transactions and the value increases all the time, though fluctuate	
Hambali	Benefit	Yes	It can be used for any transactions and the value increases all the time, though fluctuate	
	Utilization	Yes	It can be used for transactions of investments	

Islamic jurists have different opinions about which sources of wealth should be subject to zakat. According to Kahf (1997), there are three fiqhi views on zakatable wealth. First, the narrow opinion includes agricultural products, gold and silver (except for personal use), trading goods, short-term net returns, and cash in hand. This is the most agreed upon method of zakat calculation. Second, the middle opinion includes all types of assets listed in the narrow opinion plus earnings on fixed assets, as well as wages, salaries, and professional incomes.

The third opinion includes items under the narrow and middle opinions plus fixed assets, which are assets used to generate income. This would include assets such as buildings, furniture, machinery, and containers. Zakatable assets and their respectives rates are provided in Table 17.4.

From Table 17.4, as cryptocurrency can be defined as *maal*, we can analogize it to cash in hand or any liquid assets to determine the zakat

Table 17.4   Zakatable asset and its rate

Type of asset	Nishab	Rate
Gold	20 Dinar (1 Dinar = 4.25 grams of gold)	2.5%
Silver	200 Dirham	2.5%
Cash in hand or any liquid assets	Amount equivalent to 85 grams of gold	2.5%
Agricultural products	653 kg of harvest	5% (irrigated land)/10% (non—irrigated land)
Mines products	Amount equivalent to 85 grams of gold	2.5%
Rikaz	No Nishab	20%
Cattles (cow, camel, goat, sheep)	Varies	Varies (in kind)

standard of cryptocurrency. Thus, the calculation will be based on the standard of 85 grams of gold as the *nishab* and 2.5% as the rate levied. A lunar year will be used to determine the haul or minimum period of holding and owning the cryptocurrency.

One may also argue that since there is mining activity, calculation of zakat of cryptocurrency may be based on zakat of mine wealth. In the case of Bitcoin for example, although new Bitcoins are not from the bowels of the earth, but it has some similarities to minerals such as valuable and limited. Regarding this, cryptocurrency can be regarded as *ma'adin* or the mine wealth. Zakat of *ma'adin* or mine wealth has the same calculation method with zakat of money (cash in hand) and gold. However, we prefer to not analogizing cryptocurrency with mine wealth as the two have different characteristics, although calculation of both zakat on cash and zakat on mine wealth is exactly the same. Therefore, the closest analogy for cryptocurrency is with cash in hand or liquid asset.

As an illustration, a person possesses two units of cryptocurrency XX on Muharram 1438 at the value of USD 15,000 per unit. After conducting several transactions, his cryptocurrency unit is reduced to one unit on Muharram 1439 at the value of USD 19,000 per unit. In this situation, his cryptocurrency unit is an object of zakat as its value has exceeded the *nishab* of 85 grams of gold. Thus, the amount of zakat that he must pay is as follows.

Zakat payment = 2.5% × 1 unit of cryptocurrency XX × USD 19,000 = USD 475

From the given example, it is known that the amount of zakat that must be paid is equal to USD 475. This payment can be made either in the form of cryptocurrency unit with condition that the *amil* institution accepts this form of payment, or in the form of USD and other acceptable currency.

CONCLUSION

Indeed, the development of technology is unavoidable. It needs to be implemented to all sectors, including economic, to improve our life. But the question is whether the stakeholder wants to play an active role or not in this change. From the Shari'ah perspective, using technology is allowed because everything is *mubah* unless specified otherwise. So, it is permissible to apply blockchain in zakat payment. Blockchain allows in making zakat payment more efficient, reliable, manageable, and significant. Many fiqh-based arguments support that cryptocurrency is an object of zakat. This is due to cryptocurrency position as an asset (*maal*), which is analogue with gold and cash in hand. Therefore, the method of zakat calculation for cryptocurrency is similar to the standard of zakat on gold and on cash in hand.

REFERENCES

Alzubaidi, I. H., and Abdullah, A. 2017. Developing a Digital Currency from an Islamic Perspective: Case of Blockchain Technology. *International Business Research*, 10(11), pp. 79–87.

Az-Zuhaili, W. 2011. *Fiqih Islam Wa Adillatuhu*. Translated from Arabic by A. H. El Kattani. Jakarta: Gema Insani.

Bakar, N. A., Rosbi, S., and Uzaki, K. 2017. Cryptocurrency Framework Diagnostics from Islamic Finance Perspective: A New Insight of Bitcoin System Transaction. *International Journal of Management Science and Business Administration*, 4(11), pp. 19–28.

Bohme, R., Christin, N., Edelman, B., and Tyler, M. 2015. Bitcoin: Economies, Technology and Governance. *The Journal of Economic Perspectives*, 29(2), pp. 213–238.

Hosseini, H. 1988. Notions of Private Property in Islamic Economics in Contemporary Iran: A Review of Literature. *International Journal of Social Economics*, 15(9), pp. 51–61.

Kahf, M. 1997. *Economics of Zakat Book of Reading No. 2*. Jeddah: Islamic Development Bank.

Leon, D. C., Stalick, Q. A., Jillepalli, A. A., Haney, M. A., and Sheldon F. T. 2017. Blockchain: Properties and Misconceptions. *Asia Pacific Journal of Innovation and Entrepreneurship*, 11(3), pp. 286–300.

Nakamoto, S. 2008. *Bitcoin: A Peer-to-Peer Electronic Cash System.* [Online] Bitcoin. Avalaible at: https://bitcoin.org/bitcoin.pdf. Accessed 22 April 2018.

Papadopoulos, G. 2015. Blockchain and Digital Payments: An Institutionalist Analysis of Cryptocurrencies. In *Handbook of Digital Currency*. New York: Elsevier.

Qardhawi, Y. 2004. *Peran Nilai dan Moral dalam Perekonomian Islam*. Translated from Arabic by D. Hafidudin et al. Jakarta: Robbani Press.

Turner, C. 2006. Wealth as an Immorality Symbol in the Quran: A Reconsideration of the Mal Amwal Verses. *The Journal of Qur'anic Studies*, 8, pp. 58–83.

Yusoff, M., and Densumite, S. 2012. Zakah Distribution and Growth in the Federal Territory of Malaysia. *Journal of Economics and Behavioral Studies*, 4(8), pp. 449–456.

Zainal, H., Bakar, A. A., and Saad, R. A. J. 2016. Reputation, Satisfaction of Zakat Distribution, and Service Quality as Determinant of Stakeholder Trust in Zakat Institutions. *International Journal of Economics and Financial Issues*, 6(S7), pp. 72–76.

CHAPTER 18

Waqf Led Halal Cryptocurrency Model

Irfan Syauqi Beik, Muhammad Hasbi Zaenal and Priyesta Rizkiningsih

INTRODUCTION

The development of digital technology is spreading rapidly throughout the world which transforms various aspects of our everyday life from how we communicate to how we do financial transaction (McKinsey Global Institute 2016; Alzubaidi and Abdullah 2017). According to McKinsey Global Institute (2016), digital technology in the financial world will transform in three foundational form, which are: (1) Digital finance can expand customers' access; (2) digital finance can lower the cost of providing financial services by 80 to 90% particularly for serving poor customer who live in remote area; and (3) digital finance create new model of business. However, this condition has its own challenges and opportunities, as digital finance provider have to ensure that they have made a product which actively used by the customer while the opportunity

I. S. Beik (✉) · M. H. Zaenal · P. Rizkiningsih
Center of Strategic Studies, The National Board of Zakat (BAZNAS),
The Republic of Indonesia, Central Jakarta, Indonesia
e-mail: irfan.beik@puskasbaznas.com

I. S. Beik
Department of Islamic Economics, Bogor Agricultural University,
Bogor, Indonesia

© The Author(s) 2019
M. M. Billah (ed.), *Halal Cryptocurrency Management*,
https://doi.org/10.1007/978-3-030-10749-9_18

285

lies on the increasing growth using the new way of digital technology in finance.

The story of digitization started when people begin using a mobile phone as it can provide easy access to financial services, for instance, to receive and saving money, payments as well as another financial service. Moreover, digital-payment system in the future predicted will use less-cash and paper record (McKinsey Global Institute 2016; Alzubaidi and Abdullah 2017) due to all digital account can be accessed via the Internet through everyone's mobile phone. In an advance phase of digital technology, it is also predicted that the platform for financial services will be facilitated by collaborative platform, open sources, as well as peer-to-peer network which committed to social solidarity and mutual aid (Pazaitis et al. 2017; Scott 2016).

The first open source digital technology in finance network was blockchain, which is a technology behind the renowned cryptocurrency—Bitcoin.Efanov and Roschin (2018) define blockchain as a transaction record database which distributed among participating member or also known as a public ledger. In blockchain technology, each transaction should be confirmed by members' consensus therefore it can reduce fraud transactions. By using this technology, anyone can see all the financial transaction occur in the network in a real-time manner. Furthermore, all the financial records cannot be changed or removed once it is accepted by the blockchain (Efanov and Roschin 2018; Prypto 2016). Hence, the level of transparency of blockchain is better compared to traditional financial ecosystem (Prypto 2016).

As blockchain technology and cryptocurrency are becoming more popular among individual nowadays, the number of present cryptocurrency is increasing and the level of its acceptance is rising up. By using cryptocurrency, customer can have access to payment system anywhere and anytime as long as they have access to Internet and technology (Alzubaidi and Abdullah 2017; PwC USA n.d.). Hence, cryptocurrency represents the new-phase of digital technology in financial network which could be a disruption for traditional financial network. This is a valuable development in digital finance, however, whether this development could also be applicable in Islamic finance sector or not, it should be examined further.

Long before the advent of the blockchain, crypto-finance had been conceptualized in a setting with a central server trusted to prevent double-spending. Chaum (1983) proposed the idea of a cryptographically secure method of payment that would ensure privacy. This field encompasses encryption, decryption, authentication, and the distribution of keys, which is not defined by geographical location, political structure, or legal system (Babbitt and Dietz 2014).

Blockchain and Cryptocurrency in Islamic Perspective

The development of cryptocurrency and blockchain technology could shift how we do financial transaction. However, those two technologies should be assessed whether those can be applied in Islamic finance sector and in accordance with Islamic principles. This section will elaborate whether these two technologies are feasible to be implemented in Islamic finance sector.

In the case of blockchain technology, which could eliminate the possibility of fraud in transactions, increase transparency level, improving accountability, and based on trust, there are no specific Islamic principles issues as blockchain characteristics are promoting core Islamic values (Hileman and Rauchs 2017; Lacasse et al. 2017). Hence, there is no issues in implementing blockchain technology in Islamic financial system as it is in accordance with Islamic principles. Furthermore, Islamic finance industry would have great advantages by using blockchain technology as it provides the true spirit of Islamic value (Lacasse et al. 2017). In addition, Alzubaidi and Abdullah (2017) argued that blockchain technology also eliminates prohibited element in Islamic principles such as *gharar* (ambiguity) from transaction as the verification process is strong and transparent.

On the other hand, implementing the concept of cryptocurrency in Islamic finance should be considered more carefully as there are many issues arise in this case mainly because cryptocurrency does not have an intrinsic value (Alzubaidi and Abdullah 2017). Cryptocurrency can be defined as a digital currency using encryption techniques and operating independent from central bank. Cryptocurrency is designed to be utilized as a medium of exchange using cryptography to secure and control transaction as well as the additional creation of the currency (Bakar et al. 2017). Moreover, cryptocurrency is not issued by a central bank, therefore, theoretically, it immune to government intervention (Böhme et al. 2015; Prypto 2016; Alzubaidi and Abdullah 2017).

Before going further whether cryptocurrency is permissible in Islamic perspective, it has to determine in which category this cryptocurrency lies, money (currency), commodity, or assets/wealth (*maal*). To date there is no uniformity in categorizing cryptocurrency. Government in each country has to define and classify cryptocurrency based on relevant regulation in particular country. For instance, Australian Taxation office, German Federal Financial Supervisory Authority and Brazilian Law categorize cryptocurrency as a financial asset while The People's Bank of China considers cryptocurrency such as bitcoin as a virtual commodity or good.

Firstly, it has to consider cryptocurrency as a money or currency. In the economic terms, specific criteria of money are: (1) unit of account; (2) medium of exchange; and (3) store of value (Alzubaidi and Abdullah 2017; Muhammad 2017). Cryptocurrency has unit of account. For example, in bitcoin, it has decimal point as their unit of account. In addition, cryptocurrency can also perform as medium of exchange in their virtual community. Lastly, the third criteria that something can be classified as money is store of value, which means it holds the value that would appreciate and depreciate as well as can measure the amount of goods and services. These third criteria are limited in the cryptocurrency model as their price is very volatile so it becomes more difficult in terms of measuring the value of goods and services.

The other criteria to classify cryptocurrency as money or currency are widely and commonly accepted. In the case of cryptocurrency, it is only accepted through their community. Furthermore, according to Mufti Taqi Uthmani in Adam (n.d), money or currency only accepted as a currency when it is a legal tender or if it is established by legislation. However, current situation shows that cryptocurrency still not accepted by government and because the spirit of cryptocurrency are free market and decentralization which means we are all part of cryptocurrency ecosystem, therefore, cryptocurrency is difficult to comply with these criteria. To sum up, whether cryptocurrency can be classified as money or currency can be seen in Table 18.1.

Based on Table 18.1, it can be concluded that cryptocurrency does not comply with all aspects of money or currency characteristics or in other words it is not money in an accurate definition. Additionally, we have to identify whether cryptocurrency can be classified as a commodity. According to Adam (n.d.), specific criteria of the commodity are: (1) recognized by Shari'ah as valuable; (2) must have an intrinsic value; (3) identifiable; (4) transferable; and (5) can be owned. The problem in cryptocurrency is that it does not have an intrinsic value

Table 18.1 Money characteristic and cryptocurrency

No	Characteristic of money or currency	Cryptocurrency
1.	Unit of account	Yes
2.	Medium of exchange	Yes
3.	Store of value	Yes
4.	Widely and commonly accepted	Yes
5.	Legal tender	No

(Ron and Shamir 2013; Bakar et al. 2017; Alzubaidi and Abdullah 2017), henceforth, it cannot be classified as a commodity. Even though some scholars argue that the intrinsic value of cryptocurrency is the algorithm and the system they have, it still debatable among scholars (PwC USA n.d.).

Lastly, it has to be decided whether cryptocurrency is an asset or wealth. In Islamic point of view particularly from Hanafi School, wealth (*maal*) can be defined as something which is naturally desired by man and can be stored for the time of necessity—including movables (*manqul*) and immovable (*ghayr manqul*). Whereas, Maliki School define *maal* as anything can be owned. Additionally, Shafii and Hanbali School describe *maal* as something from which the owner can obtain some benefit. Having seen those criteria, cryptocurrency could be categorized as wealth as it complies with the criteria of can be owned, can be stored (in a virtual storage), as well as the owner can acquire benefit from them.

In summary, if cryptocurrency wishes to adopt in Islamic finance industry, it must comply with Shari'ah principles, which must be legalized by the government if it is categorized as currency or money. Furthermore, if it is equalized to currency so that all transactions should follow Al-Sharf ruling in Shari'ah principles. In addition, based on the explanation above, cryptocurrency cannot be classified as commodity as it does not have intrinsic value. Nevertheless, cryptocurrency can be identified as wealth (*maal*) because it conforms with *maal* criteria in Islamic perspective.

THE CONCEPT OF WAQF

Waqf is Muslim charitable endowment fund which is also termed as perpetual or continuous alms (sadaqah) (Ahmed 2007; Hassan 2010). In conjunction with it, linguistically in Arabic, waqf means hold, confinement, and stand still (Ahmed 2004; Hassan 2010). According to

Hassan (2010), waqf can be categorized based on its function. First, religious waqf which aims to maintain religious facilities such as mosque and Islamic school. The second type of waqf is philanthropic waqf which focuses in assisting the poor and needy, for instance, health services as well as education. The last category of waqf is family waqf where the benefit of waqf is distributed to the family member and its descendants first then the excess will be contributed for the poor.

There are several pillars of waqf that must be fulfilled in performing waqf, they are: (1) *Wakif*—the person who contribute the waqf; (2) *Mauquf*—the waqf property; (3) *Mauquf alaih*—the beneficiaries of waqf; and (4) *Sighat*—ijab and qabul for waqf contribution. The wakif decides for whom waqf property can be utilized include where its benefit and revenue can be allocated. In the case of waqf management and operator, wakif can determine according to themselves and they can establish governing principle as their desire (Ahmed 2004).

In waqf practice, the majority of people only know that waqf can be used only for religious purposes. This condition is really unfortunate since the potential of waqf is not only limited to religious purposes but also for the development of society particularly in eradicating poverty (Saifuddin et al. 2014). However, besides contributing waqf in the form of fixed property, waqf also can be given in cash or also known as cash waqf. This practice also performed in the first year of hijriah in which cash waqf was delivered for a free cash lending to the waqf recipient as well as distributed for investment while the earning was assigned to the beneficiaries (Hassan 2010). Later, cash waqf mechanism also becomes more popular in the Ottoman Empire (Ahmed 2004; Hassan 2010). In recent years, unlike fixed property waqf, cash waqf becomes more popular due to its flexibility in the amount to contribute so that it attracts more Muslim people to participate in waqf (Saifuddin et al. 2014).

Nevertheless, to improve the potential of waqf especially in this digital era, it could integrate the development of technology such as blockchain technology as well as cryptocurrency in the waqf collection and distribution as long as it remains in accordance with Islamic principles. It is predicted by harmonizing blockchain technology in waqf operational activities, waqf management would be more transparent to the wakif, beneficiaries as well as to the society at large. On the other hand, utilizing Shari'ah-compliant cryptocurrency could attract more Muslim population specifically Muslim young generation to participate in waqf activities. As cryptocurrency mechanism is borderless, therefore, waqf using cryptocurrency technology is expected to draw attention from Muslim population across the country. Next section will elaborate certain possibility in integrating waqf model to the recent development technology of blockchain and cryptocurrency.

In the last years, there are many innovative platforms and projects happening in the emerging "crypto-philanthropy" space. It includes crowdfunding platforms, which allows donors to make cryptocurrency donations to selected charities for their fundraising campaigns. Besides, some new tools can track the flow of donations from donor to a recipient openly, and to verify what charities have been received and achieved, all on a blockchain. Beyond cryptocurrency donations and tracking, a number of social purposes have been created to support specific nonprofit programs and endeavors.

The donation transformation by using blockchain technology and cryptocurrency medium seems to have to be considered by Islamic economist to how to utilize technology to maximize the performance, effectiveness, and efficiency in the era of digital technology. This transformation can be applied to the Islamic philanthropy instruments, i.e., waqf. Here, authors will elaborate the models that can be applied immediately by waqf institutions.

WAQF LED CRYPTOCURRENCY PLATFORMS

Waqf can be part of the provision of public goods instruments under Islamic Law in the form of donation activities that can be developed in the category of productive assets or economic and social benefits. Economic assets are generally fixed assets, income producing, including rentable shops, houses, farms, shares in companies or businesses; function facilities, e.g., halls, etc. While in the social benefit category, waqf can develop fixed or capital assets which include schools; masjids; schools; hospitals & clinics; boreholes, water and sanitation facilities; libraries; cemeteries; community centers; hostels, etc.

In the short term, cryptocurrency and blockchain platforms will significantly disrupt or displace traditional philanthropy. Reported dozens of national and international aid agencies is researching blockchain-based models for delivering humanitarian aid with fund management and distribution platform disburse. This is a transformation for the Waqf management, provides a record of all transactions and a way of determining who owns what at a given time. In the philanthropic context, it provides

donors with a new way of giving and allows charities a new fundraising channel. The waqf blockchain would act as a monitoring system to
ensure that in need while simultaneously mitigating exchange rate-based
losses. It will also make the waqf process to be transparent, fast and
which drives accountability to taxpayers and those affected by crises.

In principle, the waqf leaps on the blockchain technology platform and cryptocurrency is part of the advanced step. Connecting
from the existing transformation, i.e., cash waqf, stock *waqf*, corporate
waqf, crowdfunding waqf and so forth. If previously using a centralized technology that records only on one central (institution/*naazir*),
this transformation will bring decentralization, where the process of
recording scattered all the blockchain network. In addition, if previously
using the fiat and metal conventional currency, in this stage using the
cryptocurrency is a medium (*mauquf*).

As a charity (*Tabarru*) waqf has the meaning give of wealth (*al-mal*)
as a waqf object to help as appropriate. In Islam, *al-mal* is based on
people customs and culture. Fiqh scholars accept that *al-Maal* is goods
having value, both tangible and intangible values. Hanāfiyah scholars
define al-māl as "*Kullu Qīmatun Māliyah Baina al-Nās*" (what is considered to be human beings) tangible, physically, distinguishable from
one another and not in an emergency used only, such as carrion and liquor. *Mālikiyyah, Shāfiʿiyyah*, and *Hanābilah* expanded intangible asset.
This basis indicates that blockchain and cryptocurrency are part of *al-
mal*. Blockchain in terms of technology is an acceptable advancement of
the times and useful for realizing the effectiveness and efficiency. While
cryptocurrency, it is tangible, acceptable customarily, has value, has benefits, and can be used without emergency as land, building, plantation,
house, gold, silver, stock, and so forth.

Waqf Cryptocurrency Models

The waqf concept dates back more than a thousand years, reaching
its heyday during the Ottoman Empire. The assets in many waqf are
underutilized and earn low returns because of ineffective management,
with some waqf requiring further donations to keep running. It needs
technology to modernize and solve the problem. When waqf is applied
to blockchain and cryptocurrency model, the benefit seems very significant in solving: (1) lack of public trust transparency; (2) less operational

costs; (3) direct connection with *mauquf alaih* being helped; and (4) more funding to those in need.

In the waqf cryptocurrency ecosystem, it inseparable from the waqf pillars, there are: (1) *Waqif*—the person making the donation; (2) *Sihgat*—waqf contract in this case smart contract technology; (3) *Naazir*—an experienced person who dedicates his/her time to regularly interact with the waqif through constant updates; and (4) *Mauquf alaih*—The people in need who benefit from the donations (Fig. 18.1).

The ecosystem describes three models that can be applied in the case of waqf. This refers to the best practices of blockchain and cryptocurrency technology on current charity activities. First, blockchain-based

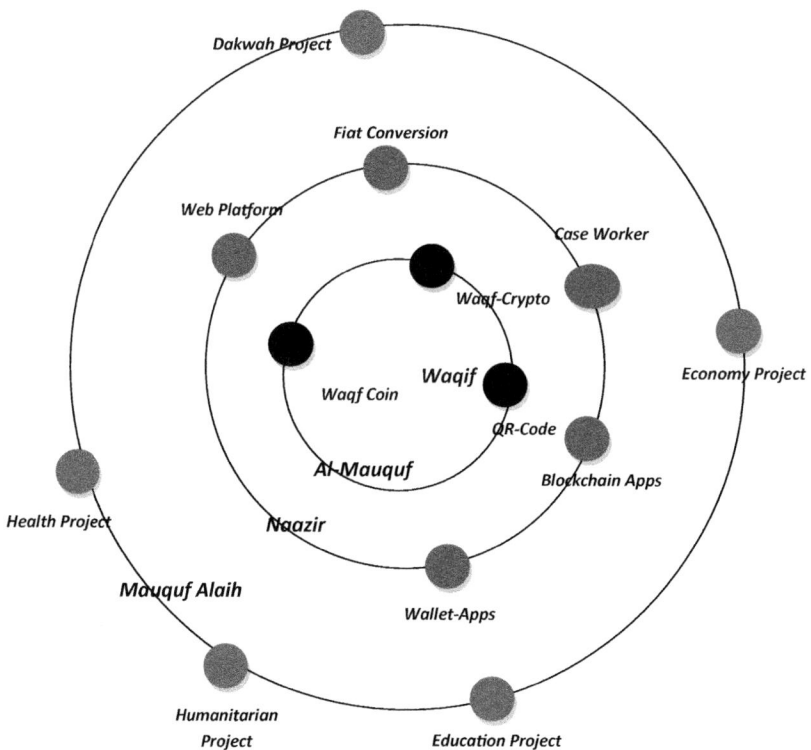

Fig. 18.1 Waqf cryptocurrency ecosystem (*Source* Authors [proceed])

waqf model—in this model, waqif can track the flow of donations from donors to a recipients openly, and to verify what charities have received and achieved, all on a blockchain; second, the *waqf* model uses the cryptocurrency crowdfunding scheme—which allows donors to obtain charities for their fundraising campaigns; and third, creating a cryptocurrency devoted to the waqf project—this digital coins have been created to support specific nonprofit programs and endeavors.

Waqf Blockchain Model

In this model, waqif can track the status of their donation and see its impact on a worthy cause. This system is full transparency about how a donation is used to support their cause. On the fund's trip, donors are notified when an update is posted to their platform tracking page. Another advantage on this platform, waqif profiles are represented in visual form that grows with every donation. Easily shareable on social media platforms and manage one-time and recurring donations seamlessly. This model described as the following paths:

- The donation process has been initiated by the *waqif*, with a fiat money medium. This could have been done by sending funds to *the nazir* (waqf organization).
- The amount of donation will be listed in QR Code, this code is processed from blockchain technology. *Nazir* has received the donation and is in the process of putting the funds to use.
- *Nazir* has used the fund from waqif to support a worthy cause (Fig. 18.2).

Waqf Crowd-Coin Model

The model is primarily two things: a Web site platform—ex: site.org and secondly a legal entity (*naazir/*a waqf foundation). The principle is that using only cryptocurrency as a medium to accumulate funds for the *mauquf alaih* (waqf project) campaigns that are hosted on the Web site platform. What the *naazir* and the platform do is actually converting cryptocurrency into tangible good for the *mauquf alaih*. The *naazir* of waqf foundation provides a place in the virtual form, where the *waqif* can find a cause as well as can associate with and help fund it, using the cryptocurrency that ever existed.

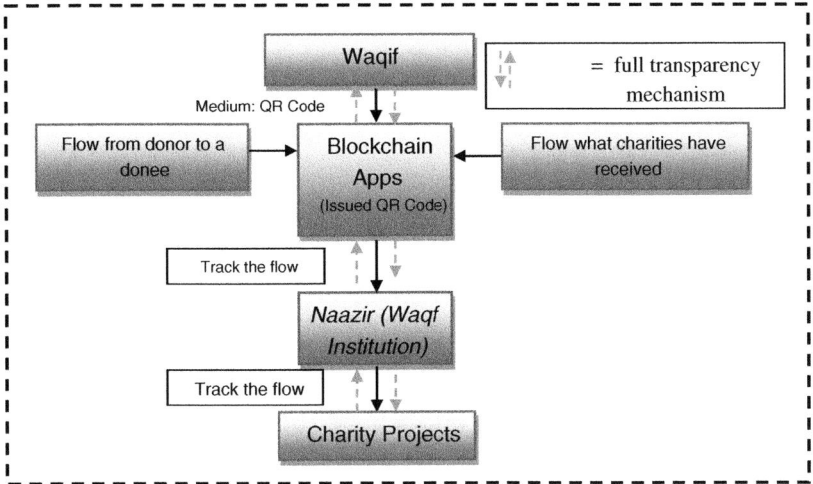

Fig. 18.2 Blockchain waqf illustration model (*Source* Authors [proceed])

This model is similar to the crowdfunding waqf project, addition with the transparency through blockchain technology in platforms/apps, described as the following paths:

- *Naazir* promotes *waqf* project campaigns in the web platform.
- The donation process has been initiated by the *waqif* by using a virtual money medium—cryptocurrency. This could have been done by sending coin to *the nazir* (waqf organization) via platform.
- *Naazir* has received the coin donation and is in the process of converting to the into tangible good.
- Waqif receives notification of the amount of money conversions donated to be processed.
- *Nazir* has used the fund from waqif to support a worthy cause (Fig. 18.3).

WAQF-COIN MODEL

This model is an inspiration, in the future, waqf foundation could produce their own cryptocurrencies, the sale of which may enable a new sustainability model. Waqf-Coin designed as unique digital currency

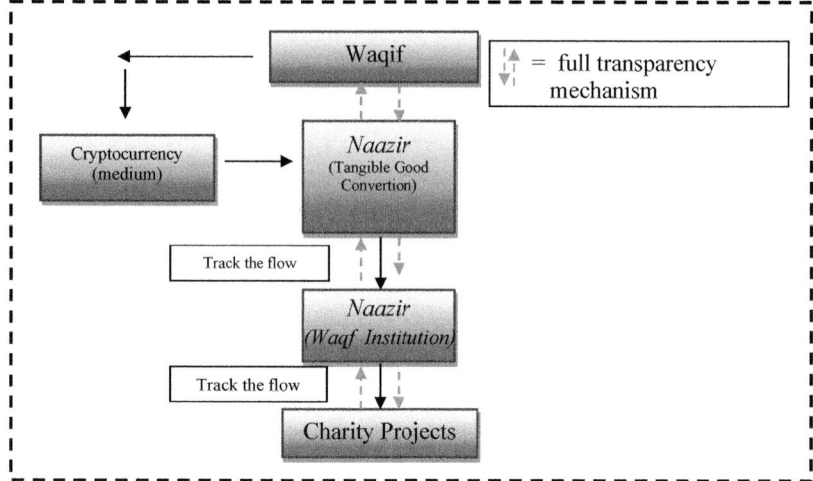

Fig. 18.3 Waqf crowd-coin model illustration (*Source* Authors [proceed])

inspired by the pursuit of Islamic philanthropy and technology cryptocurrency. Thus, offers a secure and trustless network to disrupt the non-transparent charity model.

The unique software allows *waqif* to earn proof of stake (distributed consensus) rewards as the cryptocurrency publishing system simply by running a wallet. It also allows us to automatically donate any portion of these proofs to any waqf project at zero cost. All donations will go to the charity wallet and from there it will go to Web site platform like site.org. This mechanism allows *waqif* to see the donations in real time on the blockchain that instantly goes to a waqf project.

The model is basically a hybrid system, i.e., a combination of cryptocurrency published with a waqf donation system, like the following path:

- *Naazir* publishes waqf-coin and provides a "wallet software" platform.
- The donation process has been initiated by the *waqif.* This could have been done by sending waqf-coin to *the nazir* from the wallet software.
- *Naazir* has received the any portion of these proofs donation and is in the process of converting into the tangible good.

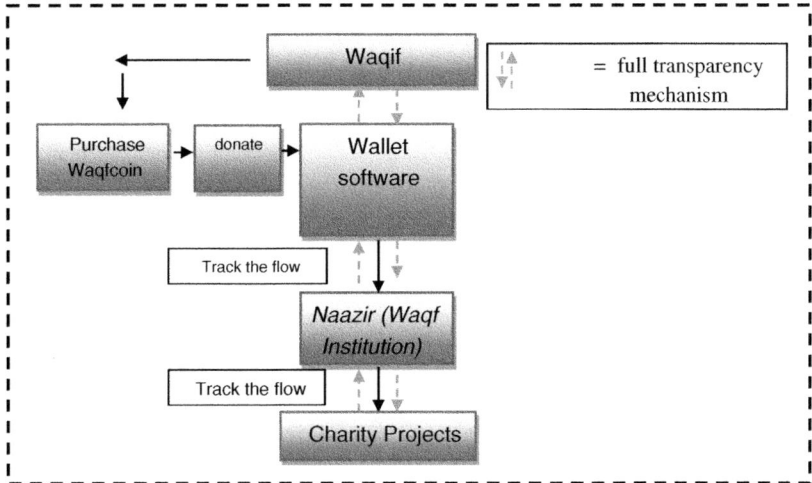

Fig. 18.4 Waqf-Coin model illustration (*Source* Authors [proceed])

- *Waqif* received a notification of the amount, the funds to use.
- *Nazir* has used the fund from *waqif* to support a worthy cause (Fig. 18.4).

CONCLUSION

Despite the unlimited opportunities, there are many challenges ahead; the most notable among them is the fact that digital currency donations and blockchain anchored systems are still new in the world of philanthropy. However, there is awareness and interest among donors and waqf institutions, how to maximize the development of this digital money as a solution to the problems of inefficiency of waqf management. This proposal can be applied immediately by the waqf institution. Initial step can be done by collaboration between *naazir* and technology providers to set and create the models.

REFERENCES

Adam, M. F. n.d. *Bitcoin: Shari'ah Compliant?* s.l.: Amanah Finance Consultancy.

Ahmed, H. 2004. *Role of Zakah and Awqaf in Poverty Alleviation.* Jeddah: IDB.

Ahmed, H. 2007. *Waqf-Based Microfinance: Realizing Social Role of Islamic Finance*. Singapore: s.n.

Alzubaidi, I. B., & Abdullah, A. 2017. Developing a Digital Currency from an Islamic Perspective: Case of Blockchain Technology. *International Business Research*, 10(11), pp. 79–87.

Babbitt, D., & Dietz, J. 2014. Crypto-Economic Design: A Proposed Agent-Based Modelling Effort. Swarm Fest 2014: 18th Annual Meeting on Agent-Based Modelling & Simulation. University of Notre Dame.

Bakar, N. A., Rosbi, S., & Uzaki, K. 2017. Cryptocurrency Framework Diagnostics from Islamic Finance Perspective: A New Insight of Bitcoin System Transaction. *International Journal of Management Science and Business Administration*, 4(1), pp. 19–28.

Böhme, R., Christin, N., Edelman, B., & Moore, T. 2015. Bitcoin: Economics, Technology, and Governance. *Journal of Economic Perspectives*, 29(2), pp. 213–238.

Chaum, D. 1983. Blind Signatures for Untraceable Payments. In Chaum, D., Rivest, R. L, & Sherman, A. T. (eds), *Advances in Cryptology*, pp. 199–203. New York: Springer.

Efanov, D., & Roschin, P. 2018. The All-Pervasiveness of Blockchain Technology. *Procedia Computer Science*, 123, pp. 116–121.

Hassan, M. K. 2010. *An Integrated Poverty Alleviation Model Combining Zakat, Awqaf, and Microfinance*. Bangi: s.n.

Hileman, G., & Rauchs, M. 2017. *Global Blockchain Benchmarking Study*. Cambridge: Cambridge Center for Alternative Finance.

Lacasse, R.-M., Lambert, B., & Khan, N. 2017. *Blockchain Technology—Arsenal for a Shari'ah-Compliant Financial Ecosystem?* Agadir: s.n.

McKinsey Global Institute. 2016. *Digital Finance for All: Powering Inclusive Growth in Emerging Economies*. McKinsey Global Institute.

Muhammad, M. 2017. *Shari'ah Analysis of Cryptocurrency: Bitcoin*. Petaling Jaya: ISRA.

Pazaitis, A., De Filippi, P., & Kostakis, V. 2017. Blockchain and Value Systems in the Sharing Economy: The Illustrative Case of Backfeed. *Technological Forecasting and Social Change*, 125, pp. 105–115.

Prypto. 2016. *Bitcoin for Dummies*. Hoboken, NJ: Wiley.

PwC USA. n.d. *Money Is No Object: Understanding the Evolving Cryptocurrency Market*. USA: PwC.

Ron, D., & Shamir, A. 2013. *Quantitative Analysis of the Full Bitcoin Transaction Graph*. s.l.: s.n.

Saifuddin, F., et al. 2014. The Role of Cash Waqf in Poverty Alleviation: Case of Malaysia. *International Journal of Business, Economics and Law*, 4(1).

Scott, B. 2016. *How Can Cryptocurrency and Blockchain Technology Play a Role in Building Social and Solidarity Finance?* Geneva, Switzerland: UNRISD.

PART VI

Risk Management in Halal Cryptocurrency

CHAPTER 19

Shari'ah Paradigm of Risk Management

Mohd Ma'Sum Billah

INTRODUCTION

No one can entirely be saved from facing an unpredicted risk, be it against one's life property or business. *Shari'ah* is a dynamic system, which does not leave one alone (among creatures) to face risk with no guidance or protection for them. For instance, during the Battle of *Uhud*, many Muslims were martyred and left their orphans and widows with no assistance. The remaining Muslims community undertook the task to look after the welfare of those helpless orphans and widows. *Allah (SWT)* commanded the community (for those who are capable of maintaining justice) to practice polygamy to provide security for those orphans and widows. Similarly, if one has a fear of risk of unfairness to the wives (for the protection of their right) restrain from practicing polygamy, but marry only one. *Allah (SWT)* says:

M. M. Billah (✉)
Finance, Insurance, Fintech and Investment, Islamic Economics Institute, King Abdul Aziz University, Jeddah, Kingdom of Saudi Arabia
URL: http://www.drmasumbillah.blogspot.com

© The Author(s) 2019   301
M. M. Billah (ed.), *Halal Cryptocurrency Management*,
https://doi.org/10.1007/978-3-030-10749-9_19

> If you fear that, you shall not be able to treat the orphans fairly, marry
> women of your choice, two or three or four, but if you fear you shall not
> be able to deal fairly (with them) then only one...[1]

In this *Ayat*, *Allah* *(SWT)* allowed polygamy for those who can uphold justice and at the same time the polygamy is prohibited for those who cannot ensure fairness and justice.

Likewise, in the provision of the fear prayer (*Solat al-Khawf*), Muslims are allowed to perform their prayer in a different style. Such ruling is for the protection of the fighters against the fear of unexpected risk of an attack by the enemy. The methods of fear prayer are as follows:

> Narrated by Yahya bin Saaid (R) ...the form of the fear prayer is that the Imam stands with the group of his companions, while another group faces the enemy. The Imam prays one Rakaah with them, including the prostration, and then stand. The remains standing while they complete the remaining rakaah by themselves. They then say the taslim, leave, and form up opposite the enemy while the Imam remaining standing. Then the other who has not prayed come forward and says the takbir behind the Imam and he prays one rakaah with them, including the prostration. He then says taslim, while they stand up and pray the remaining rakaah by themselves. Then they say the taslim.[2]

In these aforesaid examples from the holy *Qur'an* and the *Sunnah* respectively, it has been observed that the *Shari'ah* generally provides alternative provisions for the protection against unpredictable risk. An insurance policy may also be justified generally by the above-mentioned divine principles. Its prime objective is also to provide a material protection against unpredictable risk. It is clarified here that, an insurance policy dose cover a risk with material protection is needed, but not a risk against which a material chance or gain is sought.

It is again justified by the saying of the Holy *Prophet (saw)* relating to *Hijrah*. During the rise of Islam, there was a provision for Muslim to migrate (*Hijrah*) from unsafe places to peaceful locations. The provision was for the protection of faith, life and wealth for the Muslim against the risk of oppression by the *Kuffar* and *Mushrikin*, but not for the purpose

---

[1] *al-Qur'an* 4:5.
[2] *Muwatta Imam Malik.*

of any form of material gain. The Holy *Prophet (saw)* then reminded Muslims to purify their purpose of migration before making it. The purpose of migration was to achieve the pleasure of *Allah (swt)* and not for material gain. Therefore, whosever migrates for the purpose of material gain, the migration will be blotted out in the sight of *Allah (swt)*. The *Sunnah* to this effect is as follows:

> Narrated by Umar bin Khtab (r) the holy Prophet (saw) said: the reward of deeds depends on the intentions and every person will get the reward according to what he has intended. So whoever migrated for worldly benefits or for a woman to marry, his migration was for what he migrated for.[3]

In the light of this divine injunction, it may be concluded that, a risk can be covered by an insurance policy subject to the following conditions:

* It should be unexpected, but defined one;
* The purpose of having a security (insurance policy) against a risk must be for the purpose of a material protection against loss, but not purely for a material gain or chance;
* The risk should not be deliberately invented;
* No risk on unlawful subject matter should be covered by a policy; and
* The happening of risk must not be certainly known prior to the time it happens.

There are some Islamic scholars who oppose the idea of insurance practices, because it involves *al-Garar* (uncertainty). This is because a transaction which involves *al-Garar* is prohibited by the prophetic sanction. There are three aspects of the subject matter of the policy, i.e., "the subject matter itself," "the fear of the risk" and "the happening" of the risk. Hence, the opponents' arguments are general and not quite clear as whether *al-Garar* involves in the fear of risk or in the happening of the risk or in the subject matter itself? It is argued that the "subject matter" in a policy is not uncertain (*al-Garar*) as it is identified by the policyholder before the inception of the policy. Secondly, the fear of the risk in the subject matter (e.g., in a life policy, the death of the policyholder is a

[3] *Sahih al-Bukhari.*

fear of risk likewise, in a general policy, the incident on the subject matter is a fear of risk) is not vague and it is identified before the commencement of each policy.

Therefore, it is submitted here that, there is no element of *al-Garar* involved in these two situations of the subject matter of the policy. But, the element of *al-Garar* involved only in the *"happening"* of the risk (e.g., in a life policy, the time, place and cause of death or the risk itself on the life of the policyholder and whether it happens within the period or not and similarly, in general policy, the time, place and cause of incident on the subject matter, are the elements of *"happening"* of the risk). Certainly, the *"happening"* of risk should be uncertain and unknown to the creatures because *Allah (swt)* is the one who has absolute possession of knowledge of the unpredicted happening of risk as has been clarified in the holy *Qur'an*:

> And verily Allah (swt) known all things unseen.[4]

It is again justified by the declaration of *Allah (swt)*:

> Certainly the knowledge of the day of the judgment is with Allah (swt), it is He who sends down rain, and He who knows what is in unseen wombs, nor does anyone know what it is that he will earn tomorrow, nor does anyone know in what place he is to die. Verily with Allah (swt) is with full knowledge and He is acquainted with all things.[5]

Among the allegations against insurance practices are: it involves the element of *al-Garar* is baseless and unfair. The question arises, since the happening of the risk is known only by *Allah (swt)*, then what is the solution of the policyholder who has an evil intention to violate the power of *Allah (swt)* by inventing a risk on the subject matter, such as suicide, setting fire on the subject matter before and after the commencement of the policy? It is a mere plan, and the policyholder also cannot ensure that his plan will be successful. In such a situation, the policy may be held invalid on the ground of breach of good faith, but not on the question of *al-Garar*.

---

[4] *al-Qur'an* 9:78.
[5] *al-Qur'an* 31:34.

There are several categories of risks according to their nature. Are all kinds of risk covered by an insurance policy? There are nine categories of risks outlined as follows.

Subjective Risk

The degree of the risk in the subject matter is varied. For example, a building is presumed to be at risk from either fire cracking or collapsing: but still it is at risk. In this category, whether there is a fear of risk against the subject matter or not, but no chance for gain.

Objective Risk

This is in which the fear of risk on a subject matter always exists. Subsequently, there is neither chance for gain nor a changed condition on the subject matter, but only loss (of an expected nature). Examples would be an education policy in which the fear of risk of future educational expenses always exists, or a social insurance policy. For instance, in retirement scheme, in which the employees, upon their retirement, are generally at risk of lacking in adequate financial support to maintain their lives and families.

Pure and Defined Risk

There is a fear of a defined risk on a particular subject matter. Subsequently, there could be either a loss or no change on the subject matter, but no chance for again either. For example, a motor car is always at a defined risk of accident, but the risk does not necessarily always occur. It may or may not occur. If however, the risk happens on the subject matter then it is a loss, otherwise there is no change on it, but of course no gain is expected on it either.

Speculative Risk

In a subject matter where the fear of risk is present, but the owner of the subject matter believes that, the risk is either of a total loss or gain on the subject matter, this kind of risk is similar to gambling, which is expressly prohibited in the Holy *Qur'an*:

O ye believe, intoxicants and gambling, dedication of stones... are an abomination of evil's handiwork so refrain from such abomination...[6]

Risk of a Certain Happening

The happening of risk on a subject matter is genuinely known by *Allah (swt)*. A person may bona fide believe that the risk will certainly happen on the subject matter. For example, if a building is cracked, and the owner upon knowing it, proceeds to buy a policy on the building. Such an attempt is considered seeking a gain, while deceiving the counter party. It is against the objective of insurance and therefore such risk will not be recognized as a risk to be covered by an insurance policy. *Allah (swt)* strictly prohibited gaining through unlawful means or by way of deceiving others.

O you who believe, do not consume your properly among yourselves by way of unlawful means.[7]

Risk Invented Deliberately

A risk is deliberately invented by the policyholder in order to gain and deceive the insurer. For example would be, committing suicide, or purposely causing a risk to happen on a particular subject matter. Such a risk shall not be coved by a policy, as it aims at deceiving the insurer, rather than cooperation. As *Allah (swt)* commanded:

...and Allah (swt) does not appreciate destruction or mischief...[8]

Risk on Unlawful Subject Matter

There are certain subject matters as unlawful in the eyes of the *Shari'ah* principles. Some of these subject matters are declared unlawful by their origins such as pigs, alcohol and dogs. While some are unlawful due to their involvement with unlawful elements, such as stolen, smuggled property, transactions involving the elements of *al-Riba* (usury),

---

[6] *al-Qur'an* 5:90.
[7] *al-Qur'an* 4:29.
[8] *al-Qur'an* 5:2.

al-Maisir (gambling), *al-Khamr* (alcohol) and so on. These unlawful subject matters may not be covered by an insurance policy, as the aim of an insurance policy is, *inter alia*, to contribute to peaceful material security, rather than creating destruction in the society considering the principles of public interest. However, if any insurance policy does allow covering those unlawful subject matters, then social destruction might take place instead of cooperation, which definitely against the teaching of *Allah (swt)* as expressed in the following *Ayah* of the Holy *Qur'an*:

...and Allah (swt) does not appreciate destruction or mischief...[9]

Risk on an Unowned Subject Matter

This occurs when an abandoned subject matter, which has got no actual owner, is at risk. Such a subject matter may not be covered by a policy as there is no certainty of ownership on it, relying on the principles of *al-Garar* (uncertainty). A subject matter may be at risk, but be possessed not by an actual owner, but by a stranger, or a mere agent or an authorized person, or a tenant, or a hirer, who has no legal authority to buy a policy against the risk on a such unowned subject matter, as the existence of ownership on a subject matter is necessary prior to buying a policy. This means the owner, who has a permanent interest in the property and not the temporary occupiers or the invites.

Risk on Unknown Subject Matter

A subject matter is at risk, but it is neither possessed nor are its physical conditions known to the person, who wishes to buy a policy on it. Such unknown circumstances are regarded as *al-Garar* (uncertain). Therefore a subject matter involving the element of *al-Garar* may not be coved by an insurance policy, as it is a transaction, which is strictly prohibited by the Prophetic sanction:

Narrated by Said Ibn al-Musyyib (r) saying that, Verily the Holy Prophet (saw) forbade from uncertain transaction.[10]

[9] *al-Qur'an* 2:205.
[10] *Sunnah*.

The first three of the aforesaid nine categories of risk (i.e., subjective, objective and pure risk) may be covered by an insurance policy, while the remaining six may not be covered due to their failure to meet the condition laid down by the *Shari'ah* principles.

THE POSITION OF CRYPTOCURRENCY RISK

In a cryptocurrency management, it involves numerous risks against the user, receiver, management, operation and the system. The risks are due to technology failure, system crash, hacks, capital loss, fraudulent acts, malpractices, war risk, natural disasters, death, insolvency, sanctions and non-compliance. These all classes of risks may fall within the above-recognized categories of risks (subjective, objective or pure risk). In a *Halal* cryptocurrency management, it is recommended that, all categories of risk shall be planned and duly covered by defined *takaful* schemes, aiming at creating a confidence in the market.

CONCLUSION

In the day-to-day life, be one one's life, physical, property or business are exposed to unpredicted risks. It is not Islamic teaching to ignore any form of risk by merely putting trust on *Allah (swt)*. The teaching of the Holy *Prophet (saw)* is to take an effective plan against any risk before putting trust (*tawakkul*) on *Allah (swt)*. Therefore, it is a moral responsibility of everyone with wisdom to maintain an effective risk plan against unpredicted risks involving life, body, property or business and the cryptocurrency is no exception. For the *Halal* cryptocurrency management, the *takaful* scheme is a recommended to be a based for one's risk plan to minimize the unpredicted risk against the cryptocurrency management as analyzed in the following chapter.

CHAPTER 20

Risk Factors in Cryptocurrency and Its *Takaful* Solution

Mohd Ma'Sum Billah

INTRODUCTION

Any commercial or financial activity is naturally exposed to numerous risks be one financial or otherwise. Any commercial entity carries on its activities without analyzing unpredicted risks is a threat to the future of the entity and its activities. Therefore, the risk management component of any commercial entity is among the prime concerns. And thus, different classes of insurance schemes are designed to facilitate the risk management. In *halal* cryptocurrency model, the risk factors may be identified due to technological hazards or technical failure in the blockchain technology, system hazards may occur in the operation, moral hazards may be anticipated in the total operation and management through malpractices, fraud, misappropriation, natural disaster or acts of God (*Qada'* and *Qadar*). The tool of risk minimization under the *Shari'ah* principle is *takaful* scheme hence, a cryptocurrency takaful scheme may be a solution to minimize the risk in the *Halal* cryptocurrency management.

M. M. Billah (✉)
Finance, Insurance, Fintech and Investment, Islamic Economics Institute, King Abdul Aziz University, Jeddah, Kingdom of Saudi Arabia
URL: http://www.drmasumbillah.blogspot.com

© The Author(s) 2019   309
M. M. Billah (ed.), *Halal Cryptocurrency Management*,
https://doi.org/10.1007/978-3-030-10749-9_20

RISK FACTORS IN *HALAL* CRYPTOCURRENCY

Legal

Currently in the cryptocurrency management, there is no legal protection by standard law, policies or guidelines available to regulate the cryptocurrency activities fairly. As for the *Halal* cryptocurrency model, there is no room for one to escape the legal or *Shari'ah* regulatory requirement, but if in case ignorantly the operation takes place with no proper regulatory compliance is a regulatory risk.

Technical

In cryptocurrency management, the technical risk may be predicted as the catastrophe by hacking, technical failure, mistake, misrepresentation, loss of data, fraud and any form of careless malpractices. If any of those catastrophes causes any harm either to the receiver, user, system or technology may be amounting to a technical risk.

Financial

Financial depreciation in any commercial or financial operation is common. Cryptocurrency management is no exception thus, if any depreciation is realized in the capital of the investors in cryptocurrency management due to unforeseeable occurrence is a financial or capital risk.

Bankruptcy

Insolvency in any commercial activity either individual or corporate or public is not unusual and unforeseeable. In cryptocurrency management, there is no so far any record of bankruptcy as at today, but it is not impossible due to many unforeseeable circumstances because of financial turmoil, price depreciation with huge losses or by regulatory sanction. Thus, those unforeseeable disasters are the risks.

Management

In cryptocurrency management, the dissolution of management by no replacement, management is sanctioned by law, disappearance of the management or failure of management responsibilities are amounting to a risk, which likely to damage the total operations and activities of cryptocurrency platform.

Code Change

The HASH code is a mandatory for any cryptocurrency platform to be maintained for recording and authentication. It is not common for a cryptocurrency to change its HASH code with no justifiable reason. But if in case due to unforeseeable situation, the HASH code is changed either by deliberately or otherwise is a risk by change of code, which likely to crash the whole system and its business activities.

Malpractice

In cryptocurrency management, the receiver has chances of malpractices in the total system and activities, which likely to cause damage to the users and the system as well by defeating the law and the legitimate purposes. Fraud, misrepresentation and violation of law deliberately are amounting to cryptocurrency risk by malpractices. Therefore, harmful malpractices in cryptocurrency shall be covered by an insurance scheme to create confidence in the market.

War Risk

War risk is a good cause of excuse, because it is an unpredicted catastrophe, which diminishes the future of not only life and property, but also commercial activities, and cryptocurrency is no exception. If any war causes harm to any cryptocurrency management particularly in its system, financial activities and or management is a war risk, which likely to cause a threat to the total cryptocurrency management.

CRYPTOCURRENCY RISK PLAN

Even though there is no any risk plan for the cryptocurrency management so far has been designed yet and, *Halal* alternative model is no exception. Basically, there are two groups in the cryptocurrency management exposed to unpredicted risks. They are the receiver or the issuer and the other is the user. In all situations, the risk shall be defined and

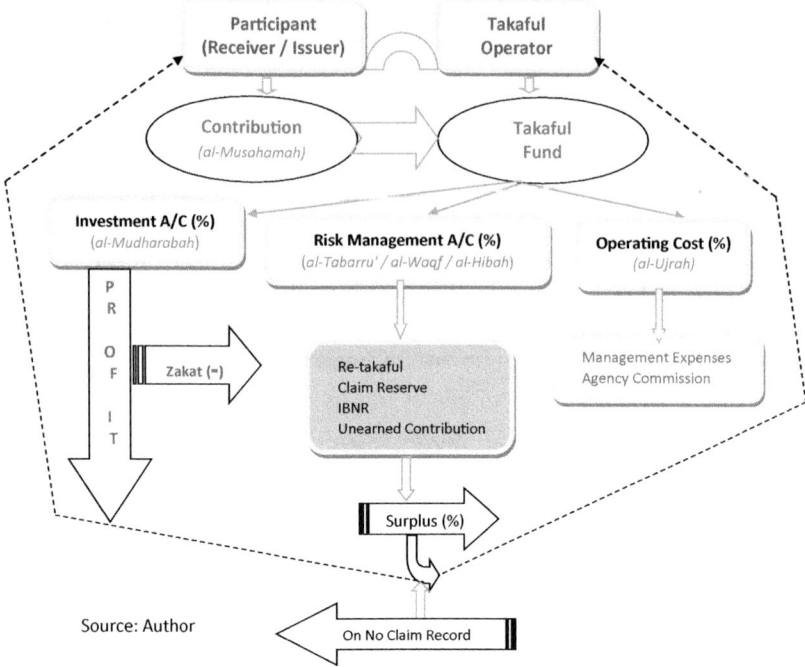

Fig. 20.1 Cryptocurrency receiver takaful model (*Source* Author)

understood before one is underwritten. However, there are two schemes recommended here under the *Shari'ah* principles to protect the victim ought to be suffered by either the receiver or the user due to unpredicted risk be one because of, the technical failure, natural disaster and or other forms of catastrophe. Hence, the schemes are suggested to be one cryptocurrency receiver takaful model while the other is cryptocurrency user takaful model. The following nutshells provide both schemes (Fig. 20.1).

In the above scheme, the participant (receiver) may hold a cryptocurrency all-risk takaful policy with a takaful operator by agreement. This policy is suggested to be a short-term one depending on the policy of the receiver and the market phenomena. The risk shall be defined prior to one's underwriting.

The receiver shall be liable to pay the agreed contribution (premium) to the takaful operator in view of managing one's cryptocurrency risk. The takaful operator in consideration of the received contribution shall undertake to manage the risk and provide the coverage (benefit) in favor of the receiver in case of any risk run over the agreed subject matter within the agreed policy period.

The takaful operator shall distribute the received contribution to three accounts with agreed proportionate by complying the operator's standard policy and manage them accordingly. These three accounts are, namely the management account for the purpose of operating costs, which shall be treated on the basis of *al-Ujrah* (service charge) or *al-Ju'alah* (reward) or *al-Wakalah* (commission). The operating costs shall include total management expenses and the commission of the agents or brokers. Secondly, the risk management account, which shall be treated based on the principles of *al-Tabarru'* (donation), *al-Hibah* (gift) or *al-Waqf* (endowment). The purpose of this account is to maintain the re-takaful requirement, claim reserve, incurred but not reported (IBNR) and unearned contribution. Thirdly, the investment account, aiming at additionally saving a portion for the future benefit of the takaful participant (receiver). This account shall be treated as *al-Mudharabah* (profit and loss sharing technique).

The profit earned in the investment account shall be subject to the deduction of 2.5% as *Zakat* before the net income is distributed between the participant and the operator. In the risk management account, the re-takaful contribution is a regulatory requirement. Similarly, the claim reserve is to meet the justifiable claims, IBNR and unearned contributions, which all are regulatory requirements. However, any surplus if so realized in the risk management account is suggested to be shared between the takaful operator and the participants (on no claim ground) in accordance with the terms of the policy agreement or the standard policy of the takaful operator (Fig. 20.2).

The participant (user) in the above scheme may hold a cryptocurrency all-risk takaful policy with a takaful operator by agreement. This policy is suggested to be a short-term one depending on the plan of the user and the market phenomena. The risk shall be defined prior to one's underwriting or policy agreement.

The participant (user) shall be liable to pay the agreed contribution (premium) to the takaful operator in view of managing one's agreed cryptocurrency risk. The takaful operator in consideration of the received contribution shall undertake to manage the risk and provide the coverage (benefit) in favor of the user in case of any risk run over the agreed subject matter within the agreed policy duration.

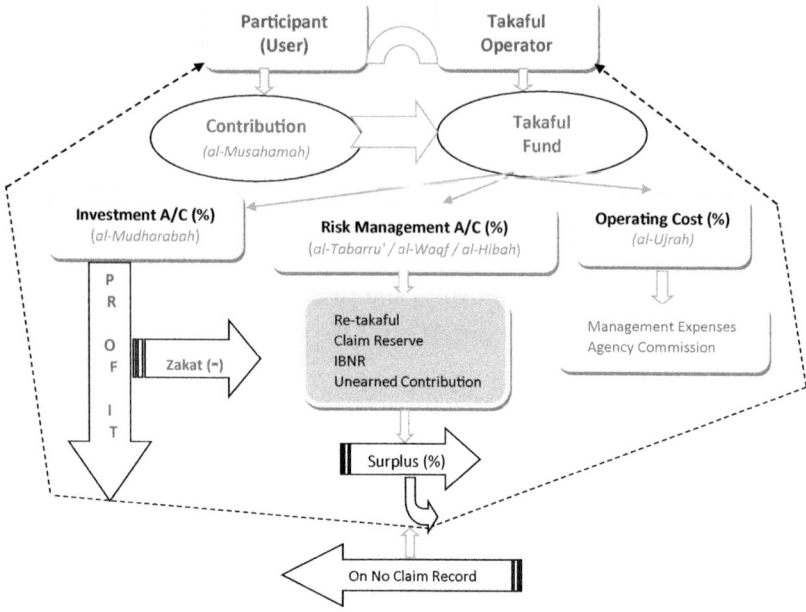

Fig. 20.2 Cryptocurrency user takaful model (*Source* Author)

In this scheme, the takaful operator shall distribute the received contribution to three accounts with agreed proportionate by complying the operator's standard policy and manage them accordingly. These three accounts are, namely management account for the purpose of operating costs, which shall be treated on the basis of *al-Ujrah* (service charge) or *al-Ju'alah* (reward) or *al-Wakalah* (commission). The operating costs shall include total management expenses and the commission of the agents of brokers. Secondly, the risk management account, which shall be treated based on the principles of *al-Tabarru'* (donation), *al-Hibah* (gift) or *al-Waqf* (endowment). The purpose of this account is to maintain the re-takaful requirement, claim reserved, IBNR and unearned contribution. Thirdly, the investment account, aiming at additionally saving a portion for the future benefit of the takaful participant (user). This account shall be treated as profit and loss sharing based on *al-Mudharabah* principles.

In the cryptocurrency user takaful scheme, the profit earned in the investment account shall be subject to the deduction of 2.5% as *Zakat* before the net income is distributed between the participant and the operator. In the risk management account, the re-takaful contribution is a regulatory requirement, similarly the claim reserved to meet the justifiable claims, IBNR and unearned contributions, which all are regulatory requirements. However, any surplus in the risk management account is suggested to be shared between the takaful operator and the participants (on no claim basis) in accordance with the terms of the policy agreement.

CONCLUSION

In cryptocurrency management, there are numerous risks be one against the user or the receiver due to capital risk, technical risk or moral hazard. In all situations, there is no any risk plan yet by any operator or provider or platform. Such weakness may hinder the growth of the cryptocurrency with sustainable existence. For the *Halal* alternative cryptocurrency model, to minimize its risks, there are two categories od takaful schemes recommended. Firstly, the user takaful model to provide protection against any defined risks. Secondly, the receiver takaful scheme to provide protection from any unpredicted defined risk. It is thus concluded that, for a sustainable growth of cryptocurrency, an effective risk plan shall be designed and thus, the takaful may be an effective solution to such risk plan particularly for the *Halal* cryptocurrency management.

Index

© The Editor(s) (if applicable) and The Author(s) 2019   317
M. M. Billah (ed.), *Halal Cryptocurrency Management*,
https://doi.org/10.1007/978-3-030-10749-9

Printed by Printforce, the Netherlands